DIVIDED, BUT NOT DISCONNECTED

# Divided, but Not Disconnected
## German Experiences of the Cold War

Edited by

*Tobias Hochscherf, Christoph Laucht
and Andrew Plowman*

First published in 2010 by

*Berghahn Books*

www.berghahnbooks.com

©2010, 2013 Tobias Hochscherf, Christoph Laucht and Andrew Plowman
First paperback edition published in 2013

All rights reserved. Except for the quotation of short passages
for the purposes of criticism and review, no part of this book
may be reproduced in any form or by any means, electronic or
mechanical, including photocopying, recording, or any information
storage and retrieval system now known or to be invented,
without written permission of the publisher.

**Library of Congress Cataloging-in-Publication Data**

Divided, but not disconnected : German experiences of the Cold War / edited by Tobias Hochscherf, Christoph Laucht and Andrew Plowman.
   p. cm.
   Includes bibliographical references and index.
ISBN 978-1-84545-751-8 (hardback) -- ISBN 978-1-84545-646-7 (institutional ebook)
ISBN 978-1-78238-099-3 (paperback) -- ISBN 978-1-78238-100-6 (retail ebook)
   1. Germany—History—1945–1990. 2. Historiography—Germany—History—20th century. 3. Political culture—Germany—History—20th century.
4. Germany—Politics and government—1945–1990. 5. Germany—Civilization—20th century. 6. Cold War—Social aspects—Germany. I. Hochscherf, Tobias, 1976- II. Laucht, Christoph, 1976- III. Plowman, Andrew, 1966-
   DD258.7.D59 2010
   943.087—dc22

2010023960

**British Library Cataloguing in Publication Data**

A catalogue record for this book is available from the British Library

Printed in the United States on acid-free paper.

ISBN: 978-1-78238-099-3 paperback    ISBN: 978-1-78238-100-6 retail ebook

# Contents

| | |
|---|---|
| Acknowledgements | vii |
| Abbreviations | viii |
| Introduction<br>*Tobias Hochscherf, Christoph Laucht and Andrew Plowman* | 1 |
| 1. Divided, but Not Disconnected: Germany as a Border Region of the Cold War<br>*Thomas Lindenberger* | 11 |
| 2. Fighting the First World War in the Cold War: East and West German Historiography on the Origins of the First World War, 1949–1959<br>*Matthew Stibbe* | 34 |
| 3. The Sideways Gaze: The Cold War and Memory of the Nazi Past, 1949–1970<br>*Bill Niven* | 49 |
| 4. Recasting Luther's Image: The 1983 Commemoration of Martin Luther in the GDR<br>*Jon Berndt Olsen* | 63 |
| 5. West German Labour Internationalism and the Cold War<br>*Quinn Slobodian* | 77 |
| 6. The German Question and Polish–East German Relations, 1945–1962<br>*Sheldon Anderson* | 90 |
| 7. From Bulwark of Freedom to Cosmopolitan Cocktails: The Cold War, Mass Tourism and the Marketing West Berlin as a Tourist Destination<br>*Michelle A. Standley* | 105 |

8. Projections of History: East German Film-Makers and
   the Berlin Wall   119
   *Séan Allan*

9. Defending the Border? Satirical Treatments of
   the Bundeswehr after the 1960s   134
   *Andrew Plowman*

10. East versus West: Olympic Sport as a German Cold War
    Phenomenon   148
    *Christopher Young*

11. Films from the 'Other Side': The Influence of the Cold War
    on West German Feature Film Import in the GDR   163
    *Rosemary Stott*

12. The Shadows of the Past in Germany: Visual Representation,
    the Male Hero, and the Cold War   176
    *Inge Marszolek*

13. Reenacting the First Battle of the Cold War: Post-Wall
    German Television Confronts the Berlin Airlift in *Die
    Luftbrücke – Nur der Himmel war frei*   190
    *Tobias Hochscherf* and *Christoph Laucht*

14. Unusual Censor Readings: East German Science Fiction
    and the GDR Ministry of Culture   204
    *Patrick Major*

15. Funerals in Berlin: The Geopolitical and Cultural Spaces
    of the Cold War   220
    *James Chapman*

Select Bibliography   233

Notes on Contributors   247

Index   250

# Acknowledgements

We are grateful to the British Academy for the award of a grant that supported speakers attending a symposium held in Liverpool in September 2006, at which many contributors to the volume were able to meet and exchange ideas. A special note of thanks must also be directed at the School of Cultures, Languages and Area Studies at the University of Liverpool, particularly to Professor Eve Rosenhaft, for the provision of financial and – above all – organizational support. We would also like to record our gratitude to Marion Berghahn and Berghahn Books for their valuable encouragement and comments from the early stages of a proposal outline to the final manuscript.

# Abbreviations

| | |
|---|---|
| AA | Auswärtiges Amt – FRG Foreign Ministry |
| Abt. Kult. | Abteilung Kultur – Culture Department |
| AIFLD | American Institute for Free Labor Development |
| AFL-CIO | The American Federation of Labor and Congress of Industrial Organizations |
| BAK | Bundesarchiv Koblenz |
| BArch | Bundesarchiv Berlin |
| BArch Film | Bundesfilmarchiv Berlin |
| BAW | Buchenwald-Archiv Weimar-Buchenwald |
| BMZ | Das Bundesministerium für wirtschaftliche Zusammenarbeit und Entwicklung – Ministry of Economic Cooperation and Development |
| CIA | Central Intelligence Agency; the US Secret Service |
| CDU | Christlich Demokratische Union – Christian Democratic Union |
| DDR-MfAA | Bestand Ministerium für Auswärtige Angelegenheiten der DDR – Records of the GDR Foreign Ministry |
| DEFA | Deutsche Film Aktiengesellschaft |
| DHfK | Deutsche Hochschule für Körperkultur – German University of Physical Culture |
| DGB | Deutscher Gewerkschaftsbund – Confederation of German Trade Unions |
| DOG | Deutsche Olympische Gesellschaft – German Olympic Society |
| DOI | Deutsches Olympisches Institut – German Olympic Institute, Frankfurt/Main |

| | |
|---|---|
| DSB | Deutscher Sportbund – German Sports Association |
| DTSB | Deutsche Turn- und Sportbund der DDR – German Gymnastics and Sports Federation of the GDR |
| EEC | European Economic Community |
| FAZ | *Frankfurter Allgemeine Zeitung* |
| FDJ | Freie Deutsche Jugend – Free German Youth, the official youth organization of the GDR |
| FDP | Freie Demokratische Partei – Free Democratic Party |
| FRG | Federal Republic of Germany |
| GDR | German Democratic Republic |
| ICFTU | International Congress of Free Trade Unions |
| IOC | International Olympic Committee |
| KJS | Kinder- und Jugendsportschulen – Children's and Youth Sports Schools |
| KMK | Kultusministerkonferenz – the collective body of Education and Culture Ministers of the states of the FRG |
| KM-Q | Kreisarchiv Merseburg-Querfurt |
| KPD | Deutsche Kommunistische Partei – German Communist Party |
| LAB | Landesarchiv Berlin |
| LSK | Leistungskommission der DDR – Performance Commission of the GDR |
| MSPD | Mehrheitssozialdemokratische Partei Deutschlands – Majority Social Democrats of Germany |
| MSZ | Ministerstwo Spraw Zagranicznych, Archiwum Ministerstwa Spraw Zagranicznych – Ministry of Foreign Affairs, Archive of the Ministry of Foreign Affairs, Warsaw, Poland |
| NATO | North Atlantic Treaty Organization |
| NOC | National Olympic Committee |
| NVA | Nationale Volksarmee – National People's Army |
| PA-AA | Politisches Archiv des AA |
| POW | Prisoner of war |

| | |
|---|---|
| PZPR | Polska Zjednoczona Partia Robotnicza – Polish United Workers' Party |
| PZPR KC | Records of the Central Committee of the PZPR, Archiwum Akt Nowych, Warsaw, Poland |
| RIAS | *Rundfunk im amerikanischen Sektor* – Radio in the American Sector |
| SAPMO-BArch | Stiftung Archiv der Parteien und Massenorganisationen der DDR im Bundesarchiv Berlin |
| SBZ | Sowjetisch besetzte Zone – Soviet Occupation Zone |
| SED | Sozialistische Einheitspartei Deutschlands – German Socialist Unity Party |
| SED ZK | SED Zentralkommitee – SED Central Committee |
| SPD | Sozialdemokratische Partei Deutschlands – German Social Democratic Party |
| SKKS | Staatliches Komittee für Körperkultur – State Committee for Physical Culture |
| SS | Schutzstaffel – Security Service, internal security force of the Nazis in Germany |
| Stasi | Staatssicherheitsdienst – GDR State Security Service |
| StKS | Staatssekretariat für Körperkultur und Sport – GDR State Secretariat for Physical Culture |
| TZ | Trainingszentren – Training Centres |
| UFA | Universum Film Aktiengesellschaft |
| UMT | Union Marocaine du Travail |
| USSR | Union of Soviet Socialist Republics |
| WFTU | World Federation of Trade Unions |
| ZAP | Zentrales Parteiarchiv der SED, Berlin – Central Party Archive of the SED |
| *ZfG* | *Zeitschrift für Geschichtswissenschaft* |

# Introduction

*Tobias Hochscherf, Christoph Laucht and Andrew Plowman*

———■■■———

On a basic level, it was its inner border that made Germany a unique place to experience the Cold War. The settlement agreed between the Allies at the Potsdam Conference not only partitioned Germany but divided the German nation, alone among the nations in Europe, along the fault lines of a new bipolar world order. With the integration of the Federal Republic of Germany (FRG) into the political, military and economic alliances of the West and the German Democratic Republic (GDR) into the Soviet bloc, the divide was cemented and the two states evolved in contrary directions.

The 'German question' in this post-1945 variant remained inextricably entwined with the vicissitudes of the Cold War until its end. Today, no event is more symbolic of the end of the conflict than the fall of the Berlin Wall, the preeminent symbol of German division following its construction in 1961. But unlike the apparent fixity – at least until 9 November 1989 – of the stone and concrete that made up the Wall, the border itself was never a wholly fixed value. This is true for the different ways in which it was experienced and in turn shaped experience within the two German states. For one thing, the meanings of Germany's inner borders were hotly contested between West and East Germany, and they changed over time, particularly in the West, where they became less important. Further, the existence of an inner border running along the fault lines of the Cold War also, as Thomas Lindenberger observes in the opening essay, assigned new and, again, different meanings to Germany's outer borders in their respective Western and Eastern geopolitical contexts. If the inner-German border, finally, was where – in Europe, at least – the two sides in the conflict stood most starkly opposed to one another, then it was also the site of competition and trade-offs between the two Germanys. The character of these interactions, which shaped the experience of the conflict so deeply (and again, unevenly) in so many areas, were owed to another unique fact about Germany in the Cold

War: namely, that the two states shared the same language and a common history, as well as kinship structures across the divide.

This book offers an analysis of divided Germany as a unique site in the global Cold War, and it focuses in particular on the various kinds of interaction between the two halves that made it so. Employing a resolutely interdisciplinary approach, the essays in the volume explore how the fact of German division shaped the various experiences of the conflict in politics, society and culture at different times, and in different places and contexts in the FRG and the GDR.[1] Because the conflict could be felt in so many walks of life, the contributions gathered here examine how the different experiences of the Cold War left their mark on a cross-section of areas, including history, memory and international relations, as well as popular culture. The chapters offer case studies in a wide range of topics, from sport to science-fiction writing to border conflicts and development aid. As a set, these range from the early years of the conflict, when the discourses that came to define the conflict were only beginning to be implemented, to its decline. Some of them – such as Bill Niven's discussion of the conflicts over the memory of the National Socialist past – compare and contrast developments in both Germanys. To the extent that specific experiences need not, and in some cases cannot, be compared on a one-to-one basis, others – like Patrick Major's account of the negotiations between authors of science fiction and pre-censors in the GDR – focus more on one side, though always with a view to the broader interpretative framework of the Cold War. Two contributions place themes relating to the conflict in later, broader contexts: Tobias Hochscherf and Christoph Laucht's and James Chapman's examinations respectively of the post-unification representation of the Berlin airlift of 1948–49 and of divided Berlin as a preferred setting for international spy thrillers. What is fascinating here is to see how specific German experiences of the conflict shade into the competing and complementary 'cultures of remembrance' that for one commentator now define the memory of it.[2]

In the years since the end of the Cold War, scholars' understanding of both the 'shape' of the German question within it and the nature of the fronts on which the conflict was 'waged' has undergone important shifts. Even shortly before the events of 1989–90, comparatively few observers might have taken issue with any expert who chose to stress the growing political, social and cultural differences between the GDR and the FRG as they became embedded in the respective ideological blocs. Above and beyond cultural elites, 'ordinary' Germans too felt these differences whenever they met their relatives from the other side. The logic of division was accepted in East and West Germany by the 1970s at the latest. The last great moment of crisis between the two states, the construction of the Berlin Wall in 1961, had in the short and medium term stabilized relations between them. By 1971, the GDR was pursuing an aggressive policy of 'demarcation' from the West that saw references to the 'German nation' dropped from its 1974 constitution. Around the same time, Chancellor Willy Brandt's enunciation of *Ostpolitik* in the West in practice acknowledged the existence of the GDR, though short of full recognition and without renouncing the FRG's claim to be the sole legitimate representative of the German nation.[3]

The construction of difference was a real and deeply entrenched process on both sides. Some years after unification, however, scholars across a range of disciplines have grasped how comprehensively previous assumptions about the development of the two parts of Germany need rethinking. A pioneer here was the historian Christoph Kleßmann. As early as 1988 he had proposed, in the face of the 'common-sense' view that the two Germanys were growing apart, that the relation between them be understood as one of 'asymmetrical entanglement'.[4] The logic of grasping postwar German history in terms of both separation *and* interconnection and in a way that reflects the greater influence of the FRG on the GDR has become widely accepted. More recently, too, Kleßmann has remained at the forefront of thinking about the issues of perspective that Germany's divided past now throws up. Primary among these is the need to avoid the temptation to read backwards from the *telos* of unification in a fashion that turns Germany's dual history into a single one in disguise, while at the same time cultivating a fresh sensitivity to the elements in it that made unification possible.[5] The notion that Germany was 'divided, but not disconnected' underpins this volume. If it can seem like a truism today, it is worth remarking how much work remains to be done to map out how specifically it shaped everyday practices and culture in the two Germanys, both in detail and across a broad range of areas.[6]

Where the wider Cold War is concerned, attention has shifted from the diplomatic towards the cultural dimension of the conflict. While the 'new' Cold War history, championed among others by John Lewis Gaddis,[7] continues to plot its course in the arena of high politics, commentators such as Patrick Major – a contributor here – and Rana Mitter have argued for examining its sociocultural aspects more paradigmatically.[8] All wars, including hot ones, have been fought using words and images, and in the case of the Cold War, film and television, books and comics, sports and music can also illuminate its cultural and psychological aspects.[9] The shift towards the sociocultural dimension of the conflict has brought with it a greater focus on the construction of ideological meanings on the home front. This is neither to suggest that the Cold War can be reduced to a number of cultural experiences (or even a specific monolithic cultural experience) nor to posit that all social and cultural phenomena are ultimately linked to the conflict, but such an approach offers rich dividends with regard to the entanglements in the German situation.[10] Nowhere else did the broader geopolitical fault lines of the conflict overlap so closely with the home front. Nowhere else, indeed, were the home fronts themselves so enmeshed as each side sought to assert its own legitimacy and to negate that of the other.

Thomas Lindenberger's concept of Germany as a *border region of the Cold War*, which he explains in this volume's opening essay, also offers a way of conceptualizing how the interfaces between the FRG and the GDR shaped the German experiences of the conflict in both a political and a broader cultural sense. What is at issue here is not simply a history of the structures that divided the two Germanys – whether in the form of the sectoral borders established after 1945, the German-German border effectively sealed off in 1952, or the Wall itself. Though these frequently come into view, the overarching emphasis is rather on the way the contradictory effects of borders as such made themselves felt in the unique situation of German division. As Lindenberger explains, borders as *lines* separate polities territorially; but as *zones* they create the need for interaction and exchange – sometimes less, sometimes more amicable. In the German case, processes of mutual delimitation on the one hand and interaction on the other influenced social and cultural experience as profoundly and widely as they did because the points at which the two states were forced to confront one another were so many, in view of their shared heritage (in both its positive and its negative dimensions).

While the increasingly lopsided character, in Kleßmann's sense, of the relationship between the two Germanys is an explicit or implicit theme in many chapters, Lindenberger's approach offers a heuristic model for understanding the ever more obvious imbalances in the ways in which they reacted to and interacted with one another. For the Federal Republic, Germany's inner border finally lost much of its signal importance in the process of its integration into the West. As its neighbours and allies there became the yardstick by which West Germany measured itself politically and socially, the 'other' Germany and division itself became less of an issue in day-to-day life. For the GDR, by contrast, the border to the FRG remained fundamental and demanded constant vigilance. As everyone knows, the Berlin Wall never provided the hermetic seal the regime desired. Whether it was the existence of West Berlin (which literally fixed the border at the heart of the GDR) or, to name just two examples, the availability of West German television and the access to

American popular culture that partly followed from this fact, the task of delimiting itself from the FRG remained a source of pressure for East Germany. Where the authorities did not, or could not, police points of contact as rigorously as they did the border, or where they were forced to enter into negotiations, they risked surrendering some of their authority. This basic lack of symmetry was reflected from the outset in the very language used to articulate the basic fact of the border in discourses on each side. A chief metaphor of the Cold War, the 'Iron Curtain' (or 'the Wall'), was charged from the Western perspective with the ideological association of restriction for the other side: one either enjoyed liberty in a privileged position 'in front of' it, or was confined 'behind' it. For its part, the official designation of *antifaschistischer Schutzwall* or 'antifascist protection wall' in the GDR was visibly always oriented towards the West in so far as it was premised on the threat and influence that was perceived to emanate from it.[11]

In Chapter One, Thomas Lindenberger thus opens up a broader theoretical space for the examination of the distinct experiences of the conflict in the chapters that follow. In addition, he himself offers a clarification of this fundamental concept in relation to three areas central to the German experience of the conflict: the question of Germany's territorial integrity, the inner-German antagonism over the National Socialist past and the intersection of the mass media public spheres of the two states. Lindenberger concludes by considering the lessons that the singular German case can offer for understanding other manifestations of the conflict and other geopolitical confrontations across the globe.

The following four chapters consider how the Cold War inflected historiography, cultural memory and politics of both sides of the border. Focusing on disputes over the decision of leadership of the Social Democratic Party (SPD) to vote for war credits in August 1914 in Chapter Two, Matthew Stibbe contrasts the interpretation of the First World War by West and East German historians. While the disputes were important for the attempts of the GDR regime to establish a Marxist-Leninist historiography able to compete with the allegedly 'bourgeois' historiography of the West, it also showed, he argues, how historians on both sides claimed to represent the national interest of all Germans. Bill Niven follows on in Chapter Three by considering the conflicts over the interpretation of National Socialism in the two Germanys between 1949 and 1969. Niven shows how these, too, became crucial battlegrounds in which each side sought to demonstrate its own legitimacy and the illegitimacy of the other: the significance of the Cold War for the memory of National Socialism was that Germans were encouraged to look 'sideways', westwards or eastwards, for the guilty party rather than confront their own responsibility. Chapter Four deals with the contested memory of Martin Luther on the occasion in 1983 of the 500th anniversary of his birth. In this chapter, Jon Berndt Olsen explores how the GDR, which had previously mistrusted Luther as a reactionary figure on account of his opposition to the peasants' uprising of 1524, sought to lay claim to the image of Luther after a shift in policy towards the past. Where Olsen deals with competition between the two German states for ownership of Germany's past cultural achievements, Quinn Slobodian, in Chapter Five, examines the struggle for influence in the developing world in the present. Slobodian's specific focus is the way organizations linked to the West German labour movement adopted stances in support of the foreign policy of the West German state abroad in the political climate of the Cold War that were at odds with their position in domestic politics at the time.

The overarching theme for the following set of chapters is the motif of the border itself in politics and culture. In Chapter Six, Sheldon Anderson looks at the controversies surrounding the GDR's external border with Poland. From the West, the GDR and Poland may have looked like part of the seamless unity of the Warsaw Pact. But as Anderson demonstrates, the Oder-Neiße border looked very different on the East German side, being a constant source of tension and antagonism between these states, deeply historically rooted and compounded by disagreements about Soviet-bloc policy towards West Germany. The next two contributions focus on Berlin and the Berlin Wall as specific Cold War sites. Examining the promotional activity of West Berlin's tourist industry, in Chapter Seven Michelle Standley explores the marketing of West Berlin as a Cold War tourist destination around the time of the construction of the Wall and the shift away from this after the 1970s as emphasis switched to presenting the Western part of the city above all to younger travellers as a trendy Western metropolis. In Chapter Eight, Seán Allan analyses the representation of the Wall in East German films. He focuses on a handful of treatments of its construction, such as Karl Gass's documentary *Schaut auf diese Stadt* (*Behold this City*, 1962), and explains the developments in cultural policy that made further engagement with the subject impossible after 1967. He then concludes with a discussion of cinematic images of the demise of the Wall. In Chapter Nine Andrew Plowman's examination of satirical images of the West German Bundeswehr illustrates the asymmetrical relations between the two German states. East German satire in matters of rearmament resolutely targeted the Bundeswehr. But whilst they mocked the ability of the Bundeswehr to defend the inner-German border, he argues, West German satirists foregrounded the debate surrounding military reform in the Federal Republic rather than the 'other side'.

The next two chapters look at the way in which the FRG and the GDR confronted one another and were of necessity forced to compete and interact with one another in the sphere of culture. Christopher Young's topic in Chapter Ten is the sporting battle between the two states at the Munich Olympics in 1972. Young examines how the staging of the Games in Germany added impetus to each side's efforts to trump the other. Whilst state sponsorship of sport ensured that the GDR ran out clear winners, Young emphasizes – in a rare example, perhaps, of the FRG attempting to match East German achievements – how sporting success on both sides was owed to the rivalry between them. In Chapter Eleven, Rosemary Stott examines a neglected aspect of cultural transfer between the two Germanys in the sphere of film. Stott argues that the case of feature-film imports from the FRG to the GDR since the 1970s not only illustrates the latter's growing reliance on imports from the hitherto most mistrusted of all Western film-producing nations, but also an increasing convergence in audience tastes on either side.

The final chapters focus more specifically on the way in which various media have both served to implement and in turn represented various German experiences of the Cold War. Inge Marszolek explores the construction of masculinity as the male hero in photographs and posters in the conflict's early years in Chapter Twelve. She demonstrates how images strongly associated with the Weimar Republic, National Socialism and the Second World War were encoded with new meanings and exploited to construct a cultural memory in tune with the respective ideology on each side. In Chapter Thirteen, Tobias Hochscherf and Christoph Laucht examine how Dror Zahavi's recent television film *Die Luftbrücke – Nur der Himmel war frei* (*The Airlift – Only the Sky Was Open*) reinterpreted the story of the Berlin airlift for contemporary viewers in 2005. They show how a popular contemporary film in many respects exemplary of a wider trend in German culture constructs the events of 1948–49 as a German foundation narrative that is both Americanized and characterized by a search for a new, independent national identity. Patrick Major considers how literary censors dealt with the science fiction produced by GDR authors in Chapter Fourteen. A preeminently though not exclusively Western genre, science fiction often sold well in the East, where it was a telling example of the negotiation of cultural power. While authors were forced to navigate the tension between the futurological speculations associated with the genre and the supposedly more 'scientific' predictions of Marxism-Leninism, Major argues, official readers often chose to promote a commodity that was in short supply as well as the claims of a limited public sphere. Finally, Chapter Fifteen reminds us that the perception of Germany as a border region was also part of a wider experience of the Cold War. In an examination of the representation of Berlin as a geopolitical space, James Chapman shows how Anglo-American spy novels by the likes of John le Carré and Ian Fleming, and the films based on them, forged an iconography of the conflict that persists in audience memories beyond Germany's own frontiers.

Given both the interdisciplinary nature of the collection and its breadth, many readers will approach it with a view to finding out more about specific topics that are treated here. But while it may be presumptuous to prescribe any manner of reading a text, we as editors hope that it should be approached also as a whole. To this end, we have included a number of cross-references throughout the volume that are designed to highlight central thematic continuities across it and to illuminate some of the many facets of Cold War culture. While some of the chapters engage with existing debates, others seek to open up new and neglected areas of study. In both respects, the volume is intended to act as a stimulus to scholars wishing to develop their own work on Cold War Germany in key political, cultural and even transnational contexts. In a Germany in which the legacy of division in the conflict forms an important part of cultural memory, the need to understand the past will always have an urgent resonance; thus the scholar who approaches it has a special responsibility. The divided *memory* of the Cold War past has become an important field in German cultural studies in its own right and need not be fully entered into here.[12] Yet here too, a clear grasp of the way in which past experiences do and do not filter into the construction of present memories can only further our understanding of the lasting impact of the inner-German border.

A recent example pertinent to one of the final contributions to the volume illustrates this. As US and British air veterans, former West German support staff, politicians and journalists from various nations descended on Berlin in June 2008 to commemorate the sixtieth anniversary of the start of the Allied airlift, one may reflect on the dynamics at work as the Germans remembered the events. Was the act of remembering one in which the end of the airlift had become overlaid with the memory of the fall of the Wall and the end of the Cold War itself? What justice did the commemorations do to East German memories of the event? In short, were these memories that were shared by all Germans or that continued to divide them? This anniversary of the airlift perhaps offered only an inkling of the questions that *the* German memorial year

2009 would throw up as the unified nation marked both the sixtieth anniversary of the foundation of the two German states and the twentieth anniversary of the fall of the Berlin Wall. There is a very real risk that in Germany today the asymmetry that once characterized the relation between the two German states may be writ large in the form of a public memory that privileges the point of view of a Federal Republic that was on the side of the 'victors' of the Cold War. In the face of such pressure, it is important to insist on the diversity of Cold War experiences as the conflict unfolded. A fresh consideration of the manifold ways in which Germany was 'divided, but not disconnected' can form an important part of this process.

## Notes

1. Holger Nehring makes a similar point about the experience of the conflict when he describes the pluralistic 'cultures of the Cold War'. See 'The British and West German Protests against Nuclear Weapons and the Cultures of the Cold War, 1957–64', *Contemporary British History*, 19.2 (2005), 223–41 (p. 224).

2. Jost Dülffer, 'Cold War History in Germany', *Cold War History*, 8.2 (2008), 135–56 (p. 135).

3. Konrad H. Jarausch, Hinrich C. Seeba and David P. Conradt, 'The Presence of the Past: Culture, Opinion and Identity in Germany', in *After Unity: Reconfiguring German Identities,* ed. by Konrad H. Jarausch (Oxford: Berghahn, 1997), pp. 25–60 (pp. 40–42).

4. Christoph Kleßmann, *Zwei Staaten, eine Nation: Deutsche Geschichte 1955–1970*, 2nd rev. edn (Bonn: Bundeszentrale für politische Bildung, 1997), p. 13.

5. Christoph Kleßmann, 'Introduction', in *The Divided Past: Rewriting Postwar German History,* ed. by Christoph Kleßmann (Oxford: Berg, 2001), pp. 1–9 (pp. 1–3).

6. An attempt to unravel the issues in the case of consumer culture is *Consuming Germany in the Cold War,* ed. by David Crew (Oxford: Berg, 2003).

7. John Lewis Gaddis, *We know now: Rethinking Cold War History* (Oxford: Oxford University Press, 1997).

8. Rana Mitter and Patrick Major, 'East is East and West? Towards a Comparative Socio-Cultural History of the Cold War', in *Across the Blocs: Cold War Cultural and Social History,* ed. by Rana Mitter and Patrick Major (London: Cass, 2004), pp. 1–20 (pp. 1–2).

9. Tony Shaw, 'The Politics of Cold War Culture', *Journal of Cold War Studies,* 3.3 (2001), 59–76 (p. 59).

10. Not least in a classic study of the influence of American culture on both sides of the divide such as Uta Poiger, *Jazz, Rock and Rebels: Cold War Politics and American Culture in a Divided Germany* (Berkeley: University of California Press, 2000).

11. Christian Koller, 'Der "Eiserne Vorhang": Zur Genese einer politischen Zentralmetapher in der Epoche des Kalten Krieges', *Zeitschrift für Geschichtswissenschaft*

[hereafter *ZfG*], 54.4 (2006), 366–384 (p. 367). Patrick Major examines the impact the Berlin Wall had on everyday life in the GDR in *Behind the Berlin Wall: East Germany and the Frontiers of Power* (Oxford: Oxford University Press, 2010).

12. See for example Paul Cooke, *Representing East Germany since Unification: From Colonization to Nostalgia* (Oxford: Berg, 2005).

# 1

# Divided, but Not Disconnected
## Germany as a Border Region of the Cold War
### Thomas Lindenberger

### 'Cold War Experience' and 'Cold War Predicament'

Within historical literature, it has increasingly become standard practice to refer to the 'Cold War' as an 'experience' rather than just a brute fact. From a strictly methodological point of view this may seem banal, since 'experience' is the way in which humans confront, form and remember any 'reality'. To emphasize the dimension of subjectivity and perception here recognizes, of course, the paramount weight of the seemingly 'objective' and life-threatening 'facts' through which the Cold War marked world history for more than four decades. Bernd Stöver has convincingly made the case for considering the Cold War as a 'system' constituted by the basic ideological conflict between the two hegemonic powers on the one hand, and the threat of extermination through nuclear warfare on the other.[1] With the establishment and stabilization of this system after 1945 a number of non-hegemonic countries and societies were forced to align themselves within it. This occurred on essentially nonvoluntary grounds in the Soviet, and on an essentially voluntary basis in the American sphere of influence, reflecting an asymmetry that was itself a constituent of the ideological conflict. The inevitability with which the bipolar world order imposed itself on its spheres of influence relied on a fundamental fear of absolute and unlimited violence that was shared in particular by those nations that had survived the devastations of the Second World War. These were driven less by the American 'fear of defeat'[2] than by a 'fear of repeat' that conditioned their postwar reality in an existential fashion. They all had to develop their own specific ways of dealing with what I propose to call the Cold War predicament.

Adaptation to the Cold War predicament took many forms and had far-reaching consequences for the development of the countries implicated in the conflict. It shaped not only the world view of elites and professionals who were engaged in this antagonism more or less directly. As with any war, mobilization and commitment of the population at large were key to the relative strength of the respective protagonist. And since the Cold War – by definition – lasted longer than most 'hot' wars, it had to be integrated into the fabric of everyday life as something determining, or at least codetermining, relevant parts of societal and cultural reality, its representations and belief systems. On this level the Cold War tended to be associated with basic attitudes and norms such as human rights, civil liberties, the pursuit of happiness, solidarity, autonomy, justice, welfare, gender relations, aesthetics, peace and, in the end, the existence of humanity. This encompassing aspect is mostly referred to as 'Cold War culture' in the literature.[3]

But although there are good reasons to highlight the systemic logic of the Cold War in its entirety, this does not preclude its historicity. On the contrary, its continuous reproduction as a system relied on the capacity of its regional subsystems to re-adapt regularly to changing conditions. A first phase of overcoming the material and mental consequences of war and genocide was followed by the transition to relative affluence and material security, and by structural changes accompanied by a secular trend of mental reorientation towards a postmaterialist and increasingly individualist world view.[4] This process took many forms and produced contrasting results in the various regions within the highly differentiated and uneven landscape of the Cold War battlefield. In order to render the notion of 'Cold War experience' meaningful, it must be specified in time and space. The ways to live the Cold War predicament varied greatly depending on the place, and this refers not just to the hemisphere and continent under consideration, it applies to every level of geography down to countries, and even regions and localities within a country.

These variations over time and place concern both the intensity and the quality of experience. There were periods and places in which the Cold War was 'lived' in an acute and existential manner, in contrast to others in which it was only present as something rather remote, in the background rather than the foreground. Cold War experience is not a homogeneous quality to be encountered in similar consistency in all places affected by the Cold War. To conceive of Cold War experience as contingent on time and space implies concretization and specification. The Cold War cannot explain everything. Rather than departing from a default assumption that all experience during the epoch of the Cold War was essentially conditioned by the conflict, the explanatory limits of the concept of Cold War experience must be born in mind. The linkage between 'experience' on the one hand and the Cold War as an overarching structure and predicament on the other must not lead to Cold War reductionism.⁵

## Divided Germany: A Peculiar Place of Cold War Experience

It requires little justification in order to identify Germany, East and West, as a highly peculiar place to have experienced the Cold War. Any discussion of its peculiarity must depart from the obviously unique fact that Cold War Germany was a divided country and that – in the European theatre – it was the only divided country. The following observations about its particular border situation thus apply to a case that, though exceptional, was tightly interwoven with the mechanisms through which Europe as whole functioned as a stake in the Cold War.

Germany's 'divisibility' followed from the way in which it had initiated, fought and lost the preceding hot war. By and in itself, this way of warfare, which was geared towards annihilation, was not causally linked to the international fault lines or ideological motives of the Cold War, which had been already established before the Second World War. The expansion of Soviet hegemony and the Americans' commitment not to return to isolationism as they had done after the First World War led to the partition of the European continent, and by virtue of being dismembered by Allied occupation anyway Germany lent itself to 'hosting' the European frontier-line of the new bipolar world order. One might suggest that this fact contributed decisively to the specificity of the Cold War in Europe in comparison to other world regions, namely the four-decade long and complete absence of international warfare.

Paradoxically, the division of Germany between the two antagonistic camps, which made it an exceptional place to experience the Cold War, nevertheless makes it difficult to speak of 'the' German Cold War experience. The longer it lasted, the more the conflict acquired different meanings in East and West, to some extent even within the two German polities. Yet it is evident that these differing experiences remained much more intimately linked to each other than were the experiences of other European states separated from the other half of the continent by the Iron Curtain. In no other country did the Cold War predicament maintain such a presence in everyday life as in Germany, at least in relevant parts of it. In no other country was concrete knowledge about the conditions of life under the 'other' system so widespread, both among elites and specialists and among those segments of the population that happened to have relatives on the other side. In order to address this paradox of conflicted intimacy I suggest treating the whole of Germany, East and West, as a *border region of the Cold War* within the European theatre. To elaborate on this idea, a short remark on borders and border regions is in order.

Borders between states or other entities are potentially contradictory in their functions and effects. As *borderlines* they separate distinct polities spatially. At the same time they define a distinguishable zone in which the same polities are closest to each other: *border zones*. When the entities in question share a history of previous antagonism, for instance war or attempts at mutual conquest, borderlines serve to stabilize a state of delimitation and/or separation that has been reached and agreed. Under specific conditions, however, border zones also allow for possibilities of mutual perception and practical necessities of continuous interaction that do not occur in the same way outside them. In particularly favourable conditions, border zones may even engender productive relations that undermine or at least counterbalance the state of separateness itself.[6]

Within the European Cold War theatre Germany was a region where these in principle generic features of borders and their adjacent territories deeply impregnated Cold War experience. The fact that the deeply polyvalent potential of state borders could develop to the full within one nation organized in two states sets Germany apart from other nations' border experiences. The fact that the partition of Europe was achieved by dividing the territory of the largest nation state in the middle of the continent created a space where interactions, both antagonistic and constructive, between the two opposed camps could and inevitably did occur more frequently and on more different levels than elsewhere. I will discuss the concrete consequences of this specificity by looking at three dimensions of interaction: the relevance of territorial sovereignty and border regimes for the respective political systems of the two German states; the triangular logic of dealing with the Nazi past as a source of legitimacy; and Germany as a site of the densification of the Cold War mediascape.

## Redefinitions of Territoriality and Border Regimes

With Germany becoming a – if not *the* – border region of the Cold War, its own internal and external borders assumed historically new meanings and functions. Towards the East, the new Oder-Neiße borderline fixed basic outcomes of the Second World War, in particular the loss of the Eastern territories and the ensuing expulsion of their remaining German population. Within the remaining German territory the internal state border served to stabilize the East German dictatorship and – especially after the construction of the Berlin Wall in 1961 – the international balance of atomic powers. For the Western world, West Germany's borders became a site of its gradual economic and cultural integration into Western Europe and the transatlantic alliance.

Following the unconditional surrender, the German state's territory was divided, the resulting parts separated by borders defining the four occupation zones and the four sectors of Berlin, and thereby the respective jurisdiction of the four military administrations. *Zonengrenzen* (zonal borders) equipped with checkpoints and passport controls surveyed and managed the movement of people and goods between these territories – a basic technique to (re-)institute centralized authority.[7] With the Cold War unfolding and the East-West schism producing two distinct projects of state-building in Germany, the inner German border became a key site in the further implementation of such new executive powers. The borderline between the territories occupied by the Western allies and the Soviet Union became the *Zonengrenze* (zonal border) in the singular in western, or *Staatsgrenze West* (state border west) in eastern terminology. It was rendered more or less impermeable by the East from 1952. Only the sector border in Berlin remained a highly visible opening in the attempt to close the GDR off from West Germany. This was sealed by the Berlin Wall in 1961, which made *Republikflucht* (flight from the Republic) across the Western borders extremely dangerous for the rest of the GDR's existence.

What is essential about these two operations to make the state border towards the West impermeable are their far-reaching internal repercussions within the GDR itself. The ramifications were felt even in the remotest areas of the social fabric of everyday life. The first operation in May 1952, characteristically called *Aktion Ungeziefer* (operation vermin), was accompanied by a massive purge of the population living near the zonal borders of 'elements' the regime regarded as unreliable and potentially dangerous. This included people who had an anti-communist reputation or a 'bourgeois' background, and also 'asocial' individuals who did not conform to the expectations of the German Socialist Unity Party (SED – Sozialistische Einheitspartei Deutschlands). Thousands of families had their homes expropriated and had to pack their things within twenty-four hours to be resettled at an assigned place in the hinterland. Near the border, a regime of surveillance was established that restricted access to the local population. Visitors from other parts of the country had to apply for permission to enter this border area (*Grenzgebiet*), which was five kilometres wide. Access to an even smaller strip, only five hundred metres wide, along the demarcation line was restricted further.[8] The border site itself was off-limits to civilians and staffed by specialist military border guards – the *Grenztruppen*. In order to enlist the resident population in this control regime the border guards recruited units of voluntary assistants, a fact that served to intensify the day-to-day control of citizens living in these highly sensitive areas.[9]

Nine years later, the construction of the Berlin Wall was accompanied by the institution of a similar border regime. In its aftermath came another severe crackdown on elements of the population considered unreliable by the SED state. In the area around Berlin this first of all affected those who had regularly commuted to West Berlin for work, visiting schools and universities or doing more or less legal business. These former *Grenzgänger* (border crossers) became victims of a harsh course of enforced integration into the state-owned socialist economy. It is no coincidence that the legal procedures to assign obligatory workplaces to this particular group were subsequently developed into a new norm of the East German penal code that defined abstention from regular work, that is from making one's living through officially sanctioned gainful employment, as the crime of 'asociality'.[10] Both closure operations, 1952 and 1961, were part and parcel of the overall SED politics of violent social transformation, including expropriation, terror against specific groups of the population, and the overall strengthening of the executive powers of the party and the state. While such procedures to construct, identify and exclude imaginary 'enemies of the people' are a generic feature of communist dictatorships, their specifically German realization was inextricably entwined with the perception of the 'imperialist' other: all 'asocial' and 'negative' elements were in one way or another considered to represent the imminent danger of West German intrusion and thereby served to embody all conceivable evils from which the first antifascist (later, socialist) state 'on German soil' had to be systematically purged and kept free.

The significance of the operations accompanying the closures of the border in 1952 and 1961 transcended the physical act of sealing off GDR territory. They were paradigmatic for the making of the SED state itself. The border regime embodied the methods of the exercise of authority in the GDR in essential form. As in the border region, where every person had to legitimize his or her presence at any given point in time by showing his identity card to any representative of state authority, the make-up of the SED dictatorship relied essentially on a close regulation of where exactly individuals were allowed to be and where not. This principle was, of course, applied most consequently to the cities, counties and districts with borders to the West, which were therefore better staffed with security personnel, be they from the Stasi, the regular police or the National People's Army, not to mention the border troops.[11] But it was extended also to the remaining parts of the GDR.

From the regime's perspective the problem was that the counties that bordered on West Germany were by no means the only spaces where GDR citizens could come in contact with the West. Due to the existence and the particular status of West Berlin alone, tens of thousands of transit travellers crossed the GDR every day. Most of them travelled across the GDR in their cars via the transit autobahn; others took the railway.[12] Waterways too, which played a vital role in the transportation of goods to and from West Berlin, constituted potential sites of illegal *Kontaktaufnahme* (establishing contact) with agents of the class enemy and were thus also taken under special control. In this way the particular regime of the border zone was projected into the inner territory of the GDR, creating additional special areas with higher numbers of security personnel and more rigid controls of the resident and nonresident population.

Policing actual or potential contacts to the West thus became an integral part of the GDR dictatorship, permeating all spheres of life there. Wherever contact or exchange with the West was anticipated, the state multiplied its efforts to keep these contacts under tight control, which implied keeping unreliable persons away from zones of contact and imposing specific procedures for the scrutiny of those entitled to be there. For the SED, the very success of the socialist project rested on the sovereignty acquired by this technique of securing authority. Ulbricht and Honecker really believed what they said when they described the Berlin Wall as the *antifaschistische Schutzwall* (anti-fascist protection wall). In order to realize the grand project of the first truly democratic and socialist state on German soil, such protective structures needed to be established almost everywhere within the sovereign space of the GDR where Western influence was lurking around the corner. Most vulnerable in this regard, however, were the lines of virtual communication based on mass media consumption, of which more shortly.

In this way *Abgrenzung* (delimitation) became a central feature of the political culture of the East German dictatorship. Yet the SED was in the process also caught on the horns of a dilemma. On the one hand, it sought to permeate all aspects of political and social life with this rigorous anti-Western stance. On the other, it had to comply with the practical exigencies arising from the inter-Allied status of West Berlin. (Any *mourir pour Berlin* option had already been ruled out by all sides since the Berlin blockade.)[13] Since the four Allies had agreed to maintain its Allied status even after the construction of the Wall, the connection of West Berlin to the rest of the Western world became a source of constant negotiation and regulation on which East and West ultimately had to cooperate. As a result the physical – and not only the virtual, media-based – presence of the West in the East was perpetuated and became a constitutive feature of GDR reality.

On comparison, it is evident that this Cold War peculiarity – an East-West border right in the middle of the country – was complemented and contrasted by a fundamentally different experience on Germany's Western rim. There, a reverse process set in, leading as the Cold War continued to the gradual dissolution of restrictive border regimes in the context of (West) European integration. In regions like Baden-Württemberg or the Saarland, borders acquired a historically new meaning. In the context of NATO and the Western security system, the western borders themselves lost their relevance as military objects. They no longer constituted zones of potential danger for the security of the polity. Furthermore, West Germany's integration into 'the West' and the West European Economic Community in particular was accompanied by conscious efforts to overcome the mutual suspicions of former 'arch-enemies'. This secular change took place not just on the level of diplomatic and economic relations and of military alliances: it became practically relevant for millions of people throughout society. As a result of the intensification of travel with the increase of automobile traffic, borders between Germany and France, Belgium and so on came to be experienced ever more in terms of the opportunity for transition and regular mutual contact in an essentially positive sense. In everyday terms this shift took the form of shopping trips and weekend tourism for the residents near the border. It became relevant for wider parts of the West German population once travelling abroad by car for the annual holiday became a mass phenomenon.[14]

In itself this change in the meaning of borders does not appear sensational, as the same process took place also at the other borders in Western Europe. When compared to the developments in the Eastern bloc, however, the exceptional character of this 'normalization' is obvious. From its Soviet precedence, Communist rule demonstrated a particular obsession with border surveillance and thereby mobility control.[15] Travel restrictions based on the passport and visa were a basic feature of everyday life in the Soviet Union.[16] Anything else would simply have been incompatible with the lack of the structures of civil society and the predominance of centralist state planning typical for a totalitarian state project.

Nevertheless, the practice of 'opening' borders was also adopted with regard to mobility between the socialist 'brother nations'. Poland and the Soviet Union, Czechoslovakia and Hungary started to introduce passport and visa-free travel during the 1960s. The GDR joined this development only in 1972 in relation to Czechoslovakia and Poland. The surge of shopping tourism from Poland that this prompted provoked xenophobic reactions from East Germans that were in turn met by the SED leadership with a tolerance that was ambiguous to say the least. In any case mistrustful of its Polish comrades, it cancelled the visa-free travelling arrangement immediately after the rise of Solidarność.[17] This response was only symptomatic of a more general feature of the relations between states of the Soviet hemisphere. In stark contrast to the steady progress of economic and political integration in the West, they remained much more secluded from each other to the point of open mistrust and mutual delimitation.

On the whole it must be stressed that borders and their regulation remained an area of diverging experience in East and West Germany. The domestic border symbolized the hardships of the division of Germany as such and the brutality and lack of legitimacy of the SED dictatorship. But this was experienced in different ways: in the East, depending on one's standpoint, as an exclusion from the path towards freedom and affluence or as a price to pay for enjoying the privilege of being a partner within the Soviet commonwealth; in the West, as a regrettable outcome of the Second World War that was more than counterbalanced by the unique opportunity to join the club of the wealthy and free in world and European politics. Integration into the respective alliances furthered contrasting experiences with the borders towards Germany's neighbour states. While they came to signify the increasingly 'unproblematic' relations within a larger community of liberal societies in the West, they continued to be regarded as a potential source of complications and irritations in the East.

## Dealing with the Nazi Past as a Cold War Battleground

The territorial dividedness of the country was only one dimension of a specifically German way to experience the Cold War. It is possible to identify other dimensions of the German Cold War predicament in order to reconstruct this specificity. I will consider two of them briefly before concluding with a comparative discussion of the ways in which different nations were placed on the front lines of Cold War conflict.

One of the aspects characterizing Cold War Germany was the divergent way of dealing with its recent past, in particular the historical responsibility for Nazism and the crimes committed by Germany during the Second World War. From the outset, each German state claimed moral superiority over the other by negating its claim to have achieved a break with Nazism.[18] On each side the power structure of the other state was depicted as a modified continuation of the Nazi dictatorship. This also implied the possibility of a comprehensive exculpation of society in one's own state. Each German state developed peculiar narratives to represent itself as the only one in congruence with the perspective of a humanist and peaceful post–World War order. In the West the ideological tool to achieve this consisted mainly in privileging the interpretation of the Soviet system as a totalitarian one and thus related to the Nazi system. This was not just an exercise among the elite of intellectuals and politicians, but rather a truism pervading the discourses and thinking of everyday life, its appeal based not least on the vestiges of right-wing anti-socialism and more specifically Nazi anti-Slavism among Germans. The East German state claimed to be founded on anti-fascism as the world view *par excellence* that supposedly had united the resistance movements against the Nazi rule in the whole of Europe.[19]

The ideological foundations of both new states found their complement in mirroring policies of exclusion and inclusion. In East Germany constructing the 'anti-fascist order' implied removing a large part of the middle class from influential positions by means of criminalization and expropriation, and driving them out of the country. The integration of millions of 'small' Nazis notwithstanding, a record as a National Socialist became a serious career liability. The conduct of this purge lacked the qualities of a fair and just procedure; as it involved a rupture with the legal norms of the state it was therefore highly contentious. In the West, by contrast, once Allied control was reduced after the foundation of the Federal Republic, middle-class and former career Nazis were re-integrated into the reemerging bourgeois society. The cover-up of their former responsibility was complemented by anti-communist repression in more or less legal state forms. (One should remember that as positions within political philosophy, both anti-fascism and the totalitarianism thesis partly shared a prehistory that was distinct from their instrumentalization within the ideological battles of the Cold War.)[20]

This helped to install a logic in Cold War Germany according to which it was impossible to address publicly the legacy of the Nazi dictatorship without making reference to the vilified 'other'. Instrumentalizing the Nazi past became a feature of everyday polemics between 'Bonn' and 'Pankow'. To deal with the past by making polemical reference to an 'other' was most poignant in a divided nation state the separated parts of which were still quite familiar with each other, at least on the level of political and cultural elites. Although there was much imposed silence on both sides regarding the past, there was abundant knowledge too. In particular during the 1950s and 1960s, the two Germanys behaved like inimical members of a family clan who each shared knowledge about the skeletons in the closet of the other and were prepared to use this knowledge in public campaigns when necessary. Even if this intimacy was asymmetric, in the sense that the Eastern political elites on the whole were much more obsessed with the Nazi past of their West German counterparts while in the other direction the same sort of competence was limited to a relevant minority of communism experts, it nevertheless adds another feature to Germany's position as a border region between the blocs of the Cold War. It remained essential to German Cold War experience but lost in relevance in West Germany, however, as a consequence of the 'fundamental liberalisation'[21] of society and culture from the 1960s onwards, when 'anti-anticommunism' was on the rise together with the broad support for the new *Ostpolitik*. In this process, the totalitarianism thesis lost its credibility and integrative power. The conflict potential inherent in the confrontation with the Nazi past shifted to internal, that is to inner–West German relations.

As a result, the linkage of the Nazi past with the mutual perceptions of and fierce polemics between the German states lost some of its strength. Both societies developed their own distinct ways of structuring their relation to the past. In the West, *Vergangenheitsbewältigung* ('coming to terms with the past') took the paradigmatic form of a confrontation between the generations, one that unfolded the potential for political and cultural pluralism of a liberal society.[22] The affective energies that allowed '1968' to become something like a cultural revolution relied on a personalization of responsibility among the educated middle classes carefully avoided throughout the first decade of the Federal Republic. In the East, similarly open confrontations were ruled out by the party monopoly in the public sphere. The general lack of legitimacy of the SED state notwithstanding, its founders were credited in particular among the new intelligentsia socialized after the Second World War with the merit of active resistance against Nazism. Dealing with the past therefore took the form of an alliance between generations within which critical questions could be raised as long as the basic consensus about the GDR's identity as an anti-fascist state was not called into question.[23] Both ways of handling the past, however, involved a crucial evasion. They focused on the agency of elites during Nazism and tended to gloss over the responsibility of the population at large. Only during the 1980s was this problematic addressed in a broader way, fuelled not least by the universalization of the Holocaust narrative.

## Germany in the Mediascape of the Cold War

A further case where we can determine Germany's predicament as a Cold War border region is its insertion in the global extension of the infrastructure of audiovisual media with their increasing relevance in everyday life. The border-region predicament in this realm meant that both German states formed a specific subregion of the global mediascape[24] enabled by the Cold War, where media users could, thanks to the shared language, switch between East and West more easily than anywhere else in Europe.

The inherent capacity of film, recorded music, radio and television to overcome barriers of language and national-cultural tradition was a well established fact already before the Second World War. In all European nation states, this had prompted attempts to contain external intrusions, in particular from the United States. The ability to regulate the domestic public sphere was understood as intrinsic to state sovereignty. Competing and mutually exclusive claims to represent the same – German – nation logically incurred attempts to undermine the competitor's ability to control its domestic public sphere. While such control was feasible to an always limited extent with regard to print-based communication such as newspapers, magazines and books, it was doomed to failure in the realm of electronic media. As a result the media publics of the two German states were never neatly separated, but rather overlapped and influenced one another. During the early decades of the Cold War, both sides went to considerable lengths to use the available technical possibilities to interfere in the public sphere of the 'other' for explicitly political purposes. Each maintained radio stations, such as the US-sponsored station RIAS (*Rundfunk im amerikanischen Sektor* – Radio in the American Sector) or the East German '*Freiheitssender 904*' (liberty station 904), to propagate its own world view among all Germans.[25] In terms of relevant audience, however, this institutional symmetry always contrasted with the asymmetry of the prevailing orientation towards the West in both German states. Consuming West German radio and TV programmes became everyday practice in the GDR while the reverse was restricted to a tiny minority of experts and political sectarians.

Western radio and TV programmes aimed at an East German audience could rely on intimate knowledge about the area served, which was gained continuously via unofficial channels. Such media institutions could therefore become key factors of politics in moments of crisis. RIAS's role during the June uprising in 1953 and West German television on the day when the Wall came down[26] are cases in point. But in 'normal' times, GDR citizens used Western media in ways similar to those of media consumers in all advanced countries. Under routine conditions of everyday life, explicit political information ranked behind entertainment and practical orientation. Only in times of political tension would East Germans switch to Western stations in order to have access to more reliable information.[27] This observation does not imply the political irrelevance of such behaviour so much as the contrary. First of all, the SED had attempted to prevent its citizens from receiving Western stations, but without any lasting effect. At no point in its existence could the regime effectively control media consumption in its own territory. This obvious fact in and by itself only added to the endemic lack of legitimacy of the GDR as a sovereign state in its own right. Rather, the habit of 'going West' in a virtual sense was progressively more tolerated by the authorities as unavoidable. Instead systemic competition shifted to the realm of the culture industry: the vilified products of Western decadence in the realm of music and film entertainment were to be countered by home-grown adaptations of the same genres and formats. The notorious *Indianderfilme* (Native Indian films), DEFA's answer to the West German adaptations of Karl May's *Winnetou* novels, represent a standard example of this strategy, which allowed also for derivatives of genres of capitalist origin such as the spy thriller or the teenage musical. It was complemented by the increasing import of films from capitalist countries for the GDR's cinemas, including extremely popular productions both from Hollywood and from the West German industry.[28]

This was only of consequence with regard to the SED's declared aim of raising the GDR to West German standards of living.[29] By Western standards, however, the concept of 'standard of living' was inseparable from individualized consumer culture and the concomitant infrastructure of mass media consumption. Having promised its population that it would catch up with West Germany on these terms, the SED was caught in a dynamic of never-ending concessions to the expectations of GDR consumers and audiences. The continual adaptation of international trends contributed heavily to undermining the claim of the socialist project to embody an alternative to the capitalist way of life. Recent studies by Heiner Stahl and Edward Larkey on popular music have provided ample evidence of how far this renunciation of the project of creating a specifically state socialist culture industry could go. Once *Tanzmusik* (dance music) in the international vein had been accepted as an integral part of domestic radio programming in the mid 1960s,[30] the monopolistic recording studios of the Radio DDR found themselves unable to produce the output required by the 60:40 ratio permitting only 40 per cent of the material in their programmes to come from nonsocialist countries. Increasingly, private studios set up by musicians able to capitalize on their commercial successes in the West filled the gap.³¹ At the end of its existence the GDR could boast a fully commercialized pop music sector – a far cry from the claims of socialist culture policy.

On the whole campaigns of political propaganda to influence the domestic politics of the other side subsided to some degree in the period of international détente after the 1970s. In particular the West German side tried to avoid aggressive anti-communist rhetoric. The global dissemination of information and audio-visual entertainment across the inner-German border via electronic media, however, went on unhindered. In the end this had a much more devastating effect on the state socialist regime's acceptance by its citizens.³²

One could point to other aspects of the effects of continuous intra-German interaction ensuing from its involuntary role as the 'host' of a large part of the Iron Curtain. The study of economic relations, academic and cultural contacts, as well as the border-crossing structures and activities of the churches and the persistent relevance not least of private kinship and friendship relations all show Cold War Germany as a zone of intensified contact and exchange (never free of practical problems and psychological tensions, of course ) across the Iron Curtain. It is their intensity, their regularity and above all their diversity that set divided Germany apart from other regions of the Cold War theatre. Although framed by intra-German state treaties, regular interactions with the 'other' were not limited to the official sphere of state actors. On the contrary, they included also actors from civil society, professional interest groups, sports and cultural associations down to private persons and tourists. It is precisely *the potential* of such a diversity of the layers and realms in which interactions could occur that is characteristic of border regions. Whether this potential is realized or not, however, is a matter of contingency.

That Germany found itself in a privileged position not only to suffer the potential of Cold War division, but also to exploit to the full the potential of rapprochement as it ensued from its border predicament, is not in itself a new observation. On a general level, Christoph Kleßmann has coined the term 'asymmetric entanglement' (*asymmetrische Verflechtung*) in order to grasp this German Cold War peculiarity.³³ On the GDR side, both regime and population remained fixated on the West until 1989. The regime always claimed that socialism would outdo the West in terms of growth and wealth while avoiding its disadvantages – for instance, social insecurity, unemployment, high crime rates, or the sell-out to American imperialism. This claim was both complemented and contrasted by an essentially positive notion of the West among the GDR population at large. What both the regime and population shared was, of course, the unquestioned notion that the yardstick for the GDR's achievements and its future prospects lay in the West.

In the Federal Republic, however, the more or less uncontested priority of political and economic integration into the Western hemisphere increasingly marginalized the interest in relations with the other part of the German nation – but only in society more generally. In regions marked by close vicinity to the East, such as West Berlin and the notorious *Zonenrandgebiet* (zonal border area), relations with the East remained an everyday issue, not least due to the technical necessities of official interaction with the East. This became a speciality of its own within West and East German politics. Notwithstanding the fact that West German society on the whole looked westwards, this went in hand with the rise on both sides of 'specialists' in spheres such as culture, sports, trade and international relations. This too was conditioned by numerical factors, of course: the proportion of people with relations in the other part of the divided country was much higher in the East than in the West, a state of affairs reinforced by the massive exodus to the West during the 1950s. East Germans' Cold War experience thus remained permeated by the sense that they were living in a state bearing the marks of imposed partition. By contrast, FRG citizens progressively learned to see their state as a saturated and sovereign nation state, entering into a process of growing *Selbstanerkennung* (self-recognition) with the beginning of détente. This polity did not need the permanent reference to the other Germany any more. Where West German society was concerned, the division of the nation seemed to have lost the status of a pressing burden.[34]

## The German Division – a Global Peculiarity?

It is not, however, enough simply to state the uniqueness of the German Cold War predicament. For the sake of comprehensiveness, the German Cold War experience must be compared with other regions of the Cold War. Territorial partition may serve as our first dimension of comparison.

Here divided Korea provides an interesting combination of commonalities and differences. The historical circumstances of division were entirely different from the German case. Korea came out of the Second World War on the victors' side and as a nation liberated from Japanese colonial rule. Its partition ensued from hot and devastating warfare that led to the establishment of dictatorships on both sides of the ideological divide. But the longer the partition has lasted, and in particular the more democratic South Korea has become since the 1980s, the greater the similarity between basic features of the interaction between parts of Korea today and that of the two German states after the construction of the Wall. Especially since German unification South Korean scholars have developed a keen interest in German research on the GDR, divided Germany and the process of unification, prompting a series of German-Korean conferences and publications.[35]

But one need not limit oneself to the most evident case in the search for parallels. The divisive effect of the Cold War on nation states and their territorial integrity can also be observed elsewhere, albeit to a lesser extent. Another case in the Asian region would be China. One could also name Cuba, where territorial integrity is intact, though relativized by the presence of a colony of exiles just across the sea. In both cases we find interactions and types of conflict typical for the situation of the border region. Problems arising from militarily sensitive areas overlap with recurrent attempts at flight from the communist side, as well as the activities of exile communities on the capitalist side and attempts to maintain a minimum of economic and cultural relations, whether through small-scale diplomacy or through mass media communication.[36]

When we look at the European theatre, however, the German case remains unique in the way the territorial partition of the nation coincided with its status as a border region between the blocs. Elsewhere these elements occurred separately from one another. The highly sensitive and conflicted border region between Italy and Yugoslavia provides an example for the possible conversion of initial crisis-ridden confrontation into a long-term status quo of proactive transborder cohabitation. Prior to 1954 it constituted a political body in its own right, the UN-controlled 'Free State of Trieste', which bore the potential for severe ethnic and political conflict. Following its partition between Italy and Yugoslavia it eventually became a zone of exchange that developed some of the typically 'positive' characteristics of a border region between the two systems, such as shopping tourism and private travelling.[37] To some extent specific border relations remained relevant in the Northeastern Baltic between Finland and the Baltic republics of the Soviet Union, owing to Finland's formal neutrality in the Cold War and to some extent also to the linguistic similarities between Finnish and Estonian, which might have furthered the understanding of Finnish radio and television on the Estonian side.[38] To what extent the former members of the Habsburg Empire could draw on their heritage of historic entanglements in their respective border regimes still remains to be researched in more depth. First results rather suggest the impermeability of the borderline in everyday life up to the very end of communist rule.[39]

But the divisive effect of the Cold War on nation states was not limited to territorial partition. More often, its disintegrative effects occurred *within* a single country. Important nation states in Europe such as Italy and France were deeply marked by the East-West conflict and had to 'house' both ideological camps. In these liberal democracies the communists were the largest or second-largest political party. They were extremely well organized and commanded a hegemonic position in the trade union movement, among intellectuals, and in specific regions where they governed numerous local and regional administrations as mayors and in city councils. At the peak of the Cold War, regions such as the Parisian *banlieues* and the mining district in Northern France, or in Italy the Emilia Romana and Tuscany, constituted something like extraterritorial red areas with regard to the Western power centre.[40] It is no empty rhetoric when French scholars specializing in the history of the GDR or other Eastern bloc countries point to this lived experience as a factor that made them sensitive to the social and cultural practice of communism on the level of everyday life.[41]

By looking at cases of nation states in which the Cold War exerted a highly divisive pressure on the political culture, we can thus identify Germany as a case the specificity of which consisted in 'acting out' (and in the beginning rather 'being forced to act out') this divisive potential through *territorial disintegration* and a resultant *sociodemographic segregation*. The latter term refers to the uneven population exchange between the two German states at the early stage of the Cold War, with communists migrating to the East and the middle class and other anti-communists migrating to the West.[42] This contributed considerably to the obvious political and social homogeneity of the two German halves when contrasted to other European societies. While in other societies in the Soviet hemisphere proletarization was achieved overwhelmingly by instituting downwards social mobility of members of traditional upper classes by enforcing their political compliance, in Germany up to 1961, regional mobility played a significant role in reshaping the sociopolitical make-up of the society. Thereby the officially acclaimed *Arbeiter-und-Bauern-Macht* appearance of the GDR, which it shared with the other 'people's republics', was complemented by a distinctively embourgeoized (*verbürgerlicht*) pendant derived from the same demographic and ethnic 'stock' on the other side of the continent's divide.

With regard to the confrontation with the past, it is impossible of course to find a similar constellation in another European nation state. No other nation had to face a similar burden of responsibility for the crimes and destruction of the Second World War. But this absence of a comparable constellation has heuristic merits that also apply to other national cases. The entanglement of confrontation with the Nazi past and Cold War policies inside Germany shows that Cold War ideology and its logic were always intricately interwoven with other agendas. Ideological representations and legitimizing discourses about the past never stood neatly in a one-to-one relation. Besides, other nations had haunting pasts, albeit fundamentally different ones: national defeat, occupation and collaboration during the Second World War; the partial loss of sovereignty and of global power; the painful process of decolonization. In the case of France, for instance, it is clear that on the level of domestic politics, the Cold War agenda overlapped with the issue of a precarious political and cultural sovereignty with regard to the US and the traumatic experience of decolonization, to the point that the latter two issues prevailed at the cost of the former. A similar observation can be made about Poland, where the recreation of a Polish state as such (although under adverse conditions) and the maintenance of its integrity were at least as important as the fact that this state regained its historical existence several hundred kilometres westwards of its original site and within the communist camp, which restricted its sovereignty. Or to put it more generally, the bipolar, ideological nature of the Cold War cannot be taken as a solitary determining factor that made Cold War experience specific at a given place at a given time.

This is most evident when set in relation to the example of the overlapping public and media spheres of the two German states discussed above. From a comparative perspective the specific German dimension is reduced simply to the fact of a shared language. The global dissemination and adaptation of Western media products – American ones in particular – was neither unique to Europe among the regions of the world nor to West or East Germany within their respective camps. When this process was initiated as an intrinsic element of American international politics after the end of the war, this meant resuming strategies of economic and cultural expansion from the interwar period.[43] The challenge of this expansion was thus nothing new for 'Old Europe'. It predated the Cold War but played out its logic most forcefully within peculiar ideological front lines of this conflict. By opting for peaceful coexistence and competition in the field of consumer culture in order to maintain their regimes' stability, the leaders of Eastern bloc countries tacitly accepted mass media and the dynamics of its usage as an intrinsic element of social life within their sphere of domination.

## Conclusions

Far from becoming 'two nations', Germany was marked by a unique paradox in its Cold War experience. In formal terms, the two parts developed all the traits of two nation states going separate ways in the world system. This was complemented, among other things, by totally different notions of the concept of 'nation' within the official discourses on each side. The more sovereign and self-assured West German political culture became, the more it tended on the one hand to deemphasize the concept in favour of its transnational ties to the Western world. On the other hand, the GDR leadership proclaimed a new socialist and somehow also German nation without mentioning Germany at all. Meanwhile GDR citizens remained firm believers in a traditional ethnic idea of the nation, based on shared cultural values and traditions.[44]

But the more this separateness established itself as routine within the system of international relations, the more these former halves of a defeated state developed an array of specific relations in the realms of economy and culture, as well as private life. Their intensity and frequency set them apart from other countries involved in the Cold War. Division could never overrule the practical necessities of interaction within the highly industrialized heart of a war-weary Europe where people did not want to run the risk of global warfare again, and where leaders in both East and West were forced equally to prioritize a peaceful path to security and welfare. In the German case, the shared national past proved to be an enabling moment in making the best out of the lasting division of the continent; it would therefore be totally misleading to categorize their relations as 'transnational'.

As it turned out, to the frustration of many postnational intellectuals, 'the imagined community' of Germans was more alive after four decades of living in separate states than had been expected. There were no chances for the 'third way' solution of an 'alternative' GDR once Europe was about to be reunited. At the same time, this persistent unity of Germans as an ethnic group turned out to be highly problematic, since it was more a product of fantasy and expectations than it was real. It is precisely with regard to their ethnic qualities that the two German societies developed so differently during the Cold War. Strict ethnic homogeneity on the one side and increasing multiethnicity on the other have given rise to conflicts and contradictions in unified Germany that are well-known facts.[45] Divided, but not disconnected: it is perhaps this permanent instability of national belonging, of coherence and self-evident identity as a nation, that can be determined as a very specific, if not *the* specific, Cold War experience in Germany.

## Notes

1. Bernd Stöver, *Der Kalte Krieg 1947–1991: Geschichte eines radikalen Zeitalters* (Munich: Beck, 2007), pp. 463–77.

2. Lary May, 'Victory's Shadow: Cold War Culture and Transnational Memory', keynote speech at the conference 'European Cold War Cultures? Societies, Media, and Cold War Experiences in East and West (1947–1990)', Zentrum für Zeithistorische Forschung Potsdam, Potsdam, 26–28 April 2007.

3. For example *Rethinking Cold War Culture*, ed. by Peter J. Kuznick and James Gilbert (Washington, DC: Smithsonian, 2001); *The Cultural Cold War in Western Europe, 1945–1960*, ed. by Giles Scott-Smith and Hans Krabbendam (London: Cass, 2003); *Across the Blocs: Cold War Cultural and Social History*, ed. by Rana Mitter and Patrick Major (London: Cass, 2004).

4. François Lyotard, *The Postmodern Condition* (Manchester: Manchester University Press, 1984); Daniel Bell, *The Coming of Post-Industrial Society: A Venture in Social Forecasting* (New York: Basic Books, 1973).

5. See the caustic remarks in David Caute, 'Foreword', in *The Cultural Cold War in Western Europe 1945–1960*, ed. by Scott-Smith and Krabbendam, pp. vii–ix.

6. For a conceptual discussion of borders see Maren Ullrich, *Geteilte Ansichten: Erinnerungslandschaft deutsch-deutsche Grenze* (Berlin: Aufbau, 2006), p. 15. In a similar vein, Stefan-Ludwig Hofmann adopts the concept of 'contact zones' developed in colonial studies to understand the encounters between antagonistic polities for his seminal study of Greater Berlin as the 'interzone' of global politics in the 1940s. See his forthcoming book *Berlin unter Alliierter Besatzung: Lokale Verflechtung und globale Politik*.

7. The pioneer study here is Peter Sahlins, *Boundaries: The Making of France and Spain in the Pyrenees* (Berkeley: University of California Press, 1989).

8. See Inge Bennewitz and Rainer Potratz, *Zwangsaussiedlungen an der innerdeutschen Grenze: Analysen und Dokumente* (Berlin: Links, 1994).

9. See the research project of Gerhard Sälter, of the Dokumentationszentrum Berliner Mauer, Berlin, on the voluntary assistants of the border guards: Gerhard Sälter, 'Rituelle Inszenierung staatlicher Anerkennung: Konferenzen der freiwilligen Grenzhelfer (1956–1989)', *Horch und Guck*, 56.4 (2006), 15–16; ibid., 'Loyalität und Denunziation in der ländlichen Gesellschaft der DDR: Die Freiwilligen Helfer der Grenzpolizei im Jahr 1952', in *Der willkommene Verrat: Beiträge zur Denunziationsforschung*, ed. by Michael Schröter (Weilerswist: Velbrück, 2007), pp. 159–84.

10. Thomas Lindenberger, '"Asoziale Lebensweise": Herrschaftslegitimation, Sozialdisziplinierung und die Konstruktion eines "negatives Milieus" in der SED-Diktatur', *Geschichte und Gesellschaft*, 32 (2005), 227–54; idem, 'Asociality' and Modernity: The GDR as a Welfare Dictatorship', in *Socialist Modern: East German Everyday Culture and Politics*, ed. by Katherine Pence and Paul Betts (Ann Arbor: University of Michigan Press, 2008), pp. 211–33.

11. On the various armed units of the GDR state executive see *Im Dienste der Partei: Handbuch der bewaffneten Organe der DDR*, ed. by Torsten Diedrich, Hans Ehlert and Rüdiger Wenzke (Berlin: Links, 2004).

12. Mathias Bertram, *Enzyklopädie der DDR: Personen, Institutionen und Strukturen in Politik, Wirtschaft, Justiz, Wissenschaft und Kultur*, Digitale Bibliothek, 32 (Berlin: Directmedia, 2000), p. 1317; also Axel Doßmann, *Begrenzte Mobilität: Eine Kulturgeschichte der Autobahnen in der DDR* (Essen: Klartext, 2003).

13. Cyril Buffet, *Mourir pour Berlin: La France et l'Allemande 1945–1949* (Paris: Armand Colin, 1991); Burghard Ciesla, Michael Lemke and Thomas Lindenberger, *Sterben für Berlin? Berliner Krisen 1948–1958* (Berlin: Metropol, 1999).

14. On EURO-Regions and the transformation of the burden of border regions into an asset for the quality of life able to attract corporate investments see Silvia Raich, *Grenzüberschreitende und interregionale Zusammenarbeit in einem "Europa der Regionen": Dargestellt anhand der Fallbeispiele Grossregion Saar-Lor-Lux, EUREGIO und "Vier Motoren für Europa": Ein Beitrag zum europäischen Integrationsprozess* (Baden-Baden: Nomos, 1995); *Euroregions: The Alps-Adriatic Context*, ed. by Josef Langer (Frankfurt/Main: Lang, 2007); on the border-crossing effects of tourism in Europe see Thomas Mergel, 'Europe as Leisure Time Communication: Tourism and Transnational Interaction since 1945', in *Conflicted Memories: Europeanizing Contemporary Histories*, ed. by Konrad H. Jarausch and Thomas Lindenberger (New York: Berghahn, 2007), pp. 133–53.

15. See Andrea Chandler, *Institutions of Isolation: Border Controls in the Soviet Union and its Successor States 1917–1993* (Montreal: McGill-Queens Press, 1998).

16. See David Shearer, 'Elements Near and Alien: Passportization, Policing, and Identity in the Stalinist State, 1931–1952', *The Journal of Modern History*, 76 (2004), 835–81; and the rich collection of essays in *Frontières du communisme: Mythologies et réalités de la division de l'Europe de la revolution d'Octobre au mur de Berlin*, ed. by Sophie Coeuré and Sabine Dullin (Paris: La Découverte, 2007).

17. Katarzyna Stokłosa, 'Two Sides of the Border and One Regional Identity: The Identity Problem in the German-Polish and Ukrainian-Slovak Border Regions', in *Crossing the Border: Boundary Relations in a Changing Europe*, ed. by Thomas Lundén (Gdansk: Förlags ab Gondolin, 2006), pp. 117–33.

18. Christoph Classen, 'Fremdheit gegenüber der eigenen Geschichte: Zum öffentlichen Umgang mit dem Nationalsozialismus in beiden deutschen Staaten', in *Fremde und Fremd-Sein in der DDR: Zu historischen Ursachen der Fremdenfeindlichkeit in Deutschland*, ed. by Jan C. Behrends, Thomas Lindenberger and Patrice Poutrus (Berlin: Metropol, 2003), pp. 101–26; Daniel Fulda and Martin Andree, 'Anticommunism and (West) German Identity: An Analysis of Metaphors and Concepts of History in the F.A.Z., 1949–1952', *Yearbook of European Studies*, 13 (1999), 94–129.

19. François Furet, *The Passing of an Illusion: The Idea of Communism in the Twentieth Century* (Chicago: University of Chicago Press, 1999), pp. 266–314.

20. Ibid.

21. Jürgen Habermas, *Autonomy & Solidarity: Interviews with Jürgen Habermas*, ed. by Peters Dews, rev. edn (London: Verso, 1992), p. 234.

22. See *Wo 1968 liegt: Reform und Revolte in der Geschichte der Bundesrepublik*, ed. by Christina von Hodenberg (Göttingen: Vandenhoeck & Ruprecht, 2006).

23. See Sigrid Meuschel, *Legitimation und Parteiherrschaft* (Frankfurt/Main: Suhrkamp, 1992); Lutz Niethammer, Alexander von Plato and Dorothee Wierling, *Die Volkseigene Erfahrung: Eine Archäologie des Lebens in der Industrieprovinz der DDR* (Berlin: Rowohlt, 1991).

24. See John Hartley, *Communication, Cultural and Media Studies: The Key Concepts* (London: Routledge, 2005); Arjun Appadurai, *Modernity at Large: Cultural Dimensions of Globalization* (Minneapolis: University of Minnesota Press, 1996).

25. See the chapters by Bernd Stöver, 'Radio mit kalkuliertem Risiko: RIAS als amerikanischer Sender für die DDR' and Jürgen Wilke, 'Radio im Geheimauftrag. Der Freiheitssender 904 und der Deutsche Soldatensender 935 als Instrumente des Kalten Krieges', in *Zwischen Pop und Propaganda: Radio in der DDR*, ed. by

Klaus Arnold and Christoph Classen (Berlin: Links, 2004), pp. 209–28 and 249–66 respectively.

26. Hans-Hermann Hertle, 'Volksaufstand und Herbstrevolution: Die Rolle der West-Medien 1953 und 1989 im Vergleich', in *Aufstände im Ostblock,* ed. by Henrik Bispinck and others (Berlin: Links, 2004), pp. 163–92.

27. See the seminal work of Michael Meyen, *Denver Clan und Neues Deutschland: Mediennutzung in der DDR* (Berlin: Links, 2003); also Michael Meyen and Ute Nawratil, 'The Viewers: Television and Everyday Life in East Germany', *Historical Journal of Film, Radio and Television,* 24.3 (2004), 355–64.

28. Jon Raundalen, 'A Communist Takeover in the Dream Factory: Appropriation of Popular Genres by the East German Film Industry', *I: Slavonica,* 11.1 (2004), 69–86.

29. See *Überholen ohne einzuholen: Die DDR-Wirtschaft als Fußnote der deutschen Geschichte?,* ed. by André Steiner (Berlin: Links 2006).

30. Heiner Stahl, *Jugendradio im Kalten Ätherkrieg: Berlin als eine Klanglandschaft des Pop (1962–1973)* (Berlin: Landbeck, 2010); ibid. 'Mediascape and Soundscape in Cold War Berlin', in *Berlin Divided City, 1945–1989,* ed. by Philip Broadbent and Sabine Hake (Oxford: Berghahn, 2010), 55–66.

31. Edward Larkey, *Rotes Rockradio: Populäre Musik und die Kommerzialisierung des DDR-Rundfunks* (Münster: LIT, 2007).

32. See Thomas Lindenberger, 'Geteilte Welt, geteilter Himmel? Der Kalte Krieg und die Massenmedien in gesellschaftsgeschichtlicher Perspektive', in *Zwischen Pop und Propaganda,* ed. by Arnold and Classen, pp. 27–44.

33. Kleßmann, *Zwei Staaten, eine Nation,* p. 13.

34. See Andreas Wirsching, *Abschied vom Provisorium: Die Geschichte der Bundesrepublik Deutschland 1982–1990* (Munich: Deutsche-Verlagsanstalt, 2006); Konrad H. Jarausch, *After Hitler: Recivilizing Germans, 1945–1995* (Oxford: Oxford University Press, 2006).

35. *Geschichte der Teilung. Wie ist sie zu betrachten? Vergleich der Nordkorea- und DDR-Forschung,* ed. by Un-Suk Han (Seoul: Sangji University, 2004).

36. See Melanie M. Ziegler, *U.S.-Cuban Cooperation Past, Present, and Future* (Florida: Florida University Press, 2007).

37. Sabina Mihelj, 'Drawing the East-West Border: Narratives of Modernity and Identity in the Julian Region, 1947–1954', in *European Cold War Cultures, Perspectives on Societies in the East and the West,* ed. by Annette Vowinckel, Marcus M. Payk, Thomas Lindenberger (Oxford: Berghahn, 2010).

38. See Walter C. Clemens, *Baltic Independence and the Russian Empire* (London: Macmillan, 1990), pp. 71 and 118; the extent of this influence on the Soviet side, however, still remains open to more thorough assessment.

39. See the project at the Ludwig Boltzmann Institute for European History and Public Spheres, Vienna, on 'Border Communities. Microstudies on Everyday Life, Politics and Memory in European Societies From 1945 to the Present': http://ehp.lbg.ac.at/en/research-programme/communist-and-postcommunist-times-central-europe (accessed 16 August 2010), first results in Muriel Blaive and Berthold Molden, Grenzfälle: Österreichische und tschechische Erfahrungen am Eisernen Vorhang (Weitra: Bibliothek der Provinz, 2009); Muriel Blaive and Thomas Lindenberger, 'Border guarding as social practice: a case study of communist governance and hid-

den transcripts', in *Walls, Borders, Boundaries: Strategies of Surveillance and Survival*, ed. by Marc Silberman, Karen Till and Janet Ward (Oxford: Berghahn, 2011).

40. See Marc Lazar, *Maisons Rouges: les partis communistes français et italiens de la Libération à nos jours* (Paris: Aubier, 1992).

41. Sandrine Kott, 'Der Beitrag der französischen Sozialwissenschaften zur Erforschung der ostdeutschen Gesellschaft', in *Die ostdeutsche Gesellschaft: Eine transnationale Perspektive*, ed. by Sandrine Kott and Emmanuel Droit (Berlin: Links, 2006), pp. 13–23 (p. 15).

42. Major, *Behind the Berlin Wall;* Bernd Stöver, *Zuflucht DDR: Spione und andere Übersiedler* (Munich: Beck, 2009).

43. Victoria de Grazia, 'Mass Culture and Sovereignty: The American Challenge to European Cinemas, 1920–1960', *Journal of Modern History*, 61.1 (1989), 53–87.

44. Jan C. Behrends and Patrice Poutrus, 'Xenophobia in the Former GDR: Explorations and Explanation from a Historical Perspective', in *Nationalisms Across the Globe: An Overview of Nationalisms in State-Endowed and Stateless Nations*, ed by. Wojciech Burszta and Tomasz Kamusella (Poznan: Wysza Szkola Nauk Hymanistycznych I Dziennikarstwa, 2005), pp. 155–70.

45. Patrice Poutrus, 'Die DDR, ein anderer deutscher Weg? Zum Umgang mit Ausländern im SED-Staat', in *Zuwanderungsland Deutschland: Migrationen 1500– 2005*, ed. by Rosmarie Beier-de Haan (Wolfratshausen: Minerva 2005), pp. 118–31.

# 2

# Fighting the First World War in the Cold War

East and West German Historiography on the Origins of the First World War, 1945–1959

*Matthew Stibbe*

Thomas Lindenberger's notion, in this volume, of Germany as a 'border region of the Cold War', with the intense and contradictory feelings of 'separateness' and 'togetherness' that borders can generate, is also useful in interpreting different modes of 'coming to terms with the past' in the two Germanys.[1] On the one hand, behind the scenes scholars in the GDR typically displayed a high degree of interest in developments in political historiography in the West (and in neighbouring socialist countries like Poland), although this interest was not always reciprocated, and increasingly less so as time passed.[2] On the other, until the late 1960s both East and West Germany depicted their opposite number as the embodiment of the worst features of the German past, while claiming that they themselves represented the more progressive elements within the German nation. Günter Grass's comparison of Walter Ulbricht to a concentration camp commandant in an open letter to Anna Seghers, President of the East German Writers' Association, in 1961 is a case in point.[3] Yet Konrad Adenauer, too, clearly saw the past in Cold War terms, declaring in San Francisco in 1953: 'Our previous capital of Berlin now sits like an island and outpost in the middle of a red ocean.'[4]

This chapter examines the peculiar impact of Germany's status as a 'border region' on the production of historical knowledge. It does so primarily by focusing on scholarly debates about the causes of the First World War in the two Germanys at a key period in the Cold War from 1945 to 1959. Important events during this time included the division of Germany into two states in 1949, the outbreak of the Korean War in 1950, West German rearmament and entry into NATO in 1955, the formation of the Warsaw Pact in the same year and Khrushchev's denunciation of Stalin at the twentieth congress of the Communist Party of the Soviet Union in 1956. Historiographically, these were also the years immediately preceding the debate over Germany's aims in the First World War, which began when the Hamburg historian Fritz Fischer published his controversial thesis *Griff nach der Weltmacht* (Grasp at World Power) in 1961.[5]

The chapter begins by considering historical research on the origins of the First World War, with special reference to the decisions by the leadership of the German Social Democratic Party (SPD, Sozialdemokratische Partei Deutschlands) to approve war credits in the Reichstag on 4 August 1914 and to adhere to the *Burgfrieden,* the government-sponsored truce between the political parties, employers and trade unions in the war's early stages. These resolutions caused a damaging split between the Majority Social Democrats or 'reformists' (MSPD, Mehrheitssozialdemokratische Partei Deutschlands) and a growing anti-war minority, divided in turn between moderate 'independents' or 'centrists' and the extreme left Spartacists, forerunners of the German Communist Party (KPD, Kommunistische Partei Deutschlands).[6] The chapter continues by examining the reception of the East German labour historian Jürgen Kuczynski's book *Der Ausbruch des ersten Weltkrieges und die deutsche Sozialdemokratie* (The Outbreak of the First World War and German Social Democracy), which appeared in 1957 and almost ended his academic career in the East. In conclusion it argues that the production of historical knowledge in the 1950s was directly linked to attempts by both German states to claim exclusive authorship over the past and future of the German nation. However, there were significant differences, too, in particular the greater plurality of opinion permitted in the FRG and the consequent lack of a single, all-defining historical narrative compared to the GDR.

## The West German View

Between 1945 and 1959 the historical profession in West Germany was still dominated by men who were trained under the old *Kaiserreich* and saw themselves as heirs of a national tradition stretching back to Leopold von Ranke and Heinrich von Sybel.[7] Radical and leftist voices were effectively marginalized. True, Friedrich Meinecke, the foremost representative of the liberal wing of the neo-Rankeans, wrote in 1946 of the necessity of a 'radical break with our military past', yet even he urged his contemporaries to 'discriminate between what was valuable and what was valueless' in terms of 'our historical traditions in general'.[8] In particular Meinecke singled out the

> exaltation of spirit experienced during the August days of 1914 ... [when] all the rifts which had hitherto existed in the German people, both within the bourgeoisie and between the bourgeoisie and the working classes, were suddenly closed in the face of the common danger [posed by the enemy].[9]

The conservative counterpart to Meinecke was Gerhard Ritter, the Freiburg historian who called not for a break with German militarism but for its rescue from the 'perversions' of the twentieth century.[10] Rejecting Meinecke's liberal idealism, Ritter focused on the positive example of the Prussian 'ideal of statesmanship' as an antidote to the 'demonic' abuse of power by modern 'demagogues' from Robespierre and Lenin to Hitler and Mussolini.[11] One statesman who had come close to this ideal was Theobald von Bethmann Hollweg, the Reich chancellor in 1914, who reluctantly but courageously led Germany into a 'defensive war', at the same time harnessing the desire of SPD leaders for national integration in order to create a bulwark against the extreme militarists and Pan-Germans on the right. The real crisis for German militarism during the First World War, for Ritter, came after 1916 when Hindenburg and Ludendorff irresponsibly forced through the declaration of unrestricted submarine warfare against the advice of civilian officials.[12] However, since Germany had gone to war in 1914 as an act of national defence, the *Burgfrieden* was patriotic and within the national interest, a view that Ritter shared with those on the right wing of the Social Democrats like Friedrich Stampfer.[13] On the other hand, those left-wing Social Democrats and bourgeois pacifists who resisted the war were either ignored or condemned as enemies of Germany.[14] Indeed, the standard line for conservative-nationalist historians in the 1950s was that a state unwilling or unable to defend its own borders cannot be a secure, stable state – as the Korean War also seemed to suggest. It was against this background that Adenauer moved the FRG towards closer economic and military integration with the West.

Outside of academe there were, of course, many leftist opponents of rearmament in the Federal Republic in the 1950s, including – at least until the official break with Marxism at Bad Godesberg in 1959 – sections of the SPD and trade union movement. Within the historical profession, however, conservative attitudes reigned. Only in the 1960s and 1970s, in the aftermath of the Fischer controversy, did a new generation of social historians – such as Helga Grebing, Dieter Groh and Susanne Miller – challenge aspects of the prevailing consensus. In at least two important respects they revised existing interpretations. Firstly, they demonstrated that the decision by the SPD leadership to approve war credits in 1914 was not predetermined by a long-term desire among the party's right wing for positive integration into the national community; in fact, the party's stance was still uncertain as late as 1 August 1914. And secondly, they showed that the wartime split in the party, which culminated in the formation of the Independent Social Democratic Party (USPD, Unabhängige Sozialdemokratische Partei Deutschlands) in 1917, was not the inevitable outcome of ideological divisions between left and right dating from before the war but had more to do with inflexible forms of party discipline introduced by the MSPD leadership during the war itself.[15]

Over and above this, however, much of the 'new' social history of the late 1960s and 1970s confirmed rather than challenged the earlier pro-reformist line in West German historiography. Despite the greater scope for pluralism than in the GDR, the dominant tone was still rigorously anti-communist.[16] Not until after 1989 did any clear-cut alternatives emerge to the standard line that the MSPD sincerely believed they were fighting a defensive war against 'tsarist aggression', and could not leave the Fatherland in the lurch. In short, there was little challenge to what Wolfgang Kruse terms the 'national idealisation of the outbreak of war' from either left or right in the Federal Republic.[17] Even the most vociferous critics of West German rearmament, like Wolfgang Abendroth, agreed that the 'patriotic hysteria' of August 1914 'also took hold of the German masses, and sadly not just the ranks of the petit-bourgeoisie'.[18]

## The East German View

The official position in the GDR, as can be expected, was very different. While in West Germany the SPD identified itself by and large with the 'reformist' or 'centrist' wings of the party in 1914, in East Germany the new SED, formed from a forced merger of the old SPD and KPD in 1946, saw itself as the successor to the revolutionary traditions of the German labour movement, from Marx and Engels through Lenin to the foundation of the KPD in December 1918. From their perspective, August 1914 was a 'betrayal' by the SPD of the real interests of the working class, while the revolutionary left, led by Karl Liebknecht and Rosa Luxemburg, were the true patriots who acted in the national interest by opposing Germany's deliberate leap into an imperialist war.[19]

In the immediate postwar years a variety of different historical perspectives were tolerated in the Soviet zone, provided they broadly fitted the framework of an anti-fascist and anti-militarist discourse. The year

1848 took centre stage as the starting point of the independent workers' movement and its demands for a democratization of society, while links were also claimed with other 'progressive' figures in German history, such as the nineteenth-century bourgeois medical reformer, humanist and '48er' Rudolf Virchow.[20] Indeed, the KPD's first published programme after its relegalization in the Soviet zone in June 1945 did not mention socialism at all, stating instead:

> The destruction of Hitlerism must be accompanied by the democratization of Germany, so that the transition to bourgeois democracy, which began in 1848, is completed, the last fragments of feudalism are done away with and the reactionary force of old Prussian militarism ... is destroyed.[21]

In line with broader developments in the Cold War, however, the 1950s saw the establishment of tighter forms of ideological control over the East German historical profession. The SED insisted that East German academic research should reject 'bourgeois' objectivity in favour of socialist partisanship to reflect positively on the historical emergence of a revolutionary, class-conscious proletariat within a specifically national context. Or as Ulbricht observed in a 1959 speech marking the tenth anniversary of the creation of the GDR:

> The SED has overcome and banned the barbaric ideology of German imperialism and fascism. It has set up an anti-fascist democratic system and boldly carried out the transition to the socialist revolution ... This process goes on ... It is the law of historical development that socialism will triumph in the whole of Germany.[22]

Another key theme in East German historiography in the 1950s was the 'reactionary role of German imperialism and militarism in history'.[23] The 'imperialist' bourgeoisie, it was argued, had attempted to win over the German workers to a policy of robbery and exploitation of colonial peoples, for instance through the 'scramble for Africa' in the 1880s and the establishment of spheres of influence in China and the Pacific in the 1890s. But it had lost all claim to leadership of the German nation because of its key part in causing two world wars, and its current attempts, in West Germany, Britain and the US, to start a third.[24] GDR historians thus had a 'national responsibility' to expose the past and present crimes of German imperialism while demonstrating that only a united Germany, under the leadership of the workers' movement and its vanguard party, the SED, could guarantee stability in Europe and the world.[25]

Rival interpretations of August 1914 are significant to understanding these developments for three reasons. Firstly, from the 1950s onwards the line taken by the official East German peace movement was that wars, including nuclear wars, could be prevented only by concerted proletarian action across international boundaries. In effect this meant pursuing a strategy of isolating the 'opportunistic' SPD leadership in West Germany from its working-class base.[26] Secondly, August 1914 played an important role in attempts by the SED to establish a Marxist-Leninist historiography that would compete with 'reactionary' bourgeois scholarship in the West.[27] Thirdly, and related, East German historical writing on August 1914 allows us to test a theory put forward by Stefan Berger that draws attention to the continued predominance of the 'national paradigm' in GDR as well as West German historiography. East German scholars, in other words, were anxious to focus on trends at a national level and to argue that they, as the inheritors of the progressive traditions in the German workers' movement, represented the 'national interest' of all Germans, in contrast to the 'anti-national' Federal Republic.[28] Indeed, leading West German Social Democrats like Friedrich Stampfer and Kurt Schumacher were regularly denounced as 'enemies of German unity and of the working class' in GDR publications,[29] providing an ideological legitimation for the periodic purges of Social Democrats or putative Social Democrats from the SED's ranks, and, in some instances, the prosecution and imprisonment of party members who had developed illegal contacts with the West German SPD. This was the fate, for instance, of the Berlin-based philosopher Wolfgang Harich and the head of the Aufbau publishing house Walter Janka after 1956.[30]

## The Kuczynski Affair

While political interference in academic publications was already the norm, from 1956 the SED took an even more direct role in the production of historical knowledge, largely to offset the potentially damaging repercussions of events in the Soviet Union, Poland and Hungary for the future of communist rule in East Germany. Ulbricht especially was anxious to prevent the emergence of a 'German Gomulka', a reference to the popular reformist leader who had risen to power in Poland in October 1956, and thus consciously used the writing of party history as a means of limiting the pace of de-Stalinization.[31] In 1957, however, his efforts suddenly seemed to be threatened by the appearance of a book by one of the GDR's leading scholars, the Marxist labour historian Jürgen

Kuczynski. Published under the title *Der Ausbruch des ersten Weltkrieges und die deutsche Sozialdemokratie,* the book broke with a chief tenet of previous East German writing by suggesting that not only the leaders of the SPD, but also rank-and-file members, had willingly gone to war in August 1914. 'Objective' economic developments, Kuczynski argued, had allowed a temporary, albeit false identification of the labour movement with the aggressive policies of the Prusso-German state, a point of view which, superficially at least, brought him close to the position of Karl Kautsky and other 'centrists' after 1914.[32] The subsequent crisis in German Social Democracy was the result not only of the 'opportunistic' stance taken by the SPD leadership, but also of the weak ideological commitment of millions of German workers to the cause of proletarian internationalism. As Kuczynski himself put it: 'In no other country were the organizations of the proletariat placed so fully in the service of imperialism ... in no other country was the economic and political struggle of the working class so completely abandoned.'[33]

In reality, he argued, no part of the German left in 1914 was Leninist and therefore no faction was in a position to organize revolutionary opposition to the war, regardless of any 'betrayal' by the leadership. In this respect, the traditional division of the old SPD into 'right', 'centre' and 'left' in communist historiography had turned out to be 'insufficient' and in some respects 'completely misguided'.[34] Kuczynski did not stop here. Even Lenin, he wrote, had committed errors in his 1908 pamphlet *Marxism and Revisionism:*

> Lenin had only discovered one of the roots of revisionism, but not the decisive cause of this poison, which was to be found in the working class itself ... This explains why even this great fighter against opportunism was unprepared for the sheer scale of opportunism which sucked in almost everything around it in August 1914.[35]

Such errors did not undermine the validity of Marxism-Leninism as an ideology. Rather, in Kuczynski's new, post-Stalinist interpretation:

> A genuine Bolshevik, a real Marxist, is not somebody who knows everything in advance ... [but] somebody who continually and successfully draws lessons from the experience of history, who applies these lessons in the cause of humanity and who acts with appropriate partisanship in word and deed ... And nobody knew better how to learn from the experience of the class struggle than Marx and Engels and Lenin, the authors of the classic works of Marxism-Leninism.[36]

Finally, Kuczynski turned the official East German view of Karl Liebknecht, the leader of the revolutionary left in 1914, on its head. Most GDR accounts glossed over Liebknecht's decision to vote with the rest of the SPD parliamentary group in favour of war credits on 4 August 1914, dwelling instead on his decisive break with party discipline in the following weeks. However, Kuczynski now leapt to Liebknecht's defence; if even Lenin had been taken unaware by events at the beginning of the war, then Liebknecht's later self-criticisms were unnecessary and exaggerated. In Kuczynski's words:

> It is childish to believe that every decision made by every communist party is always the correct one. Of course wrong decisions are made now and again. It is also only natural that there are comrades who recognize the erroneous nature of such decisions. And it is their duty, with all the means at their disposal, to fight for the reversal of these decisions. But a breach of party discipline can never be justified in these circumstances, *because a breach of discipline is in itself a much greater error than any false decision can be* ... For this reason it is entirely inappropriate to criticize Liebknecht because he voted for the war credits.[37]

The book hardly attracted attention in West Germany, where Kuczynski was seen as one of the 'red terrorists' (as Ritter called them) and little interest was shown in intellectual developments behind the Iron Curtain following Khrushchev's 1956 denunciation of Stalin.[38] There was no review of the book in the *Historische Zeitschrift,* the most prestigious historical journal in the Federal Republic, and no discussion of it at the 1958 Trier Historians' Congress. Instead, the challenge of GDR scholarship was dealt with by ignoring it or by denouncing it as 'pseudo-academic'.[39] Typical in this respect was the reaction of Hermann Heidegger, who, in a short review, dismissed Kuczynski as a slavish adherent of the 'Bolshevik' line and argued that the only merit of his work was the insight it offered into the 'style and methods of historiography in the Soviet zone'.[40] That Kuczynski had actually challenged much of previous communist writing on the subject seemed to escape Heidegger's attention.

In East Germany, however, Kuczynski's thesis was subject to very detailed analysis by officials from the SED Central Committee and related party institutes, who organized an immediate and vigorous response with the aim of enforcing what they saw as Leninist orthodoxy. This began in early 1958 with the appearance of various reviews in the journal *Zeitschrift für Geschichtswissenschaft* (*ZfG*) and an article by Albert Schreiner in *Neues Deutschland,* all accusing Kuczynski of 'revisionist' tendencies and of propagating a 'false view of the relationship between leftists and centrists' within the workers' movement.[41] The campaign against Kuczynski continued in the SED party cell within the East German Academy of Sciences, where Kuczynski worked. Senior and even junior colleagues were pressured into taking up an ideological position against him, and most of them did.[42] The book's publisher, the Akademie Verlag, was also forced to defend its decision to proceed with publication, and as a precaution it announced that it would be suspending sales of the book on 27 February 1958.[43]

Finally, in March 1958 the party's theoretical journal *Einheit* published a scathing attack by Rudolf Lindau, a member of the SED Institute for Marxism-Leninism and an old Spartacist who had participated in the opposition to the war alongside Liebknecht. Kuczynski, he argued, had shown lack of dialectical reasoning in relation to Liebknecht's vote for war credits, since a breach of discipline in an opportunistic party like the SPD was not only justified, but also historically necessary. Only a revolutionary, Marxist-Leninist party such as the KPD or SED had the right to demand absolute obedience. The author had also shown a 'strange predilection' for the views of 'the enemies of the Marxist workers' movement', including not only the 'renegade' Kautsky, but also the 'anarchist' Franz Pfemfert and the 'Trotskyist' Paul Frölich. Foremost, though, Lindau (and other critics) took offence at Kuczynski's claim that the masses bore the main responsibility for the failure to prevent the outbreak of war. The workers of today, it was argued, needed to know that their forebears had joined in the struggle against imperialism, and that it was the 'class traitors' inside the SPD leadership who had betrayed the anti-war movement by voting for war credits. As Lindau put it: 'The claim that "the masses" ... aligned themselves with [the forces of] chauvinism ... is a lie: the masses *were never asked* ... Only their leaders had a free vote – and they voted for the bourgeoisie and against the proletariat!'.[44]

This was a dangerous moment for Kuczynski's career. At the Thirty-Fifth Plenum of the Central Committee in February 1958 three leading German communists, including Kuczynski's close associate Karl Schirdewan, had been removed from the Politburo or the Central Committee for factionalism, and a few weeks earlier, in December 1957, the Central Committee secretary for economics, Gerhart Ziller, had killed himself after criticism from Ulbricht at a Politburo meeting.[45] This came at a time when Kuczynski was already under the spotlight for several theoretical articles he had published in party journals calling for greater scientific objectivity in historical research in line with resolutions passed by the Twentieth Party Congress of the Communist Party of the Soviet Union.[46]

Other associates of his, including the philosopher Ernst Bloch and the economist Fritz Behrens, had also lost academic and state positions in 1957 as a result of their attacks on party dogma.[47] The philologist and literary scholar Victor Klemperer even commented in his diary on 14 February 1958 that Kuczynski was a 'second Bloch case in the offing', although he personally agreed with what the historian had written: 'I saw it with my own eyes! ... the workers went to war voluntarily [in 1914], they had failed as Socialists'.[48]

Kuczynski's own position was also undoubtedly made more difficult by two additional factors: his middle-class Jewish background and the fact that he had spent the Nazi period in exile in Britain rather than the Soviet Union.[49] In his post-1989 memoirs he describes how at one point in early 1958 he was directly threatened with expulsion from the party, and that none other than Kurt Hager, the Central Committee secretary for science and culture, had taken a negative interest in the case.[50] In the end, he was saved by a partial retraction of his views in a self-critical address to the Third University Teachers' Conference on 2 March 1958, delivered in Hager's presence, although he consistently rejected charges of 'revisionism'.[51] His obvious ideological differences with the 'Harich group' also undoubtedly helped.[52] But over and above this, the reason why he escaped with an official reprimand was the undeniable fact that his book had initially been approved by the party and had passed through its own – and the Akademie Verlag's – rigorous review processes. Paradoxically, the very existence of censorship – although it could not be called such – had given Kuczynski the confidence to test the limits of what it was possible to write in a communist state without, in his own view of the world, leaving the path of the righteous.[53]

## Conclusion

What are we to make of all this? In a recent work Martin Sabrow portrays the 'anti-revisionist' campaign against Kuczynski largely as an internal matter within the GDR. For Sabrow, it was an 'argument about which direction the Marxist party should take', in which 'all participants in like manner pledged their allegiance to the Marxist-Leninist world-view and to the leading role of the SED'.[54] Furthermore, it ended neither in a vindication for Kuczynski nor in a complete recantation, as his critics demanded, but in a 'complete exhaustion of both sides'.[55] Even the question of scientific objectivity versus partisanship was not an issue, as Kuczynski fully supported the right of the party to guard against 'revisionist' tendencies and considered it only proper that ideological controls should be tighter in the GDR than in Gomulka's Poland because of the greater proximity of the border with the 'imperialist' West.⁵⁶ His case, simply, was that he himself was not a revisionist but an orthodox Marxist-Leninist, and to prove this he not only cited numerous passages from the works of Marx, Engels and Lenin, but also argued that objectivity itself was partisan and would ultimately prove the validity of the Marxist-Leninist world view without the need for crude distortions of history of the type put forward in official party publications. In other words, his objectivity was of the socialist rather than the bourgeois kind, on the side of progress rather than reaction.⁵⁷

However, as convincing as Sabrow's arguments are, I would further contend that this particular East German historians' dispute or *Historikerstreit* – which Kuczynski later referred to as 'my *Historikerstreit*' – was also fundamentally driven by issues concerning national identity and historical writing at a particular moment in the Cold War when the brief thaw following Khrushchev's 1956 speech yielded to renewed tensions over the nuclear arms race and the Berlin question. It can therefore only be understood in a German-German, and not just an East German, framework. As Alfred Meusel, among the more reluctant and restrained of Kuczynski's GDR critics, suggested:

> In the current situation we must give courage to the German workers, and fill them with the … confidence that peace will be preserved, that socialism will prosper and that our Fatherland will be reunited by peaceful means. If we want to play our part in achieving this, then we must show how already in 1914 there were men and women who clearly saw the character of the coming war and were willing to sacrifice everything [to prevent it].⁵⁸

Indeed, common to all approaches discussed above is a reworking of national paradigms to fit the new Cold War political landscape, and a tendency on both sides of the Iron Curtain, as Berger notes, to 'merg[e] the concepts of class and nation in [a] way … that de-emphasis[es] the importance of class'.⁵⁹ The Cold War, in other words, was to be fought through historical works that built on contested national myths and symbols associated with past wars and/or the internal opposition to past wars. Even Kuczynski came at the subject from a national perspective, concluding that because the SPD 'was not merely the spearhead, but the brains behind the [pre-war] International' it had a 'duty of honour' to rescue the cause of international socialism by acknowledging its weaknesses and learning from its past mistakes.⁶⁰ Here, as elsewhere, bourgeois or social democratic traditions stood against socialist traditions, the Federal Republic against the German Democratic Republic, lending a didactic overtone to historical writing on the *Kaiserreich* that was apparent even in the different political atmosphere of the late 1960s and 1970s.[61] In this way, both sides sought to carve out a distinctive Cold War identity by appropriating different parts of the national past.

## Notes

1. I would like to thank Stefan Berger and Josie McLellan for comments on an earlier draft.
2. Martin Sabrow, citing Christoph Kleßmann, describes this relationship as an 'asymmetric and interconnecting history of parallels and contrasts'. See Sabrow, 'Confrontation and Co-operation: Relations between the Two German Historiographies', in *The Divided Past,* pp. 127–47 (p. 128).
3. Grass to Seghers, 14 August 1961, repr. in *Das Günter Grass Lesebuch,* ed. by Helmut Frielinghaus (Munich: DTV, 2009), pp. 82–84.
4. Cited in Johanna Granville, 'Ulbricht in October 1956: Survival of the *Spitzbart* during Destalinization', *Journal of Contemporary History,* 41.3 (2006), 477–502 (p. 482).
5. On the Fischer controversy see my article 'The Fischer Controversy over German War Aims in the First World War and its Reception by East German Historians, 1961–1989', *The Historical Journal,* 46.3 (2003), 649–68.
6. On these divisions, see Geoff Eley, 'The SPD in War and Revolution, 1914–1919', in *Bernstein to Brandt: A Short History of German Social Democracy,* ed. by Roger Fletcher (London: Arnold, 1987), pp. 65–74.
7. Stefan Berger, *The Search for Normality: National Identity and Historical Consciousness in Germany since 1800* (Oxford: Berg, 1997), pp. 21–55, places particular emphasis on the overwhelming prevalence of the national tradition in German historiography pre- and post-1945.
8. Friedrich Meinecke, *The German Catastrophe: Reflections and Recollections,* trans. by Sidney B. Fay (Wiesbaden: Brockhaus Verlag, 1946; Cambridge, MA: Harvard University Press, 1950), pp. 106–7.
9. Ibid., p. 25.
10. See above all Gerhard Ritter, *Staatskunst und Kriegshandwerk: Das Problem des Militarismus in Deutschland,* 4 vols (Munich: Oldenbourg, 1954–68).
11. Gerhard Ritter, *Die Dämonie der Macht: Betrachtungen über Geschichte und Wesen des Machtproblems im politischen Denken der Neuzeit,* 6th edn (Munich: Leibniz, 1948), p. 9; idem, *Carl Goerdeler und die deutsche Widerstandsbewegung* (Stuttgart: Deutsche Verlags-Anstalt, 1955), p. 97.
12. See Ritter, *Staatskunst und Kriegshandwerk,* III (1964).
13. Friedrich Stampfer, *Erfahrungen und Erkenntnisse: Aufzeichnungen aus meinem Leben* (Cologne: Verlag für Politik und Wirtschaft, 1957), pp. 165–71.
14. For example, Hermann Heidegger, *Die deutsche Sozialdemokratie und der nationale Staat, 1870–1920* (Göttingen: Musterschmidt, 1956).
15. Helga Grebing, *Geschichte der deutschen Arbeiterbewegung* (Munich: Nymphenburger, 1966); Dieter Groh, *Negative Integration und revolutionärer Attentismus:*

*Die deutsche Sozialdemokratie am Vorabend des Ersten Weltkrieges* (Frankfurt/Main: Propyläen, 1973); Susanne Miller, *Burgfrieden und Klassenkampf: Die deutsche Sozialdemokratie im Ersten Weltkrieg* (Düsseldorf: Droste, 1974).

16. Exceptions included Wolfgang Abendroth, *Aufstieg und Krise der deutschen Sozialdemokratie* (Frankfurt/Main: Stimme, 1964); and Georg Fülberth and Jürgen Harrer, *Die deutsche Sozialdemokratie, 1890–1933* (Darmstadt: Luchterhand, 1974).

17. Wolfgang Kruse, *Krieg und nationale Integration: Eine Neuinterpretation des sozialdemokratischen Burgfriedensschlusses 1914/15* (Essen: Klartext, 1993), p. 12.

18. Abendroth, *Aufstieg und Krise*, p. 46.

19. For example, Walter Bartel, *Die Linken in der deutschen Sozialdemokratie im Kampf gegen Militarismus und Krieg* (East Berlin: Dietz, 1958). Also *Dokumente und Materialien zur Geschichte der deutschen Arbeiterbewegung*, ed. by Institut für Marxismus-Leninismus beim Zentralkomitee der SED, II/1-2 (East Berlin: Dietz, 1958).

20. See Jessica Reinisch, '"Zurück zu unserem Virchow!": Medizinische Karrieren, Nationalhelden und Geschichtsschreibung in Deutschland nach 1945', in *Gesundheit und Staat: Studien zur Geschichte der Gesundheitsämter in Deutschland, 1870–1950*, ed. by Axel C. Hüntelmann, Johannes Vossen and Herwig Czech (Husum: Matthiesen, 2006), pp. 255–74.

21. 'Aufruf des Zentralkomitees der KPD', 11 June 1945, repr. in *DDR-Geschichte in Dokumenten. Beschlüsse, Berichte, interne Materialien und Alltagszeugnisse*, ed. by Matthias Judt (Berlin: Links, 1997), p. 45.

22. Walter Ulbricht, *Whither Germany? Speeches and Essays on the National Question* (Dresden: Zeit im Bild, 1966), pp. 15–68.

23. Sabrow, 'Confrontation and Co-operation', p. 132.

24. Paul Wandel, *Der deutsche Imperialismus und seine Kriege – das nationale Unglück Deutschlands* (East Berlin: Dietz, 1955).

25. Rolf Rudolph, 'Die nationale Verantwortung der Historiker in der DDR', *ZfG*, 10.2 (1962), 253–85.

26. Ibid., p. 263.

27. On the emergence of Marxist-Leninist historical scholarship in the early GDR see Ulrich Neuhäußer-Wespy, *Die SED und die Historie: Die Etablierung der marxistisch-leninistischen Geschichtswissenschaft der DDR in den fünfziger und sechziger Jahren* (Bonn: Bouvier, 1996); Ilko-Sascha Kowalczuk, *Legitimation eines neuen Staates: Parteiarbeiter an der historischen Front. Geschichtswissenschaft in der SBZ/DDR, 1945–1961* (Berlin: Links, 1997); and Martin Sabrow, *Das Diktat des Konsenses: Geschichtswissenschaft in der DDR, 1949–1969* (Munich: Oldenbourg, 2001). A study that takes a biographical approach is Mario Keßler, *Exilerfahrung in Wissenschaft und Politik: Remigrierte Historiker in der frühen DDR* (Cologne: Böhlau, 2001).

28. Stefan Berger, 'National Paradigm and Legitimacy: Uses of Academic History Writing in the 1960s', in *The Workers' and Peasants' State*, ed. by Major and Osmond, pp. 244–61.

29. For example Paul Merker, *Sozialdemokratie und Gewerkschaften, 1890–1920* (East Berlin: Dietz, 1949), p. 323; and Dieter Fricke, 'Friedrich Stampfer und der "demokratische Sozialismus"', *ZfG*, 6.4 (1958), 749–74.

30. On Harich see Granville, 'Ulbricht in October 1956'.

31. Ibid., p. 490; Siegfried Lokatis, *Der rote Faden: Kommunistische Parteigeschichte und Zensur unter Walter Ulbricht* (Cologne: Böhlau, 2003), pp. 9–32.

32. See Karl Kautsky, *Die Internationale* (Vienna: Volksbuchhandlung, 1920).

33. Jürgen Kuczynski, *Der Ausbruch des ersten Weltkrieges und die deutsche Sozialdemokratie: Chronik und Analyse* (East Berlin: Akademie, 1957), p. 169.
34. Ibid., p. 147.
35. Ibid., p. 124.
36. Ibid., p. 126.
37. Ibid., p. 162 (emphasis in original).
38. Berger, *The Search for Normality*, p. 47.
39. Sabrow, 'Confrontation and Co-operation', p. 133.
40. Hermann Heidegger in *Das Historisch-Politische Buch*, 6 (1958), p. 116. Cited in Keßler, *Exilerfahrung*, p. 136. Heidegger was a former student of Gerhard Ritter and a captain in the Bundeswehr and the West German Defence Ministry (Bundesminesterium der Verteidigung).
41. For a more detailed discussion see Horst Haun, *Kommunist und 'Revisionist': Die SED-Kampagne gegen Jürgen Kuczynski (1956–1959)* (Dresden: Sächsisches Druck- und Verlagshaus, 1999), pp. 62–89; and Andreas Dorpalen, *German History in Marxist Perspective: The East German Approach* (Detroit: Wayne University Press, 1985; London: I.B. Tauris, 1986), pp. 287–90. Also Jürgen Kuczynski, *Frost nach dem Tauwetter: Mein Historikerstreit* (Berlin: Elefanten Press, 1993), pp. 90–102.
42. For example 'Resolution, einstimmig angenommen auf der Mitgliederversammlung der Grundorganisation am 11.3.1958', Stiftung Archiv der Parteien und Massenorganisationen der DDR im Bundesarchiv Berlin [hereafter SAPMO-BArch], DY30/IV-2/9.04/397, Bl. 393-97.
43. See Akademie-Verlag to Genossin Pflug of the Central Committee, 8 February 1958, SAPMO-BArch, DY30/IV-2/9.04/147, Bl. 65-67. Also Jürgen Kuczynski, *'Ein linientreuer Dissident': Memoiren, 1945–1989* (Berlin: Aufbau, 1992), pp. 113–14.
44. Rudolf Lindau, 'Arbeiterklasse und SPD-Führung beim Ausbruch des Ersten Weltkrieges: Kritik einer unmarxistischen Darstellung in einem Buch von Jürgen Kuczynski', *Einheit*, 13.3 (1958), 381-95 (pp. 381–82, with emphasis in the original). Copy in SAPMO-BArch, NY4198/92, Bl. 99-106.
45. Peter Grieder, *The East German Leadership, 1946–73: Conflict and Crisis* (Manchester: Manchester University Press, 1999), pp. 114–37.
46. For further discussion see Kuczynski, *Frost nach dem Tauwetter*, p. 10; and Heiko Feldner, 'History in the Academy: Objectivity and Partisanship in the Marxist Historiography of the German Democratic Republic', in *The Workers' and Peasants' State*, pp. 262–77.
47. Granville, 'Ulbricht in October 1956', p. 495.
48. Victor Klemperer, *The Lesser Evil: The Diaries of Victor Klemperer, 1945–1959*, trans. by Martin Chalmers (London: Weidenfeld & Nicolson, 2003), p. 506.
49. A detailed account of Kuczynski's life and career is found in Keßler, *Exilerfahrung*, pp. 91–145. See also my article 'Jürgen Kuczynski and the Search for a (non-existent) Western Spy Ring in the East German Communist Party in 1953', *Contemporary European History*, forthcoming.
50. Kuczynski, *'Ein linientreuer Dissident'*, p. 110–22.
51. See the transcript of this address in Kuczynski, *Frost nach dem Tauwetter*, pp. 103–7; also published in *Neues Deutschland*, 12 March 1958, alongside readers' letters attacking Kuczynski.
52. Keßler, *Exilerfahrung*, pp. 138–39.
53. Cf. Lokatis, *Der rote Faden*, p. 124.

54. Sabrow, *Das Diktat des Konsenses,* pp. 342–43.

55. Ibid., p. 343.

56. In this sense, I disagree with Horst Haun's suggestion that Kuczynski's aim was to undermine 'Stalinist' forms of party control over the historical profession and achieve a 'de-ideologization' (*'Entideologisierung'*) of academic research in the GDR In my view, his intention was simply to assert *his* interpretation of Marxism-Leninism against that of his critics within the SED, while avoiding a full confrontation with Stalinism and its continued manifestations. See Haun, *Kommunist und 'Revisionist',* pp. 78 and 88.

57. See Jürgen Kuczynski, 'Parteilichkeit und Objektivität in Geschichte und Geschichtsschreibung', *ZfG,* 4.5 (1956), 873–88; reprinted in idem, *Frost nach dem Tauwetter,* pp. 22–41.

58. Alfred Meusel, 'Der Ausbruch des Ersten Weltkriegs und die deutsche Sozialdemokratie – kritische Betrachtungen zu dem Buch von Jürgen Kuczynski', *ZfG,* 6.5 (1958), 1049–68 (p. 1058). Copy in SAPMO-BArch, NY4198/92, Bl. 68-97.

59. Berger, 'National Paradigm and Legitimacy', p. 251.

60. Kuczynski, *Der Ausbruch des ersten Weltkrieges,* p. 169.

61. See the comments made by Richard J. Evans, 'Introduction', in *Society and Politics in Wilhelmine Germany,* ed. by Richard J. Evans (London: Croom Helm, 1978), pp. 11–39 (p. 15).

# 3

# The Sideways Gaze
## The Cold War and Memory of the Nazi Past, 1949–1970

*Bill Niven*

It is a commonplace that the early, 'classic' phase of the Cold War prior to the advent of Willy Brandt's *Ostpolitik* in the 1970s is unthinkable without the Second World War and its aftermath. The very alliance between Soviet communism and Western liberalism during the war ultimately served to throw into relief and intensify the irreconcilable tensions between the two systems. In the postwar period, with control over Europe at stake, these tensions fractured and then split the alliance, and Germany found itself cut apart along the line of that split.

But the Cold War was not only causally linked to the Second World War. It is imaginatively linked to it too. As this chapter demonstrates, the Cold War struggle between West and East Germany was in many ways a struggle over the right to ownership of the positive aspects of recent German history, and over the right to determine the course of unification on the basis of that legacy. In the following, I show that the Cold War battle for legitimacy was emphasized not just with reference to the putative superiority of each respective political system, but also with reference to the past. East Germany maintained that it had emerged from the anti-fascist resistance of the communists and was untainted by Nazism. West Germany, while acknowledging its status as legal successor to the Reich, stressed its connection to pre-1933 democratic traditions as its political parties traced their history back to the democratic parties of the Weimar Republic smashed by Hitler in 1933. West Germany also, over time, came to identify with Christian, liberal, conservative and military resistance to Hitler.

The obverse side to legitimacy, of course, is illegitimacy. This chapter shows how each Germany did its best to mire the other in allegations that it embodied the bad German traditions that had led to dictatorial rule, and was therefore illegitimate. For the GDR, the FRG was a pseudo-democratic continuation of fascism by other means. For the FRG, the GDR was the continuation of dictatorship under a socialist rather than a National Socialist banner. The Cold War, in other words, was a continuation of the Second World War, only now both Germanys stood on the right side, rather than the wrong one – a reasoning that hardly invited self-critical reflection on past or present. Overall, I argue, the GDR's attacks on the FRG were more persistent and vitriolic than those of the FRG on the GDR. I also contend that the GDR's attacks on the FRG, because they were apparently hypocritical, often backfired.

A well-known axiom among critics of the German Democratic Republic is the contention that it was not German, not democratic and not a republic. No one – except the GDR – would have accused the Federal Republic of not being federal, republican or German. There is little doubt that the FRG did become a place where most West Germans wanted to live, one that, whatever its failings, was essentially democratic. This is not true of the GDR. Faced with a shrinking population as its citizens voted with their feet by moving to the West, the GDR leaders resorted to three measures of self-defence: repression of opposition, the incarceration of the population and propaganda. Like the younger brother who stands in the shadow of his older, more successful brother, the GDR's sense of inferiority was palpable. Its self-defensiveness was manifest in its endless smear campaigns against the FRG. Throughout the 1950s and the 1960s, the SED – particularly through the Committee for German Unity and Albert Norden's Propaganda Department – launched a series of attacks against West German politicians, state administrators and judicial representatives with a Nazi past. And there were plenty of them, given that Adenauer's *Vergangenheitspolitik* ('politics of the past') of the 1950s had led to widespread rehabilitation of former Nazis.[1] A number of these campaigns were accompanied by the publication of so-called 'brown books' designed to expose the Nazi pasts of West Germans in positions of responsibility. Some also took the form of *in absentia* show trials. The West German Expellees' Minister Theodor Oberländer, for instance, was sentenced by an East German court in 1960 for his part in a massacre of Jews at Lviv in 1941. Oberländer resigned in 1960. His resignation prompted chief GDR propagandist Albert Norden to write to Walter Ulbricht recommending 'the continuation of attacks of this kind'.[2]

If the FRG's 'politics of the past' was directed towards integrating former Nazis or Nazi sympathizers in the hope of binding them into the democratic system, those of the GDR were directed towards confronting these former Nazis with their pasts and establishing a counter-interpretation, according to which the FRG, far from democratizing through integration, was being systematically 'refascistized'. That the GDR itself integrated former Nazis, not least into the Ministry of State Security's network of spies and informants,[3] was not something it was so willing to confront. The GDR's view of the FRG as inherently fascist was certainly consistent with the long-standing communist belief that capitalist countries would inevitably resort to fascism to protect their exploitative and imperialist interests. Equally, the GDR's enormous investment of energy in the propaganda war against the West represented an extension of the wartime activities of its founders: once an anti-fascist, always an anti-fascist ran the implicit slogan, and without fascism, anti-fascism would be redundant. But in the atmosphere of the Cold War legitimacy struggle between the two Germanys, this understanding of the Federal Republic took on a particular, sometimes almost desperate stridency. Over time it became clear that the GDR, lacking support from its population – lacking *internal* legitimacy – needed to legitimize itself by convincing the world of the *illegitimacy* of West Germany.

Throughout the 1950s and 1960s, state commemoration of the Nazi past in the GDR was in many ways a form of anti-Western propaganda. East German citizens were to be persuaded that *theirs* was the better state. After all, the GDR had preserved the memory of Ernst Thälmann and other anti-fascists. More importantly, it was prepared to continue the struggle, which would only end when the FRG was liberated from fascism and reunited with the GDR under socialism. When Otto Grotewohl spoke to the masses assembled in September 1958 for the inauguration of the Buchenwald Memorial Site, his speech was laced with anti-Western invective. 'Irredeemably caught up in NATO alliance politics', he said, 'the forces of yesterday in West Germany are preparing to take revenge for defeat and plunge the nations into another terrible war … to this end the old fascist system is today being made "respectable" again in West Germany'.[4] In an article for the West German newspaper *Die Welt,* the reporter Bernt Conrad wrote that, had Adenauer, Strauß or any other West German politician attended the ceremony, they would have been 'torn apart by a wave of hatred'. Conrad found this hatred 'frightening'.[5] Long before 1958, in fact, Buchenwald had been transformed by the authorities into an anti-Western propaganda weapon, not least in an exhibition in the former camp gatehouse, which pointed to the threat of West German fascism and militarism. As of 1958, a massive set of statues on the Ettersberg near Buchenwald, representing a group a self-liberated prisoners, gazed out over the Thuringian landscape towards the West, calling to mind that the liberation would not be complete until the oppressed brother beyond the German-German border had been freed.[6]

The FRG could hardly remain impervious to these attacks. Moreover – at least in the 1950s – there were those in Britain and the US who were alarmed by the ease with which the GDR was able to provide apparently incriminating material on the Nazi past of West German politicians, administrators and judges. Was the FRG really doing enough to face its past? When the Conference of West German Justice Ministers met in Bad Harzburg in October 1958 and decided on the setting up in Ludwigsburg of a central agency charged with judicial investigation of Nazi crimes, this was not least the result of the GDR's smear campaigns. The GDR soon uncovered the problematic past of a number of the agency's representatives; its first head, Erwin Schüle, had to stand down because of his Nazi past.[7] But the effectiveness of the GDR in using the Nazi past to unseat West German politicians was arguably limited: State Secretary Hans Globke (CDU, Christlich Demokratische Union – Christian Democratic Union), a particular target of vilification, only left office with Adenauer in 1963; another target, Hans-Christoph Seebohm (first of the Deutsche Partei – German Party – then the CDU) can, as Pertti Ahonen has observed, be 'counted among West Germany's most durable politicians, with seventeen consecutive years as federal Minister of Transport'.[8] West German politicians with a Nazi past were able to prove (or at least appear to have proven) they had put that past behind them: democratization had worked. Moreover, the GDR was not the only moral watchdog. Within the FRG itself in the 1950s and early 1960s, SPD politicians, writers such as Heinrich Böll, and the media constantly picked up on the dubious past of West Germans in positions of authority. In 1955, for instance, the West German weekly *Der Spiegel* played a part in exposing the Nazi past of a high-ranking official in the Foreign Office, Otto Bräutigam.[9] With the advent of the 1968 generation of West German students who openly criticized their parents' generation for its role in Nazism, the critical stance of some became the policy of many; the FRG had internalized vigilance towards the past as a democratic process.

Whether the GDR's campaign helped indirectly to foster this critical stance within the FRG remains debatable; certainly the more it developed, the less relevant it appeared. In any case, the Western Allies were acutely aware of the propagandistic intent of the 'revelations'. And of course FRG politicians routinely denied their validity. Throughout the 1950s and early 1960s, the GDR offered West German political and judicial authorities access to GDR archives to view incriminating Nazi-period documents relating to West Germans. Yet until the mid 1960s these authorities largely turned down such offers for fear that high-level interaction in judicial matters might be interpreted as a form of diplomatic contact. Given that the FRG, according to its Hallstein doctrine, was committed to eschewing diplomatic ties to countries that developed diplomatic links to the GDR, it could hardly breach its own principles. In public it was argued that one could not in any case trust the GDR: material could have been forged, tendentiously selected or tampered with. In this way the campaign to delegitimize the FRG was redirected by the Federal Republic towards a campaign to discredit the GDR. This was particularly the case following the SED's attempts to bring down Federal President Heinrich Lübke for his alleged part in the construction of concentration camp huts and the procurement of slave labour. When the SED supplied incriminating photocopies, the Federal Criminal Office dismissed them as fakes, a view persistently reiterated by the Federal President's Office, the Ministry of the Interior and the West German government. Lübke himself issued a statement dismissing the documents as 'crass forgeries'.[10] Lübke was particularly adept at presenting the GDR attacks against him as an attack against West German democracy itself.

What also took the sting out of the GDR's attempt to sully the Federal Republic's moral reputation was its hypocrisy. In the 1950s, the SED liked to claim that more former Nazis had been brought to justice in the GDR than in the FRG. But a number of those sentenced by GDR courts had not received a fair trial, while others were sentenced on the basis of their Nazi Party membership alone.[11] The seemingly more vigilant judicial system in the East was shot through with injustice. Similarly, the GDR's repeated allegation that the FRG was a hotbed of anti-Semitism was a case of throwing stones from a glass house. In the early 1950s, Stalinist show trials in Prague led to the sentencing and execution of high-ranking communists accused of being agents of US imperialism and 'Zionism'. In reaction, the GDR stepped up its campaign to weed out the alleged influence of 'Western cosmopolitanism' and Zionism within the SED. The most famous target was the Central Committee member Paul Merker, who had survived the war in Mexican exile and had actively promoted plans to compensate Jews.[12] In 1953, following an increase in state-orchestrated anti-Semitism, the president of the Jewish Community in the GDR, Julius Meyer, fled to the West with other leading Jewish representatives. By 1955, the total number in the Jewish communities of the GDR had sunk to 1,715; by 1976 it had fallen to 728, and by autumn of 1990 to 372.[13] By contrast, between 1955 and 1965 the FRG's Jewish community increased by some 10,000 members (remaining stable after that at about 26,000).[14] While there were more leading politicians of Jewish background in the GDR (e.g. Albert Norden and Hermann Axen) than in the FRG, they lived largely in denial of their origins, Norden becoming one of the most virulent in his condemnation of Israel. And while it is true that anti-Semitism existed in the FRG, there was sometimes the suspicion that the GDR was involved in fomenting it.[15] Generally speaking, the Federal Republic was perceived in the international community as more welcoming towards Jews than the GDR, where official hostility towards Israel undoubtedly also generated scepticism, even coolness, towards East German Jews.

Despite an initially positive Soviet response to the foundation of Israel, attitudes to the new state were soon split down Cold War lines, and the politics of the past in both Germanys were influenced by this split. Here again, the GDR, in attacking West German anti-Semitism, laid itself open to charges of hypocrisy. The SED's condemnation of Israel as an aggressor state and tool of US imperialism did little to convince the world of its commitment to fighting the Nazi legacy of anti-Semitism (which it claimed to have banished from the GDR). The refusal to pay restitution also undermined the credibility of its stance. On 10 September 1952, West Germany agreed to pay 3 billion Marks (in goods) to Israel and 450 million Marks to the Jewish Claims Conference as restitution for Jewish suffering at the hands of the Nazis.[16] The GDR never compensated Israel. The SED argued that the GDR had fulfilled its obligations as laid down by the Potsdam Treaty, thus compensating 'a large number of Jewish victims … who were or are Polish or Soviet citizens'.[17] Because Israel did not exist when this agreement was drawn up, there is no reason to pay restitution to it now, ran the argument. Putting a further spin on this, it was argued that because the GDR had fulfilled the spirit of the Potsdam Treaty and ensured that there would be 'no repetition of the military-fascist past',[18] it had provided a more effective form of restitution than the FRG (as if the assurance that the Holocaust would never recur constituted a form of compensation). It is true that Adenauer pushed through the restitution agreement against massive opposition, and that it served as a *quid pro quo* for acceptance into Western alliances. Moreover, later West German economic and military aid to Israel in the 1958–1964 period was a more dubious form of compensation, namely for Bonn's reluctance to establish diplomatic ties: the FRG, fearful that recognizing Israel would prompt nonaligned Arab states to recognize the GDR, shilly-shallied on the issue of recognition until 1965.[19] But the fact remained that the FRG *did* offer restitution and aid, and it *did* eventually recognize Israel; the GDR did not.

In general, then, the GDR's efforts to undermine the FRG's democratic image and thereby its right to speak for Germany as a whole failed. Moreover, West German politicians, far from simply deflecting the flak from over the border, did all they could to call into question the legitimacy of the GDR. For decades the political community in the FRG referred to the GDR as 'the Soviet zone', or just 'the zone', and portrayed East German citizens as oppressed and enslaved. West German politicians, by and large, did not indulge in accusing East German politicians of being Nazis, or in describing the GDR as 'fascist'. Rather the method was to state or imply that SED rule was the 'red variant' of totalitarian praxis that had replaced the 'brown variant'. If the GDR viewed the FRG as a continuation of fascism in the guise of liberal democracy, the FRG viewed the GDR as a continuation of dictatorship in the guise of democratic socialism. Comparisons with National Socialism were never far away in West German condemnations of the GDR – especially following the construction of the Berlin Wall on 13 August 1961. The governing mayor of Berlin at the time, Social Democrat Willy Brandt, claimed that the 'barrier wall of a concentration camp' had been drawn through the city;[20] and in a memorandum of 23 August 1961, the federal government referred to the '16 million Germans ... in the Soviet-occupied zone' now 'trapped in one enormous concentration camp'.[21] Throughout the 1950s and especially 1960s, the anti-GDR rhetoric in the West evoked sympathy for the 'victims of the rule of violence' in the GDR, and for the steady stream of fugitives who risked their lives in attempting to reach West Berlin or the FRG. This sympathy was surely combined with anger at Soviet communism and its 'colonization' of East Germany. No doubt many West Germans felt encouraged to compare the situation to that at the end of the war, when areas east of the Oder-Neiße line had fallen under Soviet control and millions of Germans had been forced to flee.

As in the GDR, commemoration of the Nazi past within the FRG was also bound up with Cold War propaganda. Commemorative ceremonies in the FRG and GDR were manifestly competitive. Built into official rituals to mark its end was the claim that the war would not truly be at an end until the other Germany had been liberated – from Soviet communism, according to the West German version, or from Western imperialism, according to the East German version. Adenauer summed up the commemorative position of the FRG when he stated on 6 May 1955 in reference to the East Germans: 'you can always rely on us, because together with the free world we will not rest until you too have regained your human rights and live peacefully with us in one state'.[22] West German politicians speaking at remembrance ceremonies for victims of concentration camps found it hard to resist referring to the continuing oppression over the border, even if such reference was rarely as crudely propagandistic as in the East. Federal President Lübke, remembering the German resistance during a speech at Bergen-Belsen on 25 April 1965, couched his most elegantly: 'we would not be worthy of the sacrifice of these and other fighters against injustice and the rule of violence, if we did not feel obliged to bring to a conclusion what they wanted to achieve'.[23] The term 'victims of the rule of violence' was a standard expression in West German commemorative rhetoric, often in connection with 'victims of war'. Given the association of 'rule of violence' with both Nazism and communism, remembering the victims of Hitler using this term automatically meant remembering the SED's victims – to whom, in any case, were dedicated specific memorials and street names, and even a day of commemoration: 17 June became a national holiday in the FRG in the early 1960s in honour of the 17 June 1953 uprising in the GDR.

The infiltration of Cold War propaganda into acts of remembering or coming to terms with Nazism sometimes led to unseemly squabbles in which remembering Nazi victims seemed less important than scoring points against the Cold War enemy. A case in point was the ceremony to inaugurate Nandor Glid's international memorial at Dachau in September 1968. The presence of NATO military bands infuriated those attending from socialist countries. Then the governing mayor of Berlin, Klaus Schütz (SPD) – unpopular among West German students for his stance against the student protest movement – held a speech in which he described Dachau as a 'symbol of the memory of the victims of international crimes', a hardly veiled reference to communism. Schütz was heckled, former prisoners left the podium in protest, and even fighting erupted. The events at Dachau reflected a certain collaboration between socialist organizations of former prisoners, and left-wing West German student groups, who saw both NATO and Schütz as the embodiment of neofascism.[24]

A few years earlier, during the Frankfurt Auschwitz trials (1963–1965), proceedings had similarly threatened to turn into a West-East battle. The GDR sent Friedrich Karl Kaul to the trials to act as co–plaintiff attorney in the interest of six GDR Jewish citizens. Kaul had expressly been given the task of turning the trial into a tribunal against the industrial conglomerate IG-Farben, which had used Auschwitz labour in its factories.[25] Some of its former representatives had since reestablished respectable careers in the Federal Republic. None of these people was actually on trial; the Auschwitz trials focused largely on killers working for the SS. Besides, an IG-Farben trial had already been conducted by the Americans. Kaul's attempt to use the trial to discredit the FRG for rehabilitating industrialists who had profited from Nazi slave labour led to constant tussles with the defence counsel, Hans Laternser. One particularly egregious example illustrates this. In early 1965, Kaul called on GDR Building Minister Erich Markowitsch, a former Auschwitz prisoner, to present material to the court. Markowitsch proceeded to incriminate Walter Dürrfeld, who had been the works manager of the IG-Farben factory at Monowitz and had already been sentenced by the Americans; now he was on several boards of directors. Laternser, as West German defence counsel, immediately retorted to Markowitsch: 'If you're responsible for the building industry, then aren't you also responsible for building the Wall?'[26] Establishing the guilt of individual Germans for crimes at Auschwitz receded at such moments into the background as the Cold War took centre stage.

Whether it was the GDR accusing the FRG of continuing fascism or the FRG accusing the SED of replacing the 'brown' with the 'red' dictatorship, the net result was the same: each Germany labelled the other as the perpetrator state. Both Germanys contributed so eagerly to the rhetorical battle of the Cold War because it shifted the burden of guilt. Whether it was the GDR dismissing the FRG as the lackey of American imperialism, or the FRG dismissing the GDR as the shabby shop-window of Soviet imperialism, the result was comparable. These views automatically served to undermine the legitimacy of the other Germany across the border, and they encouraged the Germans living in one state to regard those in the other as victims. Moreover, because both Germanys tended to a somewhat too exclusive view of the Second World War as shaped by the interests of the future Cold War antagonists, they invited their citizens to reimagine themselves as victims of the war. In the FRG, the prevailing view in the 1950s and 1960s was that the fundamental responsibility for the expulsion of ethnic Germans from the Eastern territories must be laid at the door of Soviet imperialism (as well as Czech and Polish nationalism).[27] In the GDR, the prevailing understanding was that blame for the bombing of eastern German cities such as Dresden must be laid at the door of 'Anglo-American terror bombing' designed to lay waste to that part of Germany soon to be occupied by the advancing Red Army.[28] Too little attention was devoted to the question of German guilt for the process that led to the expulsions and the bombings. To a degree, the Cold War also hindered a focus on Germans as victims, at least in the GDR, where subjects such as the rape of German women by the Soviets were not openly discussed.[29] But by and large it encouraged German self-pity rather than undermined it. To an extent, the respective identification with the Americans or the Soviets depended on such perceptions of victimhood.

The victims held up as examples in East and West, of course, were 'active' victims, those who had staged resistance against Hitler. Here too the Cold War left its imprint. In the FRG, the 20 July 1944 circle involved in the unsuccessful bomb plot against Hitler was lionized. The existence of a conservative and military opposition to Hitler was seen to demonstrate a sound moral core within those social and professional groups whom Adenauer called upon to reconstruct and rearm the nation – groups who could be relied upon to draw on their traditional anti-communism.[30] In the GDR, the victims in the communist resistance were lionized. The SED claimed to have fulfilled their legacy by creating a socialist state and continuing the fight against fascism. The flip side to the focus on specific resistance groups in West and East Germany was the neglect and 'disqualification' of others. In the FRG, communist resistance was understood as pro-totalitarian activity of a 'red' rather than a 'brown' hue, while in the GDR the 20 July circle was seen largely as a group of opportunists committed to saving their skins and attempting to salvage Hitler's empire (although the GDR did subsequently attempt to rehabilitate Stauffenberg because of his links to left-wing groups).[31]

With East and West Germany so focused on German victims of one sort or another, political and public memory of Jewish victimhood in the 1949–1969 period was never prominent. In the GDR, as is well known, the Nazi persecution of Jews was long understood as an epiphenomenon of capitalism. Insofar as anti-Semitism was regarded as an attempt to distract the workers, it appeared incidental to the history of class struggle. And because the Holocaust was regarded as one form of industrialized inhumanity alongside others, Jewish victimhood was not viewed as distinct from, say, that of Russian and Polish slave labour.[32] The supposed lack of examples of Jewish resistance, and the need for a 'combative' memory during the Cold War led to an overpreoccupation with 'active' communist victims. But it was not just in the GDR that Jewish suffering was either overlooked in commemoration of the war, or subsumed under that of other groups (including German civilians). This was also typical of the FRG, despite the fact of Adenauer's commitment to restitution. The People's Day of Mourning revived there in 1950 and dedicated to all 'victims of war and violence' focused mainly on the memory of German soldiers.[33] The Christian iconography often deployed in such commemorations implicitly excluded the memory of Jews. Certainly subsuming the Jews into a wider category of victims including German soldiers and civilians helped to obscure the extent to which the former had been victims of Germans (including the Wehrmacht). In the context of this chapter, it should be noted that the focus on German victimhood was enhanced by the Cold War. It would not have been so easy for the West Germans, for instance, to imagine German POWs still incarcerated by the Soviets in the 1950s as victims had not the anti-communism underlying this view been politically useful both to Adenauer and the Western Allies (see also Inge Marszolek in this volume).

The significance of the Cold War for German perceptions of the Nazi past was that it directed the focus of memory *sideways* and *forwards,* not *backwards.* Rather than reflect on their own role in it, Germans were encouraged to look East or West respectively for the guilty party. Nazism as a historical phenomenon was not of primary importance. More important was the form it supposedly took in the FRG or in the GDR. The threat came from the present and the future – a future overshadowed by the fear of a 'nuclear holocaust' launched in the name of Western imperialism or Soviet communism. The past was conceptualized as a warning against that present and future. The Cold War matrix was a key factor in the development of strategies of transference and deflection that constituted a form of evading it.

This chapter has focused on the period before Brandt became chancellor in 1969, because that is the period when the Cold War matrix evolved and was most forceful in its impact on memory of Nazism. The advent of *Ostpolitik* in the 1970s and the gradual development of improved relations between the Western world and the Eastern bloc took the virulence out of the GDR-FRG propaganda war, significantly reducing its extent. But it never went away entirely, and in the 1980s it flared up again. An important difference between the GDR and other Eastern bloc countries, moreover, was that too great a rapprochement with the West endangered its survival, whereas countries such as Poland hoped that closer ties with the West would enhance their chances of independence. Unlike the GDR, Poland was not faced with the prospect of being absorbed into another Poland.

Given that the GDR ceased to exist in 1990, German unification brought an end to the ideological war between two opposing German states and generated great potential for a more open confrontation with the Nazi past. As I have argued previously, this potential was to a considerable extent realized.[34] Yet the Cold War itself has bequeathed a legacy, as did National Socialism before it – a legacy, for instance, of a history of killings at the German-German border, of political imprisonment by the SED and Stasi brutality. Over the last two decades, united Germany has been confronting its 'double past'. What is noticeable, however, is that while SED injustice has become a central focus of critical memory (quite rightly), less attention is paid to the history of political injustice in the Federal Republic (for instance, the notorious Emergency Decrees of 1972). Cold War neuroticism, it seems, is remembered only as an East German phenomenon. Since 1990, coming to terms with the past has also meant coming to terms with the SED's instrumentalization of antifascism (as any visitor to the Memorial Site at Buchenwald will observe).

There seems little will to confront the FRG's instrumentalization of anti-communism during the Cold War era. Because the GDR was clearly the illegitimate state dependent for its survival on the practice of injustice, it seems fair to most that it should bear the brunt of post-Cold War opprobrium. However, the present critical imbalance is also the result of the fact that the FRG won and the GDR lost – and West Germans are now calling the memory shots. The Cold War has not passed without an element of 'victors' justice'.

## Notes

1. On the concept of *Vergangenheitspolitik*, see Norbert Frei, *Adenauer's Germany and the Nazi Past: The Politics of Amnesty and Integration*, trans. by Joel Golb (New York: Columbia University Press, 2002).

2. Norden to Ulbricht, 21 May 1960, SAPMO-BArch, DY30/IV 2/2028/21; also quoted in Annette Weinke, *Die Verfolgung von NS-Tätern: Vergangenheitsbewältigungen 1949–1969, oder, eine deutsch-deutsche Beziehungsgeschichte im Kalten Krieg* (Paderborn: Schöningh, 2002), p. 151. While the GDR's attacks contributed to Oberländer's downfall, he resigned following the SPD's instigation of a parliamentary investigation into his wartime role.

3. See Henry Leide, *NS-Verbrecher und Staatssicherheit: Die Geheime Vergangenheitspolitik der DDR* (Göttingen: Vandenhoeck & Ruprecht, 2005).

4. 'Rede des Ministerpräsidenten Otto Grotewohl zur Weihe der Nationalen Mahn- und Gedenkstätte Buchenwald am 14. September 1958', Buchenwald-Archiv, Weimar-Buchenwald (hereafter BAW), Bu 48(2):1, p. 11.

5. Bernt Conrad, 'Durch das Tor von Buchenwald', *Die Welt*, 18 September 1958, photocopy in Bundesarchiv Koblenz (hereafter BAK), Nachlaß Hermann Brill, N1086/52.

6. For photographs of Fritz Cremer's statues, see *Buchenwald*, ed. by Committee of Anti-fascist Resistance Fighters (Berlin: Kongress, 1959).

7. Ulrich Brochhagen, *Nach Nürnberg: Vergangenheitsbewältigung und Westintegration in der Ära Adenauer* (Hamburg: Junius, 1994), p. 257.

8. Pertti Ahonen, *After the Expulsion: West Germany and Eastern Europe 1945–1990* (Oxford: Oxford University Press, 2003), p. 34.

9. Brochhagen, *Nach Nürnberg*, p. 228.

10. 'Wortlaut der Erklärung des Herrn Bundespräsidenten vom 1. März 1968', BAK, B122/38182, Bl. 63–65 (Bl. 65).

11. Alfred Streim, 'Vorwort', in Christa Hoffmann, *Stunden Null? Vergangenheitsbewältigung in Deutschland 1945 und 1989*, Extremismus & Demokratie, 2 (Bonn: Bouvier, 1992), pp. 7–24 (pp. 18 and 19).

12. See Jeffrey Herf, *Divided Memory: The Nazi Past in the Two Germanys* (Cambridge, MA: Harvard University Press, 1997), pp. 106–61.

13. Angelika Timm, 'Juden in der DDR und der Staat Israel', in *Zwischen Politik und Kultur: Juden in der DDR*, ed. by Moshe Zuckermann (Göttingen: Wallstein, 2002), pp. 17–33 (p. 18).

14. According to the Central Council of Jews in Germany: see < http://www.zentralratdjuden.de/de/article/764.html > [accessed 17 October 2008].

15. On anti-Semitic incidents in the 1950s, see Michael Wolffsohn, *Die Deutschland Akte: Tatsachen und Legenden* (Munich: Edition Ferenczy bei Bruckmann, 1995), pp. 20–27.

16. On compensation issues, see Peter Reichel, *Vergangenheitsbewältigung in Deutschland: Die Auseinandersetzung mit der NS-Diktatur von 1945 bis heute* (Munich: Beck, 2001), pp. 81–96.

17. Ministerium für Auswärtige Angelegenheiten, 'Stellung der DDR zur Frage der Wiedergutmachung gegenüber Israel und den Juden', 18 March 1966, SAPMO-BArch, DY57/660.

18. Draft letter from the Committee of Anti-fascist Resistance Fighters to the Jewish Victims' Organization in New York. See the attached draft, Spielmann to Becker (Büro Norden), 2 November 1962, SAPMO-BArch, DY57/660.

19. On Bonn's relationship to Israel, see Hannfried von Hindenburg, *Demonstrating Reconciliation: State and Society in West German Foreign Policy toward Israel, 1952–1965* (Oxford: Berghahn, 2007).

20. 'Erklärung Brandts' (13 August 1961), in *Deutschland 1949 bis 1999*, ed. by Archiv der Gegenwart, 10 vols (Sankt Augustin: Siegler, 2000), III (October 1957–May 1962), 2890.

21. 'Zweites Memorandum' (23 August 1961), in *Deutschland 1949 bis 1999*, III (October 1957–May 1962), 2907.

22. Quoted in Bill Niven, *Facing the Nazi Past: United Germany and the Legacy of the Third Reich* (London: Routledge, 2001), p. 103.

23. Bundespräsident Lübke, 'Vor dem Mahnmal in Bergen-Belsen: Ansprache des Bundespräsidenten beim Staatsakt am 25. April 1965', *Bulletin des Presse- und Informationsamtes der Bundesregierung*, 29 April 1965, BAK, B122/4937, Bl. 60–62 (Bl. 61).

24. For a West German report see 'Marschmusik und Schlägerei', *Abendzeitung*, 9 September 1968, p. 18. For an East German one see 'Dachau-Mahnmal eingeweiht', *Neues Deutschland*, 9 September 1968 (photocopies of these articles are in SAPMO-BArch DY57/153). For a critical account of postwar memorialization at Dachau, see Harold Marcuse, *Legacies of Dachau: The Uses and Abuses of a Concentration Camp, 1933–2001* (Cambridge: Cambridge University Press, 2001).

25. 'Information über die ersten Ergebnisse des Auftretens der DDR-Vertreter im Frankfurter Auschwitz-Prozess', 14 May 1964, SAPMO-BArch, DY30/IV A 2/2.028/10.

26. 'So wurde Laternser schachmatt gesetzt', addendum to letter, Rehahn to Norden, 5 February 1965, SAPMO-BArch, DY30/IV A 2/2.028/10, Bl. 30–32 (Bl. 31).

27. On views of expulsion in postwar West Germany, see Ahonen, *After the Expulsion*, and Hans Lemberg and K. Erik Franzen, *Die Vertriebenen: Hitlers letzte Opfer* (Munich: Propyläen, 2001), pp. 221–31.

28. See Bill Niven, 'The GDR and Memory of the Bombing of Dresden', in *Germans as Victims: Remembering the Past in Contemporary Germany*, ed. by Bill Niven (Basingstoke: Palgrave Macmillan, 2006), pp. 109–29.

29. That the issue of rape was totally taboo in the GDR is overstated. It found its way, sometimes in the form of 'rumours', into East German literature even before Christa Wolf's novel *Kindheitsmuster* (Berlin: Aufbau Verlag, 1976). Rape by the Red

Army features briefly in Hildegard Maria Rauchfuß's novel *Schlesisches Himmelreich* (Leipzig: List, 1968), p. 610.

30. On the politicization of the memory of resistance, see Peter Steinbach, 'Widerstand im Dritten Reich – die Keimzelle der Nachkriegsdemokratie?', in *Der 20. Juli: Das andere Deutschland in der Vergangenheitspolitik nach 1934*, ed. by Gerd R. Ueberschär (Berlin: Elefanten Press, 1998), pp. 98–124.

31. Ines Reich and Kurt Finker, 'Reaktionäre oder Patrioten? Zur Historiographie und Widerstandsforschung in der DDR bis 1990', in *Der 20. Juli*, ed. by Ueberschär, pp. 158–78.

32. See Thomas Fox, *Stated Memory: East Germany and the Holocaust* (Rochester, NY: Camden House, 1999).

33. See Alexandra Kaiser, 'Performing the New German Past: The *Volkstrauertag* and 27th January as Commemoration Days in United Germany', in *The Dynamics of Memory in Contemporary Germany*, ed. by Eric Langenbacher, Bill Niven and Ruth Wittlinger, forthcoming special edition of *German Politics and Society*.

34. Niven, *Facing the Nazi Past*.

# 4

# Recasting Luther's Image
## The 1983 Commemoration of Martin Luther in the GDR

*Jon Berndt Olsen*

Germany's relationship with the past entered a period of fluctuation during the late 1970s and early 1980s. The success of West German Chancellor Willy Brandt's *Ostpolitik* brought new challenges to East Germany's claims of legitimacy and forced it to reassess the categorization of many historical events and figures as belonging to either the 'progressive' or the 'reactionary' camp. Until then, the GDR had continually professed the so-called dual-line theory of history, in which it inherited the progressive elements of German history while West Germany inherited the reactionary ones. During this period of reassessment an increased number of historical subjects previously deemed 'reactionary' were transferred into the 'progressive' category for use by the East German state in broadening its own legitimizing narrative.

A good example of this can be seen in the preparation and commemoration of the 500th anniversary of Martin Luther's birthday in 1983, which is the subject of this chapter. An examination of the commemoration not only reveals how the SED attempted to appropriate the historical figure of Martin Luther and attach its own socialist policies to his legacy, but also shows how the new parameters of the Cold War in the 1980s had a direct impact on how Luther was celebrated. The crisis over the stationing of Pershing II missiles on West German soil spawned peace movements in each state. East Germany's economy was worsening, forcing it into negotiations with West Germany over a new line of credit – negotiations hampered in turn by the Cold War interests of the superpowers. All the while, East Germany struggled to maintain an independent sense of identity, one that was simultaneously 'German' and still 'socialist'.

## Heritage and Tradition from the Historian's Perspective

Official interpretations of Luther in the first decades of the GDR were based on works published by Marxist historians during the early 1950s.[1] But in the 1970s this traditional Marxist interpretation of Luther and other 'bourgeois' historical figures began to change. Among East Germany's professional historians, the reassessment of Germany's past became the centre of a theoretical debate that ran throughout the 1970s and 1980s concerning the difference between 'heritage' (*Erbe*) and 'tradition' (*Tradition*). The intention of this theoretical shift in defining the appropriate lineage of national history was to further develop the sense of a uniquely socialist identity in the GDR, one not only based upon different historical traditions from West Germany but able to draw upon a much wider and deeper conception of heritage, too.[2] This new conception of history allowed the GDR to venture into areas of commemoration previously outside its political parameters. The reemergence of Frederick the Great in 1980, the 'Prussian Renaissance' of 1981, the commemoration of Goethe in 1982, Luther in 1983, Schiller in 1984, Bach, Händel and Schütz in 1985, and the celebrations of the 750th anniversary of Berlin in 1987 were all part of this new interest in broadening the historical and cultural heritage of the GDR[3]

Despite the interest of academics and the party leadership in broadening the view of the national history of the GDR, there were voices within the SED that expressed their difficulty understanding the party leadership's sudden interest in historical figures previously categorized as reactionary who were now being heralded as equal in importance to the heroes of the German working class. For example, Ursula Ragwitz, head of the SED's cultural department, found it hard to account for this shift while writing an informational pamphlet for local party leaders about the role of the cultural heritage in the GDR. With regard to two questions that were particularly difficult to explain to the party masses, she turned to the SED's chief ideologue, Politburo member Kurt Hager:

> What are the reasons why the GDR recently turned two bourgeois and noble Germans, the religious leader Luther and the General Clausewitz, into national heroes? The treatment both of these great men of German and European history and their social engagement have recently received in the GDR has previously been solely reserved for the heroes of the communist movement. As you know, General Clausewitz was an enthusiastic supporter of the monarchy, while Martin Luther has been vilified for years in the GDR as a traitor to the rebellious peasants. And even you personally recently

chaired a meeting that dealt with the preparations for the 500th anniversary of Martin Luther's birthday in 1983.[4]

Hager's lengthy reply articulated the SED's position on the subject, refuting the idea that this signalled any change in the party's approach towards the past or its heritage. He stated:

> We are in no way ignoring the historical and class boundaries of these or other personalities from German history, their negative traits, their contradictory behaviour or sometimes the historical tragedy in which they find themselves trapped. It corresponds with our world view to study history in its objective and factual progression and in its entire dialectic ... Thus, we judge such personalities through the way in which their influence extends beyond their time, what they have contributed to societal progress and to the development of humanist culture. At the same time we raise the question of how we can make this heritage productive for our time and our society. Martin Luther is without a doubt one of the greatest sons of the German people and a man of worldwide progressive influence.[5]

Hager clearly aligned the new understanding of political figures such as Luther and Clausewitz within the more established interpretation of the cultural heritage that has existed in the G.D.R. since the 1950s. Through widening the definition of culture to include not only creative figures such as Goethe, Schiller, Beethoven and other 'high culture' personalities, Hager was able to extend the concept of cultural legacy to a broader grouping and rationalize the inclusion of figures previously judged out of bounds.

Ragwitz's second question raised the issue of competing with West Germany for control over common historical figures: 'Are you not running the risk that the GDR and the FRG are partially celebrating the same national heroes of the past?'[6] In response, Hager insisted that the new assessment was part of the sustained development of Marxist-Leninist historical interpretation aimed at providing the masses with access to history's treasures.[7]

With new ideological parameters in place, the stage was set to transport this new interpretation of the past out of the realm of professional historians and into the public sphere. To this end, the GDR began the process of preparing one of the largest commemoration events in its forty-year history. The importance ascribed to this commemoration by high-ranking officials within the SED should not be underestimated. Luther provided a new avenue for bolstering its cultural legitimacy in a period when other contributing elements of legitimacy (such as political performance and social welfare) were in steep decline.

## Commemorating Luther in the FRG

Before focusing on the commemoration activities in East Germany, it is necessary to note that parallel Luther celebrations were taking place in West Germany. In stark contrast to the elaborate plan of events in the East, the commemoration activities in the Federal Republic were much less centrally coordinated, yet played just as significant a role in the public sphere. The West German media arguably dedicated more coverage to the celebrations than to any other event in 1983 or certainly any previous Luther commemoration. Johannes Rau, the minister president of North Rhine-Westphalia, noted that, in contrast to the well-coordinated, centralized planning undertaken by East Berlin, the volume of information regarding the figure of Martin Luther circulating in the West could give rise to confusion, since the various pieces of literature, films and articles all presented different points of view.[8] However, within the pluralistic society of West Germany, this was admired as a sign of diversity and openness.

The Luther celebrations in the West included many special events organized by the West German Evangelical Church as well as local events, such as those in Worms and Nuremberg. There were official state acts commemorating aspects of Luther's life and teachings, lecture series, radio broadcasts, academic conferences, television programmes and even a street festival in West Berlin. Despite the diversity of the activities in the West some common themes emerged, such as the idea that Luther and his teachings had the ability to unify the German people. In the West Luther appeared as a symbol of unity in a divided Germany. At the opening of an exhibit in Nuremburg, Federal President Karl Carstens gave a speech titled 'Vom Symbol der Spaltung zum Symbol der Einheit' ('From a Symbol of Division to a Symbol of Unity') in praise of Luther as a figure whom Protestants and Catholics in both German states could celebrate.[9]

West German Chancellor Helmut Kohl spoke in Worms of Luther's theological teachings and his contribution to Germany's humanist traditions, especially his teachings about the freedom of beliefs. Kohl was reserved when mentioning national unity; however, he did venture to mention that Luther was an important figure 'for both parts of our fatherland'.[10] Likewise, Willy Brandt emphasized that Luther belonged to all Germans and that his legacy could not be divided into Western and Eastern portions. Such examples from West German politicians emphasize a concerted effort not to politicize the Luther commemoration, in stark contrast to the events in neighbouring East Germany. Ironically, though, by collectively asserting the nonpolitical nature of Luther, they were indeed politicizing Luther within the context of the Cold War.

## Commemorating Luther in the GDR

Preparations for the commemoration officially began in June 1980 with the first meeting of the Martin Luther Committee of the GDR. In his opening speech, Erich Honecker lauded Luther as one of the 'greatest sons' of the German people, a term more often reserved for Karl Marx that was being applied to Luther for one of the first times. Honecker began his speech by articulating the role of commemoration events within the political context of the GDR, stating that days of remembrance were not mere formalities but rather an opportunity to understand a historical event, the deeds of great individuals, and to apply them to the present.[11] He made specific reference to Luther's 'historic deed' of initiating the Reformation, which was an integral part of the bourgeois revolution, and his role in creating an atmosphere for social progress. He praised Luther's contribution to the standardization of the German language through his translation of the Bible into German and the fact that this translation allowed his progressive ideas to spread. Luther's ideas found mass appeal among the peasant population, who rose up in battle under the leadership of Thomas Müntzer. Traditionally, GDR historians limited their praise of Luther to this earlier period, after which their attention was transferred to the work of Thomas Müntzer. Yet at the point where traditional GDR acceptance of his contributions stopped, Honecker praised the older Luther too. Although Luther had not supported the peasants during the Peasants' War, he nonetheless continued to push an agenda of reform in sermons, schools and universities. Moreover, Luther's desire to help the poor and redistribute church land was seen as nurturing the roots of social consciousness in contemporary Germany. Overall, Honecker's speech lacked any controversial criticism of Martin Luther and highlighted only the positive, progressive aspects of Luther and his legacy that the GDR could claim as part of its tradition.

These basic premises concerning Luther's new place within the GDR's conception of the past were fleshed out in the publication in September 1981 of the official 'theses' for the Martin Luther Year. The theses were written by a commission of social scientists and historians drawn from the GDR Academy of Sciences and universities under the leadership of Horst Bartel, the director of the Central Institute of History at the academy. Numbering fifteen in all, they articulated the SED's new interpretation of Luther and his importance for the present political system of the GDR. Most notably, they claimed: 'The Reformation became an essential element of the start of the revolution, the ideological support for the highly different class forces behind it, and provided the framework for its rapid differentiation over the future course of the revolutionary process.'[12] Throughout, emphasis was placed on portraying Luther's struggle with the Pope as one of theology, which within the social circumstances of the time led to a revolutionary attempt to alter the dominant political system. Even Luther's role after the Peasants' War, from 1526 to 1546, was now viewed relatively positively. Luther, it was argued, continued the Reformation from above with the help of the princes.[13] In all, the theses represented a major shift in the interpretation of Luther and signalled his integration into the GDR's revolutionary line of tradition.[14]

The publication of the official state theses, however, only covered the theoretical side of preparing for the year-long commemoration activities. Attention now turned towards coordinating and planning the commemorative events and festivities, while maintaining state control over the process. In order to facilitate this new level of cooperation, leading church officials were invited to attend the state Luther Committee meetings as guests and members from both church and state committees took a tour in 1982 of Luther-related sites in the GDR to assess the progress of various restoration projects.[15] Amongst all the projects, particular care was given to the complete restoration of Luther's birthplace in Eisleben, including the first-floor room known as the '*schöner Saal*' ('the beautiful room'), and of the portraits of Luther, Melanchthon and several Electors of Saxony there.[16] Other restoration projects in preparation included the fourteenth-century monastery in Erfurt where Luther joined the Augustinian Order in 1505, Erfurt Cathedral, where Luther was ordained, and the Wartburg Castle in Eisenach, as well as buildings in Wittenberg such as the Church of St. Mary, the Collegium Augustinum (part of the former University of Wittenberg) and the Augustinian monastery that became Luther's residence in 1532.

Although the Evangelical Church of the GDR solicited international funds for some of the renovation and restoration projects, the state's contributions were estimated to have cost roughly 9 million Marks. The SED was confident that the GDR could recoup this investment through increased tourism during the Luther Year and after. Over a million visitors from abroad, most spending hard currency, were expected to visit the Luther sites in 1983 alone. Indeed, to accommodate the expected increase in foreign tourism, the national tourist board in the GDR prepared seven different tourist packages for 'following in the steps of Martin Luther'.[17]

Official preparations were not, however, limited to restoration projects nor completely inspired by hopes of improving the GDR's image abroad. The commemorations were accompanied by publishing houses' launch of over 100 books, sound recordings and picture books relating to Luther and the Reformation. Universities, museums and the educational society Urania organized exhibits, lectures and concerts. The East German DEFA even produced a television series about Luther in preparation for the celebrations.[18]

## Coordinating the Commemoration at the Local Level

The work involved in preparing for the anniversary celebrations extended beyond coordinating commemoration festivities with church officials, producing new history texts, and the restoration of Luther-related sites. As early as 1980 the organizing office of the celebration activities circulated an 'Order for the Coordination of Measures for the Cultural-Political Propaganda, Agitation and Public Relations Work on the Occasion of the Martin Luther Celebration of the German Democratic Republic' to all of the district government offices.[19] In general, the guidelines recapitulated the overall conception of the state-sponsored celebrations and the steps necessary to accomplish them with the greatest political impact.

The specific directives of the order were designed to affirm the political and moral unity of the country through providing a clear line of continuity from Luther's theological and social contributions to the present situation in the GDR With explicit reference to the domestic audience, it called for the 'integration of Martin Luther's life work and his importance for the upheaval in which the German states and Europe entered the bourgeois revolution from the decline of feudalism into the national cultural heritage of the German Democratic Republic'.[20] Such integration was tied to the increased effort to popularize the Marxist-Leninist interpretation of history and link Luther's works to political events and social issues in the GDR

The coordination order also contained specific goals for external relations with nonsocialist as well as socialist countries. Accordingly, the Luther celebration was intended to win support from Christian groups and individuals who had formerly dismissed any association with East Germany. Additionally, the GDR aimed to portray 'how Luther's humanistic ideals and his aspiration for a just society are preserved and realized through the politics of the party of the working class and for the welfare of the people in peace'.[21] The order stressed the importance of portraying the preservation of memory sites, monuments and works of architecture associated with Luther as an integral part of the socialist cultural heritage policy of the GDR. In stark contrast, the directives aimed at relations with socialist states referred only to ideological aspects of the celebration, such as Luther's progressive social politics and his place within the German tradition of revolution and democracy, as well as the celebration as an example of a progressive cultural heritage policy in the GDR.

In order to guarantee a cohesive interpretation of information regarding Luther, his work and his importance to the current situation in the GDR, the organizing office included a detailed list of examples and interpretations for use by members working in their official capacity to prepare local events, speeches and publications. The information profile was based on the official position developed in Berlin, but some aspects were expanded to include contextual information and simplified arguments to make the theses more accessible to a wider public.

Following the guidelines set down by the organizing office of the Luther celebration, each political district formulated its own plan of action and interpreted the directives and information profile for implementation in its own region. Of all the political districts in East Germany, the Halle district had the greatest role in translating the state celebration into action at the local level because of the number of Luther-related memory sites within its borders, including both the 'Lutherstadt-Wittenburg' and the 'Lutherstadt-Eisleben'. Accordingly, the Halle district council prepared a local plan for the popularization of Luther in the region and for specific preparations needed to fulfil the state's goals. Beyond the large restoration projects in Wittenburg and Eisleben, the action plan also incorporated cultural and political programmes aimed at spreading the word about the new interpretation of Luther.[22] Concretely, the district council called for the coordination of efforts by groups working in public relations, and in cultural, artistic and educational institutions. On the cultural front, the district called for the distribution of literature and its popularization through local libraries and bookstores, as well as the production of theatrical plays and orchestral concerts intended to highlight Luther's legacy.[23] All of these elements combined to form a cohesive programme for translating the SED's new interpretation of Luther as a historical figure into tangible acts of commemoration.

## Competing Commemoration Activities

Although 10 November 1983 marked the official day of commemoration for the quincentenary anniversary, minor events took place throughout the year. The GDR hosted a series of political, academic and cultural events aimed at examining Luther's life. The Evangelical Church of the GDR also held conferences and hosted smaller celebrations at historic places where Luther lived, such as Eisleben, Wittenburg and Eisenach.

Almost a million foreign tourists from around the world flocked to the historic sites during the spring and summer months.

The first event on the state's commemorative calendar was the opening of the newly restored house in Eisleben where Luther was born and died. The date chosen for the opening event fell on the anniversary of Luther's death, 18 February 1983. The symbolism of this date for marking the state's first act of commemoration set the tone for all future state events: the most important aspect of Luther was his legacy for the current GDR society. In stark contrast, the first church-sponsored event of the Luther Year took place a few months later on 4 May 1983 at the Wartburg in Eisenach, where Luther had translated the New Testament into German. The church celebration was attended by representatives of seventeen Protestant churches as well as the Russian Orthodox, Roman Catholic, Baptist and Anglican faiths. The message and tone of this initial celebration was clear. The church intended to honour the religious and theological contributions of Luther, rather than his historical or national importance, and to stress the significance of Luther's teachings for individual Christians.[24]

Some members of the church leadership had feared that the state would usurp the church's theological interpretations of Luther. Of great concern was the emphasis placed by the state on Luther's deference to political leaders. Others were worried that the state's official theses were too anti-Catholic, which could lead to decreased cooperation between the two churches. Another concern revolved around the perception that the church's involvement in the celebration might come at the cost of not fighting other, more important, social issues in the GDR, such as discrimination against Christians in education and the military or the censorship of church publications.[25] Thus the church used its commemorative events to maintain its own steady interpretation of Luther as a religious reformer and interpreter of the Bible, distancing itself from the state's desire to appropriate Luther's theological reforms as political ideology.

The church's commemoration festivities continued on 15 May 1983 with the first of seven regional congresses, each dedicated to a different cause, such as peace and disarmament, environmental issues, education and other social issues.[26] The first congress, held on the square in front of the cathedral in Erfurt, was dedicated to the GDR's youth and sent a message of nonviolence aimed at the emerging peace movement.[27] Overall, such commemorative events organized by the Evangelical Church in the GDR attracted over 200,000 participants and significantly aided the church's efforts to reinforce its institutional independence and ownership of its interpretation of Luther's legacy.

The state, however, did not completely withdraw from the commemorative events. In the summer of 1983, the Museum for German History in Berlin created a special exhibit dedicated to Luther, his work and the role of the Reformation as the ideology behind the Peasants' War. The exhibit portrayed Luther within the larger social and economic context of the time before and after the Peasants' War. The general layout of the exhibit paralleled the chronology and the main points addressed in the official theses about Luther, placing considerable emphasis on his theology as the ideology of a social movement. The exhibit was hugely popular among the general public, which demonstrated a clear desire to learn more about Luther. Within the first few days it had been viewed by over 30,000 visitors. Whether or not each visitor understood and accepted the state's interpretation of Luther cannot be ascertained, yet the sheer volume indicates that the state's celebratory programme and attempts to popularize the figure of Luther had a significant impact.[28]

The culmination of the GDR's official state celebration of Luther came on 9 November 1983 in the form of a ceremony held at the Staatsoper, the opera house, in Berlin. Present were the members of the state Luther Committee, the SED, the East German parliament, representatives from the Evangelical Church and other invited foreign dignitaries. However, several high-profile international guests who had been invited, such as West German Federal President Karl Carstens, Queen Margarete of Denmark and the kings of Norway and Sweden, decided not to attend, thus thwarting Honecker's hopes of maximizing the international prestige of the event. Although Honecker did not speak during the official celebration, he did take a moment during the reception afterwards to reiterate the official stance that 'the socialist historical and national consciousness of the citizens of the German Democratic Republic receives great impulse through the creative appropriation and continuation of the progressive and humanist heritage of the history of the German peoples, in which our workers-and-peasants-state is deeply rooted'.[29] Clearly, the importance of this event for the regime was not simply to honour the figure of Luther, but again to emphasize the importance of those elements of Germany's past that were beneficial for building support for the SED's current political and social aspirations.

A day later, on 10 November – the actual anniversary of Luther's birth – the Evangelical Church of the GDR held its final commemorative celebration in Eisleben, Luther's birthplace. By hosting the final event, the church was able to have the final word on Luther and his legacy in the GDR. The event in Eisleben was the culmination of five years of preparation by the church and marked a high point in its history. The commemoration ran all day, beginning with a service at the city's central church and continuing with festivities on the city's market square.³⁰ The church service was broadcast live throughout the GDR as well as in West Germany and other European countries with high percentages of Protestants. Indeed, the Evangelical Church was more successful than the GDR state in gaining international support for its celebrations. Church dignitaries came from around the world to participate in the ceremony – including archbishops and bishops from over twenty countries, representing most of the Western European states; several hailed from Eastern Europe and even such far-away places as Brazil and Tanzania.³¹ Although the state attempted to alter the popular perception of the great reformer, its efforts were continually confronted with the alternative view of Luther put forward by the Church. And even though the state now offered a more positive image of Luther, it was unable to completely take control of his legacy and attach its own interpretation to his popular image.

## Conclusion

The 500th anniversary of Luther's birth occurred at a crucial moment in German-German relations. The effects of Willy Brandt's *Ostpolitik* had begun to take form. Brandt's concept of 'two states, one nation' was being challenged by East Germany's attempt to delineate itself from West Germany and propagate its version of 'two states, two nations'. Although Luther was a great 'German son', an attempt was made to present the image of Luther as one of the GDR's greatest sons, denying ownership over his image to West Germany. It was primarily the new context of détente that made it possible for the East German state to extend and alter its interpretation of Luther. With the division of Germany now accepted as stable (at least from the perspective of 1983), the East German state allowed and encouraged its historians to rethink the position of Luther and how he and his teachings related to current East German society. The views that emerged seem to comprise two main elements. First, Luther was interpreted as a necessary precondition of the early bourgeois revolution. And whilst the Peasant's War, second, had been led by Thomas Müntzer, it had been made possible through the absorption by the people of Luther's teachings of self-governance.

It was now acceptable to look at the whole of Luther's life and teachings and attempt to relate them to the current situation in East Germany. Luther was no longer divided into progressive and reactionary parts; instead his legacy was inherited by East Germany in its entirety (as opposed to projecting the reactionary elements onto the West German state). However, such efforts were challenged by the Evangelical Church, which sought to differentiate itself from the state's interpretation and resist attempts to usurp its own interpretation of Luther's legacy. Ultimately, the message presented to the East German public was a confusing one – a state image of Luther as a critical figure on the long path of German history that led directly to the founding of the East German state and the current 'triumph' of communism, and on the other hand the East German Evangelical Church's image of Luther, which was free of political meaning. For the church, the most important things were to ensure that Luther's teachings of peace, community and humanism were understood as timeless and to make these teachings relevant to the current population.

In vivid contrast to the massive coordination effort in the East, the celebrations in West Germany were purposefully uncoordinated. This was an effort on the part of the FRG to distance itself from the official celebrations in the East while subtly asserting that Luther's legacy was inherited by all Germans. In the end, we see a very complex web of memories that drew on distinctly different elements in order to cultivate different aspects of historical consciousness. The success or failure of the efforts of the East German state is impossible to gauge in the absence of opinion polls from the time. However, the massive information campaign and the high numbers of visitors to the year's commemoration events demonstrate that there was indeed large-scale interest in the figure of Luther that probably would not have been sparked without the active participation of the East German state. Yet instead of further bolstering the cultural legitimacy of the state, one may speculate, the long-term effect was more likely the establishment of the East German Evangelical Church as an independent institution. It was this institution that would gain the trust of the leading figures of the popular opposition, who would find support and refuge within the church throughout the 1980s and especially during the crucial year of 1989.

## Notes

1. For example Alfred Meusel, *Thomas Müntzer und seine Zeit* (East Berlin: Aufbau, 1952) and Leo Stern, *Martin Luther und Philipp Melanchthon* (East Berlin, Rütten & Loening, 1953).

2. See *Erbe und Tradition in der DDR: Die Diskussion der Historiker,* ed. by Helmut Meier and Walter Schmidt (Cologne: Pahl-Rugenstein, 1989).

3. Martin Sabrow, 'Der Sozialistische Umgang mit dem Erbe', lecture in the series 'Potsdam in Europe' held at Altes Rathaus, Potsdam, 4 December 2003, unpublished manuscript.

4. Ragwitz to Hager, 26 June 1980, SAPMO-BArch, DY 30/IV B2/9.06/87, Abteilung Kultur [hereafter Abt. Kult.].

5. Response to questions from Hager to Ragwitz. Undated comments that accompanied a hand-corrected version of Ragwitz's original memo of 26 June 1980, SAPMO-BArch, DY 30/IV B2/9.06/87, Abt. Kult.

6. Ragwitz to Hager, 26 June 1980, SAPMO-BArch, DY 30/IV B2/9.06/87, Abt. Kult.

7. Response to questions from Hager to Ragwitz, n.d., SAPMO-BArch, DY 30/IV B2/9.06/87, Abt. Kult.

8. Hans Süssmuth, 'Luther 1983 in beiden deutschen Staaten: Kritische Rezeption oder ideologische Vereinnahmung?', in *Das Luther-Erbe in Deutschland: Vermittlung zwischen Wissenschaft und Öffentlichkeit,* ed. by Hans Süssmuth (Düsseldorf: Droste, 1985), pp. 16–40 (p. 16).

9. Ibid., p. 38.

10. As quoted in Süssmuth, 'Luther 1983 in beiden deutschen Staaten', p. 39.

11. Erich Honecker, 'In der DDR wird die historische Leistung Martin Luthers bewahrt'. Speech by Erich Honecker delivered to the Martin Luther Committee of the German Democratic Republic, 13 June 1980. Reprinted in *ZfG,* 28.10 (1980), 927–31 (p. 927).

12. 'Thesen über Martin Luther: Zum 500. Geburtstag', *ZfG,* 29.10 (1981), 879–93 (p. 880).

13. Ibid, p. 886.

14. See Jan Herman Brinks, *Paradigms of Political Change: Luther, Frederick II, and Bismarck* (Milwaukee: Marquette University Press, 2001), pp. 232–34.

15. '"Socialism Fulfils Humanist Legacy": From the Report Given by Gerald Goetting, Deputy Chairman of the Martin Luther Committee of the GDR', *Foreign Affairs Bulletin,* 19 November 1982, pp. 254–55.

16. 'Anniversary Preparations Well Under Way', *Foreign Affairs Bulletin,* 29 October 1982, p. 239.

17. Ronald Asmus, 'Opening of Luther Celebrations in the GDR', in *Radio Free Europe RAD Background Report,* 100 (German Democratic Republic), 9 May 1983.

18. 'Mit Herrn Luther ist alles in Butter', *Der Spiegel,* 7 March 1983, p. 103.

19. 'Ordnung für die Koordinierung von Maßnahmen der kultur-politischen Propaganda, Agitation und Öffentlichkeitsarbeit anläßlich der Martin-Luther-Ehrung der Deutschen Demokratischen Republik 1983', distributed by the Organizationsbüro Martin-Luther-Ehrung 1983 der Deutschen Demokratischen Republik, Kreisarchiv Merseburg-Querfurt (hereafter KM-Q), Archiv Nr. 9786.

20. Ibid., p. 4.

21. Ibid., pp. 4–5.

22. Bezirksrat Halle, 'Maßnahmen zur Würdigung des 500. Geburtstages Martin Luthers im Jahre 1983 für den Bezirk Halle', KM-Q, Archiv Nr. 9787, p. 5.

23. Ibid., pp. 5–6.

24. Asmus, 'Opening of Luther Celebrations in the GDR'.

25. Robert F. Goeckel, 'The Luther Anniversary in East Germany,' *World Politics,* 37.1 (1984), 118–20.

26. B. Welling Hall, 'The Church and the Independent Peace Movement in Eastern Europe,' *Journal of Peace Research,* 23.2 (1986), 193–208.

27. 'Kirchentag in Erfurt findet bisher nicht gekannten Anklang', *Frankfurter Allgemeine Zeitung* (hereafter *FAZ*), 16 May 1983, p. 5.

28. Detlef Urban, 'Luther-Ausstellung in Ost-Berlin', *Deutschland Archiv*, 16.8 (1983), 790–93.

29. As quoted in 'Für sozialistische Grundsätze vereinahmt', *FAZ*, 11 November 1983, p. 6.

30. 'Luthergedenken des deutschen Protestantismus in Eisleben', *FAZ*, 11 November 1983, pp. 1 and 6.

31. Peter-Jochen Winters, 'Staatliche Lutherfeier ohne Bischof Forck', *FAZ*, 11 November 1983, p. 6.

# 5
# West German Labour Internationalism and the Cold War

*Quinn Slobodian*

━■■■━

To West Germans at the turn of the 1960s, the decolonizing world represented both an opportunity and a threat. Business interests eyed overseas markets hungrily but were concerned about the advantages of Western European nations such as Great Britain and France, which maintained preferential trading arrangements with former colonies. Politicians in the Federal Republic were excited about the potential for making new allies in the struggle with their East German rival, but at the same time they were anxious that postcolonial leaders might favour the more radical politics of the GDR to their own.[1] Most West Germans believed that loyalties in the Third World had to be bought, and when surveyed, a majority of West Germans saw preempting the Soviets as the primary reason to support an enormous package of long-term loans to developing countries passed in 1960.[2] Not surprisingly, perhaps, the West German government believed that the leverage of foreign aid had to be joined by other forms of currying favour with the developing world. As an internal memo in the foreign ministry put it in 1964: 'in the age of East-West conflict, numerous varieties of influence in the international sphere have developed – from legal publicity work all the way to illegal subversion'.[3]

This chapter explores how, against the background of German-German competition in the developing world, union leaders and political foundations in the Federal Republic became important vehicles of so-called soft power in the 1960s.[4] In marked contrast to the mistrust and sometimes antagonism that defined the relations between the labour movement and the government at home in the Federal Republic, Social Democrats and labour leaders worked enthusiastically with both the West German and United States governments to dam the influence of the Soviet bloc in general and the GDR in particular in the developing countries. Through a discussion of the international work of the

Deutscher Gewerkschaftsbund (DGB, the Confederation of German Trade Unions) and the Friedrich-Ebert-Stiftung (The Friedrich Ebert Foundation, the central educational organization of the Social Democratic movement) this chapter shows how the shared paternalistic task of guiding the 'young nations' into the future helped unite West German political leaders across the spectrum in a contentious period. Only as inter-bloc conflict lost some of its edge in the era of détente during the later 1960s, the chapter concludes, did West German labour internationalism shift its focus slightly from anti-communism to sporadic support for independent socialist parties and workers' rights. This was a trend that would increase in the 1970s as the relations between the FRG and the GDR normalized to some extent.

## The DGB in Africa and Asia

It is a striking feature of Cold War politics that inter-bloc competition in the developing world enabled a degree of understanding between the labour movement and the conservative government of the Federal Republic scarcely imaginable at home in West Germany. In the second half of the 1950s in particular, cooperation between the umbrella trade union organization in the FRG, the DGB, and the West German Federal government would have seemed unlikely. The DGB had consistently taken positions opposed to Chancellor Adenauer's Christian Democrat government in matters of foreign policy and political-economic organization throughout the decade. Leftist members of the DGB leadership had mobilized opposition against the incorporation of West Germany into NATO in 1955, and the DGB, with the SPD, had launched the Struggle against Atomic Death (*Kampf dem Atomtod*) campaign in 1958 with some union leaders calling for a general strike to oppose the placement of nuclear weapons in West Germany.[5] Within the DGB, the leadership debated intensely whether unions should act as a 'counter-force' to the market, willing to adopt methods defined necessarily by conflict and class struggle, or as an 'element of order' within a model of consensual capitalism that circumscribed labour's right to act in the name of economic stability and growth.[6]

When the DGB turned its eyes and efforts to the Third World beginning in 1958, it was, crucially, representatives of the latter tendency within the DGB, the centrist reformers, who took the initiative. Key figures in this campaign were Ludwig Rosenberg, who was head of the DGB's international section until 1962, and Bernhard Tacke, the head of the DGB's education section and leader of a DGB delegation to Asia in

1958.⁷ Rosenberg would go on to become chairman of the DGB in 1962 and vice-chairman of the International Congress of Free Trade Unions (ICFTU) in 1963. Founded in 1949 as the US-led alternative to the Soviet-supportive World Federation of Trade Unions (WFTU), the ICFTU provided the stage for much of the DGB's emerging self-understanding as an actor on the international scene. From 1958 on, West German labour internationalism began in earnest as the DGB sent delegations overseas and launched a major fund-raising campaign in support of the developing countries while the pages of the union journal filled with discussion of development and decolonization.

Thomas Mitschein has argued that international activity offered the DGB the opportunity to prove to the dominant US superpower that it had shed its radical nature and would not introduce the conflict-based frameworks of class struggle on either the national or the international level.⁸ Major DGB delegations to Asia in 1958 and 1961 indeed gave evidence to support this thesis as West German labour leaders preached discipline and anti-communism to Third World unions. The DGB trips were planned jointly with the Foreign Ministry and the ICFTU, and it is significant that they targeted specifically those unions with which the GDR had developed contacts. A case in point was Burma, where DGB delegates were taken aback to learn that a group of labour leaders and government officials felt a stronger feeling of connection to the communists than to the West.⁹ The Burmese explained that they were invited to Soviet bloc states more often and better taken care of once there. Furthermore, East German union delegations stayed longer in Burma itself than the couple of days that the West German DGB were willing to spare.¹⁰

During such visits, the DGB representatives notably met with government elites far more frequently than they did with labour leaders. According to the report of the West German embassy, the DGB delegation refused 'without hesitation' to make a sympathy visit to a workers' hunger strike at a large local company while in India. Yet they held a long meeting with a Bombay labour minister who passed on his book, which he thought would be of mutual interest. This was entitled *Peaceful Industrial Relations, Their Science and Technique,* and with it, he claimed, he hoped to carry on Gandhi's legacy of anti-communism.¹¹ West German ambassadors were often unsure initially about the presence of representatives of the West German left in the Third World, but in the end they were uniformly pleased by the way the DGB followed the state line. The ambassador in India, for example, was particularly pleased, on the occasion of a 1958 visit, with the way that West German trade union delegates took up the FRG's claim to be the sole legitimate representative of the German nation. He reported: 'They acted throughout as independent representatives of a German labour force rooted within the entire people.'[12] In addition, he noted that:

> This first close contact between German and Indian unionists has proved very useful. The German visitors were able to be personally convinced in numerous discussions about the difficult situation of the free Indian unions created by the growing communist influence in the factories. On the other hand, they were able to offer their Indian colleagues valuable advice based on their own experience of many years in the struggle against communist subversion.[13]

If sceptical at first, West German diplomats overseas were soon won over to the conviction that the DGB was capable of acting as an important intermediary in building transnational anti-communist blocs that linked state leaders and labour leaders. Thus it is no surprise that diplomats came to see the DGB as a useful substitute for the West German state in politically touchy situations. A good example is Morocco in 1960, where the ambassador of the Federal Republic suggested using the DGB to create ties to the oppositional Union Marocaine du Travail (Moroccan Labour Union, UMT), which had been outspoken in its criticism of the GDR. The ambassador proposed that an invitation to the UMT to visit West Germany be sent through the DGB. His reasoning was that 'some members of government [in the Federal Republic] might not look happily upon the invitation of the UMT but they would probably not be able to raise effective objections as long as the invitation came from a private organization and the support of the German authorities did not emerge publicly'.[14] The West German embassy in Tunisia also remarked on the effectiveness of union connections in this capacity. It suggested – and the Cold War interest is evident here – that the DGB should host more delegations on the grounds that 'it has been repeatedly shown that inviting prominent Tunisian politicians, union leaders and journalists to the Federal Republic is the best means to interest the Tunisian public in the German question'.[15]

As the DGB acted as cultural diplomats building sympathy for West Germany, they also prescribed a particular model of political-economic organization commensurate with this task. The DGB formula for the Third World was the subordination of specific workers' demands to the greater cause of national economic development. An article on the DGB in Africa in an official press report of the West German government reflected the message of consensus by approvingly paraphrasing the application a labour leader from Nyasaland had made to participate in a DGB seminar:

'Africa's union members must be trained, not to become troublemakers in industrial life but as people who co-operate in producing and maintaining a harmonious atmosphere between employer and employee.'[16]

Indeed, the ICFTU publication *Free Labour World* published two more accounts from African labour leaders following their visits to West Germany that further illustrate the model of capitalism the DGB hoped to represent in the Third World. Under the title 'What can we learn from Germany?', a 1962 piece by A. M. Kailembo of the Tanganyika Union of Public Employees recounted how Kailembo had spent the summer in West Germany studying the structure of the trade unions and their relationship to the political parties. During this time he had visited factories and industrial firms, addressed meetings and spoken to workers on the shop floor, in works councils, factories and cooperative societies.[17] Kailembo observed that the most important elements of the West German model for Kenya and Tanganyika were the insurance policies of the welfare state and the practice of codetermination between employer and employee in coal, steel and other industries. He cited the fact that 'the Kenya Federation of Labour has demanded that the principle of adequate social security be incorporated in the Kenya constitution' and added that in 'Tanganyika and other parts of Africa, the question is under consideration'.[18] The codetermination mechanism could, he argued, 'eradicate the abuse of concentration of economic power. This abuse exists in such African industries as mines, railway and electricity; the only real solution is to give the worker a say and a responsibility in the running of these industries'.[19] The editors' choice of these accounts for publication articulated a narrative that the DGB wanted to tell about itself on the international stage, with an emphasis on the benefits of the welfare state, the mechanism of codetermination and the need to replace the 'troublemaking' of labour action with 'cooperation' with the employer.

In another article of 1962, Nigerian trade unionist R. A. Adams delivered a different message, but one that also reflected the concerns of the DGB in its work in the Third World. Adams complained about the use of African unions as a 'political weapon' that was often 'entirely under their government's thumb'.[20] 'We should be warned', he wrote, 'by those African countries where the trade unions exist only to serve the political parties and to feather the nests of their leaders'.[21] Adams's frustration reflected that of the DGB and the ICFTU at having to negotiate postcolonial politics in their own attempts to use unions as 'political weapons'. African leaders, in particular, rapidly grew intolerant of the apparent attempts of Western trade unions to interfere in internal domestic politics, an interference that was coupled with ongoing NATO support for the South African apartheid state and Portuguese colonialism. In June

1963, in an event reported in detail in the DGB monthly journal *Gewerkschafliche Monatshefte*, African labour delegates walked out of an International Labour Organization conference in protest at the presence of South African and Portuguese delegates.[22] The All-African Trade Union Federation, founded in 1961 and led by Ghanaian President Kwame Nkrumah, called for autonomy from the ICFTU and began accepting funds from the WFTU, which represented the interests of the Soviet bloc, in 1964.[23] By the mid 1960s, unions in Thailand, Nepal, Algeria, Morocco, Kenya, Upper Volta, Ghana and Tanzania had cut ties to the ICFTU either voluntarily or through state pressure as most national leaders in Africa and Asia curtailed the independence of unions internally to consolidate political power.[24]

The DGB's support for the ICFTU faded with the signs of its relative failure. The member contributions of the DGB to its International Solidarity Fund would drop by half from 1963 to 1964 and by a further quarter in the next year, and the DGB leadership would withhold contributions to register their dissatisfaction with the management of the ICFTU.[25] The importance of Third World work, which was in any case always secondary for DGB leaders who were more concerned with questions of rearmament, NATO and European economic integration, further waned as union leaders began to soften their anti-communist rhetoric and take the lead in calling for a *modus vivendi* with the GDR and the Soviet bloc.[26] Antagonistic competition with communist delegates in the Third World, they recognized, would not be helpful in this opening of a kind of *Ostpolitik avant la lettre*, which culminated in the DGB opening relationships to Eastern European unions outside of the GDR in 1966, an act that caused considerable anger in the bloc-minded ICFTU.[27] By 1962 the DGB had transferred its overseas responsibilities to the political foundation connected to the SPD, the Friedrich Ebert Foundation. This foundation quickly became the organization that the West German foreign ministry relied on for connections to Third World labour.[28]

## The Cold War Function of the Friedrich Ebert Foundation

Originally established in 1927 and banned by the National Socialists in 1933, the Ebert foundation was reestablished by the SPD in 1947. It was one of three foundations connected to the major West German political parties active in the early 1960s, the others being the Politische Akademie Eichholz (Political Academy Eichholz) connected to the CDU, which was founded in 1957 and renamed the Konrad-Adenauer-Stiftung (Konrad Adenauer Foundation) in 1964, and the Friedrich-Naumann-Stiftung

(Friedrich Naumann Foundation) associated with the Freie Demokratische Partei (FDP, Free Democratic Party), which was founded in 1958.[29] The West German political foundations are unique organizations. They are formally independent from both government and party but receive 90 per cent of their funding from the federal budget. Characteristically, they act as extensions of either the political party to which they are affiliated or the larger state.[30] The work of the political foundations in the Third World began in earnest in the early 1960s with some activity in Africa and Asia but a particular focus on Latin America, where multiparty democracies were perceived as providing more viable partners. In the first years in its new leading role, from 1962 to around 1966, the Ebert Foundation fulfilled the same function that the DGB had done previously, aggressively fighting communist influence in the Third World and disseminating a message of discipline and discretion to unions there.

The Ebert Foundation's strategy varied according to the region and the political form of the states in which it operated. In Africa, as many nations moved to incorporate the unions into one-party systems, the foundation adapted its support to local systems of patronage. In the second half of the 1960s, it helped found the Kenneth Kaunda Foundation in Zambia and the Milton Obote Foundation in Uganda, both named after national leaders, and used them to publish newspapers and textbooks for the ruling parties.[31] Similarly, in Ghana after the introduction of television in 1965, the Ebert Foundation helped produce programmes for broadcast that promoted the nation's industrial and educational achievements such as the Volta Dam and the Accra Polytechnic Institute.[32] In this way, the West German Social Democrats, and by extension West Germany, preserved their influence in Africa in the 1960s by deepening their infrastructural relationship to the parties and elites in power.[33]

In Latin America and Asia, the message of union discipline was combined with warnings against the influence of communism. In India, for example, a West German consul in 1964 welcomed the activity of the Ebert Foundation in training labour leaders, in part for the positive contribution this made towards securing West German overseas investment. He wrote:

> Daily praxis continues to show the damage and setbacks caused to Indian industry through the irresponsible activity of many unions, often only the momentary success of organized splinter groups. The education of Indian union leaders about the fundamentals of democratic union policy will contribute to avoiding the economic losses on projects built also with German help, and above all to counter the growing danger of a union movement leaning towards communism.[34]

Indeed, the first major expenditure by the foundation in Latin America was a pair of conferences in Costa Rica and Mexico on 'The Intellectual Encounter with Communism' in 1962.[35] The SPD began to use the foundation to build up systematically its contacts to Latin America, with West Germany becoming, in the words of specialists on Latin America, a 'junior partner' to the United States in their efforts to penetrate local labour movements.[36] The SPD took steps to place Erich Herzog, a professor close to the Ebert Foundation, at the Interamerican Institute of Political Education in Costa Rica, describing the intention behind the move as being 'to create new contacts with socialist parties in Latin America and through this means enlighten and campaign for German problems', by which, of course, it meant the question of West German competition with the GDR.[37]

Not coincidentally, 1962 was also the year of the founding of the American Institute for Free Labor Development (AIFLD) by the AFL-CIO (The American Federation of Labor and Congress of Industrial Organizations), the major US union that chose, like the DGB, to carry out its overseas work bilaterally.[38] In the following years, the AIFLD founded a series of institutes throughout Latin America through which money was funnelled to centrist unions and occasionally used to help replace governments through nondemocratic means, as in both the Dominican Republic and Guyana in 1963.[39] Representatives of the Ebert Foundation coordinated their efforts with the AFL-CIO, the AIFLD and the US state. In 1962, Secretary of State Dean Rusk apparently 'warmly welcomed' the entrance of the Ebert Foundation into collaboration on the 'political and mental development of Latin America'.[40] The SPD followed the pattern of AIFLD intervention closely, establishing its first institute of several through the Ebert Foundation in Chile in 1964.[41] The Foreign Ministry, which along with the Ministry of Economic Cooperation and Development (Das Bundesministerium für wirtschaftliche Zusammenarbeit und Entwicklung, BMZ) funded the Ebert Foundation's activities, noted internally in 1963 that the foundation seemed to have 'borne pleasing fruits in the defence against communist influence in the developing countries. Through diligently tended contacts, the Friedrich Ebert Foundation has secured a private source of intelligence that has been of great significance for German diplomatic posts as well.'[42]

In the Cold War context of the early 1960s, the Ebert Foundation, which consistently claimed its independence from the Federal government, thus acted in fact as a 'private source of intelligence' and partner against the common communist enemy. Yet by the second half of the 1960s, there were occasional instances of the Ebert Foundation acting to support forces in opposition rather than those in power in Latin

America and Asia. As the US itself pushed West Germany to improve relationships with the Soviet bloc over the course of the decade, the anti-communist imperative that had been so central to the pursuit of labour internationalism weakened.[43] In the small space for manoeuvre opened up by the beginnings of détente, West German labour overseas was able to deviate at times from its rigid anti-communist line. It was first in those countries with regimes so conservative that there was no danger of recognition of the GDR that the Ebert Foundation began to support more left-wing organizations. In Pakistan, a country with a government 'that has engaged itself like scarce any other for our standpoint in the German question', as the embassy there put it in 1964, the Ebert Foundation caused concern in diplomatic and industrial circles when two West German delegates from the metal-workers' union IG Metall began organizing within a Siemens factory and encouraging Pakistani workers to show 'firmness and consistency in making their demands' against their West German employers.[44] In 1965, the West German consul in Paraguay reported that the East Germans were holding a seminar for the insurrectionist Febrista party, only to find out that it was in fact the Ebert Foundation, which went on to develop a long-term relationship with the minority party despite its occasional calls for the overthrow of the pro–West German Stroessner regime.[45] In Guatemala, the foundation created a partnership after 1967 with the Democratic Revolutionary Unity, which had been banned by the right-wing regime for its supposed communist tendencies.[46]

By 1968, representatives of the foundation were telling West German ambassadors boldly that they were 'not tied to the state standpoint on the German question'.[47] In some of these cases the foundation representatives were disciplined for their maverick activity, as in Pakistan, where the two delegates were forced to cease organizing by the Foreign Ministry, the Ebert Foundation leadership and Siemens factory managers.[48] In others, representatives of West German labour defied the Foreign Ministry, as in Paraguay in 1968, when Harald Simon of the DGB defended the foundation's activity, saying that support for the Febristas 'was about the propagation of democratic and social thinking and forms of organization and these goals must come before the principle of non-involvement [in internal affairs]'.[49]

These isolated cases and statements, which had been unthinkable at the high point of Cold War competition around 1960, multiplied with the advent of détente in the 1970s, when Willy Brandt initiated a campaign through the Ebert Foundation and the Socialist International to reorient West German labour internationalism away from its Cold War instrumentalization.[50] In Latin America in particular, the Ebert Foundation began to act as a counterforce to US efforts, providing institutional support to the Sandinista Party in Nicaragua and the leftist National Revolutionary Movement in El Salvador in the late 1970s.[51] By 1980, the US National Security Council was complaining internally of the 'unhelpful, and possibly destructive' role of the Ebert Foundation in Latin America. This was a 180-degree turn from Rusk's 'warm welcome' in 1962.[52]

## Conclusion

West German labour leaders and Social Democrats first travelled to the Third World as anti-communist Cold Warriors, often representing a political stance abroad that was at odds with the one they had adopted at home in the FRG. In the Third World they willingly took on their role as agents of the foreign policy of the Federal Republic, and like many West Germans in the early 1960s, they viewed the diverse processes of the postcolonial world first through the lens of interbloc conflict. The first African or Asian leader to appear on the cover of the news magazine *Der Spiegel* in the decade was Guinean President Sekou Touré, who was pictured slyly smiling above the caption 'Friend of the GDR'.[53] The Cold War lens necessarily ordered developments into the dichotomy of the pro-Western or pro-Soviet camp. In the years of the high Cold War, West German labour internationalism was confined by the strictures of this dichotomy, which disallowed social-political experimentation beyond narrowly defined alternatives. Yet by the end of the 1960s, reconciliation with the GDR through *Ostpolitik* had begun to open up possibilities beyond Europe and North America as well, as West German labour leaders and Social Democrats recognized that binary Cold War categories were inadequate to capture the breadth of political imagination. They started to forge political alliances with oppositional organizations in a way that would have been unthinkable at the high point of Cold War competition, when anti-communism was the major imperative driving the pursuit of labour internationalism. Made visible first through the Cold War, the Third World became the site of novel political collaborations only as the Cold War faded.

## Notes

1. On West German attempts to court postcolonial leaders, see William Glenn Gray, *Germany's Cold War: The Global Campaign to Isolate East Germany, 1949–1969* (Chapel Hill: University of North Carolina Press, 2003).

2. *Allensbacher Jahrbuch der öffentlichen Meinung 1958–1964*, ed. by Elisabeth Noelle and Erich Peter Neumann (Allensbach: Verlag für Demoskopie, 1965), p. 572.

3. See Overbeck, Auswärtiges Amt (FRG Foreign Ministry, hereafter AA), 'Vermerk', 3 January 1964, Politisches Archiv des AA, Berlin (hereafter PA-AA) PA-AA/B90/524, p. 2.

4. Soft power describes the capacity to influence other nations indirectly through cultural and ideological means rather than by exercising hard – that is, military and economic – forms of power.

5. Klaus Schönhoven, *Die deutschen Gewerkschaften* (Frankfurt/Main: Suhrkamp, 1987), p. 327; Holger Nehring, 'National Internationalists: British and West German Protests against Nuclear Weapons, the Politics of Transnational Communications and the Social History of the Cold War, 1957–1964', *Contemporary European History*, 14.4 (2005), 559–82 (p. 564); Helga Grebing, 'Gewerkschaften: Bewegung oder Dienstleistungsorganisation – 1955 bis 1965', in *Geschichte der Gewerkschaften in der Bundesrepublik Deutschland: Von den Anfängen bis heute*, ed. by Hans-Otto Hemmer and Kurt Thomas Schmitz (Cologne: Bund, 1990), pp. 149–82 (pp. 159–60).

6. Julia Angster, *Konsenskapitalismus und Sozialdemokratie: Die Westernisierung von SPD und DGB* (Munich: Oldenbourg, 2003), p. 12; Grebing, 'Gewerkschaften', p. 154.

7. Grebing, 'Gewerkschaften', p. 172; Interview with Tacke, in Wolfgang Schroeder, *Gewerkschaftspolitik zwischen DGB, Katholizismus und CDU 1945 bis 1960* (Cologne: Bund, 1990), p. 39.

8. Thomas Mitschein, *Die Dritte Welt als Gegenstand gewerkschaftlicher Theorie und Praxis* (Frankfurt/Main: Campus, 1981), p. 173.

9. Richter to von Brentano, 8 August 1958, PA-AA/B85/410; FRG Embassy, Rangoon, to AA, 31 May 1961, PA-AA/B85/410.

10. Ibid.

11. FRG General Consulate, Calcutta, to AA, 5 November 1958, PA-AA/B 85/410; FRG General Consulate, Bombay, to AA, 13 October 1958, PA-AA/B85/410.

12. FRG Embassy, New Delhi, to AA, 17 October 1958, PA-AA/B85/410.

13. Ibid.

14. FRG Embassy, Rabat, to AA, 26 September 1960, PA-AA/B85/512.

15. FRG Embassy, Tunis, to AA, 20 September 1960, PA-AA/B85/512.

16. *Bulletin des Presse- und Informationsamtes der Bundesregierung*, 10 September 1960, p. 1644.

17. A. M. Kailembo, 'What Can We Learn from Germany?', *Free Labour World*, 145 (1962), 244–46 (p. 244).

18. Ibid., p. 245.

19. Ibid., p. 246.

20. R. A. Adams, 'African Reflections', *Free Labour World*, 145 (1962), 246–47.

21. Ibid.

22. Bruno Kuster, 'Afrika stellt eine Gewissensfrage', *Gewerkschaftliche Monatshefte* (October 1963), 481–84 (p. 481); Werner Plum, 'Internationale Rundschau', *Gewerkschaftliche Monatshefte* (February 1964), 107–9 (p. 107).

23. Yvette Richards, 'African and African-American Labor Leaders in the Struggle over International Affiliation', *International Journal of African Historical Studies*, 31.2 (1998), 301–34 (p. 333).

24. Anthony Carew, 'Towards a Free Trade Union Centre: The International Confederation of Free Trade Unions (1949–1972)', in *The International Confederation of Free Trade Unions*, ed. by Anthony Carew and others (New York: Lang, 2000), pp. 187–339 (pp. 289–90); Internationaler Bund Freier Gewerkschaften, *Zwanzig Jahre IBFG* (Brussels: Internationaler Bund Freier Gewerkschaften, 1969), p. 20.

25. Kersten, DGB, to Dr. Werner, AA, 24 November 1965, PA-AA/B85/410; John P. Windmuller, 'Cohesion and Disunity in the ICFTU: The 1965 Amsterdam Congress', *Industrial Labor Relations Review*, 19.3 (1966), 348–67 (p. 358).

26. Angster, *Konsenskapitalismus und Sozialdemokratie*, p. 385.

27. Werner Link, *Deutsche und amerikanische Gewerkschaften und Geschäftsleute 1945–1975* (Düsseldorf: Droste, 1978), p. 96.

28. Dr. Werner, AA, to FES, 10 December 1962, PA-AA/B90/521; Christoph Wagner, 'Die offiziöse Außen- und Entwicklungspolitik der deutschen politischen Stiftungen in Lateinamerika', in *Deutschland – Lateinamerika: Geschichte, Gegenwart und Perspektiven*, ed. by Manfred Mols und Christoph Wagner (Frankfurt/Main: Vervuert, 1994), pp. 167–228 (p. 167); Carew, 'Towards a Free Trade Union Centre', p. 305.

29. Michael Pinto-Duschinsky, 'Foreign Political Aid: The West German Political Foundations and their U.S. Counterparts', *International Affairs*, 67.1 (1991), 33–63 (p. 33).

30. Wagner, 'Die offiziöse Außen- und Entwicklungspolitik der deutschen politischen Stiftungen in Lateinamerika', p. 167.

31. Stanley Meisler, 'Unions Use U.S. Funds to Expand Role in Africa', *New York Times*, 10 October 1968, without page number.

32. Werner Wolf, *Untersuchungen über Schulen und Unterrichtsmittel in Ghana* (Berlin: Verein zur Förderung der Bildungshilfe in Entwicklungsländern e.V., 1966), pp. 110–11.

33. On the use of development aid to create influence see Brigitte Schulz, *Development Policy in the Cold War Era: The Two Germanies and Sub-Saharan Africa, 1960–1985* (Münster: Lit, 1995).

34. FRG Consulate, Madras, to AA, 8 July 1964, PA-AA/B90/521.

35. Dr. Witte, FNS, to AA, Referat IV/1, 15 September 1966, PA-AA/B90/695.

36. Kenneth Paul Erickson and Patrick V. Peppe, 'Dependent Capitalist Development, U.S. Foreign Policy, and Repression of the Working Class in Chile and Brazil', *Latin American Perspectives*, 3.1 (1976), 19–44 (p. 34).

37. Bindewald to FRG Embassy, San José, 3 August 1962, PA-AA/B90/521.

38. Hobart A. Spalding, *Organized Labor in Latin America* (New York: Harper & Row, 1977), p. 259. The AIFLD also had the support of the ICFTU. Mitschein, *Die Dritte Welt als Gegenstand gewerkschaftlicher Theorie und Praxis*, p. 114.

39. Spalding, *Organized Labor in Latin America*, pp. 268 and 273.

40. Hardenberg, FRG Embassy, San José, to AA, 4 October 1962, PA-AA/B90/521.

41. Erickson and Peppe, 'Dependent Capitalist Development, U.S. Foreign Policy, and Repression of the Working Class in Chile and Brazil', p. 34.

42. Röhreke, AA, 'Vermerk', 11 July 1963, PA-AA/B90/760.

43. Werner Killian, *Die Hallstein-Doktrin: Der diplomatische Krieg zwischen der BRD und der DDR 1955–1973* (Berlin: Duncker and Humblot, 2001), pp. 319–26.

44. Scholl to AA, 4 September 1964, PA-AA/ B85/665; Scholl to Thierfelder, AA, 13 August 1964, PA-AA/B85/665.

45. Grunwald, FES, to AA, 3 June 1965, PA-AA/B90/522.

46. FRG Embassy, Guatemala, to AA, 8 April 1968, PA-AA/B90/710.

47. FRG Embassy, Colombia, to AA, 25 March 1968, PA-AA/B90/710.

48. Ref. V6, re: 'Tätigkeit zwei von der FES entsandter Berater in Pakistan', 1 September 1964, PA-AA/B85/665.

49. FRG Embassy, Paraguay, to AA, 24 April 1968, PA-AA/B90/710.

50. Eusebio Mujal-Leon, 'The West German Social Democratic Party and the Politics of Internationalism in Central America', *Journal of Inter-American Studies and World Affairs,* 29.4 (1987–88), 89–123 (pp. 94–95).

51. Ibid., p. 98.

52. Memorandum for Zbigniew Brzezinski. From Latin America/Caribbean ([Robert] Pastor), 30 June 1980, Digital National Security Archive.

53. 'Der Elefant', *Der Spiegel,* 16 March 1960, pp. 15–23.

# 6

# The German Question and Polish–East German Relations, 1945–1962*

*Sheldon Anderson*

There is an old Polish saying that 'As long as the world is whole, no German will be a brother to a Pole'.[1] This fraternal reference is an apt metaphor for East German–Polish relations after the Second World War. The East Germans and Poles were like siblings born into the Soviet family. They curried favour with the paternal centre while pursuing conflicting national interests, yet no matter how much they quarrelled, they could not leave this family. This chapter examines a number of conflicts between the GDR and Poland from 1945 to 1962. It starts by exploring how East Berlin's recurrent calls for a revision of the German-Polish border fixed as an outcome of the Second World War were a constant source of ill will between the two states. Poles and Germans were never fully able to resolve the dispute over Poland's administration of German territories east of the Oder and Western (Lusacian) Neiße border. The conflict over Germany's borders to the East was compounded by disputes over policy towards West Germany as Warsaw, to the consternation of the East German authorities, sought better relations with Bonn.

The chapter continues by examining how these and other disagreements intensified during the 'Polish October' of 1956, when upstart Wladyslaw Gomulka and other Polish 'national communists' challenged Moscow by asserting Polish interests. The differences that emerged between the Poles and an East Germany more attuned to the foreign policy imperatives of the Soviet Union would resurface repeatedly until the Solidarity movement toppled communism in Poland in the 1980s. The

---

\* This chapter is based on research published previously in Sheldon Anderson, *A Cold War in the Soviet Bloc: Polish–East German Relations 1945–1962* (Westview Press, 2000), used with kind permission from Perseus Books Group.

final part examines tensions between the two states over rearmament in Eastern and Western Europe. While East Germans thought the Poles uninterested in West Germany's entry into NATO in 1955, Warsaw met East Germany's rearmament in 1956 with fear and trepidation. Despite their purported ideological affinity, the Soviets were powerless to reconcile these two historic enemies. The result was a 'cold war' of mistrust within the Cold War. Like the wider Cold War, there were times of détente and times of crisis, but in the end the East German and Polish communist parties had irreconcilable national differences.

## The Oder-Neiße Border

Tensions over the border between Poland and the GDR were shaped by a long history of border conflicts between the Poles and their Prussian-German neighbours. Prussia, alongside Russia and Austria, had partitioned Poland out of existence at the end of the eighteenth century. The resurrection of Poland after the First World War came partly at the expense of those parts of Germany that Poland had lost over a century before. The Second World War had begun with Germany's attack on the so-called Polish Corridor and Gdansk (Danzig), German territories awarded to Poland at the Paris Peace Conference; then, at the Teheran Conference in 1943, Roosevelt and Churchill agreed to Stalin's demand to move Poland's borders westwards. Running largely along the Oder and Neiße rivers, the border between Germany and Poland was confirmed at the Potsdam Conference in 1945.

After 1945, the primary obstacle to better relations between the Polish and German communists was the loss of German territories to Poland. The equivocation of the KPD and the SPD over accepting the Oder-Neiße border undermined Polish confidence in the German left from the start and was not resolved until the demise of the GDR and the Federal Republic's recognition of the border in 1990. In September 1945, the Polish Workers' Party organ *Glos Ludu* (*Voice of the People*) wrote that 'all Poland is of the opinion that there is no place for the Germans in these territories, and that they should be expelled from them as soon as possible'.[2] Party leader Wladyslaw Gomulka, too, eschewed proletarian internationalism by declaring that 'we must expel all Germans because countries are built on national lines and not on multinational ones'.[3] When he promised that no 'enemy or foreign' elements would be allowed to live in Poland, he meant the Germans.[4] As for Poland's borders, Gomulka declared that 'Poland no longer wants to be a football that is kicked around from place to place'.[5]

East Germany's communist leaders did not initially recognize the Oder-Neiße border. After the SED was forged out of the KPD and the SPD in the Soviet zone in April 1946, the Polish Workers' Party hoped that the communists Wilhelm Pieck and Walter Ulbricht, who were key figures behind the formation of the SED, would prevail upon the party to recognize the border. But the SED adopted a position more closely reflecting the SPD's blunt revisionism. Although the SED could not promote national interests as openly as the Poles, the party's stubborn opposition to the new border confirmed Polish communists' fears that the ghosts of the Rapallo Treaty between Weimar Germany and the Soviet Union in 1922 and the Nazi-Soviet Pact of 1939 would return in the form of a deal between Stalin and the SED at Poland's expense. It is uncertain to what extent the Soviets pressured the SED to accept the Oder-Neiße border, but the SED leaders undoubtedly drew their own conclusions from the breakdown of Allied cooperation in Germany.[6] In 1948, the SED cast its lot with the other Eastern European communist parties, which after the Czechoslovak communist coup in February controlled all of the governments in the region. When the SED eventually accepted the border, the Poles retained lingering doubts about its change of heart. They suspected that the Soviets had ordered an end to the SED's revisionism and were fully aware that many members did not accept the party's official position.

Thus the Polish-German border remained a source of friction between the Poles and East Germans long after the creation of the GDR in October 1949 and its formal recognition of the Oder-Neiße border in Görlitz in 1950. Though it accepted the fact of the border, the SED refused to recognize Poland's historic rights to territories that had been part of prepartition Poland. The Poles suspected that the SED wanted to retain the option for a border revision in the event of German reunification. Moreover, Polish officials were repeatedly angered by East Germans' persistent references to the GDR as *Mitteldeutschland* (Middle Germany), as though Poland's western territories constituted East Germany. Polish officials suspected that the SED referred to the GDR as Middle Germany to pander to the East German settlers from Poland, many of whom still expected to get their land back. A functionary in the SED's propaganda section told Polish diplomat Stanislaw Kopa that 'the view is rather widespread of the necessity to revise the border drawn in the Potsdam agreement ... Recognition of the right of Germans to return to these areas is justified mainly by the difficulties Poland has had in administering them'.[7]

The tenth anniversary in 1960 of the Görlitz agreement between Poland and East Germany was an opportunity to proclaim the solidarity of the two peoples, but differences immediately surfaced over the site of the celebration. Polish Foreign Minister Adam Rapacki proposed a summit and a demonstration in support of the border at Zgorzelec on the Polish side; the East Germans refused, saying that they wanted to avoid giving the West the impression that Poland and the GDR needed to reconfirm their recognition of the border. In reality, the East German communists wanted to evade a big public show of support for a border that was unpopular among the East German people. East Berlin was losing the propaganda war with Bonn here because the Federal Republic still refused to recognize the Oder-Neiße border. East German Foreign Minister Lothar Bolz instead recommended a modest ceremony in Magdeburg that would be devoted largely to condemning West German revanchism. For the East Germans, there was symbolic importance in holding the commemoration on the Elbe and not on the Oder, because they wanted tacit Polish agreement that an attack on the GDR's western border would be considered an attack on Poland.[8] Polish Ambassador Roman Piotrowski reluctantly agreed to the Magdeburg demonstration, which linked acceptance of the East German–Polish border to Polish support for the GDR's border with the FRG.

This act of mutual recognition led only to a fragile rapprochement between the two sides, however. The controversy resurfaced in 1961 when the Poles criticized Ulbricht for adhering to the old SED line that Hitler had gambled away the eastern territories, and for continuing to ignore Poland's historical claims.[9] A year later the East German government issued a document that made positive reference to German General Hans von Seeckt's support of the Rapallo Treaty of 1922. The document cited Rapallo as part of the tradition of friendly Soviet-German relations, which the GDR was now perpetuating, and blamed German capitalists and landowners for fighting Hitler's war and losing German territory.[10] For years Polish officials had expressed their strong objection to any positive references to Rapallo, which they interpreted as a precedent to the 1939 Nazi-Soviet Pact. They were especially angered by this document because Seeckt was a confirmed enemy of Poland.[11] East German diplomats explained that the publication was for West German consumption, but one Polish official responded that the price for this kind of propaganda was too high: 'Poland feels hit on the head by it. Whom does that help?'[12] The document heightened Polish fears that if a German confederation became a reality, East Berlin would work with Bonn to revise the Oder-Neiße border. The GDR had accepted the border between Germany and Poland, but the perception of the Polish communists was that if push came to shove they would have to rely on fellow Slavs in the Soviet Union to guarantee it.

## The Polish October

In addition to the tensions over the Oder-Neiße border, the 'Polish October' of 1956 presented a further challenge to Polish–East German relations as Polish and East German communists clashed over Poland's challenge to Stalinist orthodoxy. After his death in 1953, the coerced normality that Stalin had brought to communist party relations in the early 1950s had started to break down. In addition to their greater political autonomy, the satellites soon began to reassert their economic interests. As the political and economic fault lines dividing Europe weakened somewhat, the Polish government reassessed the benefits of its trade with the Soviet bloc. Many Polish communists grumbled about the SED's obedience to Stalinism, while the SED distrusted the Polish United Workers' Party (Polska Zjednoczona Partia Robotnicza, PZPR) for alleged social democratic, capitalist and bourgeois tendencies. East Berlin was especially critical of Warsaw's tolerance of the Catholic Church and Poland's lack of collectivized agriculture.

These rifts broke open after Nikita Khrushchev's de-Stalinization speech in February 1956. In October, Gomulka returned to power on a platform that directly contested the tenets of Stalinism. Gomulka's election set a dangerous precedent for the Stalinists in the other communist parties, including Ulbricht. Gomulka's national brand of socialism was a direct challenge to the SED's orthodox Marxist-Leninist-Stalinist policies. When the PZPR had purged Gomulka in 1949, the SED had obediently echoed the Kremlin by condemning Gomulka's mistakes. Ulbricht had often lumped Tito and Gomulka together, castigating them for various 'criminal activities'.[13]

The SED's sharp condemnation of Gomulka's allegedly un-Marxist and nationalist policies and the Polish communists' vituperative criticisms of Ulbricht's unrepentant Stalinism soon erased what little goodwill the two parties had developed. The SED suppressed news reports coming out of Poland. *Trybuna Ludu* (*People's Tribune*) alluded to Gomulka's expulsion from the party and arrest in 1949, but the East German press made no mention of Gomulka's past, or of the frank public discussions in Poland about the party's past errors. East German Ministry of State Security official Richard Schmöing told Polish diplomats that things were not going well in Poland if everyone could say what they pleased, a state of affairs that only weakened the power of the state authorities.[14]

In the two weeks between Gomulka's election on 20 October and the Soviet suppression of the Hungarian revolt, the SED leadership was clearly on the ideological defensive as the PZPR taunted it about its Stalinist leanings. The SED's propaganda apparatus geared up to defend the party's policies. Condemnation of the 'counterrevolution' in Hungary dominated the pages of the party organ *Neues Deutschland* in late October, and the SED Politburo boasted that it had taken steps to avoid the kind of upheaval taking place in Poland and Hungary. The Politburo tried to keep the party rank and file ignorant of developments in these states, and even Central Committee members were not informed. Alfred Neumann, the head of the SED in Berlin, specifically told East German journalists in Berlin not to ask about Gomulka.[15] At the end of October the SED Politburo notified the Central Committee that it had restricted access to news from Poland because of the uncertain situation within the PZPR. The Ulbricht regime had reason to censor reports from Poland. Ulbricht knew that there was widespread support among the East German populace and in the SED itself for Polish-style reforms. Many party members wanted the GDR to embark on its own road to socialism. According to the Polish diplomat Jan Pierzchala, East German security officials were monitoring a rise in anti-Soviet attitudes in East Germany. He reported that 'almost everyone is making comparisons between [the] 17 June [1953 uprising] in Berlin and present events in Poland ... Everyone has much sympathy for Poland. The general attitude [is] against Ulbricht'.[16] Bruno Baum, who headed the SED district office in Potsdam, told a West German journalist that the East German people were whispering that 'we need a German Gomulka, a German Nagy'.[17]

Gomulka's attempt to make the PZPR more reflective of workers' interests also challenged the SED's Leninist view of the party's leading role in building socialism. Gomulka rejected the notion that all workers' protests in a people's democracy were inherently anti-socialist, including the Poznan demonstrations that summer. Gomulka declared in his speech to the Eighth Plenum that

> the workers in Poznan, when they went out on the streets of the city, were not protesting against People's Poland [or] against socialism. They were protesting against the ills which had vastly multiplied in our social system, which had also painfully affected them, [and] against the warping of fundamental socialist principles.[18]

By contrast, East German officials, such as the director of the SED's party schools, termed Poznan 'a failed fascist putsch'.[19] Thus the SED and the PZPR were clearly headed in different ideological directions in 1956. Intense debates ensued between reformers in the PZPR and hardliners in the SED. Polish and East German officials made unprecedented public denunciations of each other – the Poles chiding the East German communists for their blind devotion to Stalinist political, social and economic policies, and the East Germans the PZPR for deviating from orthodox Marxist-Leninist principles.

The Oder-Neiße issue also resurfaced during the unrest in Poland in 1956. After ten years as the dominant party in the Soviet zone, the SED had made little headway in convincing East Germans, who sometimes openly expressed their dissatisfaction with Poland's occupation of German territories, to accept the border. They doubted whether Poland could make the efficient use of the territories that Germany had before the war, and some East German officials continued to insinuate that the border could be revised.[20] In November, Politburo member Karl Schirdewan warned Polish communists who had raised the possibility of regaining Poland's lost eastern territories that their concern with the eastern border to the Soviet Union should not lead them to forget others' claims on their border to the west.[21] Schirdewan's statement elicited protest from the PZPR, as did his attribution of the Polish and Hungarian revolutions to 'bourgeois ideologues and their collaborators'. Schirdewan vehemently rejected suggestions from PZPR members that the SED should adopt similar reforms.[22]

Gomulka and Ulbricht met in Berlin in June 1957. The atmosphere surrounding the talks was reserved, according to East German officials.[23] It was immediately apparent that the two sides diverged in their conceptions of socialism. The East Germans adhered to a strict Stalinist line, while Gomulka's appeal to the masses was his promise to de-Stalinize the system. The Poles asked the East Germans to declare their agreement with the resolutions of the Eighth and Ninth Plenary Sessions of the PZPR Central Committee, but the East Germans refused on the grounds that the resolutions were not based on Marxist-Leninist principles.[24] The Poles baited Ulbricht and other East Germans hardliners by asking them if there was really a free and unconstrained atmosphere in the SED, in contrast to the democratization of the PZPR. The East Germans thought that Gomulka naively underestimated the dangers of class conflict in Poland, and that his policies did not promote Marxist-Leninist social, economic and political development. They were particularly critical of Gomulka's agricultural policies and toleration of the 'reactionary' and 'counterrevolutionary' Polish Catholic Church.[25] A sharp exchange ensued when Ulbricht accused the Poles of passing top-secret East German documents to Western governments.[26] He was also dissatisfied with Warsaw's trade policies, which he blamed for jeopardizing the GDR's economic plan.[27]

The Ulbricht-Gomulka summit clearly failed to normalize relations. The SED's year-end report on relations with Poland reiterated earlier criticisms of the PZPR for ignoring ideological and political propaganda and for conducting a half-hearted campaign against revisionism. Although the GDR had established diplomatic relations with Yugoslavia in October 1957, the report criticized Warsaw for favouring connections to Belgrade and the West over ties to Soviet-bloc countries. The East Germans also faulted the Poles for refusing to declare that the Soviet Union was the first and the mightiest socialist state. According to the report, the Polish communists not only were reluctant to recognize the leading role of the Soviet Union but misjudged the role and character of the GDR. In contrast to the cooperative attitude of the Czechoslovak communists, the East Germans found it virtually impossible to conduct ideological discussions with the Polish communists on the basic foundations of Marxism-Leninism. The East Germans even accused the Poles of arrogance, though it was usually the East Germans who displayed an air of superiority about their supposedly superior economic and political development.[28]

## The Problem of West and East German Rearmament

In the 1950s, German remilitarization on both sides of the Iron Curtain further threatened to undercut the relations between the GDR and Poland as military allies in the Soviet bloc. If West German rearmament threatened the entire postwar settlement in Central Europe, it left the Poles worried about a potential clash between NATO and the Soviet-bloc alliance on the inner-German border and the unsavoury prospect of fighting alongside an East German army. It also prompted fears that the Soviets might bargain away the Oder-Neiße border to stave off West German rearmament and entry into NATO. The East Germans, by contrast, feared that the Soviets might sacrifice the GDR itself to prevent the FRG from entering NATO. They feared that Polish troops would lack commitment to defending the border between the GDR and West Germany in the event of conflict. Alarm over the potential for conflict on the inner-German border engendered a climate of mistrust also along the East German–Polish border such that, when NATO announced plans to deploy nuclear weapons in West Germany in 1957, East Berlin and Warsaw competed for diplomatic leadership to prevent this.

In the autumn of 1954 representatives of the Czechoslovak, Polish and East German parliaments met in Prague to discuss West Germany's entry into NATO, among other security issues.[29] The head of the SED's Department of Foreign Affairs complained that the Poles did not show any interest in strengthening cooperative diplomatic efforts against West

German militarism. He concluded that the Poles needed to be better informed about the threat the Bonn government posed to the GDR and to peace in Europe.[30] Ambassador Heymann, the GDR's representative in Poland, was even convinced that Warsaw was ignoring East German interests in favour of better ties to the West.[31]

When the Soviet Union declared an end to the state of war with East Germany in January 1955, Poland dutifully followed suit. The original draft of Poland's declaration warned that if the Western powers and the West German government ratified the Paris Treaty to rearm Germany, 'the People's Republic of Poland will further strengthen its relations with the GDR and take any measures with the other peace-loving states which will guarantee the security of Poland and other nations'. There was no special mention of the GDR in the final declaration, however, which left Heymann to conclude that the Poles lacked enthusiasm for a tripartite pact between the GDR, Poland and Czechoslovakia.[32]

Following West German entry into NATO in 1955, Moscow proceeded with plans for an East German army. It was a controversial subject for the Poles, who, still living with fresh memories of the German attack and the brutal five-year occupation by the Wehrmacht, were vehemently opposed to the plans.[33] Bolz assured Warsaw that the East German people would fight alongside Poles to defend the Oder-Neiße border.[34] But few Poles trusted an East German army whose existence depended on Soviet power. The Polish government was so concerned about people's reaction to East German rearmament that during a simultaneous radio broadcast from factories in Warsaw, Prague and East Berlin in 1955, Polish officials asked the East Germans not to play any military music.[35] Heymann speculated that Polish officials had cancelled a tour of East German musicians to Poland that summer for fear that their concerts would be disrupted by demonstrations against the creation of an East German army. The Poles also denied an East German request for a performance of the band of the Kasernierte Volkspolizei (KVP, People's Barracked Police) at the fifth anniversary celebration of the Oder-Neiße agreement in July 1955.[36] The Poles rejected any unified high command with East German army officers, and they surprised East Germans with a plan for a joint Polish-Czech command of an army group 'north'.[37]

The Polish government knew that if war broke out against NATO, it would be virtually impossible to ask Polish soldiers to sacrifice their lives in defence of the GDR. Relations between the East German and Polish militaries were punctuated with embarrassing confrontations, such as a rancorous meeting between German sailors and the crew of the Polish ship *Baltik* at Sassnitz in May 1957. The head of the GDR's navy, Vice-Admiral Waldemar Verner, was shocked at the Poles' negative attitude towards the Soviet Union, as well as their attacks on socialism generally in the wake of the 'Polish October'. To his surprise, they interpreted the Poznan strikes in June 1956 as a genuine workers' revolt rather than a fascist provocation. Polish officers claimed that Poles lived better under capitalism before the war. They said that Soviet concentration camps were worse than Hitler's, and that Stalin was a criminal who had exploited the Polish economy. One Polish sailor concluded that socialism was 'shit'.[38]

The Polish sailors displayed no signs of the politically correct behaviour that East German communists expected from their partners. According to the East Germans, the Polish sailors did not address each other as 'comrade' and were more concerned with finding prostitutes than attending 'friendship meetings' to discuss Marxism. The Poles made fun of the SED's strict control over Western influences and boasted that they could smoke American-made Lucky Strike and Camel cigarettes whenever they liked. East German officers took from this confrontation real doubts about the loyalty and fighting capability of the Polish armed forces. One concluded that the Poles had no interest in the Warsaw Pact, and that an East German soldier sitting in a foxhole with a Pole had better be ready 'to get a knife in the ribs'.[39]

Gomulka was reluctant to allow the East German army to participate in Warsaw Pact manoeuvres in Poland, knowing that Poles would shudder at the sight of German military convoys rolling down Polish motorways. Gomulka asked Ulbricht why East German soldiers had to wear uniforms so similar to the old Wehrmacht issue. Ulbricht admitted that it was a sop to East German feelings of nationalism.[40] Polish officials responded by chiding the East Germans for allowing nationalist and anti-Polish elements to play a significant role in East German military, political and economic affairs, and for coddling former Nazi and neofascist elements in the army, party, government and intelligentsia.[41]

In 1957 NATO began deliberations on stationing nuclear weapons in West Germany. US President Eisenhower hoped to extricate American troops from Europe and even considered putting nuclear forces under West German control.[42] The idea sent shock waves through the Polish and East German regimes. Grotewohl dusted off his 1952 proposal for a confederation of the two German states, now with a provision that neither would station or produce atomic bombs. The FRG and GDR would leave NATO and the Warsaw Pact, and all foreign troops would leave German soil. Bonn immediately rejected the plan.[43] Although the former Polish ambassador to the GDR Jan Izydorczyk told the Polish parliament that a confederation was a sensible solution to the German problem,[44] the Polish government did not throw its weight behind Grotewohl's proposal. Most Poles were wary of any united German state, regardless of its composition, and fearful that change in the status quo could result in a revision of the Oder-Neiße border.[45] Warsaw's foreign policy options regarding the German question were limited, but the Gomulka regime was unwilling to let the Soviet Union or the GDR dictate Poland's foreign policy towards West Germany.[46] Thus the Polish government developed its own plan to preempt the nuclearization of Central Europe. Bearing the name of Foreign Minister Adam Rapacki, the plan appeared in spring 1957. It banned the manufacture, stockpiling and deployment of nuclear weapons in the two Germanys, Poland and Czechoslovakia and prohibited the deployment of missile launchers capable of carrying nuclear weapons. After receiving formal approval from the Warsaw Pact, Rapacki and Czechoslovak Foreign Minister Vaclav David presented the plan to the United Nations on 2 October.[47] The Poles were proud of their initiative. The editor of the weekly journal *Polityka*, Mieczyslaw Rakowski, wrote that among the projects advanced in the early stages of détente the Rapacki Plan had occupied the chief place and made Poland known throughout the world.[48]

The East German Foreign Ministry immediately informed Polish officials that the Rapacki Plan made an important contribution to solving the German problem.[49] On 6 October *Neues Deutschland* carried an article on the proposal, including a telegram to the UN declaring the GDR's support.[50] Reluctant to let Poland play a key role in German affairs, however, the East Germans quickly revised their position. Subsequently *Neues Deutschland* ignored the Rapacki Plan, publicizing instead the Soviet Union's disarmament proposals.[51] One East German diplomat recalled that the Soviet Union and the GDR reacted to the plan with mistrust and did everything to let the initiative peter out.[52] East German leaders paid little attention to the Rapacki Plan, partly because it did not include guarantees for the continued existence of the GDR. They preferred bilateral negotiations with Bonn on issues affecting East Germany. Grotewohl demanded that the two German states sign a nuclear-free agreement, which of course would have meant the FRG's recognition of the GDR.[53]

The Poles meanwhile kept the East Germans in the dark about negotiations on the Rapacki Plan. In December 1957, Rapacki finally informed East German Ambassador Josef Hegen about Poland's talks with Great Britain, France, Austria and Sweden. Rapacki said that the latter two neutral countries were very supportive of the proposal.[54] In early February 1958, East German Foreign Ministry officials tried to seize the diplomatic initiative by proposing a trilateral East German-Czechoslovak-Polish disarmament plan. In an obvious attempt to loosen West

Germany's ties to NATO, Otto Winzer suggested that the four nuclear-free states (Poland, Czechoslovakia, East Germany and West Germany) pledge not to develop any weapons. The Poles rejected the idea, arguing that a joint proposal with the GDR would reduce the Rapacki Plan's chance of acceptance in the West. The Poles told Winzer that Poland had to regard the interests of countries other than Germany, not just Germany itself.[55]

The Poles were also incensed about East Germany's increasing tendency to refuse to recognize the Rapacki Plan as a Polish idea. In late 1958, the Polish Foreign Ministry observed that 'for a long time the "Rapacki Plan" was presented as an initiative of the GDR, subsequently supported by Czechoslovakia and Poland'.[56] It noted that the East German press had not paid much attention to the plan, and when it did, had emphasized the 'key role' of the GDR. *Neues Deutschland* refused to call it the 'Rapacki Plan', a stance that Polish diplomats blamed on its chief editor Hermann Axen, who had from the start been an outspoken critic of Gomulka.[57]

In the end, the Rapacki Plan was never seriously considered as a basis for addressing the arms race in Central Europe, which here at least took some of the sting out of the conflict between East Berlin and Warsaw. The Western alliance went ahead with plans to station nuclear missiles in Western Europe, including West Germany. The US was unwilling to bargain away its NATO partner for a politically and militarily nonaligned German state. Furthermore, Bonn was opposed to leaving NATO and the recently constituted European Common Market.

His next meeting with Gomulka in Warsaw in December 1958 did not alleviate Ulbricht's doubts about the reliability of the PZPR, especially with regard to the German question. Although Gomulka eventually proved a loyal Warsaw Pact partner and even supported military intervention in Czechoslovakia in 1968, Ulbricht never forgot that he was the product of a potentially dangerous reform movement.[58] However, given the strategic importance of East Germany and Poland to the Soviet Union, the Kremlin could not allow their differences over the border, West Germany and nuclear questions to develop into an open break. It almost came to that in 1956, and if not for their mutual dependence on the Soviet Union, relations between the East German and Polish communists would doubtless have gone the way of the Tito-Stalin split in the late 1940s, or the Sino-Soviet break in the 1960s. The East Germans continued to criticize Poland's economic and political links to the West in the 1970s, although East Berlin itself was becoming increasingly dependent on West German subsidies and trade. Nonetheless, the dogmatic East German communists continued to chastise the more liberal Polish communists for their friendly relations with Bonn. Evidently the Honecker government was supportive of a Warsaw Pact invasion to quash the Polish Solidarity movement in the early 1980s and rued the day when Solidarity returned in 1989 to head the first noncommunist government. The Poles set a precedent for the overthrow of a communist regime in Central Europe. East Berlin would be next.

## Notes

1. Quoted in Ines Mietkowska-Kaiser, 'Zur brüderlichen Zusammenarbeit zwischen polnischen und deutschen Kommunisten und Antifaschisten nach dem Sieg über den deutschen Faschismus (1945–1949)', *Jahrbuch für Geschichte der sozialistischen Länder Europas*, 23.1 (1979), 49–67 (p. 51).
2. *Glos Ludu*, 16 September 1945, p. 3.
3. Quoted in Norman Naimark, *The Russians in Germany: A History of the Soviet Zone of Occupation, 1945–1949* (Cambridge, MA: Harvard University Press, 1995), p. 146.
4. *Glos Ludu*, 1 January 1946, pp. 12–13.
5. Wladyslaw Gomulka, *O problemie Niemieckim* (Warsaw: Ksiazka i Wiedza, 1971), p. 105.
6. See Ralf Badstübner, 'Die sowjetische Deutschlandpolitik im Lichte neuer Quellen', in *Die Deutschland Frage in der Nachkriegszeit,* ed. by Wilfried Loth (Berlin: Akademie, 1994), pp. 114–23.
7. 'Kopa notes of meeting with Horst Heinrich', 11 February 1959, Ministerstwo Spraw Zagranicznych, Archiwum Ministerstwa Spraw Zagranicznych, Warsaw, Poland (Ministry of Foreign Affairs, Archive of the Ministry of Foreign Affairs, hereafter MSZ), 10/346/38.
8. Bolz to Ulbricht, 11 June 1960, Sozialistische Einheitspartei Deutschlands, Zentralkommitee (hereafter SED ZK), Zentrales Parteiarchiv der SED, Berlin (hereafter ZPA), Nachlaß Walter Ulbricht, NL 182/1250. Editors' note: at the time of Anderson's research all SED ZK documents were located at the ZPA under the old call numbers ('Altregistratur'). In December 1992 these documents were deposited at the SAPMO-BArch.
9. Röse to GDR Foreign Ministry, 25 September 1961, SED ZK, microfilm FBS 339/13496.
10. 'Mieszlaw Tomala notes of a meeting with Helmer', n.d., Records of the Central Committee of the Polish United Workers' Party, Archiwum Akt Nowych, Warsaw, Poland (hereafter PZPR KC), 237/XXII-1103.
11. 'Summary of a meeting with East German officials on the GDR and the future of Germany', 16 May 1962, PZPR KC, 237/XXII-1103.
12. Hilmar Schumann report, 22 May 1962, SED ZK, microfilm FBS 339/13496.
13. Dietrich Staritz, *Geschichte der DDR, 1949–1985* (Frankfurt/Main: Suhrkamp, 1985), p. 24.
14. 'Czechon notes of a meeting with Richard Schmöing', 20 October 1956, MSZ, 10/378/42.

15. 'Kopa notes of meeting of the PZPR POP on 24–25 October 1956', MSZ, 10/378/42.
16. Pierzchala to Polish Foreign Ministry, 26 October 1956, PZPR KC, 237/XXII-822.
17. 'Nasielski notes', cited in C. Urbaniak to Lobodycz, 26 October 1956, MSZ, 10/378/42.
18. *Trybuna Ludu*, 21 October 1956, p. 3.
19. 'Notes on Current Events and Relations between Poland and the GDR', unsigned, 8 December 1956, MSZ, 10/378/42.
20. 'Kopa notes of a meeting with Grünberg', 28 September 1956, MSZ, 10/378/42.
21. 'Kupis notes of his visit to Karl Marx University from 13 October to 12 November', 16 November 1956, PZPR KC, 237/XXII-822.
22. 'Polish Foreign Ministry report', unsigned, 30 November 1956, MSZ, 10/378/42.
23. 'Kopa notes of meeting with Haid on 2 July and 4 July 1957', MSZ, 10/379/42.
24. Florin to Grotewohl, 20 June 1957, SED ZK, Nachlaß Otto Grotewohl, NL 90/483.
25. 'Report of the Polish and GDR government and PZPR and SED party meetings', 20 June 1957, SED ZK, microfilm FBS 339/13423.
26. 'Record of discussions of party and government delegations in Berlin from 18 June to 20 June', 29 June 1957, MSZ, 10/309/36.
27. 'König notes on Gomulka's visit to Moscow', 31 May 1957, SED ZK, Nachlaß Grotewohl, NL 90/485.
28. 'Report on co-operation between the regional offices of the SED and counties in Poland', [c. December 1957], SED ZK, IV 2/20/31.
29. See the documents in MSZ, 10/466/48.
30. Florin to Koenen, 5 January 1955, PA-AA, Bestand Ministerium für Auswärtige Angelegenheiten der DDR (hereafter DDR MfAA), Warsaw Embassy, A3670.
31. Heymann to Florin, 1 February 1955, DDR MfAA, Warsaw Embassy, A3670; Heymann to GDR Foreign Ministry, 7 February 1955, PA-AA, DDR MfAA, Warsaw Embassy, A3670.
32. Heymann to Florin, 1 February 1955, PA-AA, DDR MfAA, Warsaw Embassy, A3670.
33. See Peter H. Merkl, *German Foreign Policies, West and East: On the Threshold of a New European Era* (Santa Barbara: ABC-Clio Press, 1974), p. 99.
34. Izydorczyk to Warsaw, 31 December 1953, PZPR KC, 237/XXII-518.
35. Heymann to Grosse, 9 April 1955, SED ZK, microfilm FBS 339/13492; Grosse to Heymann, 25 June 1955, PA-AA, DDR MfAA, Warsaw Embassy, A3670.
36. Heymann to GDR Foreign Ministry, 2 July 1955, PA-AA, DDR MfAA, Warsaw Embassy, A3670.
37. Berlin Office, FRG Foreign Ministry, to Bonn, 21 March 1955, PA-AA, Abteilung 7, Bd. 84.
38. Verner to Stoph, 9 May 1957, SED ZK, Nachlaß Ulbricht, NL 182/1249.
39. Ibid.
40. Franz Sikora, *Sozialistische Solidarität und nationale Interessen* (Cologne: Verlag für Wissenschaft und Politik, 1977), p. 161.

41. 'PZPR evaluation of the situation in the GDR', unsigned, [c. autumn 1961], PZPR KC, 237/XXII-1102.

42. Marc Trachtenberg, *A Constructed Peace: The Making of the European Settlement 1945–1963* (Princeton: Princeton University Press, 1999), pp. 185–88.

43. 'Polish Embassy report from 15 March to 31 August 1957', MSZ, 10/371/41.

44. 'Izydorczyk speech to the Polish Parliament', [c. November, 1957], PZPR KC, group Izydorczyk, file 473/6.

45. Lobodycz to Naszkowski, 3 September 1957, MSZ, 10/359/39.

46. Heymann to GDR Foreign Ministry, 29 October 1957, DDR MfAA, HA/I Secretariat, A38.

47. See Sikora, *Sozialistische Solidarität und nationale Interessen,* pp. 151–52.

48. Mieczyslaw Rakowski, *The Foreign Policy of the Polish People's Republic* (Warsaw: Interpress, 1975), p. 164.

49. 'Kopa notes of a meeting with Beling on 11 October', 16 October 1957, MSZ, 10/379/42.

50. *Neues Deutschland,* 6 October 1957, p. 1.

51. *Neues Deutschland,* 13 October 1957, p. 1.

52. Horst Grunert, *Für Honecker auf glattem Parkett: Erinnerungen eines DDR-Diplomaten* (Berlin: Edition Ost, 1995), p. 118.

53. Douglas Selvage, 'Introduction to Khrushchev's November 1958 Berlin Ultimatum: New Evidence from the Polish Archives', *Bulletin: Cold War International History Project,* 10 (1998), 200–203 (p. 200).

54. 'Hegen notes of a meeting with Rapacki on 10 December', 11 December 1957, SED ZK, Nachlaß Grotewohl, NL 90/485.

55. 'Record of negotiations between Ogrodzinski and Piotrowski, et al., and Handke and Winzer, et al.', 7–8 February 1958, DDR MfAA, HA/I Secretariat, A14759; 'Polish Embassy report from 1 September 1957 to 28 February 1958', 11 March 1958, MSZ, 10/371/41.

56. Piotrowski to Lobodzycz, 2 January 1958, MSZ, 10/371/41.

57. 'Polish Foreign Ministry report on the GDR press', [c. December 1958], MSZ, 10/464/48.

58. Winzer to Ulbricht, 12 February 1959, SED ZK, Nachlaß Ulbricht, NL 182/1250.

# 7

# From Bulwark of Freedom to Cosmopolitan Cocktails
## The Cold War, Mass Tourism and the Marketing of West Berlin as a Tourist Destination

*Michelle A. Standley*

Historically, Berlin was not one of the great travel destinations of Europe. Over the course of the nineteenth and early twentieth centuries, as mass leisure gradually extended beyond the elite classes to the bourgeoisie and petit-bourgeoisie, Berlin remained off the beaten track. Next to Rome or Paris, the city had comparatively little to attract the elite or bourgeois traveller in search of the roots of classical or modern civilization. A relatively young city, it lacked world-famous architecture, great works of art and the refined consumer pleasures of Paris or London. Nor did Berlin have sand and sunshine, which were increasingly important commodities in the early twentieth century. Because urban tourism was not yet a mass phenomenon or a major source of economic growth, city authorities lacked a compelling motive for improving the city's attractiveness as a destination or for undertaking promotional work. Yet the relative unimportance of tourism for Berlin economically began to change during the 1920s, when rates of travel increased in Europe and North America and more non-elites began to undertake shorter, more frequent trips – a practice ideally suited to the growth of urban tourism. National Socialist promotion of tourism, especially the flurry of propaganda and aesthetic improvements undertaken for the 1936 Olympics, also helped to cultivate Berlin as a tourist destination.[1]

Ultimately, it was the Cold War that transformed Berlin into a major urban tourist destination. This chapter examines the impact of the Cold War on the development of mass tourism in West Berlin and on the marketing strategies employed by West Berlin's official organization for the promotion of tourism, the Verkehrsamt Berlin (Travel Bureau Berlin).

It draws largely on the West German tourist industry trade journal *Der Fremdenverkehr* (*Tourism,* founded in 1948),[2] which reported on industry trends and on West Berlin's tourism advertising practices. This chapter argues that the travel bureau's shifting marketing strategies reflected both changes in the city's relationship to the Cold War and changes in postwar tourism practices. Specifically, in the early to mid 1960s the bureau moved away from explicitly promoting the city as a Cold War hot spot and capitalist showcase and towards marketing it as an apolitical leisure playground, suited to the tastes of both the 'new urban traveller' and the myriad target groups for whom it constituted merely a backdrop to the pursuit of their lifestyle and urban fun. The marketing of Berlin here reveals the limitations of using the Cold War as an interpretative paradigm.

## West Berlin as Bulwark of Freedom

The history of tourism in West Berlin is inseparable from that of the Cold War. West Berlin owed its birth and eventual death to the larger geopolitical struggles between the Soviet Union and the United States, and to the smaller ones between the GDR and the FRG. West Berlin emerged from the Soviet Blockade of 1948–49 as a political entity and a touchstone in the conflict. The division of Berlin left the Western part in a tenuous economic and political position, not least after Bonn became the West German capital. It was West Berlin's status as an island city-state in the midst of the socialist GDR that inspired civic leaders to turn to the overlapping projects of political propaganda and tourism promotion. The city's most urgent task was to secure political and financial support by gaining and maintaining grass-roots support in the US, the FRG and Western Europe. When the West Berlin Senate established the Travel Bureau Berlin as part of the Finance Ministry in November 1949 – weeks after the founding of the GDR – its work centred on creating a sympathetic image of West Berlin, raising its international profile and generating revenue through tourism.[3] Tourism promotion was subsumed within this greater political task and did not stand outside it.

Headed by Ilse Wolff from 1949 to 1979, the bureau approached its task from several angles. It produced slogans and cosponsored packages, creating posters and brochures for distribution in the FRG and in major Western European and North American cities. It also sent its own advertising bus around the Federal Republic and Western Europe. Posters and brochures from the 1950s illustrate how the lines between political propaganda and the promotion of tourism were blurred. Both propaganda and marketing materials centred on common themes: West Berlin as a 'bulwark of freedom' and capitalist showcase, as a place from which to view the communist and capitalist worlds side by side, and as a cosmopolitan metropolis.

The earliest promotional work explicitly sought to disseminate the message that West Berlin was the home of 'freedom' and a city to which the Cold War lent an exciting air of tension. One poster, aimed at an American audience, featured the city's 'Freedom Bell' – a replica of the Liberty Bell the US had given to West Berlin. It announced: 'Berlin is calling the world. Visit the City of the Freedom Bell.' Written across the bell, in English, were the words 'New Birth of Freedom'. To underscore the message that the fate of freedom in Berlin was the fate of freedom in the world, the bell's clapper was depicted as a globe.[4] A late-1950s poster directed rather at citizens of the Federal Republic featured, between pulsing arrowheads, the phrase 'To Berlin now more than ever!' – a message that emphasized the urgency and excitement created by the political crisis.[5] Likewise, a 1950 poster declared that Berlin was the 'the most interesting city in Europe' as it offered 'a glimpse through the Iron Curtain' and the chance to see the East and the West side by side.[6] A few years later, the travel bureau implicitly contrasted East and West Berlin as alternate civilizations in a German-language brochure that described the city's former heart, Friedrichstrasse, as banished to the Soviet sector. Using language reminiscent of National Socialism's orientalist, anti-Bolshevik rhetoric, the brochure lamented that '[t]oday [the Friedrichstrasse] appears to lie in Asia. Empty, dusty and giving the impression that one is walking in a long since abandoned settlement.'[7] Posters and brochures like this conveyed the bureau's dual purpose of cultivating support for West Berlin and advertising the city as a tourist destination.

Even in the 1950s, promotional work did not revolve solely around the Cold War. It also incorporated visual references to the modernism of the Weimar Republic. A good example is a 1953 poster featuring a solitary, well-dressed woman standing among her suitcases at the portal of a hotel. The lights of the Kurfürstendamm, the boulevard near the Zoologischer Garten's train and metro station, glisten in the background.[8] The picture hinted at the excitement of the city's night life but also communicated the message, via the travel stickers on the woman's cases, that Berlin was an attractive destination because it was international – the meeting point not only for East and West Germany but for the whole world. Allusions to the Weimar years suited West Berlin's marketing strategies because they invoked the city as the paradigm of modernist and cosmopolitan urban culture, in the process excising the horrors of National Socialism and the Second World War from the promotional image.

Appeals to anti-communist sentiment or Weimar glitz could not erase Berlin's notoriety as the former seat of Hitler's power, though. Even at the height of sympathy for the city, after the construction of the Wall in 1961, the bureau encountered some negative responses to its campaigns abroad. In April 1962 in Slagelse, Denmark, its advertising bus was vandalized, despite being parked next to a police station for safety. Daubed on it, alongside the letters 'SS', were swastikas and the phrases 'Visit Neuengamme [a concentration camp near Hamburg] and Die' and 'No war for Berlin'. Then in Copenhagen, a Molotov cocktail was thrown into the cab. In Amsterdam the information offices of the German Agency for Tourism (Deutsche Zentrale für Fremdenverkehr) were also attacked, as were cars belonging to German tourists. Tyres were slashed and windows plastered with stickers bearing the phrase 'Heim ins Reich', or 'Home to the German Reich', the slogan used by the National Socialists when they had attempted to resettle Germans from outlying regions of Europe within Germany's expanded borders.[9] Now the phrase told the Germans to go home. Faced with such attacks, the travel bureau temporarily cancelled its tour. Though isolated, such episodes suggest the difficulty the travel bureau faced in 'selling' the city as wholly new within the climate of anti-German sentiment still lingering in postwar Europe. No matter how urgent the communist threat to the city appeared, not all potential visitors were convinced that 1949 constituted a 'year zero' for West Berlin.

The Travel Bureau Berlin did not, of course, operate in a vacuum. In addition to its own promotional work, it benefited from the efforts of other private and state-sponsored individuals and organizations. Its promotional work cannot be considered in isolation from the broader competition between the Soviet Union and the United States, and between the GDR and the FRG, not merely for West Berlin but for the hearts and minds of citizens of the first, second and, to a lesser extent, third worlds. Both sides in the Cold War sought to prove the superiority of their respective ideological, political and economic systems through the display of material prosperity and technological progress. Tourism promotion and the reconstruction of the city played a part in this intrabloc competition.[10]

In divided Berlin, the political authorities employed the urban landscape itself in their competing exercises in self-promotion and propaganda. Local authorities in West Berlin, with encouragement and financial assistance from the US and the FRG, and working together with urban planners and architects, sought to rebuild the city to conform to its self-appointed symbolism as an outpost of freedom and showcase for the 'good life' offered by capitalist democracy.[11] With Berlin's historic, and more famous, boulevard Unter den Linden in East Berlin, the authorities concentrated their efforts on the area surrounding the Kurfürstendamm. Generous subsidies and tax breaks helped lure banks, insurance companies and other businesses to set up shops there. Fittingly, the city's largest department store, Kaufhaus des Westens (Department Store of the West) reopened in 1950, less than a year after the end of the blockade. The Zentrum am Zoo (Centre at the Zoo) and the Zoopalast (Zoo Palace Cinema) were completed in 1953. By 1958 the 22-storey Telefunken skyscraper was also finished.[12] The Berlin Hilton, a sign of the city's new confidence in attracting international tourists, opened to much fanfare in 1958. American architects designed the building, and numerous stars from New York attended its opening.[13] By the end of the decade the boulevard was home to restaurants, department stores and a thriving café scene. American goods, from Coca-Cola to cigarettes and jazz records, shared shop windows with West German televisions and Parisian fashions.[14] The Kurfürstendamm's reputation as a beacon of freedom shining light into the darkness of East Berlin was enhanced by the contrast at night. The lights of cars and neon advertisements turned the Kurfürstendamm into a rainbow of lights. Lacking West Berlin's many lights and also trying to save electricity, East Berlin lay mostly in darkness.[15]

Popular culture in Western Europe and North America also contributed to an image of West Berlin as an 'island of freedom' and symbol of the Cold War struggle. For many potential visitors who had watched or read spy thrillers, most famously the James Bond series, or seen British television shows like *The Saint* and *Danger Man*, divided Berlin was synonymous with international espionage, daring escapes over the Wall, menacing East German border patrols and a plucky population of freedom-loving West Berliners (see Chapman in this volume).

## The Rise of Cold War Tourism

Cold War tourism is best understood as a historical tourist culture in which visitors sought out symbols and signs of the global conflict and – consciously or not – judged the success or failure of communist and capitalist societies according to what they encountered during their visit to one or both sides of the Iron Curtain. Specific Cold War tourist sites in West Berlin included Checkpoint Charlie and its museum, the Freedom Bell and the Airlift Memorial. However, it was the Wall that became West Berlin's most popular Cold War tourist attraction. Official guests and tourists alike participated in the ritual of standing on one of the viewing platforms built alongside it to look into the GDR. Visitors also participated in 'Wall Tours' run by West Berlin bus companies like Severin + Kühn and Berliner Bären.[16]

According to a 1965 survey of overnight visits, a majority of visitors to West Berlin included a stop in East Berlin on their itinerary.[17] This fact indicates that most visitors to West Berlin were acutely aware of the contrast between the divided parts of the city. Official GDR tour guides complained that visitors to East Berlin frequently contrasted them during their bus tours, usually comparing the appearance of the East unfavourably with that of the West.[18] To cite one example, a South African visitor to East Berlin tried to persuade his East German guide that life in West Berlin was better by pointing to the Kurfürstendamm as an emblem of the 'good life'. 'Why do you have queues in front of the bakeries?' he pressed, adding, 'if only you knew all the things there are on the Ku'damm!'.[19]

Cold War tourism in West Berlin helped affirm the imagined boundaries of the global conflict. For many, seeing the Wall up close – its bleakness, the barbed wire, the no-man's-land and the watchtowers – renewed their belief in the moral superiority of the West.[20] By participating in such shared Cold War tourist practices as visiting the Wall, peering through the Iron Curtain and finishing with a shopping trip on the Kurfürstendamm, thousands of otherwise unconnected individuals could enact their perceived freedom as defined against the 'imprisoned' communist East Germany and in so doing feel, at least momentarily, that they were members of a larger community known as 'the free world'. Especially for those visiting the GDR capital as an excursion from the West, the encounter with the East German border guards, relatively little car traffic and war-damaged buildings reinforced their perception of West Berlin as freer, more modern and prosperous. Thus visitors who already equated capitalism with abundance and freedom of movement and communism with shortages and restriction of movement were confirmed in their suppositions.

Cold War tourism could extend beyond visiting specific sites or memorials into almost any activity that reaffirmed or challenged visitors' perception of the two sides of the conflict. It is impossible to pinpoint exactly where Cold War tourism ended and more generic postwar urban tourism began. This is partly because most visitors to West Berlin engaged in both obviously political tourist activities, such as the Wall tours, and in less obviously political ones, like shopping. The boundaries between such activities were blurred, the experience of one informing the way the other was viewed. A visitor to the city – like the South African above – might have understood a shopping spree on the Kurfürstendamm differently after having witnessed East Germans lining up outside state-run bakeries. What previously might have been a banal shopping experience was transformed into an exercise in freedom, specifically the freedom to consume.

## The Ambiguous Impact of the Wall on City Marketing

The Wall had an ambiguous impact on official promotional work. It contributed to the popularity of Cold War tourism yet also prompted a shift away from the Cold War in the city's official marketing. This was partly because the Wall increased the seriousness of the political climate, making it difficult to incorporate into light-hearted promotional materials. It would have seemed tasteless, even macabre, to exploit the situation. As Ilse Wolff explained, the Travel Bureau Berlin preferred that visitors understand the Wall as a political memorial, not as a three-starred Baedeker attraction – an official stance that did not stop it from unofficially encouraging Wall tours.[21] Nor did it want to scare away nervous visitors who already associated the city with Soviet tanks and East German guards. To counter such images, the bureau decided to stress the normality of life in a city that was home to a rich cultural life that visitors could enjoy regardless of the political circumstances.[22]

The first promotion after the erection of the Wall reflected this developing strategy. The '*My Fair Lady* Trip', cosponsored by the Hilton Hotel and the Theater des Westens (Theatre of the West), offered a package to West German visitors that included tickets to the musical *My Fair Lady* along with the air fare and accommodations. In a playful reference to the US and British airlift during the blockade, *Der Fremdenverkehr* dubbed it the 'airlift to the theatre'.[23] The bureau, however, made no such direct connection between the package tours and the political situation. Instead, it let the promotion itself convey the message that visitors should come to West Berlin to enjoy a taste of culture but remember its plight while doing so. In other words, visitors who purchased a package tour to West Berlin should be willing to engage in some solidarity and cultural consumption in the name of defending West Berlin.

For a time, the travel bureau continued its practice of combining propaganda and promotion. The slogan from the 1962 campaign 'For Berlin to Berlin' appealed to potential visitors to sympathize with the city because of the new political crisis.[24] Yet in contrast to previous slogans that advertised the city as a Cold War hot spot, this promotion simply appealed for sympathy. Like the *My Fair Lady* tour, the idea was to visit West Berlin as an act of solidarity but once there to enjoy the city as a backdrop to one's own pleasure, not necessarily as a political oddity or Cold War symbol.

## A Marketing and Cold War Turn: The Early to Mid 1960s

Unlike in past crisis moments – the blockade of 1948–49 or when Soviet Premier Khrushchev demanded in 1958 that US military forces leave West Berlin – the Travel Bureau Berlin never returned, after the erection of the Wall, to the Cold War as an explicit, prominent theme. Indeed, words like 'freedom' and comparisons with East Berlin eventually disappeared from its campaigns. One brochure from 1965 mentioned East Berlin only in passing, as a place where one could view the ancient Greek temple altar, the Pergamon Altar, on the museum island. It provided no additional commentary about the GDR capital, as if it were simply a benign neighbour to West Berlin without historical ties or contemporary political tensions.[25] The impact of the Wall alone cannot account for the permanent turn towards marketing strategies other than overtly promoting the city as a Cold War symbol. Numerous factors, not all directly related to the Cold War, determined the long-term shift in marketing practices.

In the early 1960s promotional work began to focus exclusively on tourism development, including attracting conferences. Propaganda became secondary to these tasks. This amounted to a significant change in emphasis compared to the 1950s, when city marketing included both political propaganda and tourism promotion. Here the Wall was indeed largely responsible. Especially after President John F. Kennedy's visit, the Wall raised the city's profile to such an extent that, at least in the short term, political propaganda was not as necessary as it once had been. Also, the Wall rejuvenated the city's Cold War mystique, ensuring West Berlin's prominence in the international media as well as in popular culture throughout the Western world. Between 1961 and 1966 over 4,000 books on West Berlin were published in the FRG.[26] The Wall, in short, generated such extensive coverage that heavy-handed propaganda was no longer needed. The travel bureau did not have to contribute to the city's Cold War propaganda when it was getting it for free.[27]

West Berlin's municipal authorities also increasingly pursued tourism as an end in itself. This changed perspective was due in no small part to the persistently strong rates of travel to the city and to the rise of international tourism in general. Between 1952 and 1962 rates of travel to West Berlin doubled.[28] Mirroring the explosion of city tourism worldwide, rates continued to climb throughout the 1960s.[29] Between 1964 and 1973 the number of visitors to West Berlin rose from 691,000 to 1,021,000.[30] From the early 1970s rates levelled out until the early 1980s, when they climbed again.[31] West Berlin's robust tourist industry stood in marked contrast to the rest of its economy. The exigencies of the Cold War made it impossible for West Berlin to mirror the success of the FRG's 'Economic Miracle'. The city was unable to overcome its dependence on subsidies from Bonn or to expand its economy beyond its increasingly antiquated manufacturing sector.[32] To invest heavily in tourism promotion and development made economic sense. One sign of the city's growing commitment to developing tourism was the travel bureau's growing budget. In 1968 the West Berlin Senate earmarked 1.5 million Marks, a significant contrast to the 30,000 Marks of 1949. This amount was necessary, Dr Wolff explained, for the continued development of Berlin's tourism and the recognition that a growing branch of the economy should not be hindered.[33]

After the construction of the Wall the city's relationship to the Cold War gradually began to change. In the short term the Wall solved the so-called Berlin Question and effectively appeased fears that West Berlin might simply be forgotten by its allies and subsumed within the GDR. It brought West Berlin a measure of confidence it had previously lacked. This was nonetheless only the beginning of a longer-term transition. Throughout the 1960s and 1970s the political climate continued to move towards strengthened stability. This was owed partly to the rise of the former West Berlin mayor Willy Brandt to the chancellorship in 1969, which provided the city with a powerful champion in Bonn. Brandt also brought with him a new foreign policy, *Ostpolitik,* which essentially accepted the division of Germany and of Berlin as the status quo. In the early 1970s, the thaw in GDR-FRG relations culminated in the signing of several treaties that further shored up West Berlin's position. All of these factors helped relegate the Cold War to the status of white noise, a constant humming in the background; it was no longer the lead percussion that consciously directed West Berliners' daily lives. Certain moments and issues, like the anti-Vietnam or anti-nuclear arms protests, or news of fantastical escapes or major developments in the socialist bloc, could temporarily renew acute awareness of the city's unique status in the Cold War. By the mid 1970s, most West Berliners had grown accustomed to living with the division of the city and accepted their communist neighbours as simply a fact of life.

## The Rise of the 'New Urban Traveller' and Niche Marketing

The factors considered above, entangled as they were with the Cold War, show how the city's marketing strategies overlapped with the city's political and economic fortunes. Yet this was not the whole story. Despite its self-conception as an island of freedom, West Berlin was not truly an island unto itself. The city's marketing practices also mirrored several key developments in postwar tourism and capitalist society that further shifted city marketing away from a Cold War emphasis: the rise of the 'new urban traveller' and the development of increasingly sophisticated marketing tactics.

Historically, a plurality of travel cultures has tended to exist side by side in a given travel destination. Nonetheless, one form will embody the zeitgeist as imagined by the mainstream media and tourist industries. In West Berlin in the early to mid 1960s 'the new urban traveller'[34] became the prime target of city marketing practices. This figure was young, well-educated, well-funded, often single and a frequent traveller.[35] In 1965, for instance, over half of West Berlin's visitors were under forty years old; about one quarter were under thirty.[36] The new urban traveller had a distinctly different world view from her or his nineteenth-century precursor – the bourgeois, almost exclusively male, flâneur. Whereas the flâneur went in pursuit of high culture, traces of the past and enlightenment about the present through quiet observation, the new urban traveller came to indulge in hedonist pursuits, including shopping, casual sex, drinking, sampling local cuisine and attending or participating in sports activities.[37] By the early 1970s, according to a 1971 survey commissioned by the Travel Bureau Berlin, themes relating to the pursuit of pleasure and the visitor's individual lifestyle were more attractive than overtly political ones.[38]

One way of appealing to this new urban traveller was through the theme of West Berlin as a cosmopolitan centre, a continuation and expansion of earlier promotions linking the city to the mythos of Weimar and to modernist aesthetics. Official marketers created advertisements suggesting that the city was home to modernist flair and characterized by a general dynamism. A 1963 advertisement aimed at attracting French visitors featured the slogan 'Berlin is worth the trip'. Why was Berlin worth the trip? The accompanying photo – a young couple bounding across the Kurfürstendamm, a city bus and modern buildings behind – suggested that it was for the enervating taste of a fast-paced metropolis. The couple appeared so energized that a slow stroll would have been out of the question.[39] An English-language brochure from 1965 likewise described the city as 'fill[ed] with a pulsating and international atmosphere'.[40]

In addition to stressing the cosmopolitan ambiance, the travel bureau also made reference to local peculiarities. Pushing the city's uniqueness was the counterbalance to marketing it as an international metropolis. The logic of tourist marketing necessitated such a two-step approach.

The bureau wanted to reassure visitors that the destination offered the amenities of a typical city and yet also something singular and distinct.[41] Advertisements represented West Berlin's local flavour with references to the city's mascot, the Berlin Bear (depicted as a cartoon or plush teddy bear), curried sausage and Berliner Weisse (a beer served with either red or green syrup), and the *Berliner Schnauze,* an idea dating back the nineteenth century that evoked an image of Berliners as rough on the edges but charming nonetheless. Such images not only painted a picture of West Berlin as enticingly different from other cities; they also helped take the sting out of potentially threatening political developments.

When student protests began to dominate international headlines and the streets of West Berlin in the mid to late 1960s, the travel bureau thus played them down as evidence of the ultimately harmless *Berliner Schnauze.* A 1968 advertisement made the city's association with the protests appear like a playful challenge or fashion statement, not a force to be reckoned with. The ad featured a photo of an attractive young woman wearing a miniskirt and ankle boots and striding confidently towards the viewer. It began:

> Some don't like us. The Berliners are too loud. The students are too radical ... The morals are too liberal ... No, you really can't build a state with us. But why in the devil's name do so many people like to come to see us, so often, in Berlin? ... Well, come over some time ... that's how we are in Berlin.[42]

Such advertisements equated youth with city chic, not with serious, sometimes violent, defiance of authority. The political unrest, they implied, added to the city's dynamic charm.

Although the new urban traveller was the main target of promotions, the travel bureau was careful not to put all its eggs into one basket. In keeping with the development of postwar marketing in Western Europe and North America, it learned to identify and market towards various consumer segments by age, income and lifestyle. To help identify market segments, it conducted increasingly sophisticated surveys and commissioned reports on West Berlin visitors. It also hosted and participated in international tourist industry conferences, which kept it abreast of the latest techniques. The new strategy reflected a global shift in marketing practices. In the early postwar period, city marketers addressed potential visitors as part of a single tourist culture. Starting in the late 1960s and accelerating in the 1970s, they addressed them as a multiplicity of target groups according to lifestyle and habits of consumption.

The endeavour to find ways to appeal to different target groups while still pandering to the target audience of the new urban traveller culminated in the 1975 campaign 'We Berliners Serve Cosmopolitan Cocktails'. Aimed at attracting visitors during the off season, every month featured a different cocktail: January, 'Partner Cocktail'; February, 'Art Cocktail'; March 'Fun Cocktail'; and so on.[43] Each represented not only an aspect of West Berlin's tourist amenities but also a target market. Thus January's 'Partner Cocktail' targeted couples interested in high culture and night life; February's 'Art Cocktail' the older generations of urban travellers who continued to come to the city in search of high culture; and in the weeks before Christmas the November and December 'Shopping Cocktail' appealed to women especially who equated a trip to the city with consumption.

## Conclusion

Notably absent from the cosmopolitan cocktails was one devoted to Cold War tourism, or to what the Travel Bureau Berlin referred to as 'political tourism'. This, according to the logic of marketing, was simply another type of tourism, and after the construction of the Wall it was addressed as such. Even though Wall tours and trips to the viewing platforms and Checkpoint Charlie museum became part of the standard tourist itinerary, the bureau increasingly focused on attracting the apolitical new urban traveller and on drawing in diverse target market groups for whom Cold War tourism was merely another item on the travel agenda. The bureau's shift away from the Cold War in the 1960s reflected West Berlin's ongoing efforts to create a politically salvageable and marketable self-image. To this end, it employed different strands of the city's past and present in accordance with the interests of changing target markets. On the whole, shifts in marketing practices reflected the tension in West Berlin's self-image as a front line of the Cold War on the one hand and a quintessentially modern, Western metropolis disconnected from past and present political struggles on the other. Though evidence of these two strands of self-justification were present in some form throughout the life of the city, the early to mid 1960s ushered in a period of increased strain between these two poles that arguably is still to be overcome.

## Notes

I thank Alexander Sedlmaier, Mary Nolan and Raymond Valley for their comments. Grants from the Berlin Program for Advanced German and European Studies of the Freie Universität, Berlin, and the German Academic Exchange Service supported much of the research for this chapter.

1. See Hasso Spode and Matthias Gutbier, 'Berlin-Reise als Berlin-Geschichte', in *Die Reise nach Berlin,* ed. by Berliner Festspiele GmbH (Berlin: Siedler, 1987), pp. 25–41.
2. See *Der Fremdenverkehr,* 5 (1966), 21.
3. Rudy Koshar, *German Travel Cultures* (Oxford: Berg, 2000), p. 117.
4. *Berlin Wirbt! Metropolenwerbung zwischen Verkehrsreklame und Stadtmarketing, 1920–1995,* ed. by Erhard Schütz, Klaus Siebenhaar and Cornelia Kunkat, (Berlin: FAB, 1995), p. 67.
5. *Berlin wirbt!,* ed. by Schütz, Siebenhaar and Kunkat, p. 84.
6. Ulrike Poock-Feller and Andrea Krausch, '"Berlin lebt – Berlin ruft!" Die Fremdenverkehrswerbung Ost- und West-Berlins in der Nachkriegszeit', in *Goldstrand und Teutonengrill: Kultur- und Sozialgeschichte des Tourismus in Deutschland 1945–1989,* ed. by Hasso Spode (Berlin: Moser, 1996), pp. 105–16 (p. 109).
7. Poock-Feller and Krausch, '"Berlin lebt – Berlin ruft!"', p. 110.
8. *Berlin wirbt!,* ed. by Schütz, Siebenhaar and Kunkat, p. 66.
9. *Der Fremdenverkehr,* 8 (1962), 17–18.
10. On US State Department promotion of tourism and foreign policy strategy, see Christopher Endy, *Cold War Holidays: American Tourism in France* (Chapel Hill: University of North Carolina Press, 2004), pp. 1–12 and 33–54.
11. Brian Ladd, *The Ghosts of Berlin: Confronting the German Past in the Urban Landscape* (Chicago: University of Chicago Press, 1997), pp. 175–215.
12. Alexandra Richie, *Faust's Metropolis: A History of Berlin* (New York: Carroll & Graf, 1998), p. 706.
13. Ibid., p. 706.
14. Ibid., p. 709.
15. Thilo Koch, *Zwischen Grunewald und Brandenburger Tor* (Munich: Langen und Müller, 1956), p. 25.
16. See reports, Landesarchiv Berlin (hereafter LAB), C REP. 123, Acc. 2401, Bd. 1.
17. *Der Fremdenverkehr,* 6 (1965), 36.
18. Reisebüro der DDR, Bezirksdirektion Berlin, Stadtrundfahrten, 'Bericht über die Tätigkeit des Bereiches Stadtrundfahrten im März 1977', LAB, C REP. 123, Acc. 2401, Bd. 1 (1977).
19. Reisebüro der DDR, Bezirksdirektion Berlin, Stadtrundfahrten, 'Bericht über die Tätigkeit des Bereiches Stadtrundfahrten im Juni 1978', LAB, C REP. 123, Acc. 2401, Bd. 1 (1978).
20. For instance Philip Shabecoff, 'Penetrating Berlin's Wall', *New York Times,* 7 March 1965, no page number available.
21. *Der Fremdenverkehr,* 9 (1962), 14–15.
22. Ibid.
23. *Der Fremdenverkehr,* 3 (1962), 26.
24. *Der Fremdenverkehr,* 9 (1962), 50.
25. *Berlin. Theater, Musik, Museen, Kunst. Berlin ist eine Reise wert. Come and See West Berlin,* ed. by Verkehrsamt Berlin (1965), p. 57.
26. 'Berlin: Das Glitzerding', *Der Spiegel,* 3 October 1966, pp. 40–61 (p. 43).
27. Harmut Häussermann and Claire Columb, 'The New Berlin: Marketing the City of Dreams', in *Cities and Visitors: Regulating People, Markets, and City Space,* ed. by Lily M. Hoffman, Susan S. Fainstein and Dennis R. Judd (Malden, MA: Blackwell, 2003), pp. 200–18 (p. 201).

28. *Der Fremdenverkehr*, 9 (1962), 14–15.
29. Cord Pagenstecher, *Der bundesdeutsche Tourismus. Ansätze zu einer Visual History: Urlaubsprospekte, Reiseführer, Fotoalben, 1950–1990* (Hamburg: Dr. Kovac, 2003), p. 316.
30. Karl König, 'Fremdenverkehrspolitik in Berlin', Artikel für die Zeitschrift *Fremdenverkehrswirtschaft*, LAB, B REP. 010, Nr. 655 (1975).
31. Ilse Wolff, 'Die Reise nach Berlin: Erinnerungen an die Wegstrecke nach 1945', in *Die Reise nach Berlin*, ed. by Berliner Festspiele GmbH, p. 316.
32. Elizabeth A. Strom, *Building the New Berlin: The Politics of Urban Development in Germany's Capital City* (Lanham, MD: Lexington, 2001), pp. 79–82.
33. *Der Fremdenverkehr*, 1 (1968), 22.
34. The phrase is mine, but I draw on Cord Pagenstecher, *Der bundesdeutsche Tourismus*, and comments made by Verkehrsamt director Ilse Wolff, 'Die Reise nach Berlin', p. 316, as well as on marketing surveys of the Verkehrsamt.
35. 'Berlin-Reisende: Untersuchung der strukturellen Besonderheiten von Berlin-Besuchern aus dem übrigen Bundesgebiet', 8 March 1972, LAB, B REP. 010, Nr. 1161.
36. *Der Fremdenverkehr*, 6 (1965), 36.
37. See Pagenstecher, *Der bundesdeutsche Tourismus*, pp. 9–12.
38. 'Berlin-Reisende'.
39. *Berlin wirbt!*, ed. by Schütz, Siebenhaar and Kunkat, p. 35.
40. *Berlin. Theater, Musik, Museen, Kunst*, p. 57.
41. Leo van den Berg, Jan van der Borg and Jan van der Meer, *Urban Tourism: Performance and Strategies in Eight European Cities* (Aldershot: Ashgate, 1995), p. 14.
42. *Berlin wirbt!*, ed. by Verkehrsamt Berlin, p. 32.
43. Karl König, 'Fremdenverkehrspolitik in Berlin'.

# 8

# Projections of History
## East German Film-Makers and the Berlin Wall

*Seán Allan*

There can be few locations in postwar Europe where the vicissitudes of the Cold War come so sharply into focus as in the divided city of Berlin. As the recent releases of Hartmut Schön's televised film *Die Mauer – Berlin '61* (*The Wall – Berlin '61*, 2006) and Dominik Graf's *Der rote Kakadu* (*The Red Cockatoo*, 2006) underline, the Berlin Wall still remains one of the enduring icons of the ideological struggle between East and West. While the inner-German border between the GDR and the FRG was effectively sealed off after 1952, the fact that cross-border transit in Berlin remained possible until the summer of 1961 gave the city a unique status not only in the history of the Cold War, but also in the popular imagination. It was in Berlin more than in any other German city that – to cite Thomas Lindenberger in this volume – Germany remained 'divided, but not disconnected'.

While cross-border exchanges permeated many areas of German-German relations during the Cold War, this was particularly true for film. The presence of cheap cinemas near the border in the western part of the city meant that GDR citizens had easy access to popular films of a kind not available in East Berlin. The pernicious influence of the sensationalist B-movies screened there is explicitly criticized in propagandist documentaries like Karl Gass's *Schaut auf diese Stadt* (*Look at this City*, 1962) and informs the plot of more sophisticated treatments of the open border, such as Gerhard Klein's *Berlin – Ecke Schönhauser* (*Berlin – Schönhauser Corner*, 1957). While cross-border traffic moved predominantly in one direction at the level of film consumption, at the level of production a significant (though often fraught) collaboration resulted in actors, film-makers and technicians from the West travelling regularly to the Babelsberg studios in the East. During the 1950s – and especially following an initiative for the preservation of German cultural unity emerging from the GDR's Ministry of Culture in March 1954 – a number of prominent actors and film-makers based in the West were involved in productions in the East. Among them were stars such as Henny Porten and Götz George, and the directors Arthur Pohl and Hans Müller, all of whom lived in West Berlin but worked extensively for the GDR's state-owned production studio, DEFA.

The employment of directors and senior personnel living in West Berlin remained a perpetual bone of contention for the studio management. During the debates about formalist aesthetics that occurred regularly throughout the 1950s, they were regarded as ideologically suspect or accused of exploiting the production facilities in the East to advance careers in the West. How far these criticisms were justified is hard to say: for many DEFA employees, the fact that GDR initiatives to encourage German cultural unity were not reciprocated by the Federal Republic meant that the prospect of a subsequent career in the West was limited. For these and other reasons, only a handful of directors based in the Western zones still had contracts with DEFA by 1960.[1] Nonetheless, the studio still remained dependent to a large extent on technical and support staff recruited from the West, and more than a third of the DEFA orchestra consisted of musicians living in West Berlin itself.[2]

The year leading up to the building of the Berlin Wall had been a difficult period for the studio. On the one hand, a new generation of film-makers including Heiner Carow, Günter Reisch and Frank Beyer was establishing itself, but on the other, there was frustration at the critical reception of certain new trends in the studio, a mood exacerbated by the controversy surrounding Gerhard Klein's *Der Fall Gleiwitz* (*The Gleiwitz Affair,* 1961), a formally innovative anti-fascist film about events in Poland on the eve of the Second World War. A report compiled less than two weeks before the construction of the Berlin Wall conveys the prevailing mood:

> It was said that none of the serious, artistically significant feature films received due recognition by the party; instead they were subjected to harsh and, in part, destructive criticism ... On the other hand, the party was seen as adopting a highly uncritical attitude towards films with obvious aesthetic shortcomings.[3]

These ongoing aesthetic debates, however, were quickly overtaken by events in the political sphere. Looking back at the political and cultural climate in the months before the building of the Wall, Kurt Maetzig, one of the GDR's best-known directors, noted:

> At that time you could sense how the atmosphere of political tension stoked up by the West was spreading ... It became clear that some kind of confrontation was inevitable and that we could not simply stand by and watch as events lurched towards a crisis.[4]

At the time, Maetzig had been working on *Septemberliebe* (*September Romance*, 1961), a film in which the tensions in the run-up to the summer of 1961 are foregrounded. While the programme accompanying the film's release avoids explicit references to the political situation,[5] the triangular relationship between the three main protagonists Hans Schramm, his fiancé Hannelore and her sister, Franka, is couched in terms that – as the *Chefdramaturg* (senior script advisor) Klaus Wischnewski pointed out to party officials[6] – were designed to invite viewers to relate the film's theme of 'trust and responsibility' not just to the lovers' predicament, but to the GDR itself. *Septemberliebe* was one of many films to exploit the metaphor of the love triangle to capture the conflicts of German-German relations during the Cold War.

Any lingering doubts GDR citizens may have harboured concerning questions of 'trust and responsibility' would be resolved by the events of 13 August 1961. As in East German theatre, many prominent figures from the cinema were quick to make a show of solidarity with the SED leadership in the official state organs.[7] In a radio interview with the station *Märkische Volksstimme* on 15 August 1961, the director Konrad Wolf claimed:

> I believe that the bulk of the population in our Republic welcomes these measures, even if, for the time being, they may result in some difficulties ... but all this pales into insignificance when set against the fact that at last we will have a period of peace and calm ... That's why I think that our creative artists will also welcome these measures.[8]

Alongside Wolf, internal reports identify Frank Beyer, Günter Reisch and Heinz Thiel among the first to respond to the emergency call sounded in the night of 12–13 August.[9] But while some studio employees threw themselves behind the new measures (directors Carl Balhaus, Kurt Maetzig, Slatan Dudow and Gerhard Klein are all praised), the attitude of others was more ambiguous. The actor Erwin Geschonneck is one of the few leading figures singled out for criticism on account of his absence at this crucial juncture: 'Comrade Geschonneck was on unauthorized leave and has not been in touch for some time.'[10] Joachim Hasler, the cameraman for the GDR's first science-fiction film, *Der schweigende Stern* (*The Silent Star*, 1960), is also taken to task for apportioning blame to both sides for the political crisis.[11]

Generally, though, open expressions of dissent were confined to those remaining employees living in the West. Cameraman Eugen Klagemann, whose association with DEFA dated from Maetzig's *Ehe im Schatten* (*Marriage in the Shadow*, 1947), is reported as stating that 'some of the West Berliners – he himself belonged to this group – regarded the recent measures as an expression of weakness and panic'.[12] Unsurprisingly, Klagemann's days at the studio were numbered; by March of the following year he left for good. Similarly, Erich Zander, who had worked for DEFA as an art director on *Das Beil von Wandsbek* (*The Axe of Wandsbek*, 1952) and the children's classic *Das singende, klingende Bäumchen* (*The Singing, Ringing Tree*, 1957), was criticized for staying away from the studio following his son's appointment to a judicial position within the West Berlin Senate; like Klagemann, Zander's association with DEFA ended the following year.[13] Nonetheless, it is striking that even after the building of the Wall, various employees based in the West continued to work at the Babelsberg studios. Accordingly, on 19 October 1961 the studio's technical director, Alfred Wilkening, wrote to Hans Rodenberg in the GDR's Ministry of Culture about the difficulties experienced by employees forced to make the journey from the West: 'The studio's Berlin-based employees are very anxious about the travel situation – especially at the rail interchanges – and there is a real danger that they will stop working for us.'[14] At the same time, the new restrictions on travel meant that assembling a cast and crew in the same location often took longer and shortened the time available for shooting.

Attributing such dissent as there was to disgruntled studio employees from the West meant that political activists at DEFA could, with some justification, assert that 'the senior employees in our studio, the senior management, the divisional heads, the heads of production etc. are right behind the government's measures because they have resulted in changes that have improved the morale of all employees'.[15] Indeed, they welcomed the new political situation on the grounds that it would put an end to 'false conceptions of democracy' and 'exaggerated demands' coupled with certain individuals' threats to leave for the West. Many saw the building of the Wall as ushering in a new, more stable phase for the Babelsberg studios, a fact evident in another document submitted to the GDR's Council of Ministers:

> The measures of 13 August 1961 have helped many employees in the studio to reach a clear position on basic political issues ... At the same time, it has become obvious to many who until now had been undecided that now was the time for them to make up their minds, and that they too would have

work through all the issues and draw the right conclusions where their artistic activities and indeed their private lives were concerned.[16]

While the studio's production schedules were not unduly disrupted by the construction of the Wall, an early casualty of the new search for ideological clarity was Konrad Petzold's *Das Kleid* (*The Robe*, 1961), a deliciously ironic children's film scripted by Egon Günther and based on Hans Christian Andersen's tale *The Emperor's New Clothes*. Although the film had been in production long before August 1961, the dialogue in its opening sequence – 'There's the Wall – it cuts right through the middle of everything; behind it lies the city – and everything you could wish for!' – would never endear the film to the *Hauptverwaltung Film*, the board responsible to the Ministry of Culture for approving film releases in the GDR. Ultimately the film's depiction of a morally bankrupt leadership presiding over a world of illusion was deemed too sensitive, and on 26 March 1962 the commission refused to grant a distribution license on the grounds that the *mise-en-scène* 'could render it subject to a hostile interpretation'.[17]

Whilst DEFA could hardly be expected to respond overnight to the new situation, by November 1962 no fewer than three major films dealing with the Berlin Wall had been released. The first, Karl Gass's 'documentary' *Schaut auf diese Stadt,* was released on the first anniversary of the building of the Wall. Subtitled 'The History of West Berlin from 1945 until 13 August 1961', the film portrays the Allies, in particular the US military, as an alien occupation force pandered to by a revanchist West German leadership. Throughout, the film rehearses the political arguments for Berlin being granted the status of a free city that were so central to the negotiations between Khrushchev and Kennedy in the first half of 1961 (though tellingly, this 'history of West Berlin' omits the blockade of 1948–49).

In seeking to provide an ideological justification for the closure of the border, the film situates the conflict over Berlin within the framework of a German militarism extending back to imperial times. Accordingly, Gass incorporates sections of documentary footage showing military parades (during both world wars) to underline the peculiar significance of the Brandenburg Gate as a site of memory in German history. At the same time, the film seeks to embed the events of 13 August 1961 within a tradition of German classical humanism: in the carefully edited sequence where images of approving GDR citizens applauding Ulbricht are intercut with images of East German soldiers sealing the border, the soundtrack plays Beethoven's Fifth Symphony. Such an organicist approach to German history and national identity stands in sharp contrast to the treatment of the Allied troops: there we see images of ethnically diverse members of the US armed forces underscored by the rock'n'roll melody of 'Yakety Yak' – 'alien sounds', the voice-over intones, 'in a German city'. Despite its overtly propagandist tenor, however, *Schaut auf diese Stadt* has become a source of some of the most iconic images of the Cold War in Germany, notably the sequence in which an American tank pulls up before a nonchalant East German policeman at Checkpoint Charlie. Not only is this sequence embedded within Frank Vogel's film *Und deine Liebe auch* (*And Your Love Too*), released later the same year, but, as we shall see, it is quoted alongside other key sequences from Gass's film almost forty years later in Jürgen Böttcher's 1990 documentary *Die Mauer* (*The Wall*).

The autumn of 1962 saw the release of two feature films about the Wall: Vogel's *Und deine Liebe auch* on 27 September and Heinz Thiel's *Der Kinnhaken* (*The Punch to the Jaw*) on 29 November. In contrast to the wider 'historical' perspective of *Schaut auf diese Stadt,* both films set out to explore the impact the events of 13 August had on the lives of ordinary individuals. Of the two, Thiel's film is more conventional in terms of form and content. This is probably the reason why, on the pre-release report for the *Hauptverwaltung Film,* there is a note suggesting that it should be released before *Und deine Liebe auch. Der Kinnhaken* – scripted by and starring the well-known actor Manfred Krug – is a love story–cum-thriller about Georg, a young man employed in a GDR electrical engineering plant who, on duty with his brigade on the morning of 13 August, encounters Carolin, a young woman living in the East and working in the West. On the pretext of helping her escape to West Berlin, Georg arranges a series of increasingly amorous rendezvous, in the course of which he dissuades her from leaving the GDR.[18]

The constellation of characters in *Der Kinnhaken* is particularly significant. Whilst Carolin is a typical representative of the *Grenzgänger* – individuals earning higher wages by working in the West while exploiting subsidized housing and food costs in the East – who were despised by both the SED leadership and sections of the GDR population, the casting of Manfred Krug in the role of a young foreman in an East German industrial plant addresses what Patrick Major identifies as the growing sense of frustration among the industrial *Nachwuchs,* the GDR's up-and-coming generation of engineering technicians.[19] At the same time, the film also goes some way towards addressing GDR viewers' desire for sensationalist images of violence and eroticism of the kind hitherto available in the cinemas over the border. While Gass's *Schaut auf diese Stadt* pulls no punches in its criticism of such lowbrow fare, *Der*

*Kinnhaken* suggests a softening of the line. Throughout the film Carolin is associated with an overt eroticism, though the contrast with her more demure GDR flatmate suggests that such overtly flaunted sexuality remained a suspect quality. Whilst the film ends with a fist fight between Georg and his male rival, the violence is condoned on account of its political character. Indeed, the report prepared prior to the film's release stresses that there is nothing gratuitous about this violent denouement: 'Bubi's comeuppance at Georg's hands represents the comeuppance of all who believe that, after 13 August, they can poison what our Republic stands for with impunity.'[20]

Whereas the conventional character of *Der Kinnhaken* reflects its indebtedness to certain generic conventions, Vogel's film *Und deine Liebe auch* is, formally at least, more innovative. Described by cameraman Günter Ost as a 'documentary feature film', it blends documentary footage from the autumn of 1961 with narrative sequences shot on location and in the studio. The film also testifies to Vogel's fascination with the work of Alain Resnais, especially *Hiroshima mon Amour* (1959). For the most part, the narrative of *Und deine Liebe auch* is conveyed by means of retrospective voice-overs in which the three main characters reflect on the Wall's impact on their lives. The film is constructed round a love triangle involving two men, stepbrothers Ulli and Klaus, who are both in love with Eva, a socialistically inclined but emotionally confused postal worker from the provinces. Vogel's film too rehearses the familiar conflict between the dissolute *Grenzgänger,* Klaus, and the young member of the industrial *Nachwuchs,* Ulli (played by a youthful Armin Müller-Stahl). As the action unfolds, the viewer is invited to draw a parallel between Eva's struggle to align her heart with her head and the universal struggle to reject the superficial temptations of Western capitalism in favour of a commitment to socialism: 'Somewhere a line [*Grenze*] has to be drawn', Ulli and Eva repeatedly remind the audience as the film seeks to embed the personal within the political.

While, superficially, the plot of *Und deine Liebe auch* has a conventional ring to it, the formal means by which it is conveyed are anything but. In part this reflects the improvised manner in which the film was assembled, which meant that the film-makers could to an extent sidestep the studio's customary controls. In the absence of anything approaching a conventional shooting script, cameraman Ost and director Vogel spent considerable time on the streets of Berlin in the latter part of 1961 and – somewhat in the spirit of the Italian neorealists Ost so admired – produced a fascinating documentary record of these times.[21] Nonetheless, what Rosemarie Rehahn, film critic of the weekly *Wochenpost,* termed 'its authentic documentary character'[22] was clearly something the viewing public struggled with, and other GDR critics went to some lengths to prepare viewers for an unusual experience. In the GDR daily *Der Morgen*, for example, Christoph Funke urged readers not to dismiss the film, but rather to see it as a successful 'step towards artistic innovation'.[23]

*Und deine Liebe auch* is a curious blend of conventional ideology packed in an unconventional format, and often the voice-overs have a propagandistic quality at odds with the film's experimental aesthetics. During the sequences depicting the construction of the Wall, it is hard, at least from a present perspective, not to smile at Ulli's observation that 'we knew why – for peace. For the right to determine our lives in Berlin just like in Havana.' It is tempting to see the extended coverage of Ulli's trip to Cuba as an attempt to imbue life in the GDR with a degree of the cosmopolitanism that seemed to be threatened by the sealing of the border in 1961. Ulli's hobby as a radio enthusiast likewise serves to locate the GDR at the hub of an international network of communications – a motif visually underscored by the map above Ulli's radio equipment that portrays the GDR quite literally at the centre of the modern world. There are also moments when the film borders (unintentionally) on parody, such as when Alfredo, Ulli's friend from Havana, visits him at his border control post, where they sing revolutionary songs while Alfredo uses the magazine from Ulli's machine gun as a set of make-shift maracas. Towards the end, when Ulli is injured by a bullet as he tries to prevent Klaus from escaping to the West, it is the East German border guards who fire into the air, whilst their West German counterparts shoot to kill.

Yet such moments should not obscure the qualities of the film as a whole. The film does not shy away from addressing the material shortcomings of the GDR. Ulli is open about the problems in his factory and the workers' dissatisfaction with pay and conditions. He draws attention to these issues in a way that highlights the discrepancy between state propaganda and the reality of lived experience: 'It was never quite as simple as it was made out to be afterwards in the press.' At the same time, in keeping with the traditions of Italian neorealism, *Und deine Liebe auch* stops short of offering full closure. With its multiplicity of perspectives showing ordinary Berliners going about their daily business, the concluding sequence bears a certain resemblance to the famous panoramic shot at the start of *Berlin – Ecke Schönhauser*, while at the same time suggesting that the fate of the two lovers is still an open question. As he reflects on what the future holds for him and Eva, Ulli observes that 'we realised this wasn't the end of it all … Nothing ever really comes to a final conclusion.'

In view of this, it is hardly surprising that the studio direction was uncertain how to act when presented with the film in its final format. Although it was approved for release on 6 June 1962, only nine days later Deputy Minister of Culture (and former head of DEFA) Hans Rodenberg received a report containing a list of misgivings that were beginning to surface within the SED's Berlin headquarters. These included comments that, first, the film did not sufficiently address the concerns of the GDR population regarding the measures of 13 August and that it 'might have damaging repercussions where the issue of West Berlin was concerned'; second, that the border was presented as a 'prison Wall' rather than a 'protective Wall'; third, that the East German labour camp where Klaus is imprisoned after his attempt to flee the GDR resembled a Nazi concentration camp; and, finally, that 'the way the crowds on the western side of the "Wall" are portrayed' – a rare use of the term in official discourse – 'could lead people to think that the police and population are unanimous in their protest against the security measures undertaken by our government'.[24] It was only after Lotte Ulbricht, Walter Ulbricht's wife and an SED official in her own right, invited Rodenberg to show the film at a private screening at the SED's secure compound in Wandlitz that the film was finally given the green light.

Although *Und deine Liebe auch* does not appear to have attracted large audiences, it is the most innovative of all the films dealing with the Berlin Wall that were released in the first half of the 1960s. While the merits of Vogel's film were being debated, another film about 13 August 1961 was in production: Gerhard Klein's *Sonntagsfahrer* (*Sunday Drivers*). Based on a script by Georg Edel and Wolfgang Kohlhaase, Klein's film premiered on 1 October 1963. The film depicts a group of individuals from Leipzig who, dissatisfied with life in the GDR, head for Berlin on 12 August 1961 to sell their vehicles and start new lives in the West. The group consists of four individuals: its leader, the interior designer Spiessack, a man with thinly concealed militaristic tendencies who harbours a deep-seated hatred of the GDR; Teichert, a professor at the University of Leipzig persuaded to leave by his ambitious wife so that 'they' can enjoy a better standard of living in the West; Rosentreter, an overweight figure of fun who dreams of opening a hairdressing salon on the North Sea island of Norderney; and Denker, a doctor frustrated by shortages of medical equipment in the GDR who fears becoming caught up in a military conflict between East and West. As the story unfolds, they are forced to overcome a variety of obstacles and disasters, most of which are deliberately engineered by two young students – Spiessack's daughter Sabine (played by a young Angelica Domröse) and Teichert's son

Gernulf – neither of whom wishes to leave a GDR where their future is secure.

Unsurprisingly the film was a flop. In large measure its failure to appeal to a wider public is a reflection of the grotesque mismatch between the complexity of the political issues posed by the events of 13 August 1961 and the crude psychology and unsophisticated politics of the caricatured protagonists. Writing in *Der Morgen,* Christoph Funke observed that

> the whole business may be amusingly exaggerated, and the 'motorized' escape from an orderly life may be deliberately portrayed as something grotesque ... but the fact remains that it all needs to be motivated somehow ... What we have is a film with many comical moments ... but which fails to provide any kind of underlying psychological thread.[25]

Looking back at the film in 1984, scriptwriter Kohlhaase attributed its failure to a mismatch between the political context in which the film was made and the attempt to embed the issues it raises within a comic framework: 'Comedy presupposes', he observed, 'that you and the spectator share the same perspective from which a given subject appears comical. I think that, regardless how one viewed the situation, it simply wasn't possible to see it in a comic light.'[26]

Four years after the debacle of *Sonntagsfahrer,* Gerhard Klein received another opportunity to tackle the issues surrounding the building of the Wall with a contribution to the four-part film *Geschichten jener Nacht* (*Stories from That Night,* 1967). Klein's contribution, *Der große und der kleine Willi* (*Big Billy and Little Billy*), stands out as the best of the four episodes dealing with the night of 13 August 1961. The two main characters – one played by the established DEFA star Erwin Geschonneck, the other by a young Jaecki Schwarz in his film debut – instantly develop an on-screen rapport further heightened by Helmut Baierl's sparkling script. As a result, Klein's contribution to the project is largely free from the obtrusive, melodramatic pathos of the preceding episodes: *Phönix* (*Phoenix,* directed by Karlheinz Carpentier), *Die Prüfung* (*The Test,* Ulrich Thein) and *Materna* (Frank Vogel). While the political message of the film is hardly ambiguous – Big Billy wins the wayward Little Billy over to the cause of socialism – what distinguishes *Der große und der kleine Willi* from the other episodes is Klein's unconventional stylistic approach – or, as he explained, 'the attempt to present a didactic narrative in an entertaining way'.[27] The viewer is constantly provoked through a series of often bizarre juxtapositions: Big Willy directs operations from underneath a huge dinosaur skeleton in the Humboldt University's Museum of Natural History; in the absence of any taxis at this moment of historical crisis a father is ferried to his wife and children in an army tank; and a group of prostitutes cut off from their western clients – the first casualties of the new political situation! – is dispatched to the local unemployment office. Not surprisingly, some members of the preview panel viewed these stylistic discontinuities suspiciously. While no one was in doubt that the film had 'a clear message', it is equally apparent that Klein's thinly concealed attempt to undermine the conventional monumentalist discourse of GDR history by highlighting occurrences of an everyday, banal and occasionally comic character did not meet with universal approval.

The political climate in 1967 was, however, very different from that of 1962–63, and the release of *Geschichten jener Nacht* – a work commissioned by the SED to coincide with the Seventh Party Congress in the GDR – had more to do with developments in cultural policy in 1964–65 than with the building of the Wall in 1961. Following the infamous Eleventh Plenum of the Central Committee of the SED in December 1965, a number of DEFA films had been banned or withdrawn from circulation on aesthetic and ideological grounds. Klein was among those singled out for criticism; his film *Berlin um die Ecke* (*Berlin around the Corner*, 1965) was not screened until 1990, after the collapse of the GDR. Klein's willingness to collaborate on *Geschichten jener Nacht* can thus be seen in the light of the studio's attempt to restore its political reputation. Nor was Klein the only figure whose standing – at least in the eyes of the politicians – had become open to question. Frank Vogel had also been taken to task for his film *Denk bloß nicht ich heule* (*Just Don't Think I'm Crying*, 1965). The actors Angelika Waller, Peter Reusse, Eberhard Esche, Johannes Wieke and Erwin Geschonneck – who all feature in *Geschichten jener Nacht* – had all had major roles in films that were condemned following the Eleventh Plenum. The remarks with which the studio's new director, Hans Bruk, concluded the internal screening of *Geschichten jener Nacht* suggest clearly what was at stake: 'With this film these comrades have demonstrated that they have learned the appropriate lessons from their experiences. Tonight we have also seen proof that our political leaders and the party are prepared to trust the artists.'[28]

*Geschichten jener Nacht* – the last film explicitly about the events of August 1961 to be released by DEFA prior to 1989 – was, partly at least, an exercise in restoring relations between the film-makers and the political establishment. It thus seems almost ironic that more than twenty years later it would fall to Jürgen Böttcher, another of the Eleventh Plenum's *enfants terribles*, to direct the studio's next major film about the Wall. Released in 1990, Böttcher's documentary, *Die Mauer – Demontage eines Alptraums* (*The Wall – Deconstruction of a Nightmare*), is anything but an upbeat account of the events set in motion on 9 November 1989.[29] By focusing as much on the camera crews from around the world as on the Wall itself, his film draws attention to the artificiality of memory and to the constructed nature of historical representation in contemporary mass media. In the opening sequences, the stark images of isolated sections of the Wall standing in an open field contrast markedly with the celebratory images that have now become clichés through their repeated exposure in news bulletins and television retrospectives. In a film almost devoid of dialogue, the soundtrack is dominated by the hammering of the so-called *Mauerspechte,* the people relentlessly chipping away at the Wall to secure personal historical mementos. Yet rather than this obsessive quest for souvenirs, Böttcher suggests, what is required is a process of critical reflection. Images of Japanese tourists being photographed in front of the graffiti, together with sequences showing young boys selling lumps of concrete from the Wall, underline the ways in which history here is being commercialized and packaged for rapid consumption. The transformation of this historical moment into something akin to a tourist spectacle is emphasized by the cosmopolitan composition of the assembled spectators – a group from which East Germans are conspicuously absent. Where they do appear in the film, their worried, puzzled expressions hint at a hidden anxiety and the feeling that a part of their history and collective memory is systematically being dismantled by souvenir-hunting intruders whose relationship to this historical moment is tangential.

Part of the fascination of Böttcher's film lies in how the Wall is treated not solely as a historical object – a piece of '*Geschichte*' – but as something that tells stories, '*Geschichten*' in its own right. This is suggested both in the collage of individual histories in the graffiti on the Wall and in the sequence showing the graves of those who died attempting to cross it (a sombre counterpoint to the carnivalesque atmosphere of the New Year's Eve celebrations of 1989–90 preceding that sequence). Perhaps the most memorable moments are the three points where a section of the Wall is transformed into a cinema screen onto which memories of the past are projected. The first contains footage of the Wall's construction in 1961; the second, a series of triumphant military parades through the Brandenburg Gate – including the Nazi torchlight parade of January 1933; and the third, documentary footage of the military parade to mark the fortieth anniversary of the GDR cut together with images of the night of 9 November 1989. These sequences – for Böttcher, the film's kernel – emphasize how history is indelibly inscribed into the very buildings and architecture of Berlin and underscore the peculiar significance of the Brandenburg Gate and the sectoral border in the historical and political development of Germany. The fact that the first two sequences are visual 'quotations' from Gass's *Schaut auf diese Stadt* serves to locate Böttcher's film within the historical context of DEFA and East German film-making as a whole. By requoting these images, Böttcher subjects them to further degrees of alienation, prompting the spectator to reflect on the role of moving images in the construction of historical narrative and on their power to shape the perception of the past. During the almost overly long static shots that are typical of Böttcher's style, the Wall is transformed into a screen onto which the viewer is invited to project his or her own memories and reflections.

*Die Mauer* ends on a sombre note, underlining the fact that the Berlin Wall is not simply a physical construction of concrete, but an ideological structure deeply ingrained in the minds of East and West Germans. The difficulties that lie ahead for those who regard its fall as heralding the promise of a new beginning are alluded to in the closing images, which show an overgrown field where sections of the Wall are strewn like abandoned headstones. Contrary to the expectations set up by the subtitle 'Deconstruction of a Nightmare', the cemetery-like setting at the close has an elegiac quality. The removal of the Berlin Wall may represent a radical break with the past; but Böttcher's film pleads that we not lose sight of the thread of historical continuity that – via the Wall – connects not only East and West, but also the past and present.

It is striking that the two most successful films dealing with the Wall – Vogel's *Und deine Liebe auch* and Böttcher's *Die Mauer* – have their roots in the GDR's rich tradition of documentary film-making. Finding a filmic genre into which such an unremitting icon of the Cold War could be successfully integrated proved a challenge to which few film-makers in either East or West could rise. Although the border between East and West provided the basis for many Cold War thrillers, images of the Berlin Wall in the cinema of the GDR remained the exception rather than rule. Following German unification in 1990 it was perhaps inevitable that German film-makers would once again turn their attention to the Wall. What makes Jürgen Böttcher's documentary stand out is its explicit critique of the sentimentalizing approach so evident in recent feature films like Hartmut Schön's *Die Mauer – Berlin '61* and Dominik Graf's *Der rote Kakadu*. Instead of creating yet another mythical notion of German unity through a sentimentalization of the events of the Cold War, Böttcher's film explicitly criticizes this tendency and reminds us that if we are to reach a proper understanding of the German nation as one that was 'divided, but not disconnected', then this can only be achieved through an acceptance of the cultural difference between East and West.

## Notes

I am grateful for the assistance of staff at the Bundesarchiv Berlin (especially Michael Müller and Ute Klawitter) for help in researching this essay.

1. Ralf Schenk, 'Mitten im Kalten Krieg', in *Das zweite Leben der Filmstadt Babelsberg: DEFA Filmspiele 1946–1992*, ed. by Ralf Schenk (Berlin: Henschel, 1994), pp. 50–157 (p. 142).
2. Joshua Feinstein, *The Triumph of the Ordinary: Depictions of Daily Life in the East German Cinema, 1949–1989* (Chapel Hill: University of North Carolina Press, 2002), p. 122.
3. Untitled report, 1 August 1961, SAPMO-BArch, DY 30/IV/2/906/204, p. 354. See also Feinstein, *The Triumph of the Ordinary*, 122–24.
4. Kurt Maetzig, *Filmarbeit: Gespräche, Reden, Schriften*, ed. by Günter Agde (Berlin: Henschel, 1987), p. 112.
5. Reproduced in *Film und Gesellschaft in der DDR*, 2 vols, ed. by Manfred Behn and Hans-Michael Bock (Hamburg: Cinegraph, 1989), II, p. 132.
6. 'Chefdramaturg an Zentrale Parteileitung der APO Spielfilme', 14 March 1961, SAPMO-BArch, DY 30/IV/2/906/204, pp. 304–5.
7. See also Laura Bradley, 'A Different Political Forum: East German Theatre and the Construction of the Berlin Wall', *Journal of European Studies*, 36 (2006), 139–56.
8. '"Jetzt gilt es für unsere Sache einzustehen": DEFA-Regisseur Konrad Wolf am Sonntag interviewt. Stellungnahme für Märkische Volksstimme vom 15.8.1961', in *Konrad Wolf: Direkt in Kopf und Herz. Aufzeichnungen – Reden – Interviews*, ed. by Aune Renk (Berlin: Henschel, 1989), p. 62.
9. 'Bericht über die Lage im VEB DEFA-Studio für Spielfilm', 5 September 1961, SAPMO-BArch, DY 30/IV/2/906/204, pp. 359–64.
10. Ibid.
11. Ibid.
12. Ibid.
13. Ironically, Erich Zander was one of the West Berlin–based employees whom the former studio director Hans Rodenberg singled out in May 1953 as personnel that DEFA should strive to retain (see Schenk, 'Mitten im Kalten Krieg', p. 81).
14. Wilkening to Rodenberg (HV Film Abteilung Filmproduktion), 19 October 1961, BArch, Abt. DDR (Kultur), DR1/4038.
15. 'Bericht über die Lage im VEB DEFA-Studio für Spielfilm', p. 362.
16. 'HV Film Abteilung Film Produktion: Informationsblatt für die Mitglieder des Präsidiums des Ministerrats', September 1961, BArch, Abt. DDR (Kultur), DR 1/4038.
17. 'Das Kleid', BArch, Abt. DDR (Kultur), DR 1 MfK-HV Film/86.
18. In June 1977 the film was withdrawn because of Krug's own emigration to the West following the Biermann affair.
19. Patrick Major, 'Vor und nach dem 13. August 1961: Reaktionen der DDR-Bevölkerung auf den Bau der Berliner Mauer', *Archiv für Sozialgeschichte* 39 (1999), 325–54 (p. 334).
20. 'Der Kinnhaken', BArch, Abt. DDR (Kultur), DR 1 MfK-HV Film, p. 552.

21. For an account of the making of the film, see Frank Vogel, '*Und deine Liebe auch*: Notizen zur Entstehungsgeschichte des Films', *Filmwissenschaftliche Mitteilungen,* 3 (1962), 421–37.

22. Rosemarie Rehahn, 'Drei in einer grossen Stadt', *Wochenpost,* 17 March 1962.

23. Christoph Funke, 'Bausteine deines Lebens', *Der Morgen,* 23 September 1962.

24. 'Und deine Liebe auch', BArch, Abt. DDR (Kultur), DR 1 MfK-HV Film, p. 408.

25. Christoph Funke, '"Flucht aus dem Wohlstand": *Sonntagsfahrer,* ein neuer DEFA-Film von Gerhard Klein', *Der Morgen,* 31 August 1963.

26. *Werkstatterfahrungen mit Gerhard Klein,* ed. by Hannes Schmidt ( = *Aus Theorie und Praxis des Films,* 2 (1984)), p. 37.

27. 'Geschichten jener Nacht', BArch, Abt. DDR (Kultur), DR 1 MfK-HV Film, p. 137.

28. Ibid., p. 137.

29. See also Marc Silberman, 'Post-Wall Documentaries: New Images from a New Germany?', *Cinema Journal,* 33 (1994), 22–41.

# 9

# Defending the Border?
## Satirical Treatments of the Bundeswehr after the 1960s

*Andrew Plowman*

In Arno Ploog and Joachim Fischer's humorous illustrated volume *Meine Dienstzeit bei der Bundeswehr* (*My Service in the Bundeswehr*, 1965), the protagonist, a conscript to the West German Bundeswehr, briefly reflects upon the difference between military service in the FRG and in the GDR: 'Our motives for serving are also superior to the East, because we have *values worth defending,* e.g. freedom', he observes, comparing his situation to that of 'young people in the [former Soviet Occupation] Zone, who are ruthlessly forced into military service'.[1] The joke, of course, is his failure to understand that conscription was a fact in both German states.

This comic remark neatly illustrates the point that in the Cold War, rearmament was a key sphere in which the FRG and the GDR were tied to, yet forced to distinguish themselves from, one another. From the 1950s on, the two states were bound in a military 'feedback loop' in which each justified rearmament and the introduction of conscription as responses to the moves of the other as they respectively embedded themselves into NATO and the Warsaw Pact. Each side presented its own policy as defensive and peace-loving, and that of the other as hostile.[2] In this process, both states were confronted with a shared military past that extended beyond the National Socialist Wehrmacht and the Weimar Republic's Reichswehr to the reforms of Scharnhorst at the start of the nineteenth century as they searched for usable military traditions.

This chapter examines the satirical representation of the Bundeswehr in West Germany from the 1960s to the mid 1970s. Texts considered include articles and illustrations in the satirical monthly *Pardon* (established 1962). Also examined are the volume *Meine Dienstzeit in der Bundeswehr* and a 'cult' trilogy published under the pseudonym Miles Bramarbas:[3]

*Die Armee auf der Erbse* (*The Army on the Pea*, 1969), *Die Offensive im Eimer* (*The Offensive down the Pan*, 1971), and *Ein Hauch von Truppe* (*A Whiff of Troops*, 1975). In the GDR, widespread unease about remilitarization was not expressed openly.[4] In officially sanctioned public representations, the Nationale Volksarmee (NVA) appeared rather as a force for socialism and peace in the face of Western capitalism and imperialism.[5] The turn to military traditions of the past occurred with a relative absence of self-consciousness as policy makers invoked the spirit of the reforms of Scharnhorst on the one hand and dressed the NVA in largely traditional uniforms on the other.[6] Satire was reserved for the Bundeswehr in the West. In the journal *Eulenspiegel* or texts like Karlludwig Opitz's *Im Tornister: Ein Marschallstab* (*Destined to Become a Field Marshall*, 1959), West German claims about the Bundeswehr were shown to conceal ideological continuities with the National Socialist Wehrmacht. In the FRG, by contrast, satirists took surprisingly little heed of the NVA; Soviet forces tended to figure as the primary adversary. But satire did establish itself as an important mode of reflection upon the controversy and soul-searching that accompanied rearmament. In the FRG, remilitarization was the major political and moral question of its day; few other issues shaped the fledgling democracy more decisively.[7]

This essay shows how the Bundeswehr throughout the 1960s provided satirists with themes that touched centrally upon the self-understanding of the West German state. Satirical treatment, it is argued, crystallized around two broad sets of topics. One concerned the defence of the FRG's external borders. The perception of the Bundeswehr's subordinate role in NATO, controversies over nuclear and conventional strategy and anxieties about the combat-readiness of the army provided rich material. The other – ultimately major – theme was military reform. The concept of the soldier as *Staatsbürger in Uniform* (citizen in uniform) was positioned at the 'inner front' in a battle for democratic values and indeed became the site of a struggle between reformers and traditionalists that was satirized from the perspective of first the left and then the right.

Satire is understood here in its broad sense, as an attack by ridicule across a range of discourses rather than as a genre in its own right.[8] Satirical writing had been an established feature of the cultural landscape since the 1950s: the rearmament debate had spawned notable literary satires on German militarism, including Heinrich Böll's story 'Hauptstädtisches Journal' ('Bonn Diary', 1957). But with the exception of Böll in his novel *Ende einer Dienstfahrt* (*End of a Mission*, 1966), the Bundeswehr did not itself attract the attention of leading writers after its establishment. Rather, it produced subliterary forms that underwent a striking development, moving from the news-based texts of *Pardon* to sustained narratives that positioned themselves with greater parodic sophistication towards both the military experience of the growing numbers passing through the Bundeswehr's ranks and the motifs of literary satire. Yet within the climate of politicization in the late 1960s, the essay concludes, such satirical treatments were increasingly outstripped by more direct forms of critique.

If satire is dependent on context for its interpretation,[9] then one should note that the Bundeswehr remained so controversial after its establishment that it was rarely absent from the pages of the West German press. Where the defence of the border was concerned, controversy came to a head with the *Spiegel* affair of 1962. This was triggered by an attack by *Der Spiegel* on the defensive capability of the Bundeswehr and on the defence policy of a conservative government that was predicated on atomic weapons.[10] The attack came on the eve of a major shift in strategic thinking. In the late 1950s, the doctrine of 'massive retaliation' favoured by the United States under Eisenhower had foreseen prompt deployment of 'tactical' or other nuclear weapons in a conflict with the Warsaw Pact. For the West German government, equipping the Bundeswehr – against popular opposition – to deliver NATO atomic weapons had offered the promise of leverage in the quest for parity with other nations in the Western alliance. Yet the advent of 'flexible response' under Kennedy in the mid-1960s marked a shift away from nuclear weapons as a first line against a conventional attack and exposed the shortcomings of a Bundeswehr geared towards a 'sword-and-shield' strategy that emphasized the atomic 'sword' over the conventional 'shield' designed to protect it.[11] The defensive capabilities of the military remained contentious in the wake of the *Spiegel* affair. Multiple crashes in the mid 1960s cast doubt on the ability of West Germany's American-built Starfighter jets to provide aerial support within NATO. Argument raged over the political decision, held partly responsible for the crashes, to modify the Lockheed F-104G model used by the West Germans beyond optimum capacity in order to deliver atomic weapons.[12] And from 1967, defence cuts rendered increasingly implausible the concept of 'defence forwards' designed to keep large segments of the West German population out of the potential conflict zone.[13]

Military reform, too, became an explosive issue in 1963 with the death of the recruit Gerd Trimborn and revelations about abuse in the paratroop regiment in Nagold.[14] Numerous measures since the 1950s had been intended to secure the Bundeswehr within West German parliamentary democracy and prevent the military from turning into the autonomous 'state within a state' that the Weimar Reichswehr was perceived to have become. Under the banner of the 'primacy of politics' the forces were placed under parliamentary control and the legal status of soldiers was codified.[15] Other proposals sought to anchor the democratic values of civil society within the military. Associated with Graf Wolf von Baudissin, the concept of the citizen in uniform defined the soldier as the embodiment of the democratic values he was called to defend.[16] He enjoyed the right of active and passive franchise and of free association as well as freedom of expression.[17] A related concept was *Innere Führung* (inner leadership or structure), which encompassed the training methods and command structures designed to cultivate the requisite ethos of responsibility.[18] For the reformers, the commitment of the citizen in uniform placed him at the 'inner front' in the battle to distinguish the Bundeswehr from the German armies of the past and from the NVA.[19]

The citizen in uniform indeed became the site of conflict – between the reformers and the champions of traditional military values. From the outset, the reform agenda met with resistance from officers and noncommissioned officers (NCOs) who had received their military training in the Wehrmacht before 1945. But the conflict became fiercer and more public following the revelations about the paratroop regiment at Nagold in 1963. The left went on the offensive with claims that the abuses of soldiers' rights, particularly by inadequately trained NCOs, were symptomatic of both a disregard for the reform agenda and a perverse cultivation of military tradition.[20] The later part of the 1960s saw the traditionalists regroup as conservatives argued for reform to be rolled back. In military circles opposition to the changes was expressed increasingly openly, culminating in a pamphlet by General Albert Schnez that called for a return to core military values in the interests of a credible Bundeswehr.[21] The 1969 SPD government responded by affirming the binding character of *Innere Führung* and pressing on with reform. Yet despite a degree of normalization, the conflict rumbled on.

The treatment of the Bundeswehr in *Pardon* bore the imprint both of the *Spiegel* affair and the revelations about Nagold. The magazine was launched in 1962 by Hans A. Nikel and Erich Bärmeier just weeks before the government's heavy-handed response to *Der Spiegel* had finally, as *Pardon* put it, revealed the West Germans' 'democratic boiling point'.[22] *Pardon* contained a mix of information and comment, its satirical impulse residing in the pointed way it used humour to illuminate topical events from a left-liberal perspective.

From the outset, several pieces highlighted a perceived lack of parity between the Bundeswehr and the armed forces of other NATO nations. Nowhere did this emerge more clearly in the wake of the *Spiegel* affair than where atomic weapons were concerned. Here, plans for a West German nuclear arsenal were dashed in the shift to flexible response.

A cartoon sequence of February 1965, for instance, shows two senior Bundeswehr officers discussing their 'inferiority complexes' after one has returned from a briefing in Washington: 'They still plan on a grand scale! 19 megatons on Tursk, 30 on Zarakov ... And we throw grenades about.'[23] The cartoons ridicule both the pursuit of nuclear weapons and the willingness to embrace self-destruction that these might mean, and they further suggest nostalgia for the ambitiousness of the Wehrmacht in its campaign against the Soviet Union. Yet they also seem to question the very purpose of conventional forces in a situation where conflict might quickly escalate beyond any flexible response into a nuclear one. The men are not engaged in the training they describe, but stare out of a window. The idea of a loss of function in the atomic age is underlined in the contrast with romanticized images of warfare from earlier times (e.g. lance battles in 1250), and it undermines the claim of military reformers that the challenge of nuclear warfare made the democratic commitment of the citizen in uniform essential.[24]

Nonetheless, the topic of the combat readiness of the Bundeswehr's conventional forces was recurring, and never more so than during the Starfighter crisis. A cartoon of July 1966 suggested that the frequency of the crashes robbed them of interest: the crowd in the foreground is preoccupied with a bicycle accident and ignores the smouldering wreckage behind.[25] Of course, they remained an explosive topic. Turning the usual criticisms upside down, a 1966 article disingenuously claimed that maintaining the Bundeswehr in a 'state of lacking combat readiness' might prove a blessing if it could prevent Starfighter jets from being entrusted with live rather than dummy nuclear weapons.[26] The Bundeswehr's preparedness to defend the FRG continued to feature in the pages of *Pardon* following defence cuts in 1967, when cartoons featured soldiers equipped with toys or boxing gloves.[27] Striking here, in a publication noted for its anti-establishment stance, is that government policies were under attack not on pacifist grounds, but rather on account of the poor condition in which politicians left the military.

The treatment of military reform was shaped primarily by the left-liberal critique of the failure to realize the proposals. Already prior to Nagold the concept of the citizen in uniform had been attacked as window-dressing which barely masked a continuity of military values and personnel from before 1945. The tenor is humorous in the 'Monolog eines Bundeswehroffiziers' ('Monologue of a Bundeswehr Officer') from October 1962 which suggested that nothing but the language of the military had changed. Here a veteran of the Eastern front disgruntled at having to address conscripts 'as human beings' learns that modifying his language does not mean treating them any less harshly.[28] Following

Nagold the tone became accusatory, for instance in an account of the abuse of recruits published in September 1963. In the piece, an official recruitment publication trumpeting the military's democratic credentials throws into relief the reality of the marginalization of the reform agenda in an unholy alliance between 'Hitler's generals' Heusinger, Ruge and Kammhuber.[29] The perception of a failure to respect the reform agenda also informs the approach to subjects as diverse as freedom of association in the army and, again, the Starfighter crisis. A piece from January 1966 on proposals to allow soldiers to join the public service and transport union mocked the assimilation of the military to the values of civil society by projecting the antipathy expressed by officers back into the civilian sphere: 'A factory is like a barracks. If its soldiers want co-determination, that is mutiny'.[30] The Starfighter crisis, too, highlighted the lack of accountability of the military before the law as *Pardon* asked in April 1966 whether the crashes should be prosecuted as manslaughter.[31]

Yet occasionally recruits' pedantic insistence upon their rights rendered the citizen in uniform an absurd figure. A report in July 1967 about grenadiers in Ellwangen who complained at having to slaughter a chicken during survival training suggested the incompatibility of military training and civilian niceties.[32] Underlining the incongruity is an accompanying cartoon depicting soldiers standing over the bodies of their enemies and fretting about killing the bird. Such items lent credence to the claims from the right that despite the reformers' claims to the contrary, the citizen in uniform was also a soft and ineffective soldier.

The cartoons and articles in *Pardon* exemplify the features of topical satire. Its meaning bound to the context of production, it is ephemeral and makes no aesthetic claims. It tends not to explain, instead assuming prior knowledge of events as it illuminates the gap between their appearance and their underlying meaning by means of contrasts and juxtapositions.[33] The irony of perspective and the parodic borrowing of other forms visible here take more systematic shape in Ploog and Fischer's 1965 *Meine Dienstzeit in der Bundeswehr.* This illustrated volume situates itself in relation not only to current events but also to the experience of military service, which was a formative one for many West Germans, and to the handbooks and manuals that shaped that experience. *Meine Dienstzeit* tells the story of a conscript who appears at the outset as a left-leaning reader of *Der Spiegel* and *Pardon*. In the Bundeswehr, he is instructed in field and combat skills by the NCO Kreuzberg, a veteran of Stalingrad, and in *Innere Führung*. At the close he alone returns home; his fellow conscripts have died in training incidents around him. The volume is primarily a satire on the citizen in uniform in the aftermath of Nagold. Like *Pardon* (to which Ploog contributed regularly), its defining perspectives are those of a left-liberal critique, yet it also demonstrates a heightened awareness of the comic potential of the citizen in uniform.

The incidents in which the protagonist's comrades die correspond to cases of abuse widely discussed after 1963. The circumstances of Gerd Trimborn's death in Nagold that year are mirrored when Martin Schweigler and Christoph Warnke are pushed to the point of collapse by Kreuzberg. There follow the deaths of soldiers marched off a cliff; another is driven to a breakdown after being picked on and forced to sing marching songs without respite.[34] In the figure of Kreuzberg, a representative of the NCO class generally held responsible for such abuses, the volume points to the persistence of brutal and outmoded concepts of discipline across the caesura of 1945. His experience of war and Soviet captivity euphemistically glossed as 'valuable wartime and postwar experience', Kreuzberg, like the officer in *Pardon,* has adopted the language of *Innere Führung* whilst remaining the callous '*Schleifer*' who takes sadistic pleasure in knocking recruits into shape. (A term relating to the polishing of precious stones, the '*Schleifer*' acquired fresh notoriety in the claims of officers in Nagold that their paratroopers were rough diamonds needing special attention.)[35]

Several passages deal with the instruction of conscripts in democratic values. The sessions designed to promote awareness of the constitutional values they are to defend underline the discrepancy between the ideal and the deficient reality of the citizen in uniform. Yet the concept itself is one that the recruits are unlikely to line up to. They too recite the maxims of *Innere Führung* without understanding them. Misunderstandings ensue when Lieutenant Woigle has them translate the infamous motto over the entrance to the United States Military Academy at West Point: 'Ours is not to reason why, ours is to work and die' (translated as 'Wir fragen nicht nach dem *Warum,* wir kämpfen und wir kommen um'). This idea is plainly the antithesis of the democratic awareness of the citizen in uniform. Yet the protagonist compounds the misunderstanding by treating it as a lesson learnt: 'Once the sense of this dictum has been understood one is on the way to becoming a good soldier. For as the *Handbook of Inner Leadership* puts it: *the performance of the soldier increases with his insight.*'

Such irony is stressed by the way the volume parodies the texts designed to provide a guide to the experience of military service. Though actual call-up rates remained low, the introduction of conscription created an appetite for first-hand accounts of the Bundeswehr among those eligible for service. *Meine Dienstzeit* holds up a distorting mirror up to publications like Harry Neyer's *Wie hast Du's mit der Bundeswehr* (*Where Do You Stand on the Bundeswehr,* 1963) which reached an optimistic conclusion about the prospects of the reform agenda on the basis of interviews with soldiers. Ploog and Fischer send up this optimism: their protagonist believes his experience to have been exemplary despite evidence to the contrary. Extensive citation from military handbooks issued in the Bundeswehr moreover emphasizes the contradictory claims on the soldier as citizen in uniform. Issued to all recruits, the *Taschenbuch für Wehrpflichtige* (*Handbook for Conscripts*) covered topics ranging from the role of the Bundeswehr within NATO to combat techniques. The *Handbuch Innere Führung* (*Handbook of Inner Leadership*) was issued to officers to explain the new command practices. Ploog and Fischer delight in playing out the most ludicrously self-evident statements in the former – 'Whoever shoots more quickly and accurately will emerge victorious'[36] – against the maxims of the latter, such as the one above about the relation between performance and insight.[37] The gulf between the practical imperatives of military training and the theory of *Innere Führung* appears, too, in the quotation from General Heinz Karst's 1964 treatise *Das Bild des Soldaten* (*The Image of the Soldier*) that prefaces the volume. During the 1960s Karst distanced himself from the concept of *Innere Führung*, which he had helped to author. He is cited to suggest that the reformers themselves harboured doubts about the limits of their creation: 'At the moment he enters into combat … rational motives for defence are indifferent to the soldier'.[38]

The element of parody and quotation here construct a space for a reader increasingly familiar with the forms in which Bundeswehr experience was being articulated. The moment of recognition is stronger still in the Miles Bramarbas satires. What distinguishes these texts, however, is their grounding in the right-wing critique of the reform agenda as well as their more elaborate fictional plots. With a grey cover reminiscent of the *Taschenbuch für Wehrpflichtige*, *Die Armee auf der Erbse* (1969) relates how World War III is averted when a Soviet invasion of the FRG is repulsed by the Bundeswehr (and former Wehrmacht) General Blaartsch. In *Die Offensive im Eimer* (1971), the disaster-prone manoeuvre 'Jagger Mick' is rescued for NATO after Karl-Eduard Trimmdich Sr, an industrialist nostalgic for his simple soldier's life before 1945, heads for the Bundeswehr wearing the uniform of his son, a lieutenant in the reserves. *Ein Hauch von Truppe* (1975) deals with a manoeuvre that goes awry following the introduction of malfunctioning new computer technology.

The texts – the first especially – address several issues relating to the defence of the FRG. Picking up traditional anti-communist stereotypes that go back to National Socialism, *Die Armee auf der Erbse* plays upon fears of Soviet aggression in the image of Soviet generals keen to run their tanks down West German motorways towards Aachen.[39] (The

East German NVA is strikingly absent from Bramarbas's texts.) Where this text sends up the doctrines of 'flexible response' and of 'defence forwards' in its inflated picture of Blaartsch's conventional victory, *Die Offensive im Eimer* exploits the tensions between NATO member states over the shift towards flexible response. Here, Blaartsch is convinced by the topsy-turvy logic of pro-nuclear French officials to throw the NATO manoeuvre. His military prowess, they argue, might convince the US of the feasibility of a solely conventional defence and so increase the likelihood of Soviet attack: 'since the only thing they feared was the complete flattening of Moscow's Sparrow Hills'.[40] By contrast, *Ein Hauch von Truppe* satirizes the effect of cutbacks on the Bundeswehr during the relative détente of the early 1970s. In the manoeuvre at the close, a gap in the front emerges when the new computer substitutes the 'planned strength' of a battalion for its 'actual strength' in a dig at the language of defence planning.[41]

The heart of the texts, though, is again the conflict over reform and military tradition. What makes *Die Armee auf der Erbse* the most compelling of the three is its proximity to Hans Georg Studnitz's polemic *Rettet die Bundeswehr!* (*Save the Bundeswehr!*, 1967), which painted a picture of a Bundeswehr crippled by half-baked reforms. In an attack on the democratic reform agenda Studnitz argued that the soldier as citizen in uniform had indeed come to embody wider social values in so far as he was spoiled by a typically West German obsession with the affluent life.[42] *Die Armee auf der Erbse* alludes to Studnitz in an observation about a critic of reform and his book *Rettungsschwimmer für die Bundesmarine* (*Lifeguards for the Navy*).[43] Its preface mimics Studnitz's bluster, which was ripe for parody: 'It cannot continue like this! ... Taxpayers finance one of the most expensive armies in German history and have every right to expect that its uniformed citizens do not start crying for a psychiatrist when bombs and grenades go off'.[44] The text offers a comic reduction of many of the views expressed by Studnitz. The left-liberal critique in *Pardon* and *Meine Dienstzeit* of a failure to take the reform agenda seriously is abandoned as the citizen in uniform emerges as a soft, inept soldier incapable of defending the FRG. In a swipe at an army in which recruits were entitled to go home most weekends, *Die Armee auf der Erbse* has the Soviets consider making their move when barracks are empty, though they finally strike when the Bundeswehr is even more likely to be helpless: during combat training. It is up to a former Wehrmacht man to save the day, and tellingly, the first step of General Blaartsch's defence plan has his tank regiment throw out copies of the *Handbuch Innere Führung*.

Blaartsch appears as a resolute opponent of *Innere Führung*, yet it is unclear, in a satire that ultimately spares no one, how much better the representatives of traditional military virtues fare. Their outlook shaped by military service before 1945, they are given to romanticizing the Eastern front, a trait exposed by the appropriately named Bundeswehr Major Nörgel, who has researched the topic and corrects the officers' tales ('Nörgeln' means to cavil at something). In this vein, Bramarbas more than once hints that the account offered of Blaartsch's defence of the FRG may itself be grossly inflated.[45]

The conflict over military reform still figures prominently in *Die Offensive im Eimer* in 1971. Jokes about the citizen in uniform and the opposition of the old guard abound in references to the establishment of Bundeswehr universities and to the long hair worn by recruits asserting their right to express their personalities freely. However there is a clear loss of focus in *Ein Hauch von Truppe* in 1975, with extraneous plot developments involving Irish republican terrorists among other things. Now the familiar comic results are produced by malfunctioning computer technology. Indeed, the narrator reflects openly on the implications for his satirical undertaking of a lessening of the old conflict upon the retirement of the officer cohorts formed by the Wehrmacht: 'But now fresh-faced lads occupy the rooms and corridors of Command Centres as Lieutenant Colonels ... More and more, the upper ranks of the Bundeswehr are ruled by an emotional sobriety which scarcely allows the satirist a point of purchase.'[46]

Here Bramarbas suggests an explanation for the decline of the Bundeswehr satire in the 1970s. But even if the retirement of former Wehrmacht soldiers did rob the conflict over reform of its charge and the satirist of material, this process cannot wholly be explained in terms of a generational shift. It also touches upon the limits of satirical discourse within the cultural context of the FRG after the 1960s. Satire was a discursive mode well suited to the oppositional mindset of the 1950s and early 1960s. But laughter could be a stabilizing as well as a critical force, and as the 1960s progressed, satirical impulses, especially on the left, fell out of step with a politicized climate favouring more direct critique and action.[47] The distinction between subversive and affirmative laughter appears particularly germane to Bramarbas's satires and their ultimately ambivalent grounding in the critiques of the right. *Die Armee auf der Erbse* and *Die Offensive im Eimer* are accomplished pieces that align themselves with a literary tradition of military satire in their self-conscious choice of figures and motifs. In the former, for example, Private Schlurf is characterized by a mixture of stubbornness and guilelessness reminiscent of the protagonist of Jaroslav Hasek's *The Good Soldier Švejk* (1921–23); in the latter, when Trimmdich Sr heads for the Bundeswehr, reference is made to the motif of the impostor in military uniform familiar from Carl Zuckmayer's play *Der Hauptmann von Köpenick* (*The Captain of Köpenick*, 1930).

Also striking is a marked reduction in the projected readership of the texts. Both the narrator and the anticipated reader are positioned within the Bundeswehr ('Companions!')[48] in works that renounce the wider social import of the critique of *Pardon* or *Meine Dienstzeit*. Frequently, these texts have the character of an obscure in-joke for the military. Satirists are often regarded as moralists who draw attention to the follies and hypocrisies of individuals and institutions, but their pervasive irony can render their statements ambivalent. Does *Die Armee auf der Erbse* satirize the right-wing views of traditionalists like Studnitz? Or does its representation of the citizen in uniform endorse such views? Probably both, but there is an element here of Private Schlurf's own 'straight posture, of which no one knew whether it was meant ironically or not'.[49]

On the left, by contrast, satire had by the late 1960s been outstripped by more direct critique. Where the Bundeswehr was concerned, the publication of Günter Wallraff's Bundeswehr diaries was the symptomatic event. First published under the title 'Von einem der auszog und das Fürchten lernte' ('Of One Who Left Home and Learned to Fear', 1970), Wallraff's diaries deal with his belated attempt to be recognized as a conscientious objector during his military service in 1963. Wallraff, the *enfant terrible* of West German investigative journalists, offers in stark form the left-liberal critique of the abuse of recruits. Significantly, however, the citizen in uniform is never mentioned, and the reform debate that provided satirists with so much material is collapsed into the assertion of the continuity of the Bundeswehr with the military before 1945 as Wallraff records the treatment meted out by former Wehrmacht officers.[50] Wallraff later described the strong identification he felt with Hasek's Švejk.[51] Yet his text strips satirical motifs (for example, the Švejk figure whose desire to avoid trouble lands him in it) of their irony. Where the satirist illuminates the difference between appearances and the reality behind them using ironic juxtapositions and wit, Wallraff employs the unambiguous gesture of revelation to tell the shocking truth about the Bundeswehr. If this gesture became the hallmark of Wallraff's signature brand of documentary literature, it subsequently also established itself as the central trope of writing about the Bundeswehr in texts from Christian Klippel's *456 und der Rest von heute* (*456 and the Rest of Today*, 1979) to Thomas Bohn's *Der Querschläger* (*Ricochet*, 1990).

Satirical representations of the Bundeswehr in the FRG, it has been argued, crystallized around two key themes: the defence of the West German border and the question of military reform, where the figure of citizen in uniform was positioned at an inner front that was supposed to mark the Bundeswehr's difference from past German armies and from the NVA. In the process, news-based satires gave way to forms that positioned themselves in more complex ways in relation to experience-based discourses, the discourses of the Bundeswehr itself and literary traditions. But if rearmament was an area where the FRG and the GDR observed each other closely in order to construct their difference from one another, the texts examined here suggest fundamental asymmetries. In the GDR, satire was reserved for the critical representation of the West German Bundeswehr and was the counterpart to positive images of the NVA. The satires in *Pardon, Meine Dienstzeit in der Bundeswehr* and the Bramarbas trilogy suggest that the Bundeswehr was never defined against the NVA in the same way. To the extent that military reform was the major preoccupation, the citizen in uniform was the site of a struggle over military tradition that had more to do with West Germany's tormented relation to the past than with its attitude to the GDR. The satirical representation of the Bundeswehr went into retreat in the climate of politicization after the late 1960s. Only recently has the Bundeswehr reemerged as the subject of satirical representation – and on a grand literary scale. Named after a district of Bremen, Sven Regener's *Neue Vahr Süd* (2004) looked afresh at the citizen in uniform as a comic, contradictory figure in a send-up of Wallraff's story of his military service. This work appeared in the context of debates about the transformation of the Bundeswehr into a global intervention force. The struggle to establish the citizen in uniform against the background of the Cold War has become the stuff of nostalgia.[52]

## Notes

1. Arno Ploog and Joachim Fischer, *Meine Dienstzeit bei der Bundeswehr* (Frankfurt/Main: Bärmeier und Nikel, 1965), unpaginated.

2. Ute Frevert, *A Nation in Barracks: Modern Germany, Military Conscription and Civil Society* (Oxford: Berg, 2001), pp. 268–69.

3. After *miles* (Latin), soldier; and *Bramarbas oder der großsprecherische Offizier*, the German translation (1741) of Ludvig Holberg's Danish comedy *Jakob von Tyboe eller den stortalende Soldat* (1722).

4. Frevert, *A Nation in Barracks*, p. 269.

5. Bernard H. Decker, *Gewalt und Zärtlichkeit: Einführung in die Millitärbelletristik der DDR* (New York: Lang, 1989), pp. 3–5.

6. Frevert, *A Nation in Barracks*, p. 269.

7. David Clay Large, *Germans to the Front: West German Rearmament in the Adenauer Era* (Chapel Hill: University of North Carolina Press, 1996), p. 3.

8. Charles Knight, *The Literature of Satire* (Cambridge: Cambridge University Press, 2004), pp. 1–15.

9. Ibid., p. 51.
10. 'Bedingt abwehrbereit', *Der Spiegel,* 16 October 1962, pp. 32–53.
11. Detlef Bald, *Die Bundeswehr: Eine kritische Geschichte 1955–2005* (Munich: Beck, 2005), pp. 51–73.
12. 'Die Starfighter-Affäre: Ein gewisses Flattern', *Der Spiegel,* 24 January 1966, pp. 21–36.
13. Bald, *Die Bundeswehr,* p. 54.
14. 'Nagold: Tiefste Gangart', *Der Spiegel,* 11 November 1963, pp. 52–59.
15. Bald, *Die Bundeswehr,* pp. 44–45.
16. Wolf Graf von Baudissin, *Soldat im Frieden: Entwürfe für eine zeitgemäße Bundeswehr* (Munich: Piper, 1969), p. 195.
17. Frevert, *A Nation in Barracks,* p. 264.
18. On this term see Large, *Germans to the Front,* p. 177.
19. *Handbuch Innere Führung,* 2nd edn (Bonn: Verteidigungsministerium, 1960), p. 31.
20. 'Nagold: Tiefste Gangart', p. 57.
21. Albert Schnez, 'Der Teufelskreis hat sich geschlossen', *Der Spiegel,* 5 January 1970, pp. 23–27.
22. 'Die Demokratie ist aufgewacht', *Pardon,* January 1963, p. 7.
23. 'Soldat, was nun?', *Pardon,* February 1965, pp. 18–19 (p. 19).
24. Baudissin, *Soldat im Frieden,* p. 221.
25. Untitled, *Pardon,* July 1966, p. 13.
26. Otto Köhler, 'Von Hassel muß bleiben', *Pardon,* October 1966, p. 12.
27. Untitled, *Pardon,* August 1967, p. 27.
28. Erhard Hunger, 'Monolog eines Bundeswehroffiziers', *Pardon,* October 1962, p. 43.
29. Otto Köhler, 'Wer sich in Uniform begibt, kommt darin um', *Pardon,* September 1969, pp. 26–31 (pp. 30–31).
30. Otto Köhler, 'Ein General wird aufgeklärt', *Pardon,* January 1966, pp. 21–24 (p. 24).
31. Rolf Lamprecht, 'Beim wievielten Absturz beginnt der Totschlag?', *Pardon,* April 1966, p. 16.
32. 'Partielle Hemmungen', *Pardon,* July 1967, p. 21.
33. M. D. Fletcher, *Contemporary Political Satire: Narrative Strategies in the Post-Modern Context* (Lanham, MD: University Press of America, 1987), p. 9.
34. 'Nagold: Tiefste Gangart', pp. 52–59.
35. Ibid., p. 55.
36. *Taschenbuch für Wehrpflichtige und die Reserve der Bundeswehr* (Regensburg: Walhalla und Praetoria, 1962), F 23, p. 5.
37. *Handbuch Innere Führung* (Bonn: Bundesministerium für Verteidigung, 1960), p. 24.
38. Heinz Karst, *Das Bild des Soldaten* (Boppard am Rhein: Boldt, 1964), p. 356.
39. Miles Bramarbas, *Die Armee auf der Erbse: Ein Schulbuch der Nation* (Munich: Moos, 1969), p. 11.
40. Miles Bramarbas, *Die Offensive im Eimer: Ein Verteidigungsgraubuch 1971/72* (Koblenz: Mönch, 1971), p. 26.
41. Miles Bramarbas, *Ein Hauch von Truppe: Eine Gegendarstellung zur neuen Wehrstruktur* (Bonn: Gerhard Haas Selbstverlag, 1975), pp. 71–72.

42. Hans-Georg Studnitz, *Rettet die Bundeswehr!* (Stuttgart: Seewald, 1967), p. 133.

43. Bramarbas, *Die Armee auf der Erbse*, p. 55.

44. Ibid., pp. 7–8.

45. Ibid., pp. 7 and 79.

46. Bramarbas, *Ein Hauch von Truppe*, pp. 12–13.

47. Friedemann Wendauer and Alan Morris, 'The Politics of Laughter: Problems of Humor and Satire in the FRG Today', in *Laughter Unlimited: Essays on Humor, Satire and the Comic*, ed. by Reinhold Grimm (Madison: University of Wisconsin Press, 1991), pp. 56–78 (p. 61).

48. Bramarbas, *Ein Hauch von Truppe*, p. 10.

49. Bramarbas, *Die Armee auf der Erbse*, p. 11.

50. For example Günter Wallraff, *Von einem der auszog und das Fürchten lernte* (Munich: Weissmann, 1970), pp. 9–11.

51. Günter Wallraff, 'Meine Lehrjahre: Als Pazifist in der Bundeswehr', *Die Zeit*, 9 November 2000, p. 78.

52. Andrew Plowman, '*Staatsbürger in Uniform*? Looking back at the Bundeswehr in Jochen Missfeldt *Gespiegelter Himmel* (2001) and Sven Regener *Neue Vahr Süd* (2004)', *Seminar*, 43.2 (2007), 163–75.

# 10

# East versus West
## Olympic Sport as a German Cold War Phenomenon
*Christopher Young*

———■■■———

Lies, damn lies and statistics! Nowhere is this maxim more appropriate than in sport, a world where figures on a spreadsheet capture little of the essence of individual brilliance and collective achievement. And nowhere more than sport is it so outrageously flouted as coaches, spectators and commentators analyse statistical information to gauge and celebrate the macro-narratives of season's bests and the micro-details of individual performance. The body cultures of sport might generate aesthetic pleasure and engender a mood of mutual respect and understanding, but their dominant hermeneutic codes reduce them all – from gymnastics to clay pigeon shooting – to the bottom line of triumph and defeat. This has always been particularly acute in the Olympic Games. Despite the movement's rhetoric of inclusion and participation and the outward disdain for medal tables since the 1960s, the mass media spectacle of the quadrennial event has offered governments and societies the opportunity to reflect publicly on their national prowess.

Olympic success was a staple of Cold War discourse, with the two superpowers and their central European surrogates, the FRG and the GDR, dominant participants. Indeed, medal tables show that from the moment the Olympics became a media event (when first televised live in 1960) up until comparatively recently, these four nations *were* the Olympics. In terms of combined medals, German athletes outperformed each of the superpowers from 1972 until the collapse of communism – but only when competing on separate teams. Leaving aside Helsinki 1952 (the first postwar Games at which Germans, though only from the FRG, competed), the German medal count was prolific from 1956 to 1964, but nowhere near that of the big two. These were years in which the International Olympic Committee (IOC) forced East and West Germany to compete on a unified team. The characteristic Cold War phenomenon of German Olympic preeminence was not simply born out of intense ideological rivalry: it came to full fruition only when the two sides faced each other as separate entities. This chapter examines the genesis of this phenomenon in the years from 1968 to 1972, explaining the relation of sport to the respective political systems and arguing that each sports structure flourished precisely because of a state of competition and mutual dependence.

## Western Anxiety

For the West Germans, the 1968 Mexico Olympics marked diplomatic defeat and sporting disappointment. Not only did the FRG lose its long battle to block full recognition of the GDR's National Olympic Committee (NOC) – thus assuring that East Germany would appear as a fully sovereign team with its own flags and anthems for the first time at, of all places, the Munich Olympics in 1972 – but, in a contest in 1968 that pitted the two separate Germanys against each other for the first time, the East ran out clear winners.[1] The GDR claimed the fifth-best medal rating (nine gold, nine silver and seven bronze) behind the US, the USSR, Japan and, surprisingly, Hungary, and came third in the overall rankings, which awarded points on a graduated scale to the top six finalists in each event.[2] The FRG reached eighth in the medal table, with more medals but fewer gold (five gold, eleven silver, ten bronze), and rated fourth overall. Taken together, a combined German total would not have challenged the hegemony of the USA (107 medals, 45 gold) and the USSR (91 medals, 29 gold), but the individual performances established both German teams in the top echelon of Olympic sport. By Munich in 1972, however, the two German teams did, taken together, outmedal the top-ranked Soviet Union. Between Mexico 1968 and Munich 1972 a significant shift had occurred within the hierarchy of world sport.

In 1968, the West German public had been left in little doubt as to their team's standing relative to the GDR. The twenty-five medals won in Mexico by a squad of 298 athletes costing 7,000 Marks per head fell short of the thirty-six predicted by the tabloid *Bild* or the forty-four forecast by the sporting news agency Sport-Informations-Dienst.[3] The press lambasted the performance, and the families of some athletes were abused, threatened and insulted as traitors and Eastern agents.[4] West German sports bodies' assessment of athletes' performance was more moderate, however, as suggested by a letter from the Olympic team manager, Siegfried Perrey, to Willi Daume, the President of the West German NOC and Organizing Committee of the 1972 Games.[5] Aside from the profligacy of the rowing four, which foundered on the involvement of two members with the team's young secretaries, there were more mundane reasons for the lack of success. A straightforward combination of bad luck and an unusually small pool of talent, of which experts had been aware, accounted for the shortfall of medals with respect to the previous Games. Nonetheless, Perrey was acutely aware that to keep up with the US, the USSR and other Eastern-bloc countries in the four years until the Munich Games would require a concerted effort. Financial support should be withdrawn, Perrey recommended, if athletes failed to fulfill their training requirements. Above all, it was necessary to identify people at the top of the individual sports associations who understood the modern management of competitive sport and could speak the same language as the coaches.

By 1972, sufficient money had been invested to avoid, as *Bild* put it, the further 'bankruptcy' of West German sport.[6] In early 1967, the Deutscher Sportbund (German Sports Association, DSB), the NOC, the Bundesausschuß Leistungssport (Federal Committee for Competitive Sport), the Deutsche Olympische Gesellschaft (German Olympic Society, DOG), and the Organizing Committee for Munich had established the Stiftung Deutsche Sporthilfe (Foundation for German Sports Aid) as the social market economy's reply to state sponsorship of sport in the Soviet bloc.[7] It was supported by donations from companies and industry, and additionally, in the 1968–72 period when it was headed by the businessman and Olympic medalist Josef Neckermann, by the sale of sports stamps and a proportion of the *Glücksspirale* lottery proceeds intended primarily to swell the coffers of the Munich event itself. The relatively poor showing in Mexico, where twenty of the twenty-five medalists had been beneficiaries, highlighted the importance of the scheme.[8] Neckermann told the press that the West German team would incur the wrath of the public with a similar performance in Munich, explaining: 'High-performance sport is an advertisement. Society is not simply represented by its elite athletes. Rather, it identifies with them too. It's not the individual who wins the gold medal, but all of us.'[9] Between 1968 and 1972, the Deutsche Sporthilfe provided 25 million Marks in sponsorship.[10] By 1972, the government had increased support for the individual sports associations to 14,438 million Marks (from 7,574 million Marks in 1969), quadrupled subventions for national coaches (to 2.77 million Marks) and taken its place in newly founded bodies such as the Deutsche Sportkonferenz (The German Sports Conference) and the Bundestag's Sonderausschuß für Sport und Olympische Spiele (Parliamentary Special Committee for Sport and the Olympic Games).[11] Such financial and political investment was not without success: in 1972, the FRG jumped to fourth in the unofficial table with forty medals in total.

Yet the systemic improvements hoped for after Mexico left something to be desired. At the end of the Munich Olympics, Horst Meyer, who represented the Deutsche Sporthilfe in the Olympic Village, offered an insider's perspective to Neckermann.[12] He found the athletes' awareness of the foundation's work lacking. Most of them were not being trained for success and were using their grants for private purposes. He also felt that West German athletes should be reminded that their performances at major championships counted more than the season's average. The director of the Bundesinstitut für Sportwissenschaft (Federal Institute for Sports Science) continued in similar vein when he reported a dearth of sports doctors, inadequate training for coaches and a lack of centralized information – all direct consequences of structural difficulties that had troubled him for over a year.[13] Before the Games, Neckermann had already known that many of the FRG's best athletes would be injured and unable to compete as a result of their coaches' inability to balance increased training loads with rest periods. Additionally, the team would be on average two years older than in Mexico because recommendations made in 1968 to concentrate on younger athletes had gone unheeded.[14] By late 1972, not only the Deutsche Sporthilfe – which had long been viewed simply as the 'supplier of steaks' to high-performance athletes – but the whole sporting establishment realized that changes were required.[15] Whilst the FRG, the only Western country to improve significantly since 1968, was widely perceived to have performed well in Munich, there was room for improvement.[16]

The urgent need for enhancement arose from the continued dramatic rise of the GDR. In the twentieth Olympic Games in 1972 both Germanys had progressed, but the centre of sporting gravity had lurched eastwards: the United States conceded first place to the Soviets for the first time since 1960, and the GDR could claim over two thirds the number of US medals as opposed to under a quarter in 1968. With twenty gold and twenty-three silver and bronze, it now outstripped the FRG in every medal category, overshadowing its total by 50 per cent. As Neckermann's comments after the Winter Olympics in Sapporo in February 1972 reveal, Eastern-bloc success was a cause of concern and perplexity in view of the FRG's economic and cultural achievements. Neckermann asked: '[W]hy is it only in sport that centralist coercion outperforms democratic pluralism?'[17] The answer lay partly in the Federal Republic's suspicious response to the National Socialist appropriation of sport. The Kultusministerkonferenz (the collective body of Education and Culture

Ministers in the federal states, KMK) promoted sport at school only ambivalently, and much was left to agencies like the DOG and the DSB.[18] Yet the 1960s saw some success, with the KMK issuing guidelines for physical education in West German schools and the DSB a charter for German sport in 1966 that promoted both leisure sport for all and specific funding and training for talented athletes. An 'Olympia' scheme (Federal Youth Games and a 'Youth Trains for Olympia' programme) was introduced in 1968–69. Nonetheless, a programme for identifying talent, agreed in principle between the KMK and the DSB in 1968, was delayed until 1972, falling victim to the awkward interfaces inherent in the federal structure.

## The East German Sporting Apparatus

There was nothing sluggish about sport in the GDR. Neckermann's comment in 1972 on the national-representational value of sport would long have been a truism in the East. In the 1950s and 1960s, the FRG government had felt uneasy with sporting success per se (a prime example being the contrast between the euphoric popular reaction and the muted official response to West Germany's World Cup victory in 1954)[19] and had expended much of its energy on 'off-field' diplomatic intrigues. The Hallstein doctrine (whereby the FRG threatened to break diplomatic relations with states recognizing the GDR) had not functioned effectively in sport, where the GDR had forced the FRG onto the back foot in bickering over flags, anthems and insignia at international events.[20] Whilst the FRG had tried to set the rules of the game, the GDR had got on with playing it. In the West, sport had been constrained by political and bureaucratic decentralization, the limits of democratic structures, insufficient medical and scientific support, and problems of identifying talent. The situation in the GDR was the reverse. If in the West authorities, trainers and athletes had to be coaxed into speaking the same language, the East already had an evolved sporting syntax.

In accordance with the high degree of interpenetration of state and society, sport was totally integrated into the social and political fabric of the GDR. Meticulous state planning, the strategic use of limited resources, and a sophisticated structural network of talent seeking, identification and development were important features.[21] Ideologically and organizationally, sport was top-down and all-encompassing. Seen as a vital contribution to the intellectual and physical development of the 'socialist personality', it was guaranteed by the constitution and the Jugendgesetz (Youth Law) in all their successive drafts. GDR sport was probably the most highly regulated in the world: in 1951 and 1952 alone, the Politburo and the Secretariat of the Central Committee of the SED passed over two hundred sport-related resolutions.[22] Walter Ulbricht's personal love of sport certainly played a part. Although responsibility for sport officially fell to the second in the SED chain of power (Erich Honecker under Ulbricht), Ulbricht, a former parallel bar gymnast in a working-class sport club in Leipzig, maintained considerable managerial interest.[23]

Sport formed an important part of East German culture. The Spartakiads, a mini national Games after the Soviet model that drew in schools and sports clubs, grew exponentially between 1965 and 1974, going from 1.7 million participants to over 4 million. Half of GDR television viewers claimed to watch only major sporting events.[24] Frequent local and national physical education displays were well-rehearsed and often spectacular ideological showcases. In 1969, for instance, Willi Daume thought it vital for a member of the Munich Organizing Committee to observe the fifth quadrennial gymnastics and sports festival of the GDR in Leipzig. Attended by twenty members of the IOC and its president, the event put everything else in the shade, including, Daume claimed, the 1936 Berlin Olympics and the Moscow Spartakiads.[25] The costs, confidential FRG sources claimed, ran to 50 million Marks and were held by some in the GDR to be wasted money.[26]

Competitive sport was organized according to the principles of the planned economy, with targets being set, mostly reached and rigorously checked via annual and five-year plans for Olympic preparation and participation and other technical and infrastructural considerations. By the Munich Games, the largely capillary sports 'economy' was underpinned by a clean division of labour between three agencies: the Deutsche Turn- und Sportbund der DDR of 1957 (German Gymnastics and Sports Federation, DTSB) and its regional and local subsidiaries; the state Staatssekretariat für Körperkultur und Sport (State Secretariat for Physical Culture, StKS), formed in 1970 out of the Staatliches Komitee für Körperkultur (State Committee for Physical Culture, SKKS), and with responsibility for the Deutsche Hochschule für Körperkultur (German University of Physical Culture, DHfK) in Leipzig and the Forschungsinstitut für Körperkultur und Sport (Research Institute for Physical Culture and Sport) established in preparation for Munich; and, linking these to the highest echelons of government, the Abteilung Sport beim ZK der SED (Department of Sport in the Central Committee of the SED), a quasi sports ministry that evolved out of the Arbeitsgruppe Sport (Working Group Sport, 1959). This tight institutional weave regulated a system for the production of high-performance athletes largely implemented by Ulbricht in the 1950s.

The system made sport the largest social sector beneficiary of material support in the GDR. Work-based sports clubs (as of 1951–52) provided the final output. In the 1970s, these were staffed by between two to three hundred full-time employees and allowed seconded sportsmen to work under professional conditions. These clubs were fed by children's and youth sports schools (Kreis- und Jugend-Sportschulen, KJS) formed in the 1950s, which in turn were supplied by the preparatory work of Trainingszentren (Training Centres, TZ) starting in the late 1960s, where children, even at this bottom rung, undertook ten to fifteen hours' training weekly. Success came from a steep pyramid: whilst one child in eight attended a TZ, only one in ten TZ athletes were selected for a KJS. In total, the tripartite system came to measure around 75,000 athletes and 2,000 trainers, and was supported by a network of around 500 sports scientists and doctors.[27] Despite the denials by athletes themselves, the organization of sport in the GDR was far from normal.

As documents from the Olympiads running up to Tokyo 1964 and Mexico 1968 reveal, the system was as effective vertically in its decision-making and regulatory capacity as it was horizontally in the breadth of its conceptions. In the first resolution to break the normal temporal patterns of the GDR and follow an Olympic four-year (rather than five-year) cycle, the Politburo in 1961 suggested increasing athletes' 'socialist education' and training schedules, as well as improving training methods, the number of squad members, and facilities in preparation for Tokyo in 1964.[28] Faced a year later with only 30–50 per cent fulfillment of its targets, the leadership vigorously reaffirmed its goals.[29] The squad was to undergo education to make it unconditionally loyal to the state and 'to hate the enemies of the people, the militarists and imperialists'. Central training courses and conferences were to be supplemented by increased input from sports/natural scientific research. The slow performance of the bureaucratic machine was to be oiled by a Leistungssport-Kommission (Commission for Competitive Sport) founded to facilitate communication between the agencies responsible for sport. Although a resolution from the end of 1962 reported pleasing results, the whip was still cracked in the direction of sports science with a catalogue of directives for improvement.[30] In the course of the 1960s, the Politburo's sports resolutions took an increasingly long-term view. In 1960, a target for the percentage of GDR participants on the all-German team was set less than a year before the Rome Olympics and was subsequently missed.[31] In preparation for Tokyo, however, longer-term initiatives were implemented, like the obligatory testing of children's potential[32] with an eye to Mexico in 1968.[33] The final analysis of Tokyo 1964 led to the investment of 17.5 million East German Marks to enable a 50 per cent boarding provision at the KJS, and in 1965 a resolution covering the following seven years (Mexico 1968 and Munich 1972) was passed to expand the number of KJS and TZ to 900.[34]

By the time the GDR had risen to unprecedented success in the 1968 Olympics, significant internal organizational changes meant that East German sport would find itself even better placed to hone its athletic potential in preparation for Munich. Since Manfred Ewald had exchanged the chairmanship of the SKKS for that of the two-year-old DTSB in 1961, sport had become – as his personal assistant Erhard Rapke put it in his informer's report for the Stasi – 'a state within a state'.[35] Having joined three political parties in as many years – the National Socialists in 1944, the Communists in 1945, the SED in 1946 – Ewald survived a suspicious past to establish himself in the young elite of the GDR. He became chair of the SKKS at the age of twenty-six and in 1963 became a member of the Central Committee of the SED, a promotion placing him, in sports matters, just below the Politbu?ro and the Secretariat. Yet the ambitious Ewald was frustrated in the exercise of his power. The Leistungskomission des DTSB (Performance Commission of the DTSB, 1959) occupied an advisory role to, and frequently saw its recommendations eroded by, the party machine. In 1963, an anonymous report noted that there was possibly ideologically driven friction between the DTSB and Ewald's former institutional home, the SKKS.[36] Although the Politbuero's seven-year sports programme of 1965 devised a strict division of competences between the DTSB and the SKKS, the former receiving full responsibility for Olympic preparation, residual tensions maintained an unacceptable level of friction.

In 1967, with Honecker taking over as the Central Committee Secretary with responsibility for sport, Ewald made his move. The 'Arbeitsrichtlinien für die Leistungssportkommission der DDR' ('Working Guidelines of the Commission for Competitive Sport') presented in November 1967 and passed with immediate effect introduced ground-breaking changes for the organization of sport, with far-reaching effects for athletes. A new Performance Commission of the GDR, with Ewald at its head, was to be given powers to make definitive sports decisions and to give their content priority.[37] It was to be responsible for all sports associations, including the financially privileged, semi-autonomous and fiercely self-protective army and Stasi clubs Vorwärts and Dynamo. For Ewald, these changes meant a consolidation and even extension of his power as he assumed the political position from which he would (after Munich) usurp the urbane Heinz Schöbel's presidency of the NOC. For GDR sport, it heralded twenty years of more direct and self-defining government. Although the constitution of the commission meant it could hardly drift beyond Honecker's reach, the days of sport merely following Ulbricht's bidding were over. Developments in sports governance thus fit interpretations of the growing dual leadership between Honecker and Ulbricht – the former with domains of power to match those of the party leader – in the later 1960s, as well as of Ulbricht's own increasingly autonomous decision-making.[38]

The newly empowered Ewald's first major decision certainly befitted the structural paradigm shift. A month before Mexico, a draft document sent to Honecker requested the doubling of sports programme funding from the 40 million East German Marks already projected for 1970. Ulbricht and the Finance Ministry countered with the prioritization of other deserving sectors.[39] The GDR's stunning performance in Mexico might well have supported Ulbricht's assessment of sport's relative good health, but it also emboldened its champions. Ewald wrote to Honecker again, emphasizing the gear-change in the country's Olympic aims.[40] Whereas before the 1968 Games the GDR had sought to outnumber the FRG on the joint German team, now it was necessary to maintain the overall third-place ranking and gain more medals in real, not just per capita terms. Given the rapid increase in competitive sports and the political significance of the Games in Munich, such efforts were deemed to have exceptional potential for the state. Honecker was convinced and, in Ulbricht's absence, pushed the decisive 'Grundlinien der Entwicklung des Leistungssports in der DDR bis 1980' ('Principles for the Development of Competitive Sport in the GDR until 1980') through the Secretariat of the Central Committee in early 1969.[41] It was a document that drew itself up to the full rhetorical height of the GDR's sports argumentation over the preceding decade and set the tone and organizational accents for the following two years. East German sport was to prepare itself for 'direct confrontation with aggressive West German imperialism which, in accordance with its global strategy, aims to use the 1972 Olympics to disguise its aggressive goals'[42]. Sporting success would promote the GDR's international authority and reputation, serve as an expression of the state's productivity and consolidate state and class awareness among the population, especially the youth. For the FRG, it was maintained, competitive sport represented a component of the new 'expansionist' *Ostpolitik*.

All this was paramount in view of recent developments in international sport. Not only was the West getting better (in Mexico the US had gained more medals than the USSR for the first time since 1952), but there was also improvement in neutrals such as Kenya, Mexico and Ethiopia and, importantly, in other socialist states. The majority of the

GDR's socialist rivals were introducing measures to accelerate the pace of change. In the majority of disciplines, it was believed, 'there was no evidence yet of decreased rates of improvement in sporting achievement',[43] a phenomenon expected to hold until at least 1980. Although this latter statement smacks of paranoia, it is open to other explanations. First, the belief that sporting development was, in the medium term at least, limitless formed a standard element of the GDR's rhetorical inventory.[44] Second, the extraordinary performances in Mexico – where, for example, all but one of the finalists in the women's 4x100m relay broke the world record and the world standard in the triple jump was broken nine times –[45] were not solely attributable to the benefits of altitude. And third, the promise of performance-enhancing drugs, introduced sparingly in 1968, was both the stuff of fantasy and still largely unpredictable. Table 1 shows how predictions made in the 1969 'Grundlinien' for the 1980 Games both under- and overestimated future potentialities:

|  | GDR record 1968 | World Record 1968 | Predicted 1980 | Actual WR / Olympics 1980 | Actual date when prediction fulfilled |
|---|---|---|---|---|---|
| 10,000m, men | 28.04.4 min. | 27.39 | under 26.50 | WR 27.22.4 (1978) Oly 27.42.7 | 1995 |
| Discus, men | 63.32m | 68.4 | over 72.0 | WR 71.16 (1978) Oly 66.64 | 1986 |
| Long jump, women | 6.57m | 6.82 | over 7.2 | WR 7.09 (1978) Oly 7.06 | 1983 |
| Shot, men | 20.08m | 21.78 | over 23.0 | WR 22.15 (1978) Oly 21.35 | 1988 |
| Shot, women | 19.61m | 19.61 | over 21.0 | WR 22.45 (1980) Oly 22.41 | 1972 |
| 100m freestyle, men | 53.7 sec. | 52.6 | under 50.0 | WR 49.44 (1976) Oly 50.4 | 1976 |
| 100m freestyle, women | 61.2 sec. | 58.9 | under 57.0 | WR 55.41 (1978) Oly 54.79 | 1974 |

**Table 1**: GDR predictions of future athletic performances[46]

The government made concrete plans to 'reach for the stars'.[47] Training and educational programmes at the DHfK were to follow strictly organized, semi-military forms. There was to be an increased and differentiated search for talent. Specific targets were set for the size and shape of the athlete pyramid: TZs, into which communes were to invest most of their sports budget, were to reach 50,000; KJSs, where training was to be increased to thirty hours, 12,000; and the national and club squads, which were to train up to forty hours a week, 2,000. The school careers of those involved in the most time-consuming training were to be extended from ten to eleven years. Sports science was to become more practice-orientated though the turn to 'bold training experiments', and its cause was to be supported by the whole of scholarship.[48] Particularly with young and female athletes the use of 'uM' ('unterstützende Mittel', 'supporting means', a euphemism for drugs) was recommended, and ideological training was to be increased.[49] Infrastructurally, there was to be a full assimilation to competitive conditions. This meant, for example, sparing no expense to build a replica of the Augsburg canoe-slalom course.[50] As a result, the East Germans won every gold medal at this discipline over the first days in Munich.

Although far-reaching, each of these measures represented a mere extension of established principles. The most important way, however, to secure superiority over West Germany and to determine world standards entailed a radical restructuring of top-level sport. Success, it was argued, could be ensured only by concentrating financial and human resources in decisive sports and disciplines. In 1968, the socialist countries' sports conference had proposed that in order to counterbalance athletes from the US and the FRG, only sports in which the socialist states were successful should be included in the Olympic programme.[51] What was intended as a working principle for future admission of new sports to the Olympic Games took on a special twist in the GDR, where the increase in support for some disciplines occurred at the expense of others. Team sports in particular, which required the nurturing of large squads for a single medal, fell victim to the GDR's Olympic plan–economy. Water polo, which took up 30 per cent of swimming pool capacity, compared unfavourably, for instance, with swimming and its 79 per cent potential of a return.[52] Its funding, alongside that of basketball, hockey, modern pentathlon and tennis, was drastically cut. In contrast to the key sports in 'Sport I', these 'Sport II' disciplines were removed from the internal tripartite structure and international circulation, even at veterans' level. Notably, the perennial underachiever football survived the cut because of its 'professional' structure and status as the people's favourite. Ice hockey initially came under threat but was pulled back from the brink to survive, incredibly, in a league of two teams. Basketball, which in 1968 had experienced the largest membership growth of any Olympic sport, was not so lucky.[53]

The division between 'Sport I' and 'Sport II' signalled not only the disinheritance of one child but the neglect of another: mass sport. Over the course of the twentieth Olympiad, Ewald would not talk seriously about the 'parlous state' of school sport,[54] nor would Ulbricht discuss the need for young people to engage in folkloric song and dance evenings at their sports meets.[55] Any trumpeting of the essential symbiosis of high athletic performance and the formation of the socialist personality, as the GDR publicly promulgated in Mexico, was empty wind.[56] As the editor of the satirical magazine *Eulenspiegel* would discover when called in for a dressing-down after some loose comments, the sports resolutions were no laughing matter.[57] Recorded levels of discontent at the depriving of mass sport had not reached the high levels of the 1980s,[58] but the seeds were being sown.

## Conclusion

When Josef Neckermann wrote to Willi Daume shortly after the Munich Olympics to congratulate him on their magnificent staging, the chairman of the Deutsche Sporthilfe put his own spin on the FRG's sporting performance.[59] Counting medals in unorthodox fashion – according to the number taken home instead of the events in which they had been won (the customary practice of the medal table) – Neckermann boasted eighty-seven medals for West Germany rather than the official forty. Only the GDR had improved its top-six performance rating more than the FRG since 1968, and this, he noted insouciantly, was hardly surprising given their rivals' intensive preparations, underpinned by political objectives. Since the GDR's success was 'to be expected', Neckermann seemed to be arguing, it could almost be discounted. The East German interpretation was, of course, the mirror opposite. As Georg Wieczisk and Wolfgang Gitter argued in *Der Leichtathlet* (*The Athlete*): whilst the FRG had done nothing but invest in the material trappings of its own self-image at Munich, the GDR's noble emphasis on health and body culture had preserved the Olympic ideals.[60] Victory in sport, the conclusion ran, laid bare the advantages of socialism and its superior conception of modern society.

Rhetorical brio on both sides, however, masked the underlying reality of German sport at this critical juncture. It was as inaccurate for the FRG simply to whitewash the GDR's achievements as it was for the East to ignore the West's improvement. One team consistently outstripped the other, but both performed exceptionally, and their respective successes were mutually dependent. The performance of the united German team rocketed through the 1960s due to competition for places on both sides of the Iron Curtain. And although the FRG was left behind by the GDR's organized and drug-fuelled programmes of the 1970s and 1980s, it nonetheless maintained its position within the elite when competing as an individual team. The scale of this achievement becomes evident when compared to that of a comparably sized and sport-ambitious Western nation such as France, which rose with heavy investment to sixth place in Mexico 1968 only to enter free-fall in the two subsequent Games (placing seventeenth in Munich, fifteenth in Montreal in 1976). Despite concerns within Deutsche Sporthilfe about the efficacy of its methods, the FRG remained the best-ranked Western European nation.

GDR sport justifiably draws our fascination, but it is often forgotten that the West Germans enjoyed consistent success during the Cold War. This was due to their intense local rivalry. The East German sports lobby would have found it difficult to secure quite so much backing had it not been able to offer its government the chance of humiliating its West German rivals at their own showcase event in Munich. The West Germans, although playing catch-up, owed their own world-class performances to the fact of their eastern neighbours' prodigious performance. In Cold War sport it is clear that competition bred mutual and prolific dependence. The fact that the medal total of the united German team has now sunk below its 1964 level (the last year of a united German team before 1990) is testimony to this former rivalry's significance.

## Notes

1. Uta Andrea Balbier, *Kalter Krieg auf der Aschenbahn. Der deutsch-deutsche Sport 1950–1972: Eine politische Geschichte* (Paderborn: Schöning, 2007), pp. 221–48; Hans-Dieter Krebs, 'Die "doppelten Deutschen" (1965 bis 1988)', in *Deutschland in der Olympischen Bewegung: Eine Zwischenbilanz,* ed. by Manfred Lämmer (Frankfurt/Main: Nationales Olympisches Komitee für Deutschland, 1999), pp. 267–99.

2. Volker Kluge, *Olympische Sommerspiele. Die Chronik III: Mexico-Stadt 1968–Los Angeles 1984* (Berlin: Sportverlag Berlin, 2000), p. 152.

3. *Bild-Zeitung,* 29 October 1968.

4. For instance *Berliner Morgenpost,* 25 October 1968.

5. Perrey to Daume, 6 November 1968, Landesarchiv Speyer, Nachlaß Siegfried Perrey, V88/1968/III.

6. *Bild-Zeitung* headline, 28 October 1968.

7. Balbier, *Kalter Krieg auf der Aschenbahn,* pp. 147–53.

8. Krebs, 'Die doppelten Deutschen', p. 269.
9. Cited in *Bild-Zeitung,* 28 October 1968.
10. 'Bericht der Stiftung Deutsche Sporthilfe zur Jahreswende 1972/73', Carl und Liselott Diem Archiv, Zentrum für Olympische Studien an der Sporthochschule Köln, p. 5.
11. Krebs, 'Die doppelten Deutschen', p. 278.
12. Meyer to Neckermann, 19 September 1972, BAK, B106/49892.
13. Managing Director, Federal Institute for Sports Science, to Neckermann, 21 September 1972, BAK, B106/49892.
14. Pelschenke, note for Neckermann, 13 August 1972, BAK, B106/49892.
15. 'Bericht der Stiftung Deutsche Sporthilfe zur Jahreswende 1972/73', p. 3.
16. Ibid.
17. 'Sporthilfe an die Presse: Ausführungen von Josef Ackermann anläßlich der Pressekonferenz am 29.2.1972', Deutsches Olympisches Institut, Frankfurt/Main (hereafter DOI), Daume Nachlaß 533.
18. Ken Hardman and Roland Naul, 'Sport and Physical Education in the Two Germanies, 1945-90', in *Sport and Physical Education in Germany,* ed. by Roland Naul and Ken Hardman (London: Routledge, 2002), pp. 29-76.
19. Paul Cooke and Christopher Young, 'Selling Sex or Dealing with History? German Football in Literature and Film and the Quest to Normalize the Nation', in *German Football: History, Culture, Society,* ed. by Alan Tomlinson and Christopher Young (London: Routledge, 2006), pp. 181-203.
20. Tobias Blasius, *Olympische Bewegung, Kalter Krieg und Deutschlandpolitik 1949-1972* (Frankfurt/Main: Lang 2001).
21. Hardman and Naul, 'Sport and Physical Education in the Two Germanies', p. 68.
22. Hans Joachim Teichler, 'Sport in der DDR: Systemmerkmale, Folgen und offene Forschungsfragen', *Deutschland Archiv: Zeitschrift für das vereinigte Deutschland,* 37.3 (2004), 414-21 (p. 418).
23. Mario Frank, *Walter Ulbricht: Eine deutsche Biographie* (Berlin: Seidler, 2001), pp. 287-90.
24. Thomas Fetzer, 'Die gesellschaftliche Akzeptanz des Leistungssportsytems', in *Sport in der DDR: Eigensinn, Konflikte, Trends,* ed. by Hans Joachim Teichler (Cologne: Sport und Buch Strauß, 2003), pp. 273-357 (p. 285).
25. Daume to Knoesel, 1 August 1969, DOI, Daume Nachlaß 530.
26. Federal Office for the Protection of the Constitution to Minister of the Interior; Minister for All-German Affairs, 1 October 1969, BAK, B137/16432.
27. Martin-Peter Büch, 'Elite Sport', in *Sport and Physical Education in Germany,* ed. by Roland Naul and Ken Hardman (London: Routledge, 2002), pp. 132-52 (pp. 136-37).
28. The major sports decisions of the East German Politburo are reproduced in Hans Joachim Teichler, *Die Sportbeschlüsse des Politbüros: Eine Studie zum Verhältnis von SED und Sport mit einem Gesamtverzeichnis und einer Dokumentation ausgewählter Beschlüsse* (Cologne: Sport und Buch Strauß 2002). This essay refers to them (without title) in this edition. Here, pp. 392-99.
29. Ibid., pp. 408-16.
30. Ibid., pp. 421-31.
31. Ibid., pp. 353-54 and 371-85.

32. Ibid., pp. 421–31.
33. Ibid., pp. 408–16.
34. Ibid., pp. 495–522.
35. Giselher Spitzer, 'Anfang und Ende der Lex Ewald 1955–1989', in *Goldkinder: Die DDR im Spiegel ihres Spitzensports,* ed. by Grit Hartmann (Leipzig: Forum, 1998), pp. 260–81 (p. 264).
36. Giselher Spitzer, 'Der innerste Zirkel: Von der Leistungssportkommission des Deutschen Turn- und Sportbundes zur LSK der DDR', *Sportwissenschaft,* 25.4 (1995), 360–75 (p. 362).
37. Ibid., pp. 364–67.
38. Andreas Ritter, *Wandlungen in der Steuerung des DDR-Hochleistungssports in den 1960er und 1970er Jahren* (Potsdam: Universitätsverlag Potsdam, 2003), p. 275.
39. Ibid., pp. 185–89.
40. Ibid., pp. 119–24.
41. SAPMO-BArch DY 30/JIV2/3/1509, reprinted in Teichler, *Die Sportbeschlüsse des Politbüros,* pp. 561–68.
42. Teichler, *Die Sportbeschlüsse des Politbüros,* p. 563.
43. Ibid., p. 565.
44. Uta Andrea Balbier, '"Die Grenzlosigkeit menschlicher Leistungsfähigkeit" Planungsgläubigkeit, Konkurrenz und Leistungssportförderung in der Bundesrepublik und der DDR in den 1960er Jahren', *Historical Social Research,* 32 (2007), 137–53.
45. Raelene Boyle and Gary Linnell, *Raelene: Sometimes Beaten, Never Conquered. The Raelene Boyle Story* (Sydney: HarperCollins, 2003), 110.
46. Omitted here is the prediction for weightlifting, as this discipline was to change in significant ways in the intervening years.
47. Teichler, *Die Sportbeschlüsse des Politbüros,* pp. 561–68.
48. Ibid.
49. Ibid.
50. Werner Rabe (Bayerischer Rundfunk), interview by author.
51. Ewald to Hellmann, 16 December 1968, attached 'Dokument, das als Schlußfolgerung der Tagung der Sportleitungen der sozialistischen Länder in der Zeit vom 10. bis 12. Dezember in Warschau von allen teilnehmenden Delegationen akzeptiert wurde', SAPMO-BArch, DY 30/IVA/18/21.
52. As argued at the Tenth Bundesvorstandssitzung des DTSB; see Teichler, 'Sport in der DDR', p. 420.
53. Ritter, *Wandlungen in der Steuerung des DDR-Hochleistungssports,* p. 209.
54. Teichler, *Die Sportbeschlüsse des Politbüros,* pp. 488–94.
55. 'Niederschrift über eine Aussprache mit dem Genossen Walter Ulbricht in Oberwiesenthal am 26.12.65', SAPMO-BArch, DY 30/IV 172/18.
56. Teichler, *Die Sportbeschlüsse des Politbüros,* pp. 540–44 and 556–60.
57. Hellmann to Honecker, 12 December 1970, SAPMO-BArch, DY 30 /IVA2/ 18-10.
58. Fetzer, 'Die gesellschaftliche Akzeptanz des Leistungssportsytems', pp. 299–309.
59. Neckermann to Daume, 20 September 1972, DOI, Daume Nachlaß 566.
60. Georg Wieczisk and Wolfgang Gitter, 'Olympisches Essay. München '72: Wo wird die Olympische Idee verwirklicht?', *Der Leichtathlet,* 49.7 (1972), 19.

# 11

# Films from the 'Other Side'
## The Influence of the Cold War on the West German Feature Film Import in the GDR

*Rosemary Stott*

Film exchange between the two Germanys reveals much about diplomatic relations between the two states, with fluctuations in distribution patterns providing a barometer of the cultural relations between the GDR and the FRG. Because film production was one of the means via which both governments developed a distinctive national culture, film exchange was a politically sensitive activity, with neither government motivated to promote the 'other' German identity. A glance at the film releases in cinemas confirms that the two Germanys were generally very much divided when it came to promoting one another's film output. In the FRG, films made by the East German DEFA were shown at film festivals but were of little commercial interest to distributors. On the rare occasions that DEFA films like *Die Legende von Paul und Paula* (*The Legend of Paul and Paula,* Heiner Carow, 1973) were released in mainstream cinemas, they were not box office successes.[1] Television provided a better outlet for East German productions, particularly those with content familiar to West German audiences, such as fairy-tale films.[2] With the increase in the number of West German television channels in the 1980s, DEFA films gained a wider exposure there.

In the GDR, film distribution, like film production, was under full control of the state. It was crucial to the endeavour in the cultural sphere to present an image of the world that matched the strategic priorities of the state and supported the socialist world view. Hence films from the Soviet Union and the other socialist countries dominated imports for mainstream cinemas as well as film festivals and television screenings. Nevertheless, imports from Western countries, including from the FRG and other German-speaking countries, were a regular feature of cinema programmes. In the 1980s the official claim was that the Helsinki agreement of 1975 was being applied more consistently to film distribution in the GDR than in the Western states. For instance, Kurt Maetzig, one of the best-known East German directors, talked of a 'one-way street', claiming that the West's willingness to import DEFA films was not equal to the GDR's willingness to promote understanding of other countries through their films.[3]

This chapter focuses on film relations between East and West Germany during the concluding phase of the Cold War. It looks in particular at West German imports selected by the East German film authorities for exhibition in mainstream cinemas and the shifting patterns of theme and genre characterizing these. It shows how the West German film import came to new prominence in East Germany during the 1980s, reflecting not only a thaw in Cold War cultural politics but also an increasing convergence between the film cultures of the two Germanys.

The statistics for film imports from Western countries confirm Maetzig's claim that the cinema culture of the GDR was genuinely international. The total number of Western imports remained steady from the early 1960s onwards, representing approximately 25 per cent of imports overall, although the levels for individual countries did fluctuate. For France and Italy they were consistently high, reflecting the relatively favourable state of political and cultural contacts between them and the GDR. The pattern of imports from the FRG, by contrast, varied the most among Western countries and mirrored the fraught relations between the two German states on the front line of the Cold War.

At an official level, the FRG was (with the possible exception of the United States)[4] the most mistrusted of all the Western film-producing nations. This is evidenced by the barrage of polemical articles in the East German print media, particularly during the 1960s and 1970s, about production there. A 1970 piece by Horst Knietzsch, the film reviewer for the official party newspaper *Neues Deutschland,* was typical. Knietzsch characterized the West German film industry as driven by commerce and sensationalism, everything that East German culture was not: 'Popular film is used to attract audiences. Film programmes are dominated by the spaghetti western, sadistic war films, entertainment at the level of Heintje [a Dutch child star popular in the FRG], speculation with naked flesh and finally – lowest of all – the pornographic film.'[5]

How were imports from the Federal Republic justified in this context? It was claimed that the films screened were exceptions to the rule, carefully selected imports representing the few humanist films worthy of distribution in a socialist state. Moral and ideological reservations, along with the fear of infiltration of undesirable propaganda or positive images of, as the East German media sometimes put it, 'the other side', resulted in a relative paucity in the number of film imports from West Germany. A total of thirty-two films from the FRG were exhibited between 1970 and 1979, compared with ninety-two from France and seventy-three from the US. In the 1950s, before the borders were sealed and when politicians in the East still held out hopes for a united socialist Germany, the situation was strikingly different: films from the Federal Republic as well as films from the Universum Film Aktiengesellschaft (UFA) studios produced during the Weimar and Nazi eras were common in the cinemas, and Western imports made up as much as 50 per cent of total screenings. Between 1945 and 1959, seventy-four films from the FRG and sixty-eight from pre-1945 Germany were screened. Moreover, those living in East Berlin could amuse themselves in the border cinemas subsidized by the West German government specifically to serve East Berliners with Western genre films. It was not until the first Central Conference for the Cinema Industry on 3 and 4 September 1959 that the notion of a socialist film programme was firmly established and the number of Western imports reduced to approximately one quarter of the total. A further caesura was marked by the building of the Wall in 1961, which cut off access to the border cinemas. From then onwards, the quota of approximately one quarter of annual film imports produced in Western countries was maintained.

In 1961 the annual number of West German imports fell to only seven, and in subsequent years it did not recover to levels comparable with the 1950s. The virtual absence of the West German import persisted into the 1970s, despite the climate of thaw resulting from Willy Brandt's *Ostpolitik* and the ensuing increase in economic and cultural exchange. From the East German perspective, it was not surprising that the West German import was of minor significance at this time. The Basic Treaty of 1972, which formally acknowledged the existence of two separate German states, and Erich Honecker's desire to break down taboos in the cultural sphere, lent new impetus to the arts in the GDR. At a time when the New German Cinema was at its creative peak in West Germany, there were no examples of the movement in East German cinemas. DEFA was enjoying its own renaissance with films that were artistically on a par, such as *Der Dritte* (*The Third,* Egon Günther, 1972), *Die Legende von Paul und Paula* and *Der nackte Mann auf dem Sportplatz* (*The Naked Man on the Sports Field,* Konrad Wolf, 1974). Genre film-making by DEFA (including comedy, westerns and science fiction) was also thriving.

The new impetus behind DEFA film-making in the early 1970s was linked to a general downturn in the reliance on the Western import, although this picture did not last. By the 1980s, levels of films from West Germany had returned to a level comparable with those of the 1950s on account of economic as well as artistic problems within DEFA and the authorities' renewed reliance on Western imports.[6] Whereas in the 1970s there were only thirty-two imports in total, this increased in the 1980s to eighty-five. What distinguished this decade from that of the 1950s, however, was that the films were not only more numerous than before; they also represented significant developments in theme and genre. Firstly, there was a flurry of West German imports dealing with Germany's Nazi past, a subject represented hitherto on the East German circuit almost exclusively by DEFA.[7]

The significance of the import of West German films about Germany's Nazi past can be understood in the context of identity formation in the two German states. The belief that fascist tendencies had failed to be eradicated in the F.R.G. after the end of the Third Reich was a central tenet of East German ideology. By contrast, the G.D.R. saw itself as having made a clean break with the past, being founded on the basis of the self-liberation of communist resistance fighters from fascist oppression. This opposition at the core of official G.D.R. interpretation of the shared past was vital to the construction of East German identity, and was shaped in part by the national film culture. The home-produced contribution towards the interpretation of the Nazi legacy was the 'anti-fascist film', which accounted for approximately 13 per cent of all DEFA feature films.[8] The official East German argument about West German film production was that the National Socialist past had been addressed only intermittently and inadequately.[9] Whilst this assertion may have been valid for the 1950s, West German cinema's later investigations of the past were as crucial to West Germany's postwar production as a whole as the anti-fascist film was to East Germany's.[10] For many reasons, however, a significant number of the West German productions dealing with the Nazi past were not acceptable to the East German selectors. One example was *Die Blechtrommel* (*The Tin Drum,* Volker Schlöndorff, 1979), which was considered very seriously by the highest echelons of the Central Film Authority (Hauptverwaltung Film) but nevertheless not released.[11]

Despite the East German selectors' reluctance to acknowledge that anything akin to the anti-fascist film could emanate from West Germany, there was a clear change in import policy in the 1980s. The decade began with the first and only West German film week, a high-profile diplomatic event closely overseen and planned by the cultural ministries in both states. The week was a significant showcase for West German film. It took place in Dresden, Frankfurt an der Oder and Potsdam from 16 to 23 October 1980. That the selectors chose the two films *David* (Peter Lilienthal, 1978–79) and *Die Ehe der Maria Braun* (*The Marriage of Maria*

*Braun,* Rainer Werner Fassbinder, 1978) could be interpreted as an official signal of the change in attitude towards West German imports dealing with the Nazi past. Whereas *David* never went on general release, *Die Ehe der Maria Braun* was subsequently given mainstream release.

The West German–American co-production *Das Schlangenei (The Serpent's Egg,* Ingmar Bergman, 1977), arguably the first 'anti-fascist' film from West Germany to go on general release in the GDR, was premiered in 1980. In 1981, *Mephisto* (István Szabó, FRG/Hungary/Austria, 1981) was screened in East German cinemas. In 1983, three more West German films with an anti-fascist theme were released: *Die weiße Rose (The White Rose,* Michael Verhoeven, 1982), *Nach Mitternacht (After Midnight,* Wolfgang Gremm, 1981) and *Malou* (Jeanine Meerapfel, 1980). In 1984, *Stern ohne Himmel (Star Without Sky,* Ottokar Runze, 1980), dealing with how Germans treated Jews who had gone into hiding, was released, and in 1985, *Peppermint Frieden (Peppermint Peace,* Marianne S. W. Rosenbaum, 1983) and *Die Grünstein-Variante (The Grünstein Variant,* Bernhard Wicki, 1984) were shown, the latter a ground-breaking co-production between DEFA and the West German Allianz film company. The year 1987 saw the release of *Das Jahr der ruhigen Sonne (Year of the Quiet Sun,* Krzystof Zanussi, Poland/US/FRG, 1984) and 1988, *38 – Heim ins Reich (38 – Back Home to the Fatherland,* Wolfgang Glück, Austria/FRG, 1986), films dealing respectively with the aftermath and the onset of the Second World War. The last West German film about the Nazi past to be released, which focused on the fate of the Jews, was *Auf Wiedersehen Kinder (Au revoir les enfants,* Louis Malle, France/FRG, 1987; GDR, 1989). The number of prints for these was not as high as for popular genre films. *Die Ehe der Maria Braun,* for instance, was circulated with fifteen prints, *Otto – der Film (Otto – The Movie,* Xaver Schwarzenberger, Otto Waalkes, 1985), which was released in the GDR in 1986 and is discussed below, with forty-eight. However, reviews suggest they were received positively by audiences.[12]

Although all the films mentioned were discussed in detail in the press, the critical reception of *Die weiße Rose* was the most overwhelmingly positive. This was rare for a Western import of any kind:

> Verhoeven's film is more than a chronicle of an inglorious chapter of German history. It is also a declaration of his commitment to the shared and decisive battle against fascism and war, irrespective of origin, religion or world view. In one scene, Hans declares, 'You have to tell the people what is really happening!' The contemporary relevance of the message of the film cannot be missed.[13]

Above all, Verhoeven's attempt to question the extent to which the FRG had fully come to terms with the issues of the past met with approval:

> With provocative directness, the director Michael Verhoeven has bravely added an epilogue to the film, the text of which proves that the demon of the German Nazi past has still not been dealt with in the Federal Republic. In the final credits the audience is informed that according to the West German Federal Supreme Court the judgements brought against the anti-fascist resistance group known as 'The White Rose' are correct and that the German Parliament has not yet been prepared to annul the judgements by law.[14]

Arguably the most significant West German release was Fassbinder's *Die Ehe der Maria Braun*. Fassbinder's nineteenth film was his first to be shown in the GDR. The film was highly critical of the way the FRG had achieved the 'Economic Miracle' of the 1950s, and it is not difficult to see why this was the one to mark the official East German recognition of Fassbinder's work. Its narrative substantiated the East German view that the Federal Republic demonstrated a dangerous amnesia about the legacy of fascism and that the 'Economic Miracle' was driven by greed and consumerism. Nevertheless, the film was a provocative work that in other ways did not sit easily with the established East German film culture. Firstly it was, alongside the other films mentioned above, proof that West German film-makers *were* engaged in coming to terms with the Nazi past in a critical manner. Indeed, the complexity of the film must have made some of the DEFA anti-fascist films seem one-dimensional and predictable by comparison. Secondly, the multi-layered narrative and *mise-en-scène* of Fassbinder's richly ironic and ambiguous film left different interpretations open to the audience. This was something the film authorities were usually uneasy about. The figure of Maria, for instance, strongly tinged by the culture of Nazi Germany, is morally suspect, yet highly seductive. Using her sexuality in a manner recalling Marlene Dietrich in *Der blaue Engel* (*The Blue Angel*, Josef von Sternberg, Germany, 1930), she is a powerful and transgressive symbol, in stark contrast to the archetypal DEFA heroine. The exceptional nature of the film was confirmed in a review by Rosemarie Rehahn in the weekly *Wochenpost*: 'The young people leaving the packed cinema alongside me expressed appreciative surprise that Progress [the East German distribution company] is showing such a provocative film.'[15] Rehahn, though not referring to the anti-fascist aspects of the film, did not agree that the film represented an unusual choice. Rather, it continued a strand of West German film-making that had begun to be imported a few years earlier, a strand that, though not explicitly referred to as such, consisted of the first examples of the New German Cinema to be released in the GDR:

> I can think of comparable West German imports in the cinemas, like *The Lost Honour of Katharina Blum* [*Die verlorene Ehre der Katharina Blum*] (directors: Volker Schlöndorff, Margarethe von Trotta), *Knife through the Head* [*Messer im Kopf*] (director: Reinhard Hauff), Ingmar Bergman's *Serpent's Egg*, which was produced in Munich and last but not least, Margarethe von Trotta's *Sisters, or the Balance of Happiness* [*Schwestern oder Die Balance des Glücks*]. Films, which come to terms with an episode of recent history via a personal story.[16]

The films discussed so far could be classified as art-house films, representing a sector of the film distribution network that had undergone expansion from the mid 1970s on. Such films were classified by the authorities as either 'problem films' or 'films with a social message' and were generally screened in 'studio' cinemas, similar to art-house cinemas in the West. The 'studio' cinemas were part of a strategy developed during the mid 1970s to diversify the cinema and appeal to individual social groups. It was not only in the art-house sector that the profile of West German imports was subject to significant change, but also in the sphere of popular genre film, which selectors were increasingly relying upon to prop up the economic viability of the cinema network as a whole. The entertainment film was a staple among the Western imports, and the West German feature film was no exception. The West German crime film, for example, appeared regularly in East German cinema programmes throughout the 1970s. The films were mainly Edgar Wallace adaptations made in the 1960s, such as *Der Hexer* (*The Sorcerer,* Alfred Vohrer, FRG/France, 1964), released in the GDR in 1970, and *Die toten Augen von London* (*The Dead Eyes of London,* Alfred Vohrer, FRG, 1961), released in 1979. However, it was the genre of the western that marked another major shift in policy with regard to West German film imports in the 1980s.

The traditional western was problematic ideologically in the GDR and consequently DEFA produced a socialist version of the genre, known as *Indianerfilme* (Native American films), which enjoyed great success domestically. The focus of the DEFA western was on native Americans rather than the white settlers, but many Hollywood conventions were retained. The first DEFA western, which set the aesthetic parameters for the East German variant, was produced in 1966 and was entitled *Die Söhne der Großen Bärin* (*The Sons of Big Bear,* Josef Mach).[17] A DEFA western was produced every year from 1966 to 1975, but in the late 1970s production began to falter, both in quantitative and qualitative terms. The 'anti-westerns' of New Hollywood provided an acceptable alternative, but by the early 1980s the supply of both these and the DEFA westerns had almost dried up. The fact that it was West German westerns based on literary works by Karl May that were selected to fill the gap left by the decline in the DEFA western was significant, as they were the negative example that had inspired DEFA to produce the homegrown variant in the first place. They had previously been dismissed by East German selectors on the grounds that they did not provide an accurate picture of the past, and critics rejected them as kitsch. The decision to import the Karl May westerns seems to be representative of an ideological compromise on the part of the selectors and an admission that westerns emanating from the FRG would after all be popular with East Germans.

The second development regarding the import of the West German genre film was another new departure: the German comedy. Examples were *Männer* (*Men*, Doris Dörrie, 1985), released in the GDR in 1986, *Seitenstechen* (*In Stitches*, Dieter Pröttel, 1985), released in 1987, and *Ödipussi* (*Oedipussy*, Vicco von Bülow [Loriot], 1988), released in 1988. Unlike the Karl May westerns, these films were set in the contemporary Federal Republic and reflected the taste of West German audiences at the time. This was true also of the series of *Otto* films, the creative force guided by the comedian Otto Waalkes, who made it his business to engage with the East German as well as the West German audience by appearing on East German television. The 1986 release of the first film, *Otto – der Film* (*Otto – the Film*, Xaver Schwarzenberger, Otto Waalkes, 1985), was subject to a type of controversy and ideological discussion at the Central Film Authority that characterized a number of potentially problematic imports. In July 1985, the film was viewed in West Berlin by Erhard Kranz, the head of the Department for Film Selection, and a 'C protocol', effectively a rejection of the film, was issued, with the comment that the decision was 'final'.[18] Nevertheless, it appears that the head of the Central Film Authority, Horst Pehnert, did not agree, since on 10 September the same year he personally authorized its release.

The justifications provided in the accompanying documents testify to the growing convergence of audience tastes in East and West Germany during the last few years of German division. The majority of East Germans were watching West German television; their preferences were shaped by what they saw and East German television and the cinema circuit were forced to compete. The film selectors acknowledged the fact that Waalkes was a popular star in East Germany. Firstly, he was referred to as an 'an extraordinarily prominent artist, who is well-known and respected in the GDR, too',[19] with particular reference being made to an appearance on the East German television variety show called *Ein Kessel Buntes (The Variety Show)*. Secondly, he was described as a 'pure' rather than a political comic: 'His humour aims at human frailties or weaknesses. Because he does not take sides, he is for this reason just still possible for us too'.[20] Finally, and most tellingly, the import was justified by pointing to the need for the East German cinema to keep up with the viewing expectations of the mass audience, which were being raised by television:

> The search for possible compromises when it comes to popular films is also necessary because on television, including East German television, more and more popular films of western provenance are screened to entertain citizens and because not all of these are judged with the usual political-ideological and aesthetic-artistic criteria.[21]

This quotation illustrates the fact that East German selectors were in competition for film premieres and screenings not only with West German but also with East German television. Although the ideological criteria governing selection for national television and cinema networks were the same, the selection committees were separate and their decisions sometimes divergent.

It was Pehnert again who was responsible for the decision in May 1986 to invite Waalkes to the premiere of *Otto* in the GDR. By then, the will to show the film was so great that the refusal by the West German distributor, Tobis Film, to permit one of the two cuts requested by the Central Film Authority was not a hindrance either (a reference to flying to Havana in Cuba was cut, another to enjoying the First World War not).[22] The premiere of the film was, according to the West German magazine *Stern*, due to take place in East and West Berlin simultaneously: 'There's no doubt that Otto's film will be released according to plan on 16 July in 350 cinemas and if Gorbachev continues his policy of détente, the formal premieres will take place simultaneously in East and West Berlin.'[23] The only reason this did not happen was that the prints for the film were not ready for that date.[24] Following the film's premiere in East Berlin on 25 July 1986, it became the most successful film on record in the GDR. In the first eight weeks of release, it was seen by almost 3.5 million East Germans.[25] It was also the most popular film of the decade in the FRG, further evidence of the convergence of tastes in East and West.

A further development in East-West German film relations was the growing number of official contacts between West German film-makers and East German cultural officials, which resulted in a number of official visits to the East. At the 1983 premiere of *Die weiße Rose* at the 'International' in East Berlin, the most prestigious of the GDR's premiere cinemas, the author Mario Krebs, the director Michael Verhoeven, the actress Lena Stolze and the cameraman Alex de Roche all attended.[26] As we have seen in Fassbinder's case, the work of most of the directors associated with the New German Cinema was hardly acknowledged in film programmes. The only film by Wim Wenders to be released – in 1984 – was the crime film *Hammett* (USA, 1982). Though neither the best-known nor the most representative of his films, it was still a breakthrough. In the same year, Wenders made an appearance at the East German Akademie der Künste (Academy of Arts), where two further screenings took place: *Der Stand der Dinge* (*The State of Things,* FRG/Portugal/USA, 1982) and *Nick's Film – Lightning Over Water* (*Lightning Over Water,* FRG, 1980).[27] Margarethe von Trotta, whose work was the best-represented of all the directors associated with the New German Cinema, also visited East Berlin among other cities to discuss her work. Hark Bohm, whose work was favoured by selectors, made an appearance at a festival of films from Hamburg held in Dresden from 6 to 10 April 1989.[28]

Finally, in terms of production, a small number of what were officially termed West German or West Berlin imports were actually collaborations between the West Berlin Allianz film company and DEFA. Made at the DEFA studios in Babelsberg, Potsdam, these productions were further evidence of the growing dialogue between the two Germanys in the sphere of film. *Johann Sebastian Bachs vergebliche Reise in den Ruhm* (*Johann Sebastian Bach's Futile Journey into Fame,* Victor Vicas, 1980; GDR, 1980), a biographical portrait of Bach, was produced by Allianz but made in the DEFA studios. Another film with a musical theme, this time focusing on the relationship between Robert Schumann and Clara Wieck, *Frühlingssinfonie* (*Spring Symphony,* Peter Schamoni, 1983; GDR, 1983), officially referred to by DEFA as a 'film made under contract', was also effectively a co-production. It was filmed on location in the GDR and starred West German actors Herbert Grönemeyer and Natassja Kinski alongside the East German actor Rolf Hoppe. Alfred Hirschmeier, one of the best-known set designers at DEFA, created the sets, and Christiane Dorst, costume designer for DEFA, the costumes.[29] According to Schamoni, the film represented a practical contribution towards peace.[30] The final of the three collaborations was the 'anti-fascist' film mentioned above: *Die Grünstein-Variante.* The script, by Wolfgang Kohlhaase of DEFA and the Swiss film-maker and actor Bernhard Wicki, was adapted from an original radio play by Kohlhaase. The contact between the two developed as a result of a mutual working relationship with the East German film-maker Konrad Wolf.[31] In the press, the film's internationalism was celebrated as a 'cinema phenomenon'.[32] Despite its East German origins, the film's 'anti-fascist' pedigree was played down in favour of an attack on the FRG:

> Although one of the themes is anti-fascism, Bernhard Wicki directs it for the sake of the contemporary associations: in West Berlin and in the FRG today, foreigners, above all Turks, who don't conform or who cause difficulties, are held on remand awaiting deportation, with no hope. The legacy of inhumanity of 1939 thus still casts shadows over the present.[33]

Further examples of collaboration during this period were: *Himmel über Berlin* (*Wings of Desire*, Wim Wenders, FRG, 1987) and the documentary films *Drehort Berlin* (*Location Berlin*, Helga Reidemeister, FRG, 1987) and *Aufrecht Gehen, Rudi Dutschke, Spuren* (*Standing Tall, Rudi Dutschke, Traces*, Helga Reidemeister, FRG, 1988).[34]

## Conclusion

In the Federal Republic, DEFA films were almost totally absent from cinema screens owing to a lack of commercial interest and their limited audience appeal. In the GDR, ideological concerns and the need to develop a distinctive film culture resulted in a comparable deficit of West German films on the mainstream cinema circuit. In the 1980s, however, changes in cinema programming policy occurred, driven largely by developments in television. Television offered more opportunities for both East and West German film productions than cinemas did. In the West, DEFA productions sold quite well to West German television companies in the 1980s. In the East, West German television was at the centre of the battle for the hearts and minds of East Germans. Feature film screenings played as decisive role as news, current affairs and popular programming did in exposing East Germans to West German popular culture. East German television and cinema selectors had little choice but to compete with it in order to maintain the viability and credibility of their own film programmes and to keep audiences satisfied. The ideological framework stayed the same, and the principles of socialist film programming were maintained. However, the actual film import policy towards the Federal Republic changed significantly in the 1980s, reflecting a thaw in Cold War cultural politics and an increasing degree of similarity between the film culture and audience preferences in the two German states.

## Notes

1. Daniela Berghahn, *Hollywood behind the Wall* (Manchester: Manchester University Press, 2005), p. 34.
2. Ibid., p. 34.
3. Kurt Maetzig, 'Für ein Klima des Vertrauens', *Film und Fernsehen*, 14.4 (1986), 6–7 (p. 7).
4. See Rosemary Stott, 'Zwischen Sozialkritik und Blockbuster: Hollywood-Filme in den Kinos der DDR zwischen 1970 und 1989', in *Umworbener Klassenfeind: Das Verhältnis der DDR zu den USA*, ed. by Uta A. Balbier and Christiane Rösch (Berlin: Links, 2006), pp. 144–60.
5. Horst Knietzsch, 'Ausverkauf und erst ein wenig Hoffnung', *Neues Deutschland*, 30 October 1971. No pagination for newspaper articles in the Bundesfilmarchiv, Berlin (hereafter BArch Film).
6. See Rosemary Stott, 'Entertained by the Class Enemy: Cinema Programming Policy in the German Democratic Republic', in *100 Years of European Cinema: Entertainment or Ideology?*, ed. by Diana Holmes and Alison Smith (Manchester: Manchester University Press, 2000), pp. 27–39.
7. A notable exception in the 1970s was the US import *Cabaret* (Bob Fosse, 1972; GDR: 1975).
8. Berghahn, *Hollywood behind the Wall*, p. 64.
9. See the discussion of *Stern ohne Himmel* (*Star Without Sky*, Ottokar Runze, 1980; GDR: 1984) in the in-house publication of the Progress distribution company, which contrasts the DEFA anti-fascist film with West German film culture. Progress, *Kino DDR*, 3 (1984), pp. 23–34.
10. Berghahn, *Hollywood behind the Wall*, p. 59.
11. The reasons why the film was not selected are not given; 'Aktenvermerk. Die Blechtrommel', SAPMO-BArch, 1V B2/2.024/83 (DEFA 1972–1980).
12. See note 15 below for the review of *Die Ehe der Maria Braun* by Rosemarie Rehahn.
13. Felicitas Knöfler, 'Eine Chronik und doch weit mehr', *Tribüne*, 22 February 1983, BArch Film.
14. Raymund Stolze, 'Denn ihr Sprengstoff waren Flugblätter...', *Junge Welt*, 23 February 1983, BArch Film.
15. Rosemarie Rehahn, 'Vom Pech der Glücksmarie', *Wochenpost*, 28 August 1981, BArch Film.
16. Ibid.
17. See Gerd Gemünden, 'Between Karl May and Karl Marx: The DEFA Indianerfilme (1965–1983)', *Film History*, 10 (1998), 399–407.
18. Hauptverwaltung Film, Berlin, C-Protokol, 11 July 1985, BArch Film, HF 5877 (*Otto – Der Film*).
19. Hauptverwaltung Film, 'Aktenvermerk', Berlin, 11 September 1985, BArch Film, HF 5877 (*Otto – Der Film*).
20. Ibid.
21. Ibid.
22. Ibid.
23. *Stern*, 5 May 1986, pp. 70–74.

24. Handwritten note on original cutting from *Stern* (5 May 1986), pp. 70–74, sent by Kranz to Otto, 6 May 1986, BArch Film, HF5877 (*Otto der Film*).

25. 'Statistics from Progress Film Distribution', BArch Film, HF5877 (*Otto der Film*).

26. Horst Knietzsch, 'Tapfer und unbeugsam gekämpft und gestorben: Zu Michael Verhoevens Film "Die weiße Rose"', *Neues Deutschland,* 25 February 1983, BArch Film.

27. Martin Mund, 'Ein Krimi von Wim Wenders', *Weltbühne,* 28 September 1984, BArch Film.

28. Ulf Mallek, 'Filme aus Hamburg in Dresden. *Yasemin* – Plädoyer für Toleranz und Verständnis: Besucher im Gespräch mit dem Regisseur Hark Bohm', *Sächsische Zeitung,* 11 April 1989, BArch Film.

29. Horst Knietzsch, 'Drama einer großen Freundschaft und Liebe', *Neues Deutschland,* 9 November 1983, BArch Film.

30. Philipp Hartung, 'Blaue Blume der Romantik blüht nicht', *Junge Welt,* 8 November 1983, BArch Film.

31. Georg Antosch, 'Schachspiel in der Zelle', *Neue Zeit,* 14 November 1985, BArch Film.

32. Hans-Dieter Tok, 'Drei Männer in einer Zelle', 9 November 1985, BArch Film.

33. Antosch, 'Schachspiel in der Zelle'.

34. Barton Byg, 'DEFA and the Traditions of International Cinema', in *DEFA: East German Cinema, 1946–1992,* ed. by Seán Allan and John Sandford (Oxford: Berghahn, 1999), pp. 22–42 (p. 36).

# 12

# The Shadows of the Past in Germany
## Visual Representation, the Male Hero and the Cold War

*Inge Marszolek*

Focusing on the visualization of the 'male hero' as the embodiment of power, this chapter deals with the significance of visual representations in the battle for cultural hegemony during the Cold War. Although the role of visual representation in this battle is acknowledged, there has been little research on actual published pictures. This fact reflects the enduring suspicion among historians about the source value of images. A hierarchy of sources obtains, and questions of interpretation remain more acute in the case of visual material than for the written word. As Gerhard Paul emphasizes, what we might term 'visual history' cannot offer a royal road to understanding. As elsewhere in cultural history, there is no single methodology, but rather a laboratory where different disciplines explore the linkage between the production and distribution of pictures, and the consumption and embedding of images within different contexts and traditions.[1]

My approach here is to explore the visual strategies deployed to represent governance. To this end the chapter concentrates on published pictures: photographs mostly, but also – and in the case of the GDR especially – photomontage, retouched photos and posters. Using the term 'body of governance' I refer to the process of government for which Foucault coined the term '*gouvernementalité*' in his account of the discourses of power.[2] The visualization of power appears as a tool with which to stabilize and generate political supremacy. In focusing on the politics of the male body as a strategy to regulate and control both individuals and collectives, the chapter explores how visual images constructed the body of governance in the FRG and the GDR in the early Cold War.

A central issue where the visualization of the Cold War is concerned is propaganda. Typically, scholars concentrate on the organization and propagandistic intentions of media products at the expense of the transfer processes through which messages are transported between the superpowers and their respective spheres of control.[3] In this chapter propaganda is defined as a communicative power tool in contradistinction, first, to research that grasps propaganda as a tool working from top to bottom, usually in the context of war or dictatorial regimes. Second, it is set against an (over-)expansion of the concept, for instance, in attempts by scholars to delimit the fields of propaganda and advertising.[4] It remains important in the GDR case to note the broad asymmetry of communication in the public sphere of dictatorships. Yet propagandistic strategies to implement power can persuasively be seen as part of a complex interaction that, in democratic and dictatorial societies alike, do not simply occur from top to bottom.

Although they occupy different positions in the respective power apparatus, the media are the key transfer mechanism within modern societies. Media products are always multifaceted, and their decoding by recipients escapes total control. There is unanimity in current research on images that the meaning of pictures is produced discursively in the way they are embedded in specific social and cultural contexts. For propaganda photography this means that the line between photos that represent direct political propaganda and other media-related photos that also serve the consolidation of power is not always clear. Social documentary photography, for instance, may be described in Rupkalwis's terms as an 'advertisement for socio-political ideas':[5] the photographers documenting farm life in the US by order of the American Farm Security Administration in the 1930s essentially supported the policy of President Roosevelt's New Deal.[6] In the GDR, however, it was regarded with suspicion where it referred to that state and did not fit the self-image of a socialist society despite its self-description as a Workers' and Peasants' State.[7] Wherever photography showed the successes of construction or of industry, it was perceived as a dynamic medium able to initiate or catalyse the process of consolidation according to the regime's intentions. But whenever photographers like Helga Paris showed the underside of towns in the GDR or threatened to exceed the official picture canon, such intentions were suppressed.[8]

The visualization strategies operating in both German societies in the initial postwar years positioned the two states in relation to the past as well as the future. Although both states started from the same point (defeat of the Nazi regime by the Allies, growing knowledge of the atrocities, the more or less vague feeling of guilt), their founding narratives soon differed completely, as did their iconography. With respect to the Federal Republic, Herfried Münkler has shown how the dominant communicative elements are rooted in the experience of the so-called 'miracle years' following the currency reform. The Berlin airlift permitted West Berliners and West Germans to regard themselves as freedom fighters within the realm of the Americanization of popular culture. For the GDR, Münkler emphasizes cultural elements in the collective memory of the anti-fascist narrative of socialist and communist resistance against the Nazis and friendship with the Soviet Union.[9]

The permanent performance of these founding narratives was a necessity. In a manner characteristic of the controlled public sphere of dictatorships, they were implemented in East German society by means of performed rituals and visual representations. Anti-fascist resistance was not part of the collective memory or experiences of most Germans. Communist elites had to invent this tradition and inscribe it into the public sphere to create a group-related fiction of continuity and to achieve the desired identification with the victorious Red Army and with Stalin, formerly the enemies of National Socialism. The building of the memorial at the Buchenwald Concentration Camp, which represented the anti-fascist (and older Christian) myth of sacrifice, resistance and redemption, illustrates how memorialization, political ritual and media transfer provided a frame for the performance of the narrative.[10] Germany's liberal-bourgeois heritage also became part of the visual repertoire, establishing a continuity from Martin Luther and the Peasants' War through the Wars of Liberation and the revolution of 1848 to the founding of the GDR itself. In the GDR, the FRG was represented as the 'other' through the suggestion of its continuity with Nazi Germany and with warmongering and anti-democratic capitalism more generally.

In the West, the political elites were sceptical of using collective symbols to fill a public space perceived as contaminated following National Socialism. The decision for Bonn, a provincial Rhineland town, as capital was itself symptomatic. Not until the 1970s did President Gustav Heinemann insist on the rediscovery of liberal-democratic traditions and symbols for the FRG too. The 1950s had seen more or less ideological notions of the 'Abendland' (Western civilization), with the ideal of Europe as its core, invoked against the 'pragmatic' values of Anglo-American democracy. But these did not impinge significantly on the outlook of the majority.[11] The economic success and popular culture of the 'miracle years' served to implement the Western way of life, promising redemption from guilt through membership of the Western system. The enemy stayed the same: the Russian Bolsheviks, though without the Jewish connotations ascribed to them under National Socialism. In the light of the prevailing totalitarianism theory, the USSR and GDR appeared of the same order as National Socialism. Stalin was like Hitler, and Ulbricht a smaller Hitler.

## The Male Body: The Case of the Soviet-Occupied Zone/GDR

The reciprocity and asymmetry that, as Thomas Lindenberger notes in this volume, characterized the Cold War predicament in Germany also defined the representation of the male body as part of the image reservoir of the Second World War. Here, the Soviet occupation zone and the GDR built on Ferdinand Lassalle's 'socialist agitation of images' (a concept widely invoked in GDR ministries)[12] and on the aesthetic forms of the labour movement of the 1920s. In the GDR, photographs were mistrusted. On the one hand, extreme forms of montage (like that of Heartfield) extended the range of communist propaganda with the intention of producing unambiguous pictures. On the other, the 'retouching' of photographs sought to refine them and eliminate their serial character.[13]

The visualization of the 'body of governance' as the male hero was important in the GDR. Under Soviet occupation the anti-fascist narrative already hinged on identification with the Red Army soldier as the liberator from fascism. This more or less sacred canon could be successfully implemented because it relied on the discursive radicalization of earlier traditions. The visual repertoire of the workers' movement was compatible with that of the Soviet Union, and with the mental images of much of the German population. The crucial difference from the Western zone was that the visualization of the Red Army's victory permitted the returning German communist elite to construct a line of continuity that legitimated both the claim of anti-fascism and communist rule.

The self-representation of the new political leadership proceeded through the construction of self-images that were condensed in allegorical elements of the labour movement and in the heroic male body. If the former aspect is illustrated by the male handshake,[14] which became the emblem of the merger of the two labour parties (the communist KPD and the social-democrat SPD) into the SED, the latter is demonstrated by a photograph that became the icon of victory in East Germany: the image of a Red Army soldier raising the red flag over the Reichstag, which had been arranged for the camera and rehearsed until the composition satisfied the photographer. This photo was distributed everywhere, from schools to the FDJ, the official youth organization of the GDR.

The victorious soldier of the Red Army – representing liberation from fascism and friendship with the USSR – became an iconic figure in the early postwar years. The building of the central memorials in Berlin and elsewhere took this figure into public spaces. These rewrote the aesthetics of nineteenth-century warrior memorials, embodying Soviet power and in the process transporting Stalinist megalomania into East Germany. In the famous memorial in Treptow Park in East Berlin, a huge soldier holding a sword and carrying a child was erected on a mausoleum. Such memorials were central to the politics of memory. On 8 May, the anniversary of the liberation from fascism, Treptow became the stage for mass ceremonies. Appearing on stamps and postcards, the memorial attained a ubiquity in keeping with the status it gained as a key instrument in the propaganda war between East and West following its inauguration on 8 May 1949, just days after the end of the Berlin blockade. The GDR newsreel *Der Augenzeuge* for May started with the inauguration of the memorial and ended with the decision at the Four Allies' Conference to stop the 'mutual' blockade, thus linking the end of the blockade to the image of the Red Army as the liberator from fascism.[15]

The nationalization of this icon of victory was facilitated in the GDR by the way it converged with a tradition of the self-presentation of labour using the figure of the male hero. The proletarian male body was coded with allegorical elements dating back to the workers' movement of the Weimar Republic and earlier. As early as 1900, the body of the male worker was foregrounded in representations such as Max Slevogt's famous untitled May Day print of 1903.[16] This contains all the elements of later images. Representing his male energy and his demand for power, two eagles (symbolizing the Reich) perch on the muscular arms of the worker with the naked torso. Though the worker with a hammer on his belt might be a craftsman, there is an industrial plant in the background; in the Weimar Republic, the proletarian male hero always appeared in an industrial landscape.[17] This figure was partly militarized in the iconography of the Communist Party as 1 May became the *Kampfmai* ('Fighting May Day'). One should also mention the issue of continuity with National Socialist iconography, which further radicalized the image. With the swastika flag in the background, the Nazi soldier typically stood at the worker's side, both figures overlooking the symbols of industry and militarized modernity: a ship, an aircraft and houses.[18]

Propaganda specialists in the SED related closely to this visual tradition. The small changes were mostly influenced by the visual repertoire of the Soviet Union, for instance in the use of female figures to depict rural society. What was new was that the proletarian hero blended with the representation of government, which had not previously been possible in Germany. A difference from National Socialism was that the figure of Hitler was rarely combined with other visual icons, whether by means of juxtaposition or photomontage. By contrast, a photo from 10 July 1958 of the SED's Fifth Party Congress showing Khruschev, Ulbricht and Grotewohl is captioned 'With cheers, the delegates welcome the president of the first German Workers' and Peasants' State, Willy Pieck'.[19] The representatives of government are elevated on a tribune, behind which a youthful male worker on a poster looks boldly to the horizon. Government was thus legitimated using the working hero, who additionally became part of the narratives of state-building and German-Soviet friendship. This male hero was also militarized. A poster for 1 May 1955 copies the aesthetics of Russian realism with its use of coloured and retouched photos.[20] The eye is caught by two men. On the right a worker places his left hand on the shoulder of a soldier with a machine gun; his right holds a flag that flutters in the wind in an evocation of dynamic power. To the background left is a woman with flowers in her hand, probably from the country. Behind and on the left is an industrial plant. The subtitle is 'May 1: Prepared for work and the defence of the Heimat!' With the worker and soldier standing shoulder to shoulder, parallels to the National Socialist poster are obvious.

The young male in particular played a key role in the self-presentation of the GDR. A 1954 poster entitled '5 years SED' shows a young proletarian with a flag bearing the heads of Marx, Engels, Lenin and Stalin; behind him there follow older men and women.[21] The iconography of the GDR, in which individuals became stereotypes, appears here in essential form. As Stefan Wolle observes, the closed society had a closed visual programme that embodied petit-bourgeois hopes for safety, peace, security and the approval of the party. The worker always stood seriously in front of the icons of heavy industry, the children played, the rotund woman farmer laughed, the earnest soldier stood ready to protect socialism, and political representatives like Ulbricht explained the political aims to them all.[22]

The representation of friendship with the USSR drew especially heavily on the imagery of Soviet posters. This strategy aimed to counteract the anti-Soviet prejudices fed both by Nazi propaganda and by the rapes notoriously committed by Red Army soldiers. Photographs of large civil events designed to stage this special friendship were widely disseminated in the media, for example on the occasion of the World Games of Youth and Students in Berlin and Moscow. But there were prohibited images too: the dismantling and relocation of industrial facilities out of the country was not publicly presentable.

The male hero of the GDR was progressively militarized. In the 1950s it became evident that West Germany would be integrated into the Western alliance. The official stance of the GDR was to accuse the FRG of forcing the process of 'remilitarization'. Visual spectacles in the GDR such as those on 1 May copied the Stalinist rituals, with the Volkspolizei (People's Police) taking on the role of the army, which did not yet exist. Yet the leaders of the GDR refrained from openly presenting the militarized special units of the police, which, as in the West, had been organized back in 1946 to protect the borders. Stalin's famous note of 1952 proposed the neutrality of a unified Germany; but it also opened the door to the establishment of an East German army. The Central Committee campaigned to promote rearmament, but willingness among workers to join the organizations designed to feed this process, such as the Gesellschaft für Sport und Technik (Society for Sport and Technology), was not great.

The pressing task facing the authorities was to adapt the discourse of anti-fascism to one of defending socialism and fighting for peace. However, in contrast to the integration of the FRG into the West, which occurred on political and cultural levels, integration into the Warsaw Pact remained controversial in GDR society, as the choice of uniform for the new army illustrates. While the police uniform copied Russian ones, that of the NVA needed to be distinct from both the Bundeswehr and the Soviet army. The adaptation of the traditions of earlier armies was not problematic for the communist elite, but rather mirrored the widespread adaptation of bourgeois traditions. Traditional uniforms and the adoption of the goose-step served to ground the NVA in Prussia's progressive heritage. In a 1956 brochure issued by the Defence Ministry, the NVA soldier was pictured in a line that included a soldier and a militiaman from 1813, a revolutionary seaman recruit and a revolutionary soldier from 1918.[23]

## Male Hero – West: German POWs in 'Russia' and the Citizen in Uniform

In West Germany, the situation was more complex. On the surface, the impression of a rupture was underlined by military occupation and by the Anglo-American programme of reeducation and denazification. But it soon became clear that the task of reconstruction lay in the hands of former members of the second tier of Weimar's bourgeois parties who had kept a low profile during the Third Reich, acting out of a mixture of opportunism and the partial approval of National Socialist politics. This outlook had been shared by most Germans, and it is precisely this affinity between political base and superstructure that helps to account for the surprising success of West German democracy.[24] It may also explain why the political class was hesitant to develop a visual language for West German democracy. There was no founding myth for the FRG beyond Americanization, consumerism and popular culture.

The visual repertoire of National Socialism was cleared out. Now, democracy and citizenship were combined with the promise of consumption held out by the Marshall Plan. The images surrounding the plan were colourful and dynamic, and their simple language was oriented towards American advertising and devoid of martial overtones. In East Germany the handshake symbolized the unity of workers under the tutelage of Marx, Lenin and Stalin; in the West a hand clasping a bottle of Coca-Cola in front of the globe stood for friendship.[25] Shadows of the past remained, however. *Der Spiegel* reprinted a caricature from the British *Daily Mirror* that was subtitled (in an allusion to the Nazi takeover of 1933) 'The Seizure of Power 1947 – new life is blossoming from the ruins'. It showed skeleton hands clinging to a damaged wall in the foreground and behind this the rising moon with a swastika inside. The article beneath reported on the Nazi past of the president of the Berlin police. Apart from the reference to the former Nazis in the postwar administration, the visualization of the past was limited largely to portraits of the perpetrators in trials.[26] In contrast to the East, the male hero appeared contaminated. Identification with the Western soldier was not supported politically, though the black GI distributing chocolate to children did become an image of Americanization and democracy in West Germany.[27] Only after the Berlin airlift could the blank be filled where the public image of the hero was concerned: first with photos of the American and British pilots, and later with that of Elvis Presley arriving as a GI in Bremerhaven, which became an icon of the ascendancy of US popular culture.

In the climate of the incipient Cold War, an image of a heroic German soldier was propagated again in the figure of the POW returning from the USSR. Starting in summer 1948 *Der Spiegel* reported regularly on these POWs, one of the first photos showing a smiling man in civilian clothes who resembled a hiker rather than a soldier.[28] Captured from below, he carries a bundle on a stick over his shoulder. In the distance one can make out the victory column erected in Berlin in 1873 to commemorate the defeat of Denmark in 1864 and France in 1871. The subtitle reads: 'The beginning of life. A citizen of Berlin.' A second photo in the accompanying article shows another POW: a young, wounded, ragged figure in one of the camps where they were accommodated.[29] Here the hero appears broken. These different images illustrate both the contradictory perception of German soldiers in general and how Stalingrad, the image of the soldier at the Russian front and the POW were reinterpreted in the Cold War. Where the visualization process is concerned, the first photograph appears less typical. It does not present the soldier as a victim of war. The perspective, the juxtaposition with the victory column, the civilian clothes and the man's appearance suggest he is filled with optimism and energy, an impression supported by the caption. This image may express the wishful thinking of wives and mothers towards the men returning, who were generally in poor condition.[30] But in contrast to the male hero in the East, the soldier in this photograph is a civilian rather than a military figure. The second image is closer to everyday experience and shows how the Cold War offered the framework for the invention of a new hero: the POW who had suffered in the Stalinist camps. It constructs this figure as the true, tragic and resistant combatant of the Cold War who 'remained human' in the face of the ultimate evil – the Russian.

The Battle of Stalingrad offered a screen for the reinterpretation of images in the Cold War. Thousands of German soldiers were taken prisoner, and many died marching to the camps. Stalingrad allowed the German soldier to reemerge as the real victim – of both the criminal elite of National Socialism and the Bolsheviks. *Der Spiegel* is full of accounts of officers in Stalingrad who recounted the scale of death in the camps and the efforts of German communists to convince them to work for the anti-fascist committees there.[31] Such reports drew on the stereotype of the decent officer trying to protect German soldiers from exploitation by the Soviets and the Germans in the anti-fascist committees. The accompanying visualizations were a curious mix: more or less idyllic images prisoners had drawn of the Russian landscape around the camps, Russians in fur hats dancing among the ruins of Stalingrad, and photographs of leading generals like von Seydlitz and Paulus, the former talking with the Führer, the latter at the Nuremberg trial. There is criticism here of the military elites connected to the National Socialist regime. The new heroes were those who remained decent under severe conditions. The discourse of 'decency' established itself in popular culture in films like *Der Arzt von Stalingrad* (*The Doctor of Stalingrad*, Géza von Radványi, 1958), in works by authors like Rudolf Krämer-Badoni and Heinrich Böll and in the myth of the 'clean' campaign waged by the Wehrmacht.[32]

Frank Biess argues that this view of the POWs as a victimized anti-Bolshevik community, which confirmed Nazi predictions of catastrophic consequences should the Soviets ever emerge victorious, had symbolic and practical uses in postwar West Germany. However, the integration of POWs, he observes, presented a problem with the emergence of a consumerist society in the 1950s. The discourse of Stalingrad partly militated against the shift towards the construction of a masculine citizen capable of participating in the task of reconstruction. POWs who had not collaborated with the anti-fascist committees had proved their moral strength in their resistance to totalitarian propaganda. Who else should the ideal citizen of the new democracy be but the man who had proved immune to totalitarian temptation?[33] But in this configuration, the POW was a bulwark against consumerist, Americanized society, too. Because he was linked to older German masculine moral values like honour and virtue, he stood at odds with an increasingly Americanized popular culture. On a poster for the documentary *Die Glocke von Friedland* (*The Bell of Friedland,* Gerhard Klüh, 1957), for instance, the melancholic face of the returning POW in the foreground looks sorrowfully into the future. He has left the war (a tank in the background) behind. But the present is symbolized by a jazz band and a young couple dancing to rock'n'roll.[34]

Even if the image of the civilian ready to participate in the reconstruction of West Germany did not dominate the visual repertoire in the early years, it represented a hope for the future and eased the introduction of the soldier as a 'citizen in uniform'. *Der Spiegel* and other magazines commented regularly on the new Bundeswehr and its precursor organization, the Bundesgrenzschutz, founded in 1951 as a force to protect West Germany's borders. A photograph of 10 March 1954 showed an elegant couple dancing, he in uniform, she in a fashionable dress. 'Free and self-assured', the subtitle reads. The text continues: 'Future officers of the Bundesgrenzschutz should behave well at public events. Learning to dance is thus part of the training.' The photo was taken at a graduation ball held by the training school of the Bundesgrenzschutz in Lübeck. One year before the Bundeswehr was established, this picture staked out the discursive field for the new German soldier. Integrated into society and domesticated by the modern Americanized woman (wearing make-up, the man's partner resembles cover models of women's magazines), he was able to protect West Germany's borders against the enemy in the East and to represent democratic society in public.[35]

In a photo-story entitled 'They came as volunteers', the magazine *Stern* redrew this figure shortly after the Bundeswehr was founded.[36] The story captured the arrival of the first recruits to the army in Andernach, the air force in Nörvenich and the navy in Wilhelmshaven. The accompanying report stressed that the young men had arrived in their fathers' cars and that their light cases, which carried international hotel stickers, contrasted with the luggage once carried by Wehrmacht soldiers. There is a discrepancy between the photographs and the text. The images show soldiers standing in rows, their hands to the side, some wearing helmets and others in their working uniforms, which, the report explained, were copied from the US Army. However, the text emphasizes how civilianized the life had become: the soldiers were served by women in the canteen, they did not wear the old-fashioned Wehrmacht-style boots and so on.

But the figure of the 'citizen in uniform' was controversial and ran against the demands of army discipline. Shortly after this a *Stern* journalist spent time with the various armed forces in West Germany. He wrote that compared to his precursors, the new German soldier enjoyed substantial liberties and the training was less arduous. Photographs showed the soldiers' nicely furnished rooms, yet the reporter wrote that the women servants and comfortable foam mattresses had disappeared. Another photograph showed soldiers obeying the order to stand still: the fact that their arms were not straight by their side was attributed, rather ironically, to the absence of a seam on the trousers of the working uniforms. A further image presented five good-looking, laughing men hugging each other. In dark and light jackets, ties and bow ties, they were dressed as if for a party. The comment reads: 'These soldiers are "citizens in uniform", as people in Andernach mockingly call them. Next year these easy-going young men will, as officers, instruct our young soldiers.' The question the reporter discussed with the young soldiers in Andernach was whether more discipline, which he thought necessary, could be introduced without reverting to the Prussian drill.

Parallel to rearmament and the debate about the ideal of the democratic soldier came the popularization of the figure of the 'Landser' (a low-ranking soldier in the Wehrmacht). This had its roots in the discursive network of the POW and Stalingrad. Habbo Knoch presumes that in the process of the reconstruction of civil society the 'Landser' became 'the medial alter ego' of part of the male population with a disturbed relation to the Second World War.[37] The *08/15* films based on the novels by Hans Hellmuth Kirst are a case in point, but photographs published by magazines like *Revue* or *Kristall* are also indicative. Published later in the 1950s, the magazines regularly featured photo-stories and soldiers' memories. Photographs were partially selected from the National Socialist propaganda units, but they differed from those published by the Nazis. In the Third Reich, the visual image of the soldier was that of the determined fighter. The mass media now presented a different type, who stood relaxed, a cigarette hanging from his mouth and his uniform unbuttoned, looking not into the horizon of battle but quizzically at the spectator. For Knoch, this deviant and nonmilitary body, which referred visually to values linked to German labour culture, offered 'a non-bourgeois mode for the post-totalitarian reconstruction of values'.[38]

A close look at the photographs reveals that they are compatible with the Americanized 'soldier in uniform' as well as with working-class American stars of pop culture in the mid 1950s such as James Dean or Elvis Presley.

## Conclusion

This examination of the visual representation of the male hero in postwar Germany underlines the asymmetric strategies underpinning visual representations in East and West Germany. However, both German states faced difficulties in positioning themselves using images. The dilemma for both was that the repertoire of images that was implemented in the collective memory was contaminated by the Nazi past. Although the GDR situated itself in relation to the heritage of anti-fascism by appealing to the visual traditions of the communist movement, the representation of the male hero sometimes verged on the aesthetics of National Socialism. Two decades after the collapse of communism, one can ask more freely how such similarities should be interpreted. The images were embedded in different ideologies. In the context of competition between capitalist and communist systems, the official anti-fascism at the heart of the socialist project revealed evident limitations. The extent to which the regime drew on the visual repertoire of the Soviet Union was not always welcome in the GDR. Reinforced by the memory of the brutality of Russian soldiers during the Second World War, the old National Socialist image of the enemy had deep roots in both Germanys. But the biggest problem was the gap between everyday experience and the messages of the pictures. Most images represented socialism optimistically, picturing a utopia that necessarily had to compete with consumerism in the West.

The visual strategies involved in dealing with the past and representing the heritage of the FRG were more complex. The process of democratization and Westernization was linked both to economic reconstruction during the 'miracle years' and to the gap between official policies concerning the National Socialist past and private memories. The discovery of the POW as the male hero promised to redeem public memory by means of private experiences and to avoid a discussion about guilt. For the majority, the experience of victimhood was reinforced by the Cold War. Magazines published mostly private photos, so visual representations detached soldiers from the context of National Socialism. Discourses about the 'citizen in uniform' show how contested the representation of the soldier still was in West German society. Yet images of

Elvis Presley arriving in his GI uniform perhaps shaped the discourse on the new male hero even more.

The impact of visual representation in both societies is ultimately hard to gauge. What is important here is the asymmetry between them. Whereas in the GDR the mass media and visual representations were under the control of the SED, there was no state control of the West German media, even if they were initially under the observant eyes of the Western Allies and, until the *Spiegel* affair of 1962, associated informally with the government. But in both societies the limits of visualization became obvious as the images of the victims of National Socialism were erased. Where the GDR could position itself within anti-fascist traditions, for the FRG the problem of reinventing its identity remained more acute. For West Germany the larger framework of Europe was required – but this is another story.

## Notes

1. Gerhard Paul, 'Von der historischen Bildkunde zur Visual History: Eine Einführung', in *Visual History: Ein Studienbuch,* ed. by Gerhard Paul (Göttingen: Vandenhoeck & Ruprecht, 2006), pp. 7–36 (pp. 26–27).

2. On this term see Susanne Krasmann, 'Gouvernementalität: Zur Kontinuität der Foucaultschen Analytik der Oberfläche', in *Geschichte schreiben mit Foucault,* ed. by Jürgen Martschukat (Frankfurt/Main: Campus, 2002), pp. 79–98.

3. For example Frances Stonor Saunders, *Who Paid the Piper? The CIA and the Cultural Cold War* (London: Granta, 1999).

4. For example Rainer Gries, 'Zur Ästhetik und Architektur von Propagemen: Überlegungen zu einer Propagandageschichte als Kulturgeschichte', in *Kultur der Propaganda: Überlegungen zu einer Propagandageschichte als Kulturgeschichte,* ed. by Rainer Gries and Wolfgang Schmale (Bochum: Winkler, 2005), pp. 9–35.

5. Jörg Rupkalwis, 'Soziologie und Fotografie: Das Bild als Dokument, Fotografie als Methode. Grundlage zu einem Handbuch für optisch-visuelle Kommunikation und Sozialwissenschaften', (unpublished MA dissertation, University of Hamburg, 1994), p. 71. Cited in Jens Jäger, *Photographie: Bilder der Neuzeit. Einführung in die Historische Bildforschung* (Tübingen: Edition Diskord, 2000), p. 107.

6. See Lili Corbus Bezner, *Photography and Politics in America: From the New Deal into the Cold War* (Baltimore: John Hopkins University Press, 1999).

7. Stefan Wolle, 'Die Welt der verlorenen Bilder: Die DDR im visuellen Gedächtnis', in *Visual History,* ed. by Paul, pp. 333–52 (p. 346).

8. Albrecht Wiesener, 'Halle an der Saale – Chemiemetropole oder "Diva in Grau": Zur bildlichen Repräsentation einer Stadt im Sozialismus', in *Die DDR im Bild: Zum Gebrauch der Fotografie im anderen deutschen Staat,* ed. by Karin Hartewig and Alf Lüdtke (Göttingen: Wallstein, 2004), pp. 51–68 (pp. 64–65).

9. Herfried Münkler, 'Das kollektive Gedächtnis der DDR', in *Parteiauftrag: Ein Neues Deutschland: Bilder, Rituale und Symbole der frühen DDR,* ed. by Dieter Vorsteher (Berlin: Koehler & Amelang, 1996), pp. 458–68 (pp. 460–61).

10. Thomas Heimann, *Bilder von Buchenwald: Die Visualisierung des Antifaschismus der DDR (1945–1990)* (Cologne: Böhlau, 2005).

11. Axel Schildt, *Zwischen Abendland und Amerika: Studien zur Erfolgsgeschichte der Bundesrepublik* (Munich: Oldenbourg, 1999), pp. 7–9.

12. Katharina Klotz, 'Foto – Montage – Plakat. Zur politischen Ikonographie der "sozialistischen Sichtagitation" in der frühen DDR', in *Die DDR im Bild*, ed. by Hartewig and Lüdtke, pp. 29–50 (p. 29).

13. Ibid., pp. 31–32.

14. Ibid., p. 35.

15. *Der Augenzeuge,* May 1949, AZ20_1949, < www.wochenschau-archiv.de > (accessed 3 December 2008). I thank Petra Henzler for this suggestion.

16. Udo Achten, *Zum Lichte empor* (Bonn: J.H.W. Dietz Nachf., 1980), p. 82.

17. In *100 Jahre Zukunft: Zur Geschichte des 1.Mai*, ed. by Inge Marszolek (Frankfurt/Main: Büchergilde Gutenberg, 1990), p. 166.

18. Ibid, p. 233 for a front page of the *Bremer Zeitung* from May 1935.

19. *Parteiauftrag,* ed. by Vorsteher, photo 113 (unpaginated).

20. Ibid., photo 190.

21. Ibid., photo 337.

22. Wolle, 'Die Welt der verlorenen Bilder', p. 339.

23. Klaus-Peter Merta, 'Uniformierung als Mittel der Politik', in *Parteiauftrag,* ed. by Vorsteher, pp. 175–86 (p. 181).

24. Wulf Kansteiner, *In Pursuit of German Memory: History, Television, and Politics after Auschwitz* (Athens: Ohio University Press, 2006), p. 184.

25. Peter Zec, *Mythos aus der Flasche: Coca-Cola Culture im 20. Jahrhundert* (Essen: Design Zentrum NRW, 1994), p. 40.

26. Habbo Knoch, *Die Tat als Bild: Fotografien des Holocaust in der deutschen Erinnerungskultur* (Hamburg: Hamburger Edition, 2001), p. 248.

27. Lutz Niethammer, 'Privat-Wirtschaft: Erinnerungsfragmente einer anderen Umerziehung', in *Lebensgeschichte und Sozialkultur im Ruhrgebiet 1930–1960,* ed. by Lutz Niethammer, 3 vols (Bonn: J.H.W. Dietz Nachf., 1983–85), II (1983), pp. 17–105 (p. 22).

28. 'Das war hart genug: 40 Minuten von Frankfurt', *Der Spiegel,* 26 June 1948, pp. 16–17.

29. Ibid., p. 17.

30. Frank Biess, 'Survivors of Totalitarianism: Returning POWs and the Reconstruction of Masculine Citizenship in West Germany, 1945–1955', in *The Miracle Years: A Cultural History of West Germany, 1949–1968,* ed. by Hanna Schissler (Princeton: Princeton University Press, 2001), pp. 57–82 (p. 65).

31. For instance Philipp Humbert, 'Ich bitte erschossen zu werden', *Der Spiegel,* 5 February 1949, pp. 14–16.

32. Knoch, *Die Tat als Bild,* p. 356.

33. Biess, 'Survivors of Totalitarianism', pp. 64–69.

34. Ibid., p. 74.

35. 'Frei und sicher', *Der Spiegel,* 10 March 1954, p. 8.

36. Jochen Grossmann, Ich war Soldat in vier Armeen', *Stern,* 21 April 1956, pp. 11–13.

37. Knoch, *Die Tat als Bild,* p. 449.

38. Ibid., p. 453.

# 13

# Reenacting the First Battle of the Cold War

Post-Wall German Television Confronts the Berlin Airlift in *Die Luftbrücke – Nur der Himmel war frei*

*Tobias Hochscherf* and *Christoph Laucht*

In an episode of the comedy show *Pastewka*, the actor and film producer Til Schweiger offered his host Bastian Pastewka a role in a fictitious historical drama based on the 1973 oil crisis entitled *Der autofreie Sonntag* (*The Car-Free Sunday*). Schweiger explains the project to Pastewka: 'You know the major two-part television films about important events in German history, right? *Sturmflut, Dresden, Die Luftbrücke, Der Tunnel* ... they always follow the same pattern: a historic event, a love story, a woman has to choose between two men, one of them played by the actor Heino Ferch.'[1] With their formulaic narratives and aesthetics, the films Schweiger ridicules –*Die Sturmflut* (*The Flood*, Jorgo Papavassiliou, 2006), *Die Luftbrücke – Nur der Himmel war frei* (*The Airlift – Only the Sky Was Open,* Dror Zahavi, 2005), *Dresden* (2006) and *Der Tunnel* (*The Tunnel,* both Roland Suso Richter, 2001) – illustrate a current trend in German television. The new 'historical event film' or 'histotainment' genre features nostalgically dramatized and romanticized productions loosely based on events in recent German history, especially the Cold War period.

The fact that Schweiger includes *Die Luftbrücke* in his list of such films is no coincidence: not only did Heino Ferch star, but the dramatic story of the Soviet blockade of West Berlin in 1948–49 possessed inherent potential for filmic exploitation. As the Cold War almost turned hot, the airlift presented the Western Allies with a serious strategic and logistical challenge and revealed West Berlin's pivotal geostrategic role in the emerging conflict. To prevent a human tragedy in the Western sectors of the city, American and British forces launched the biggest air transportation operation in history, supplying over two million people with staple foods, coal, petrol and medicine.

While the Berlin blockade cemented the division of Germany and marked the first battle of the Cold War, the perception of the event has undergone remarkable transformation since the late 1940s. Established as the first West German foundation myth in the 1950s, its significance was revived after unification. With considerably fewer eyewitnesses alive at its sixtieth anniversary in 2008, media representations have assumed a crucial role as agencies of popular memory. Putting Germans in the mood for the anniversary, *Die Luftbrücke* plays an important part in the formation of what Alison Landsberg terms 'prosthetic memory', a process through which 'a person does not simply apprehend a historical narrative but takes on a more personal, deeply felt memory of a past event through which he or she did not live'.[2] Since *Die Luftbrücke* does not attempt to provide an accurate historical account of the events surrounding the airlift but blends fact with fiction, it contributes to the 'postmodern' blurring of distinctions between memory and history.

This chapter focuses on *Die Luftbrücke* as the latest attempt to visualize and reinterpret the airlift for a new generation of Germans about fifteen years after unification. It shows how ambivalently the so-called Berlin Republic confronted early Cold War history. Our analysis is divided into three parts, the first of which locates the film within its production context. The second part then examines how the television film partly adopts the West German and American viewpoints of the events of 1948–49 from the time itself, before the final section shows how it simultaneously maps a post-Wall German perspective onto the story of the airlift.

## Production Contexts: TeamWorx's 'Historical Event Films'

In order to tie in with the Berlin airlift's approaching sixtieth anniversary and exploit its dramatic potential, Nico Hofmann's company TeamWorx Television und Film GmbH produced *Die Luftbrücke* for the private broadcaster Sat1 in 2005. Since its foundation in 1998, TeamWorx has emerged as a major player in the German television market through a specialization in 'historical event films' under the umbrella of the UFA company. By relying on conventionalized aesthetics and formulaic storylines, the company was able to produce cost-effective films with high production values within a relatively short filming period. In this way, it made premium television films and miniseries that attracted family audiences at prime time, especially weekends and public holidays, and allowed for the amortization of production costs through expanding ancillary markets such as DVD releases. TeamWorx soon developed into a preferred cooperation partner for various television networks on this account.

Following Sat1's takeover and reorganization by the American media mogul Haim Saban in 2003, *Die Luftbrücke* – which cost €7.5 million – served as a figurehead production for the network. The film was part of a wider strategy to position Sat1 within the competitive German television market between public-service broadcasting and the resourceful Bertelsmann/RTL Group.[3] Aired in two parts at the beginning of the Christmas television season, *Die Luftbrücke* was designed to demonstrate a dedication to 'quality' television. Its high production values are apparent in the use of a number of cinematic devices, including a detailed set design, crane and dolly shots, computer-generated imagery, stunt scenes and a cast of renowned German actors including Ferch, Ulrich Noethen (who received the German Television Award for his performance), Ulrich Tukur and Bettina Zimmermann. The fact that *Die Luftbrücke* was not produced in-house was indicative of Saban's quest for a slimmer organizational structure. Outsourcing helped secure his investment group a profit of some €1.6 billion when he sold the Pro7/Sat1 Group shortly after the premiere.[4]

While the production of the two-part film in Germany exclusively for Sat1 followed the network's strategy of reducing its dependence on American imports in favour of 'home-grown' material, it did not mark a turning away from popular American formats. The network's tactic was rather to copy narrative and aesthetic elements of historical films and, in particular, television dramas made in the US. American television films such as Robert Harmon's biopic of General Dwight D. Eisenhower, *Ike: Countdown to D-Day,* which premiered on Memorial Day 2004 on the private A&E Network to commemorate the sixtieth anniversary of the Allied invasion of Normandy, served as a model for TeamWorx productions like *Die Luftbrücke, Die Mauer – Berlin '61* (*The Wall – Berlin '61,* Hartmut Schoen, 2006), *Das Wunder von Berlin* (*The Miracle of Berlin,* 2008) and *Mogadischu* (2008, both Roland Suso Richter) as well as the biopics *Der Mann aus der Pfalz* (*The Man from Palatinate,* Thomas Schadt, 2009) and *Dutschke* (Stefan Krohmer, 2009). The imitation of American models found graphic expression in the company's name, TeamWorx. This echoed Steven Spielberg's production company DreamWorks, which was itself behind films involving historical subjects such as *Munich* (2005) and *Saving Private Ryan* (1998).[5]

In accordance with their 'American' take on historical drama, Zahavi and Martin Rauhaus, the director and scriptwriter respectively of *Die Luftbrücke,* reduced the political implications of the early Cold War period in favour of a personalized and dramatic storyline. The subtitle *Only the Sky Was Open* is itself suggestive of the commercial and sensationalist exploitation of the story of the Berlin blockade. The film's tendency to overdramatize events is apparent, among other instances, in the historically inaccurate suggestion that the Truman administration used nuclear weapons as a bargaining chip during the crisis.[6] In line with TeamWorx's production strategy, which was aimed at female and male prime-time audiences, such dramatic elements are counterbalanced by romantic ones.[7] Since Hofmann publicly renounced being 'Germany's history teacher',[8] *Die Luftbrücke* transforms the Berlin airlift into a narrative background against which the love story and family drama revolving around US Air Force (USAF) General Turner (Heino Ferch), his German secretary Luise Kielberg (Bettina Zimmermann), her husband Axel (Ulrich Noethen) and their son Michael (Jannis Michel and Leo Natalis) unfolds.[9] With its hybrid formula combining elements of romance, family drama, action film and historical epic, the two parts of *Die Luftbrücke* attracted a high audience share of 31 per cent (8.97 and 7.86 million viewers respectively).[10] Additionally, the DVD release through Warner Brothers guaranteed wide distribution.

## Screening Victors' History: The Berlin Airlift through a West German and an American Lens

*Die Luftbrücke* not only occupied a central place among 'historical event films', it also served contemporary audiences as a chief instance of the 'prosthetic memory' of early postwar German history. One of the picture's most problematic aspects is the way it combines reedited archival footage with new images in the style of the actual newsreels aired by the American-sector broadcaster RIAS at the time. (An example is the use of an actor to play a 'talking head' in the fictitious newsreel 'Berlin Aktuell' ['Berlin Now']). This manipulation of archival footage allowed the producers to reinterpret the events of 1948–49 without any loss of verisimilitude, and serves to portray the airlift exclusively from West German and American perspectives. This is reflected, too, in the concentration on characters from West Berlin and the US alone; Germans living in the Soviet occupation zone are absent and only a few Soviet military leaders, notably Joseph Stalin (Hans-Jürgen Hürrig), appear.

*Die Luftbrücke* establishes its American point of view especially through its heroization of US military personnel. This is apparent, for instance, when Generals Clay (Ulrich Tukur) and Turner, the two officers heading the operation, discuss their strategy. Combining an orchestral soundtrack, an airborne fleet of computer-generated aircraft and cheering West Berliners, the sequence turns American military personnel into heroes. The figure of Turner – almost certainly modelled on the actual USAF General William H. Tunner – is identified as *the* man responsible for the airlift, however. With its focus on an American officer as a central protagonist, the film built on the popular iconography of US soldiers in West Germany during the early postwar years (see Marszolek in this volume). It draws on some of Tunner's achievements as the logistics mastermind behind the airlift and exploits his supposedly charismatic leadership style,[11] for instance when Turner improves the aircrews' motivation by letting them compete against each other to achieve the quickest delivery of goods into West Berlin.

To the extent that the picture focuses on the US military as the driving force behind the operation, it also neglects the contributions of the other two Western occupation powers, Great Britain and France. During a discussion about possible French support, General Clay dryly expresses his opinion that 'the French would perhaps rather help the Russians to build an airfield'. When Turner suggests that it would perhaps help to remind them who had liberated France, Clay replies: 'Colonel, in France the Communists are the second most powerful party – they don't want to hear that the Americans have freed their capital.' Let down by the French who are sympathetic to socialist ideas, Turner and his crews seem to be the free world's last line of defence.

While the French government indeed played no significant role, omission of the British part in the operation reveals a more profoundly distorted interpretation of the events. Although the US provided more material and manpower, Whitehall still contributed considerably to the operation, and British planes flew fuel and salt in particular into West Berlin.[12] *Die Luftbrücke* even manipulates one of the best-known speeches of early German Cold War history in order to excise any reference to British support for the airlift: when Ernst Reuter, the mayor of Berlin, gave his famous address in front of the Reichstag on 9 September 1948, he appealed to the 'People of the world, people of America, England, France and Italy! Look at this city and realize that you cannot, and must not, abandon this city or its people!'[13] The film, by contrast, leaves Reuter to address only the US, France and Italy. While Britain was certainly relegated to the rank of a second-class power after the Second World War, *Die Luftbrücke*'s Americanized version of the foundation myth of the

Berlin airlift is also in part rooted in a general underestimation, in Germany and elsewhere, of Whitehall's early commitment to West Berlin and of British involvement in the early Cold War period more widely.[14]

Just as the film glorifies the US military and ignores the British efforts, it also vilifies the Soviet Union and especially the figure of Stalin – the aggressor behind the blockade. Frequently, its perspective is assimilated to a Western Cold War gaze of 1948–49 in its sinister characterization of the Soviet Union. At the time, Frank Howley, the commandant of the American sector in Berlin, called Stalin's decision to isolate West Berlin 'the most barbarous in history since Genghis Khan reduced conquered cities to pyramids of skulls'.[15] While Stalin was indeed the driving force behind the blockade, *Die Luftbrücke* tends to assign him and his military blame in excess of the historical evidence. It claims, for instance, that Stalin ordered the complete sealing off of the Western sectors of Berlin even at the price of starving women and children and spreading diseases like tuberculosis. In another sequence, two Soviet fighter planes violate one of the three aerial corridors to West Berlin and encroach upon an American plane transporting children, almost forcing it to crash.[16]

In aesthetic terms, *Die Luftbrücke* relies on its set design and gloomy cinematography to reinforce its anti-Soviet ideology. In the scenes set in the Kremlin, dimly lit, smoke-filled, sparsely furnished rooms work together with a monochrome colour scheme and an absence of music (notable in a film heavily reliant on its emotive score) to create a stereotypically 'authoritarian' atmosphere of claustrophobia and oppression. In another sequence, Michael Kielberg refers to the Soviets as an 'evil' people who intend to 'kill us all' when his father Axel, who has just returned from captivity as a POW in the Soviet Union, shows sympathy for the Russians. Although Axel Kielberg explains to his son that it was in fact the Germans who attacked the Soviet Union and left millions dead, many of them fathers like him, his reply seems tokenistic and scarcely detracts from the picture's anti-communist tenor. Axel Kielberg's warning that 'the world is not just black and white' fails to provide a corrective and even appears cynical in the face of the film's overt anti-communism.

While *Die Luftbrücke* marks the Soviet Union as the common enemy of both Americans and West Germans, it presents West Germans as the new allies of the US. The film includes the motif of the so-called *Schokoladenflieger* (chocolate flier) to present the United States' dedication to its former enemies in a most sympathetic light. Shocked by the plight of children in Berlin, First Lt. Gail S. Halvorsen had conquered the hearts of young Berliners by dropping candy bars (using handkerchiefs as parachutes).[17] *Die Luftbrücke* alludes to this incident in a slow-motion scene of children picking up the little parachutes and waving to the USAF pilots. The enduring popularity in Germany of the story of the *Schokoladenflieger* was demonstrated in June 2008 by the media coverage accompanying Halvorsen's visit to Berlin for the sixtieth-anniversary commemorations of the airlift.[18] Like *Die Luftbrücke*, the commemorations themselves drew on an established narrative about the event as a turning point in German history (notably expressed in Henry Ries's iconic photograph 'Landeanflug auf den Flugplatz Berlin-Tempelhof während der Berliner Blockade 1948/49'): away from the Nazi past and the devastation of the Second World War, through the present challenge of confronting Soviet totalitarianism towards an optimistic future under American patronage.[19]

*Die Luftbrücke* uses Halvorsen's candy drops to connect the United States military and its new West German allies. It also follows on from earlier Hollywood productions, including George Seaton's *The Big Lift*, the first major airlift film (1950), Billy Wilder's *A Foreign Affair* (1948), Henry Koster's *Fräulein* (1958) and Norman Taurog's *GI Blues* (1960), in the way it links the stories of the US military operation and its beneficiaries in West Berlin to Turner's romance with his German secretary.[20] Like these films, *Die Luftbrücke* uses an American–West German love affair as a metaphor for foreign relations between the countries. In particular *GI Blues,* starring Elvis Presley, offered a ready precedent for an inflated depiction of fraternization between the US forces and West Germans.[21] Significantly, however, *Die Luftbrücke* shows West Germans on a par with Americans: when General Turner treats Luise Kielberg as an equal partner in their romance, she comes to embody a (retrospectively) emancipated FRG.

## A View from the Berlin Republic: Projecting the Image of a New Germany

The fact that Turner and his secretary are shown as equal partners not only suggests that the Germans in the West acted in a self-confident and (limitedly) sovereign manner even before the foundation of the FRG. It also illuminates how, over a decade after unification, the so-called Berlin Republic now views itself and its prehistory. The years since unification witnessed both the emergence of an Americanization of cultural remembrance (of which the film's reinterpretation of the airlift is a good example) and of a new self-confidence in the FRG. Whilst the Nazi past and the ideological and physical divide of the Cold War had previously dominated postwar German national identity, voices calling for a new, positive patriotism based upon the FRG's achievements before and since unification now became louder. Historical event films like *Die Luftbrücke* often reflected this development, turning Cold War narratives into (West) German foundation myths. In their attempts to retrospectively reinvent the image of post-Wall Germany, they constructed highly subjective accounts of postwar German history by focusing on success stories such as the West Berliner's resilience to the Soviet blockade of Berlin or the West German victory in the 1954 World Cup.[22]

The projection of the image of West Germans as a liberated people through a strong female main character is illustrated particularly well at the end of the second part, when Luise Kielberg and Turner bid farewell as he leaves for Guam. Here *Die Luftbrücke* pays homage to *the* Hollywood wartime classic *Casablanca* (Michael Curtiz, 1942) by restaging – at the close, and in an early postwar German setting at Tempelhof airport – the iconic parting of Rick Blaine (Humphrey Bogart) and Ilsa Lund (Ingrid Bergman) on the Casablanca airfield. Although *Die Luftbrücke* borrows heavily from the cinematography and content of *Casablanca* here, it does not simply replicate this famous sequence but reinterprets it to fit its overall ideology. The scene in *Die Luftbrücke* does not per se reenact the one from *Casablanca,* but rather applies its classic melodramatic ending of renunciation to the context of the airlift in an endeavour to appeal to the emotions of the audience. Unlike Rick Blaine, who insists that Ilsa Lund leave with her husband because otherwise she 'will regret it, maybe not today, maybe not tomorrow, but soon for the rest of [her] life', Luise Kielberg is now the one to confront Turner, saying: 'You know that I can't come with you!' Turner replies understandingly: 'Yes, I know! After some time, I would have seen in your eyes that you paid a price too high for this happiness.' In the end Luise Kielberg – like *Casablanca*'s Ilsa Lund, who leaves the love of her life for the greater good – returns to her husband to reshape postwar (West) Germany.

In *Die Luftbrücke,* the Kielbergs as a family thus symbolize the nucleus of the postwar West German society, past and present. Here the film follows in the vein of recent German films such as *Das Wunder von Bern* (*The Miracle of Bern,* Sönke Wortmann, 2003) and *Good Bye, Lenin!* (Wolfgang Becker, 2003) that combine the fate of an exemplary family with a specific historical event.[23] West Berlin, as the story's setting and a West German 'enclave' in the Soviet zone of occupation, becomes the cradle of the FRG and, ultimately, the Berlin Republic. The final scene of Luise Kielberg and General Turner's parting thus also marks the transition of power from the Allied occupation troops to a democratized (West) German people.

The film promotes a new German identity built on a sense of community and citizenship that was needed in 2005 as much as it was in the late 1940s themselves. It thus suggests that the spirit of the early postwar years might serve as a model for today's Germany as it confronts pressing issues such as unemployment, slower economic growth and the search for a new identity. This is especially apparent in the longing for harmony the film expresses, following a recent trend that Eric Rentschler has referred to as the 'post-wall cinema of consensus'.[24] Potential conflicts such as Michael Kielberg's initial refusal (before his own father's return from a Soviet POW camp) to accept Turner as a surrogate father are usually resolved within a few scenes or left undeveloped. Michael Kielberg, who briefly resorts to alcohol because of his mother's affair, stops drinking as suddenly as he started. After this he even gets along well with the new man in his mother's life, although the overall domestic situation remains difficult.

As part of this quest for harmony, *Die Luftbrücke* neglects Germany's tainted history and is evidently less critical in its representation of Germans than are earlier Hollywood films such as *The Big Lift*. It makes no reference to the Holocaust, and none of its leading characters, it seems, either joined, supported or sympathized with the Nazi Party. By contrast, many show a humanistic commitment that renders Allied reeducation programmes almost unnecessary. Axel Kielberg's selfless efforts following his return from captivity to help patients at a Berlin hospital where he had worked before being drafted into the Wehrmacht illustrate the point particularly well. Instead of confronting his past engagement with National Socialism, *Die Luftbrücke* focuses entirely on his postwar integration into society. Kielberg rehabilitates himself as a democratic West Berliner purely on the basis of his actions as a physician and in caring for his family.

This deflection of war guilt allows a post-Wall German audience to feel empathy for Germans as victims of the Second World War and in the early postwar years. *Die Luftbrücke* pointedly exploits Axel Kielberg's fate as a so-called *Spätheimkehrer* – one of the POWs who returned from Soviet prison camps only years after the war – to this end. While the POWs who returned late were a marker of German defeat in the early postwar era, in the film they embody German victimhood alone. In addition, scenes showing the plight of patients at Axel Kielberg's hospital depict German suffering in a larger dimension. The West Berliners who suffer as a result of the Soviet blockade are depicted as victims of the early Cold War period. In this way, the film extends to the Cold War period the recent discourse about German victimhood in the Second World War that found expression in Günter Grass's novel *Im Krebsgang* (*Crabwalk*, 2002), Jörg Friedrich's book on the bombing of German cities, *Der Brand* (*The Fire: The Bombing of Germany, 1940–1945*, 2002), as well as *Die große Flucht* (*The Great Flight,* 2002), a four-part television documentary by Germany's populist television historian Guido Knopp.

Alongside the striving for harmony, the allegory of the *Wunder* or 'miracle', which has become a common feature of historical films for cinema and television such as the *Das Wunder von Bern* or *Das Wunder von Berlin,* imparts a further and magical element of wish-fulfilment to the treatment of history. The twin processes of economic recovery and Western integration. which were palpable, *Die Luftbrücke* suggests, in West Berlin on the eve of the blockade, mark a 'miraculous' historical turning point. In referring to the currency reform, which saw the introduction of the German Mark to the Western occupation zones in 1948 and indeed marked an economic upturn, the film establishes a direct connection to the so-called 'Economic Miracle' of the 1950s. *Die Luftbrücke* further incorporates the idea of the miracle through the motif of the 'miracle bag', a paper-bag present for children with a surprise inside. When Luise Kielberg explains the significance of these bags to Turner in an emotional and romantic moment, their sudden disappearance during the war becomes a powerful symbol for the loss of hope during National Socialism:

> General, do you know what miracle bags are? When I was eight, they had suddenly appeared: small colourful bags available for five Pfennigs each with liquorice or little animal model figures – once I even got a whistle. But the moment before opening the bag was best because you didn't know what was in it apart from the fact that it must be something nice. But then, suddenly, during the war there were no more bags. There was no time for miracles any longer.

A turning point comes when Turner gives her one of the bags after a happy stopover in the countryside towards the end of the first part of the film. Handed over by the American soldier, the miracle bag becomes a symbol for the airlift operation (which is referred to as a possible miracle in a brief newsreel insert) and for new hope in a postwar Germany that is again learning to be optimistic about the future. Through the use of the symbol, *Die Luftbrücke* acquires the fairy-tale-like quality of melodrama or a romantic comedy. By showing West Berlin as the site where miracles happen, the film rewrites the story of the airlift using the model of 1940s and 1950s-style melodrama, not only as a contemporary urban fairytale but also as a fantasy of reassurance and unity.

The handing over of the miracle bag, like the farewell between Luise Kielberg and Turner, symbolizes the transition of power from the US military to democratized and assertive West Berliners. In the broader political arena, the figure of Mayor Ernst Reuter (Burghart Klaußner) embodies the image of the democratic West Berlin that makes such a handover of power possible. This is particularly clear in one scene when Reuter confronts General Clay shortly after the start of the Soviet blockade and warns him that the continuation of Washington's initial passivity in Berlin will have a detrimental impact on the 'free world'. The film then shows Reuter as the architect of President Dwight D. Eisenhower's 'domino theory' when he explains to Clay how easily 'free countries' would fall like dominoes if Soviet expansionism was not 'contained' or even 'rolled back'.[25]

*Die Luftbrücke* thus creates a powerful myth of resilient West Berliners who defend basic democratic values against Soviet communism. In its portrayal, the film borrows from British myths about the Second World War, especially the 'Blitz spirit' of London's East End that serves to emphasize a sense of belonging and purpose in the fight against a common enemy. *Die Luftbrücke* suggests that West Berliners (and in fact all West Germans) had regained a place among the democratic nations at the time of the airlift precisely at the time the Berlin Republic was asserting its intention to play a more important international role, for example by becoming a permanent member of the United Nations Security Council.

At the same time, Luise Kielberg's abandonment of Turner and her final return to her husband demonstrate that the film is informed by Germany's often contradictory relationship with the United States, which oscillated between strong anti-American sentiment on the one hand, in particular from the educated left, and a significant cultural and often subconscious Americanization on the other. The fact that the Berlin Republic has become a 'critical friend' of the United States – a partner still sympathetic towards America but also critical of its claim to cultural and political hegemony – has become manifest in its refusal to blindly accept the course of US foreign policy, most notably in Chancellor Gerhard Schröder's refusal to support the Iraq War in 2003. *Die Luftbrücke* incorporates the ambivalent transatlantic relationship when it portrays West Germans as grass-roots democrats.

## Conclusions

With its ambiguous portrayal of the saga of the Berlin airlift, *Die Luftbrücke* proved to be a crucial agent in forming post-Wall Germans' 'prosthetic memory'. It thus helped to manufacture a mythical foundation story of the Berlin Republic that was largely based on West German achievements. Its success spawned a number of 'historical event films' based on Cold War history. Private channels such as RTL and public broadcasters such as ZDF and ARD imitated Sat1 by showing comparable films such as *Prager Botschaft* (*Prague Embassy*, RTL, 2007), *Suchkind 312* (*Foundling 312*, ARD, 2007) and the miniseries *Die Frau vom Checkpoint Charlie* (*The Woman from Checkpoint Charlie*, ARD, 2007), as well as the many aforementioned TeamWorx productions. Since *Die Luftbrücke* served as a blueprint for other historical television films and TeamWorx worked for both commercial and public service broadcasters, the film contributed to the blurring of the boundaries between private and public television channels. Admittedly, the interchangeability of recently televised historical dramas, which demonstrate a high degree of convergence in their interpretation of postwar German history, raises questions about whether public service broadcasters are in the end fulfilling their remit to offer alternative views. Given the impact of televised history, this is particularly important. As Robert Brent Toplin has argued in a different context, 'historical films help to shape the thinking of millions'.[26] Nonetheless, Germans were creating a new image of their country when they hosted the 2006 World Cup and celebrated a hitherto unseen new feeling of peaceful and hospitable patriotism. Perhaps here lies *Die Luftbrücke*'s ultimate legacy as a film that is symptomatic of such wider developments.

## Notes

1. *Pastewka*, 'Der Wecker', Sat1, 9 November 2007.

2. Alison Landsberg, *Prosthetic Memory: The Transformation of American Remembrance in the Age of Mass Culture* (New York: Columbia University Press, 2004), p. 2.

3. Andrea Kaiser, 'Schaut auf diese Quote: "Die Luftbrücke – Nur der Himmel war frei," zweiteiliger Fernsehfilm von Dror Zahavi (Regie) und Martin Rauhaus (Buch), Kamera: Gero Steffen, Produktion: TeamWorx (Sat1, 27./28.11.05, 20.15-22.20 Uhr)', *epd Medien*, 7 December 2005, 28–29 (p. 29).

4. See Martin Scheele, 'Haim Saban: Milliardär, Medienmogul, Menschenfänger', *Manager-Magazin*, 5 August 2005, < http://www.manager-magazin.de/koepfe/|artikel/0,2828,368380,00.html > [accessed 10 November 2008].

5. On TeamWorx and Hollywood, see Paul Cooke, '*Dresden* (2006), TeamWorx and *Titanic* (1997): German Wartime Suffering as Hollywood Disaster Movie', *German Life and Letters*, 61.2 (2008), 279–94.

6. See Roger G. Miller, *To Save a City: The Berlin Airlift 1948–1949* (Washington, DC: GPO, 1998), pp. 23–25.

7. On the company's ratings-driven production strategy, see Nico Hofmann interviewed by Martin U. Müller and Thomas Tuma, '"Letztlich geht es nie um Größe"

Der TV-Produzent Nico Hofmann, 50, über Quotenflops, seine aktuelle Sinnkrise, den Blumen-Etat für Schauspieldiven und die Zappeligkeit der Zuschauer', *Der Spiegel*, 26 April 2010, pp. 160-63.

8. Nico Hofmann, interview by Andreas Borcholte and Christian Buß, *Spiegel Online*, 30 November 2008, < http://www.spiegel.de/kultur/gesellschaft/0,1518 ,593049,00.html > [accessed on 3 December 2008].

9. See the interview with Barbara Thielen, 'Weniger ist mehr: Die neue RTL-Fiction-Chefin Barbara Thielen über Events nach der "Sturmflut"', *FAZ*, 19 February 2006, p. 31.

10. Kaiser, 'Schaut auf diese Quote', pp. 28–29.

11. Michael D. Haydock, *City under Siege: The Berlin Blockade and Airlift, 1948–1949* (Washington, DC: Brassey's, 1999), pp. 180–88.

12. Miller, *To Save a City*, pp. 38 and 87–88. Guido Knopp's documentary *Die Luftbrücke – Legende und Wahrheit* (ZDF), which was aired on 24 June 2008, two days before the sixtieth anniversary of the beginning of the airlift, provides a corrective and gives appropriate credit to British contributions.

13. See Ernst Reuter, 'Berlin ruft die Welt', Berlin, 9 September 1948, Stiftung Deutsches Rundfunkarchiv, Frankfurt/Main and Potsdam-Babelsberg, DRA Ffm B4893289. The address can be found online at: < http://www.berlin.de/imperia/ md/audio/rbm-skzl/reuter-rede/ihr_voelker_der_welt.mp3 > [accessed 10 November 2008].

14. Peter Weiler, *Ernest Bevin* (Manchester: Manchester University Press, 1993), p. 179.

15. Frank Howley, *Berlin Command* (New York: Putnam's Sons, 1950), p. 3.

16. William Stivers has shown that the Soviet Union never sealed the city hermetically off; 'The Incomplete Blockade: Soviet Zone Supply of West Berlin, 1948–49', *Diplomatic History*, 21.4 (1997), 569–602.

17. Miller, *To Save a City*, pp. 56–58.

18. For example, Peter Badenhop, 'Süße Freiheit am Himmel über Berlin', *FAZ*, 26 June 2008, p. 3; Christian Mayer, 'Ein Sommer voller Rosinen', *Süddeutsche Zeitung*, 25 June 2008, p. 9. The *Tagesschau*'s evening edition on 26 June 2008 also featured a report on Halvorsen.

19. On the iconography of Ries's photograph, see Christoph Haman, 'Visual History und Geschichtsdidaktik: Beiträge zur Bildkompetenz in der historisch-politischen Bildung' (unpublished doctoral dissertation, Technical University of Berlin, 2007), pp. 86–92.

20. See Georg Schmundt-Thomas, 'Hollywood's Romance of Foreign Policy: American G.I.s and the Conquest of the German Fräulein', *Journal of Popular Film and Television*, 19.4 (1992), 187–97 (p. 187). Scriptwriter Martin Rauhaus also stressed the intentional use of this metaphor on the 'making-of' featurette on the DVD.

21. Here see also Raymond M. Weinstein, 'Occupation G.I. Blues: Post-war Germany During and After Elvis Presley's Tour', *Journal of Popular Culture*, 39.1 (2006), 126–49 (p. 128).

22. On *Das Wunder von Bern* and the creation of a (West) German foundational myth, see Tobias Hochscherf and Christoph Laucht, '"Every Nation Needs a Legend": *The Miracle of Bern* and the Formation of a Postwar Foundational Myth', in *All-Stars and Movie Stars: Sports in Film & History*, ed. by Ron Briley, Michael K.

Schoenecke and Deborah A. Carmichael (Lexington: University Press of Kentucky, 2008), pp. 279–302.

23. See Matthias Uecker, 'Fractured Families – United Countries? Family, Nostalgia and Nation-building in *Das Wunder von Bern* and *Goodbye Lenin!*', *New Cinemas: Journal of Contemporary Film,* 5.3 (2007), 189–200.

24. Eric Rentschler, 'From New German Cinema to the Post-Wall Cinema of Consensus', in *Cinema and Nation,* ed. by Mette Hjort and Scott MacKenzie (London: Routledge, 2000), pp. 260–77.

25. 'Eisenhower Press Conference, April 7, 1954', in *Public Papers of the Presidents of the United States: Dwight D. Eisenhower, 1954* (Washington, DC: GPO, 1960), p. 383.

26. Robert Brent Toplin, *History by Hollywood: The Use and Abuse of the American Past* (Urbana and Chicago: University of Illinois Press, 1996), p. vii.

# 14

# Unusual Censor Readings
## East German Science Fiction and the GDR Ministry of Culture

*Patrick Major*

> It is necessary to dream!
> —Lenin

Science fiction (sf) in East Germany was always a double-edged sword. It was, first, a propagandistic means of inculcating young, mainly male readers with the virtues of science in general, and of Soviet endeavour in particular. After all, this was the age of the atom and Sputnik. This brand of writing reflected a long tradition of 'hard' sf, realist in approach and not limited to Germany, in which rationality and technology solved social problems. Ever since the *Kaiserreich,* the 'production novel', pitting engineering know-how against nature, had flourished in a rapidly modernizing country at the forefront of the second industrial revolution. Bernhard Kellermann's *Der Tunnel* (1913), the epitome of this technocratic subgenre, was among the first pre-war sf novels to be reprised in the GDR in 1950. The positivistic, problem-solving hero fitted neatly into a forward-looking ideology of historical materialism, which itself claimed scientific validity, and he fulfilled the literary expectations of socialist realism. In the 1950s reality appeared to be getting ahead of fantasy, culminating in the manned orbit of Earth by Gagarin in April 1961. The better future that socialism promised its citizenry was presented as an extrapolation of the present, and sf as a blueprint of a proximate and realizable future. Yet even within the GDR's lifetime, East German fans looked back with bemusement on the 'heroic' phase of space travel and 'scientomania' of the late 1950s and 1960s, when optimism reigned.[1]

However, sf had developed another strain of 'soft', social sf, using a virtual future as a safe vantage from which to criticize the present. Fiction had long rehearsed various false utopias, but recently under the Weimar Republic political sf had flourished on both left and right.[2] Moreover, in the postwar Soviet Union the Strugatsky brothers, widely available in the GDR, pioneered their brand of 'social fantasy', which has been labelled 'apocalyptic realism'.[3] In Poland, Stanislaw Lem, the giant of Eastern-bloc sf, perfected a variant of tongue-in-cheek satire, poking fun at mankind's grandiose attempts to control nature and evolution. It was no surprise that, from the 1970s and into the 1980s, East German sf became more critical of aspects of GDR society, a tolerated vehicle for 'safe' satire in which dystopias, too, could appear in coded analogues.[4] Nonetheless, even positively couched utopias had faced ideological problems ever since Engels disowned utopian socialism in the 1880s. There was also a suspicion that any 'dreaming ahead' showed too much affinity with Ernst Bloch's humanist Marxism, outlined in his 'principle of hope', which had fallen into official disfavour in the later 1950s. Instead, sf supporters had to cite Lenin's words: 'Yes, dream, young man! Dream! … Dreams drive forward progress. The greatest dream is socialism'.[5] Yet just as Marxism-Leninism was suspicious of utopian visions that might compete with its own purportedly more scientific futurology, it was hostile to dystopian prognostications. The 'awful warning' story familiar to Western readers, where fictive nuclear devastation or genetic mutation occurred with almost monotonous regularity, was reserved to the imperialist opposition in the cultural Cold War. Socialist sf preferred to look on the bright side. Despite this containment of cultural pessimism, and despite GDR authors' willingness to locate 'negative' stories in the so-called 'non-socialist exterior', however, these could easily be read as criticisms closer to home.

An excellent overview of East German sf literature, offering case studies of the salient works by decade, has recently been provided by Sonja Fritzsche, and DEFA's sf film repertoire has been ably covered by Evan Torner.[6] What follows is more limited in scope – a brief exploration of the negotiation of cultural power between sf writers and the state, in the shape of the Ministry of Culture and its publishing section.[7] Fritzsche did not ignore this relationship but it remained tangential to her textual analyses and was presented as largely consensual. The ideological contortions before publication were often as interesting as the texts. From 1951 on, every mainstream publishing house in East Germany had to vet manuscripts submitted to it and provide at least one external reader's report to the ministry, as well as its own in-house assessment, prior to licensing. Although those involved did not like the word, preferring to view their activities as a form of editorializing, this was pre-censorship.[8] Where for Western publishers the selection of texts was more informal and market-driven, the formalized socialist system has left a rich archival seam that illustrates the state's sensitivities to potential criticism. Initially, sf had been denigrated by the socialist literary establishment as part of the pulp fiction allegedly endemic to 'bourgeois', capitalist publishing. It struggled for a place among the 'entertainment literature' eventually deemed necessary for GDR popular enlightenment, never entirely escaping the stigma of the 'smut and trash' literature associated with the Anglo-Saxons since long before the Cold War.[9] Consequently, even the poor table manners of fictional heroes could strike a prim censor as 'American brashness'.[10] This culturally subordinate status actually protected sf politically, allowing more deviant ideas to slip through the net than occurred with the more closely scrutinized *Belletristik* or 'high' literature.

There were also reasons specific to the recent past as to why sf was a suspect genre. Some bestselling earlier authors had lent their talents to National Socialism.[11] Above all, Hans Dominik, a Siemens engineer writing from 1922 to 1945, had championed the colonial domination of racial inferiors by the technocratic leadership principle and was bound to strike GDR cultural critics as politically incorrect.[12] The dilemma for the country's literary guardians was the recognition that popular fiction sold well and was a potentially valuable mass communicator. As a later GDR history of the genre admitted: 'New ideas had to be inserted into an ever popular but discredited mantle – the unspoken demand for an "anti-fascist Dominik"'.[13] Even beyond 1945, the GDR's continuity thesis suggested fascistoid tendencies in the FRG and its popular culture. Creations such as Perry Rhodan, the popular space adventurer launched in the West in 1961 by the Moewig publishing house, were attacked as intergalactic imperialists who treated species on other planets as the new 'subhumans' or *Untermenschen*.[14] For the GDR's moral police, sf always smacked of past and present fifth columnism.

Sf is of further Cold War significance for the transnationalism of the writers and readers who made up the sf community, continuously in touch with developments elsewhere, even beyond the Iron Curtain. Until the building of the Berlin Wall in 1961, Western pulp fiction was directly accessible in West Berlin, and early GDR efforts had a compensatory function. Nevertheless, the open border meant that wholesome alternatives could not be too strait-laced. Some of the cover illustrations for the 'yellow series' by the publishing house Das Neue Berlin, in lush four-colour offset, were unusual in a deprived GDR economy, apparently designed to compete with Western glitz. Sf transnationalism even permeated the corps of lectors who reviewed the manuscripts. These were, at least in the GDR's later years, a group of cultural functionaries and co-opted experts who interceded for a limited liberalization of utopian writing and an opening of the literary scene.

Though the various publishers in East Germany were involved in self-censorship, they were increasingly aware, with bestsellers often selling out within days, that they were brokering a cultural shortage item and could invoke the economic factor, thus undermining the ideological orthodoxy of earlier years.[15] In some cases, publishing rights were syndicated to publishers in West Germany, Austria or Switzerland, adding the lure of hard currency to decision-making. Since in the early years publishers were competing for scarce paper supplies, they were under internal pressure to see their authors through, perhaps bending the rules in the process. One publisher argued: 'A good reader's report is ideal. But it is not always good to have a good reader. He hardly leaves space for one's own thoughts, removing insights and forcing repetitions.'[16] Thus editors and lectors, many of them aspiring authors, walked a tightrope between satisfying readership demand and controlling cultural supply. Moreover, as Angela and Karlheinz Steinmüller, the favourite sf authors of the 1980s, admitted, there was considerable self-censorship by writers themselves. Passages bound to meet resistance could be offered as sacrificial decoys to get others through.[17]

As long as the barbs were aimed at the West, satirical sf could be justified within the system. The very first futuristic novel published in the GDR, Ludwig Turek's *Die goldene Kugel* (*The Golden Sphere,* 1949), was a vehicle for attacking American militarism and atomic diplomacy. The Venusian aliens visiting Earth in their giant sphere have the power to mind-read and thus reveal the capitalist aggressors' supposed war plans, concluding: 'Those who began with the invention of the atomic bomb belong to the family of Faschissapos [an amalgam of *Faschismus,* SS, SA and *Gestapo*]'.[18] In a typical GDR sleight of hand, 'antifascist' is extended into the present to include US global imperialism. It was also possible to translate liberal authors from the West and publish them in the East, but with guidance for the reader. One of these was Ray Bradbury, viewed as a critic, albeit inconsistent, of capitalism. According to the supportive publisher's report for *Fahrenheit 451,* Bradbury manifested 'the <u>condemnation</u> [original emphasis] of the imperialist system as an anti-human system', yet was trapped in his bourgeois humanism, which 'dissipates itself partly in fatalism, partly in the refuge of warning. Bradbury does not see how the world has changed in our century and is still changing and that a real long-term future for humanity is emerging in the form of real socialism.'[19] Consequently, Western authors usually came with a health warning in form of an afterword by a literary scholar. It also suited East Germany's purposes to publish self-critical West German authors as evidence of the 'inhumane nature of imperialism', including one collection under the instructive title *Thought Control*.[20] Yet the so-called 'new wave' of 1960s writing by Western authors, like the fiction of J.G. Ballard or the paranoid world of Philip Dick, usually remained off-limits, although forbidden works circulated via the samizdat network.

## Policing the Future

To return to the initial category of 'hard' sf in the pioneering days of the 1950s, or what Fritzsche calls 'utopian realism',[21] one usually encounters more straightforward variants of the production novel, typically set at a research institute, in which technocratic elites solve the social problems of the future. These include Klaus Kunkel's *Heißes Metall* (*Hot Metal*, 1952) and Heinz Vieweg's *Ultrasymet bleibt geheim* (*Ultrasymet Stays Secret*, 1955), in which a new wonder substance is coveted by Western intelligence services in what is effectively a futuristic spy novel, the classic Stalinist subgenre. In line with Soviet restrictions on utopian writing, many of these works represent a proximate future, and their ulterior object is to recruit young, mainly male readers to take an interest in the natural sciences. Vieweg's *Die zweite Sonne* (*The Second Sun*, 1958), for instance, contains helpful diagrams more reminiscent of a physics textbook than a fictional work. Authors like H.L. Fahlberg and Eberhardt del'Antonio were themselves working scientists who placed a premium on realism. Del'Antonio's *Gigantum* (1957) was perhaps the GDR's classic sf paean to progress, where in a Germany of circa 1980 we encounter a Paris-Moscow monorail, weather control and a Dresden Rocket Works (an extrapolation of the real but ill-fated Saxon air industry), as well as the superfuel 'transuran gigantum', a uranium derivative.[22] For the ministry's readers it was important that technical feats remained in the realm of the plausible, or as one lector put it: 'not so much "literature of the stars" as earthly utopia with its feet on the ground'.[23] Flights of fancy could be given harsh reality checks by literal-minded lectors. Readers with a scientific background (and a slide rule) sometimes prepared their own calculations to disprove flight times or orbits. One complained that a photon spaceship was behaving 'as if a hussar was shooting from a T-34 with bow and arrow and steering the tank with reins'.[24]

Nor did the scientific optimists ignore the conditions of social reproduction. But the future was depicted in the way communism liked to see itself, with automation having overcome the alienation of production-line work and permitting a degree of leisure activity in a GDR that in reality was struggling to produce enough bath-plugs. In Günther Krupkat's *Die Unsichtbaren* (*The Invisible Ones,* 1958) we read of a future Berlin where:

> Magically, a new city had arisen on the banks of the Spree from the smoke-blackened ruins of the last world war. In bold architecture rose buildings with shimmering porcelain facades and glass walls ... At first sight not much was reminiscent of the old Berlin. Those who turned off the great new traffic arteries into the new capital, found amidst dreamlike parks many a place from the past: the Red Rathaus or the famous avenue 'Unter den Linden' with the Brandenburg Gate and other historical buildings.
>
> Colourful life swirled through the streets of the metropolis. Some Berliners had just finished their four-hour work day and were sitting comfortably under the multi-coloured awnings and umbrellas of pavement cafés or park restaurants, promenaded along the avenues by the Spree, went shopping or visited the universities to hear the afternoon lectures ...
>
> Some early birds had headed north in their mini-planes for a quick sunbathe at the Baltic. It was only a twenty-minute flight to the Big Beach, Berlin's 'bathing strip'. There, too, as in the capital, atomic climate conditioners pleasantly prewarmed the cool sea breeze before it was allowed to touch the skin of the Athenians of the Spree.[25]

One may smile at such optimism, or suspect that super-technology was creating hostages to fortune in a technically backward GDR. From the 1970s on, technological utopias were increasingly banished to the realms of parody.[26] But for Krupkat's lector, technocracy was in danger of usurping party rule: 'Thus can the world of tomorrow evolve in an author's head who throughout the novel, consciously or unconsciously – at any rate systematically – avoids the terms 'socialism' and 'socialist'. Instead he presents the reader (in whom he wishes to bring out the humanist [which smacked of neutralism to SED hardliners] – or are we mistaken in this assumption?) with a veneer of anti-capitalism and ideologically co-existential pseudo-democratism.'[27] This reader called for a ban, but the work appeared nevertheless. Popular authors evidently had more leeway than hardliners liked.

The other great trend in technocratic sf into the 1960s was space. Sputnik's launch in October 1957, a Soviet lunar probe in 1959 and Gagarin's spaceflight in April 1961 delivered an obvious propaganda theme. Astronomy even entered the school curriculum and the popular imagination, if we are to believe Wolfgang Becker's film *Good Bye, Lenin!* (2002), which is framed by the protagonist's schoolboy idolization of Sigmund Jähn, the GDR's only cosmonaut. Krupkat especially fictionalized a space race in which the Soviets were superior (as they were, in the early years at least). In *Gefangene des ewigen Kreises* (*Prisoners of the Eternal Circle*, 1956) Soviet cosmonauts scored points by rescuing stranded US astronauts. *Die große Grenze* (*The Great Frontier,* 1960) depicted a US that stooped to dirty tricks to foil rival socialist missions to the moon. Here, the geopolitical realities of the opposing power blocs in the 1960s are still discernible in the future and have not been overcome in a total utopia of world government. The East German authorities were also keen to exploit the enthusiasm surrounding the space race. Under pressure from the FDJ leadership, its house publisher, Neues Leben, explained how it was going to make its home-grown comic, *Mosaik,* less humanist and more socialist, using space:

> Voyages in spaceships and landings on other planets will, besides utopian-fantastical aspects, be depicted as the real possibility of a not all-too distant future which is theoretically worked out even today. The Sputniks have finally proven that in the socialist societal order the creative forces of man are unfolding at an unheard-of pace. Dig and Dag [the comicbook heroes of *Mosaik*] will experience the formation of the solar system, the development of organic life, the construction, significance and function of artificial satellites, rockets with photon drive etc., and alongside them the reader will understand that the materialist explanation of the world leaves no place for religious superstition.[28]

Indeed, at the end of 1958 *Mosaik* produced its space series, in which its diminutive heroes, Dig and Dag, visited the planet Neos, which bore striking similarities to an idealized GDR.[29] Moreover, there were gentle reminders that there could not even be implied criticism of the Soviet space programme. Where Eberhardt del'Antonio had written in *Gigantum* 'fled to a safe distance' before a launch, the ministry suggested 'withdrew', 'since during a rocket launch in a socialist country surely no one needs to flee'.[30]

Yet space sf meant more than spaceships. The exploration of other planets raised the thorny issue of 'space colonialism'. It was expected that capitalist astronauts would oppress other planets. But socialist cosmonauts? Lectors agonized over whether visitors should be allowed to intervene in more primitive societies.[31] There could be difficulties over the reasons for the move into the cosmos: too much emphasis on (Western) Malthusianism and the need to evacuate an overpopulated home planet, and the censor's blue pencil could intervene.[32] Outer space was also the only place where GDR authors could address the nuclear threat, suggesting that 'capitalist' civilizations on other planets had wiped themselves out or been held in check by 'socialist' cultures. In Lothar Weise's

*Das Geheimnis des Transpluto* (*The Secret of Transpluto*, 1962) the reader encounters all-too-rare GDR imagery of mushroom clouds and fleeing people, though quarantined to outer space. Otherwise, the atom was reserved exclusively for peaceful means, a glorified form of dynamite to blast away obstacles or even turn the moon into an artificial sun, minus the inconvenient truth of fallout. More problematic was the encounter with more advanced alien species. Were they completely alien, or cosmic cousins of the earthlings? Almost invariably Eastern-bloc sf decided that not only were aliens humanoid, they were communist too. Only the most progressive humanoids of the future would be capable of the technological advancement and moral detachment to make the leap into the cosmos. Like the first aliens encountered in Soviet sf in Ivan Efremov's 1959 story 'Cor Serpentis', they were friendly and part of the intergalactic human family.[33]

Breaking this rule could mean trouble. A minor storm erupted around the publication of Horst Müller's *Kurs Ganymed* (*Vector Ganymede*, 1962), which illustrates many of the official hopes and fears surrounding utopian literature in the GDR. Here an Earth spaceship, the *Terra*, discovers humanoid life on one of Jupiter's satellites: survivors of the planet Phaeton, destroyed in a nuclear accident. The Ganymeders live a perilous existence, bombarded by the radioactive rays of Jupiter and ruled autocratically by a council of elders that uses hypnotic beams to impose its will. In the first draft, infanticide was even endemic in the collapsing society, over which a caesarist dictator, Admiral Gotan, emerges. The Ministry of the Interior's reader had reservations about whether the manuscript reflected 'the glowing perspective of the free humanity of socialism and communism, of a great community of scientifically, morally and culturally superior men and women'. The crew of the *Terra* did not live up to these high ideals, exhibiting 'a decidedly vulgar, sloppy and common mental attitude' and 'vestiges of a hostile ideology'.[34] This was typical of Ministry concerns that sf was too closely tied to pulp fiction, with its hard-boiled idioms and instinct to sensationalize. Müller, a librarian, had been at pains to make his novel accessible to a teenage readership, but as one assessor saw it: 'This is teddy boy slang with a racial superiority complex. Again and again we encounter how repulsively, vulgarly and primitively the 'best astronauts' and scientific heroes of the earth converse with one another. Can one imagine Titov and Gagarin seeing their goal in such conversations?'[35]

Other 'inconsistencies' included the Ganymeders' banning of theatres, refusal to show old films and closure of state archives – all issues too close to home in the second wave of de-Stalinization in late 1961, months before the book appeared. The newspaper *Neues Deutschland*, the SED's house organ, published a negative review, pointing out the dangers of sf in the wrong hands: 'Even today imperialists use utopian literature to heighten war hysteria. The polemic "1989" [sic] by Orwell was already notorious, an insult to the socialist future which even the author held to be "inevitable".' The novel's suggestion of mind control under socialism raised concerns that it might be a belated attack on Stalinism, since 'here, too, it is deemed possible that in the most advanced social order a single person attains dictatorial power and endangers the existence of an entire people.'[36] The publisher, VEB Domowina, a provincial press catering for the Sorb minority in the GDR, was held to account. One representative remained adamant, citing Walter Ulbricht's call for the right of the socialist citizen to be well entertained, while another recanted, condemning the Marxist inconsistency of a barbaric Ganymedan superstructure and a technologically advanced infrastructure. Domowina published no more fiction.[37]

The problem with *Kurs Ganymed* was that several of its barbs pointed too obviously eastwards. Other authors became adept at writing political fantasies in which the *overt* target was the US. or the 'West', but where *covert* 'side swipes' were aimed against real, existing socialism. For instance, Gert Prokop's hugely successful Timothy Truckle novels, written in a hard-boiled, Chandleresque style but set in a twenty-first century US that had sealed itself off behind a giant security dome, had resonance closer to home. Prokop introduced an American secret police that, with its 'security officials on public transport, the house and private police, undercover people in the leisure centres, the street and house monitors', must for many readers have evoked parallels with the GDR.[38] Consumerism was another double-edged topic. It was routine to parody the West's mindless consumerism, but as Honecker's 'unity of economic and social policy' became the mantra of the 1970s, materialism as a means to social pacification had domestic resonance, too. A range of taboo themes, such as environmental pollution, bureaucracy and dictatorship, could be tackled indirectly in the utopian novel – themes other contemporary literature would not touch. Rarely did authors directly challenge the system per se, and when they did there was an immediate response. When Peter Lorenz attempted to satirize the GDR's appalling environmental record by having a fictional biologist deal with the contaminated river 'Elaas' (easily recognizable as 'Saale'), a visit from the Stasi ensured that this became 'Elaat'.[39]

The organization of sf fans in clubs was another source of official concern, for the authorities did not quite know what to make of these otherworldly aficionados. Initially, these were outgrowths of existing GDR cultural organizations such as the Kulturbund, or of libraries, like the

Utopia-Klub set up in Hoyerswerda. A minor stir occurred in 1973 with the closing down of the Stanislaw-Lem-Klub at the Technical University in Dresden. Professors in the physics department suspected individuals of harbouring anti-Soviet views in their literary discussions, and one student-author, Rolf Krohn, was exmatriculated for life.[40] Significantly, editors at the Verlag Neues Berlin such as Ekkehard Redlin took the alienated student authors under their wing, publishing a number of works against the grain after the mid 1970s.[41] By the 1980s – despite an attempt to canalize alternative sf into a series of official *Lichtjahr* (*Light Year*) anthologies – a series of home-produced fanzines, essentially a form of semi-official samizdat, were being produced, in which fans unashamedly used the English term 'science fiction', rather than the preferred 'utopian literature' or 'novel of the future'.

By the early 1970s GDR sf was growing out of its fixation with the space age to become aimed at an audience of not only adolescents and science students, but adults with higher literary expectations. The main exponents of the satirical social fantasy were Johanna and Günter Braun. Their debut sf novel, *Der Irrtum des großen Zauberers* (*The Grand Sorcerer's Mistake*, 1972), established their theme of the querying of technology as an end in itself. The technocratic dictator at the heart of the novel, Multiplikato, ultimately fails to manipulate the populace in a machine culture. According to the lector:

> The book is a social satire on dictators who bet everything on cybernetics in their fascist or neo-fascist power craze, and so see the means of eternal rule. At the same time the authors portray the case of a reactionary symbiosis of man and machine (robots) and make clear that cybernetics is not the panacea for progress, but that it is up to the social order in which it is applied. This is stated clearly, there are no nebulous passages, no theorizing about utopian visions and no demonization of cybernetics.[42]

It was clear the censor realized there were problems with technology in the GDR too, and it was permissible to make tongue-in-cheek criticism. In the context of the handover of power from Ulbricht to Honecker in 1971, however, the novel had more than allegorical significance. Ulbricht's discredited 1960s modernization programme, the New Economic System, would appear to have been the unspoken target. But more fundamental criticism of socialism per se was not encouraged. Other authors such as Gerhard Branstner or Herbert Ziergiebel pursued instead a line of picaresque whimsy, though short of the biting irony of Lem in Poland, let alone the macabre humour of Philip K. Dick in the West.[43]

The Brauns became the flagship writers of the 1970s, critiquing the problems of overproduction in *Unheimliche Erscheinungsformen auf Omega XI* (*Uncanny Creatures on Omega XI*, 1974) or the sexual tribulations of adolescence in a prudish society in *Bitterfisch* (*Bitter Fish*, 1974). As the Verlag Neues Berlin lector Adolf Sckerl wrote, the former contained acceptable 'small satirical asides against weaknesses in contemporary society, such as too many formalities or obstructing creativity. Justifiable side swipes and incidental reader pleasure without having to delve too deeply.' Humour, for Sckerl, was a means to convey 'something of the Brechtian "friendliness of socialism" to the reader'.[44] In 1974 Neues Leben even printed a Western edition of *Irrtum* for publication in the FRG. Yet by the late 1970s titles such as *Conviva Ludibundus* (1978) encountered more readers' resistance to the 'ironic scattergun fire at many deficiencies in our own society'.[45] The controversial topics of environmentalism or bureaucratic obstructionism touched a raw nerve. Eventually, in 1983, the Brauns applied to have their next work, *Das kugeltranszendentale Vorhaben* (*The Spherical Transcendental Project*), licensed for publication in the FRG. Its suggestions of a state subliminally putting words into the mouths of its citizens proved too much. After nine months of prevarication by the Ministry of Culture, the Brauns went ahead unilaterally with their 'tamizdat' option ('publishing over there'), to be followed by two other Western publications in 1984 and 1985, which both adopted a more critical tone against the GDR. Curiously enough, Braun manuscripts were still submitted in the East, but editors at Neues Berlin were becoming increasingly concerned that criticism was moving from the particular to the general and relying on the assumption that the 'average reader' would misunderstand the subtext: 'He or she will chortle at the critically intended passages and read past the misinterpretations. More worrying is that false conclusions will penetrate into the unconscious and lodge there as truth.'[46] In this case, a reduced print run and an explanatory jacket text were thought a wise precaution.

The Steinmüllers, another married couple working as a successful authorial team in the 1980s, also fought running battles with the censor. Their major work, *Andymon: Eine Weltraum-Utopie* (*Andymon: A Space Utopia*, 1982), voted the most popular GDR sf work ever, was also celebrated by the Verlag Neues Leben as an 'anti-end-of-time-story', refuting the cultural pessimism prevalent in the West.[47] Nevertheless, suggestions in early drafts that the Earth from which the novel's ark-like spaceship was travelling had been consumed in a nuclear conflagration had to be excised. Instead the couple had to insert passages suggesting that any civilization capable of launching an intergalactic starship must have been benign:[48] 'Would a state with high military spending or a crisis-riven society be able to afford such fantastic investments?'[49] But gone was the blithe optimism of the 1960s space operas of their older colleague Krupkat. When the Earth colonists arrive at Andymon, the project of terraforming the planet proves to be a more difficult proposition than previous novels had suggested. The spaceship orbits the planet for years, 'going round in circles', as do the crew, who start to factionalize. The better future becomes a holy grail that is permanently on the horizon, until a section of the crew decides to start the thousand-year trip back to Earth. Other younger authors parodied the impossibility of utopia even more blatantly. Andrea Melzer's short story, 'Vorstoß nach Andromeda' ('Advance to Andromeda'), published in the GDR's final year, presents the absurd situation in which each of a series of spaceships sent to Andromeda is overtaken by another superior craft, until the final mission aborts the project. Likewise, the aliens appearing in GDR sf became ever more inscrutable, 'degenerating' from the insectlike to the plantlike and to a collective entity with which no meaningful contact was possible.[50]

## Conclusion

Just like Western sf, the genre underwent a journey from propagandistic tool to subversive medium between the 1950s and the 1980s. This was partly the result of real shortcomings in the Eastern bloc's space programme after the initial successes, as well as economic failings in the GDR. But it also reflected an international dialogue within the genre, invoking more critical voices like the Strugatskys and Lem in the East, who were to some extent protected by their reputations in the West, and US authors such as Ursula LeGuin and Ray Bradbury, who became part of the critical sf canon available in the GDR. Indeed, despite the censorship of authors like George Orwell, Philip Dick or the angry young men of the British 'new wave' such as Brian Aldiss and J.G. Ballard, Eastern sf was penetrated by Western styles to a far greater extent than vice versa. The setting of so many Eastern novels in generically 'Western' environments, overtly to lampoon them, in fact provided a form of escapist tourism for the Eastern reader denied the real possibility of travel, who may thus have read them for the 'wrong' reasons.[51] Yet limited satire became tolerated within the ministerial censorship remit. The GDR's present problems came increasingly to inhabit the imagination of the future. There was also a 'knowing' internal discourse between lectors on the open secret of social problems within the GDR that could not be simply ignored. As long as basic taboos such as the failings of bureaucracy or environmental pollution were observed, it remained possible to satirize GDR society. In most cases the censor clearly realized what was being stated but preferred to promote a limited public sphere, if only to show that there was no total censorship. We can thus speak of a mutually interdependent relationship between writer, reader and censor who inhabited a rather closed but safe world, not unlike the fictional universe generated in the process. All the while, publishers' growing reliance on the sale of popular literature to meet their production plans meant an exponential growth in the number of novels and short stories. Whereas the 1950s and 1960s had seen a handful of stories appearing each year, by the 1980s it was dozens. Quality control and ideological policing came under increasing pressure, and many forgettable works were published.

At the same time it was possible for mainstream authors to cross over to sf to experiment with ideas barred from conventional works. Anna Seghers and Christa Wolf produced one fantasy story each, in Wolf's case exploring gender identity through sex change.[52] When Franz Fühmann wrote his *Saiäns-Fiktschen* (1981), the ministry's lector immediately realized that the text 'referred all too linearly to [GDR] reality and acts as cheap satire'.[53] Nevertheless it was deemed worth the risk of publication, if only to call Fühmann's bluff and 'break off the barbs' of his virtual criticisms, and on the assumption that Western journalists reviewing it would find it too dense to comprehend. (Again, we see the censor consciously acting as the average and not the discerning reader.) And despite the relative ghettoization of the genre, sf followed the same introspective trends as 'high' literature. As the Steinmüllers later observed, contrary to the GDR's project to promote collectivism: 'Like the literature of the GDR overall, science fiction trod the path from We to Me.'[54]

As an exercise in censorship history, sf also demonstrates the rather blurred borderline between writers and publishers. The latter were painfully aware that in the GDR there was a shortage of the sort of literature abounding in the West. This was partly a problem of physical reproduction. Most fiction in the GDR still appeared in hardback. The even greater shortage of popular authors meant that these could exploit their scarcity value. Publishers, and to an extent external readers, who earned fees for their reports, had an interest in bending the rules to bring their commodity onto the market and justify their existence. The Ministry of Culture itself appears to have exercised an arm's-length arbitrating role, intervening only in extreme cases. Of course, there are methodological problems when dealing with a source that only records its successes and those manuscripts that were published. The 'desk drawer' manuscripts that never made it into print are more difficult to reconstruct, and there were surely many of these. Nevertheless, one frequently encounters cases where publishers were encouraging greater marketability and less didacticism from authors: the medium was beginning to take control of the message. Finally, however, East German sf's paradox was that it was too predictable and tied to the present to achieve genuinely great status, so it rarely rose above the average. But that meant that inevitably it dealt more with the here and now of the GDR, and thus, as the grandiose predictions of the 1950s failed to materialize, even the most 'positive' of futures must have felt like criticisms of the present.

## Notes

My thanks to Warwick University's Humanities Research Centre for funding to conduct research for this article.

1. Erik Simon and Olaf R. Spittel, *Die Science-Fiction der DDR: Autoren und Werke. Ein Lexikon* (East Berlin: Das Neue Berlin, 1988), p. 40.
2. Peter S. Fisher, *Fantasy and Politics: Visions of the Future in the Weimar Republic* (Madison: University of Wisconsin Press, 1991).
3. Yvonne Howell, *Apocalyptic Realism: The Science Fiction of Arkady and Boris Strugatsky* (New York: Lang, 1994).
4. Karsten Kruschel, *Spielwelten zwischen Wunschbild und Warnbild: Eutopisches und Dystopisches in der SF-Literatur der DDR in den achtziger Jahren* (Passau: EDFC, 1995).
5. Heinrich Taut, 'Träume, Träume, wo ist eure Wonne: Wie soll unsere Zukunftsliteratur aussehen?', *Sonntag*, 44 (1962), p. 11.
6. Sonja Fritzsche, *Science Fiction Literature in East Germany* (Bern: Lang, 2006); Evan Torner, 'To the End of a Universe: The (Brief) History of the DEFA Science Fiction Film', in *From Weimar to Christiania: German and Scandinavian Studies in Context*, ed. by Florence Feiereisen and Kyle Frackman (Newcastle upon Tyne: Cambridge Scholars Publishing, 2007), pp. 89–106.
7. See Simone Barck, Martina Langermann and Siegfried Lokatis, *'Jedes Buch ein Abenteuer': Zensur-System und literarische Öffentlichkeiten in der DDR bis Ende der sechziger Jahre* (Berlin: Akademie, 2002).
8. Robert Darnton, *Berlin Journal, 1989–90* (New York: Norton, 1991), pp. 188–203.
9. Patrick Major, '"Trash and Smut": Germany's Culture Wars against Pulp Fiction', in *Mass Media, Culture and Society in Twentieth-Century Germany*, ed. by Karl-Christian Fuehrer and Corey Ross (London: Palgrave, 2006), pp. 234–50.
10. Ursula Kroszewsky-Tschesno, 'Gutachten', 2 December 1961, BArch, DR-1/5102.
11. *Sun Koh oder der Erbe von Atlantis und andere deutsche Supermänner: Paul Alfred Müller, alias Lok Myler, alias Freder van Holk – Leben und Werk*, ed. by Heinz Galle and Markus R. Bauer (Zurich: SSI, 2003).
12. William Baldwin Fischer, *The Empire Strikes Out: Kurd Lasswitz, Hans Dominik and the Development of German Science Fiction* (Bowling Green: Bowling Green State University Popular Press, 1984).

13. Simon and Spittel, *Die Science-Fiction der DDR*, pp. 20–21.
14. Adolf Sckerl, 'Zu dem Manuskript "Gedankenkontrolle",' 5 May 1978, BArch, DR-1/5432.
15. Star authors sometimes complained at inadequate print runs. See Del'Antonio to Baum, 11 April 1957, BArch, DR-1/3941.
16. Günther Claus, 'Verlagsgutachten', n.d., BArch, DR-1/3635.
17. Angela Steinmüller and Karlheinz Steinmüller, *Vorgriff auf das Lichte Morgen: Studien zur DDR-Science Fiction* (Passau: EDFC, 1995), pp. 164–65.
18. Ludwig Turek, *Die goldene Kugel* (East Berlin: Dietz, 1949), p. 141.
19. Prof. Dr. Bussewitz, 'Gutachten', n.d., BArch, DR-1/3630. Original emphasis.
20. Ekkehard Redlin, 'Verlagsgutachten', 16 March 1978, BArch, DR-1/5432.
21. Fritzsche, *Science Fiction*, pp. 83–84.
22. Paul Friedländer, 'Eberhard del'Antonio "Gigantum"', 30 November 1956, BArch, DR-1/3941.
23. Ruth Greuner on del'Antonio's *Heimkehr der Vorfahren* (1966), 1 November 1965, BArch, DR-1/3626a.
24. Rudi Schönfeld, 'Einzelbemerkungen zu dem Manuskript (Müller's *Kurs Ganymed*) nach den jeweiligen Seiten', 12 November 1961, BArch, DR-1/3360.
25. Günther Krupkat, *Die Unsichtbaren* (Berlin: Das Neue Berlin, 1958), pp. 117–18.
26. This is not to claim technology disappeared from later stories. See Thomas Hartung, *Die Science Fiction der DDR von 1980–1990: Eine unterhaltungsliterarische Bestandsaufnahme unter thematischem und wirkungsspezifischem Aspekt* (Magdeburg: Block, 1992).
27. Arno Hausmann, 22 December 1957, BArch, DR-1/5019.
28. Verlag Neues Leben, 'Information an das Sekretariat des Zentralrates über MOSAIK', n.d., BArch-SAPMO, DY 30/IV 2/9.04/684.
29. Hannes Hegen, *Die Reise ins All* (reprint; Berlin: Junge Welt, 1999).
30. Ministry of Culture (Sektor Schöne Literatur) to Verlag Das Neue Berlin, 20 July 1959, BArch, DR-1/3941. A year later Marshal Nedelin, head of Soviet missile forces, and 100 ground crew were killed in the Baikonur disaster of October 1960. See James Harford, *Korolev: How One Man Masterminded the Soviet Drive to Beat America to the Moon* (New York: Wiley, 1997), pp. 119–20.
31. Dr Hubert Laitko, 'Bemerkungen zum Erzählungsband "Marsmenschen"', 8 August 1967, BArch, DR-1/3626a.
32. Dr Siegfried Seidel on Richard Groß, *Der Mann aus dem anderen Jahrtausend* (1961), 17 January 1961, BArch, DR-1/3988.
33. Patrick Major, 'Communist Science Fiction in the Cold War', *Cold War History*, 4.1 (2003), 71–96 (pp. 81–85).
34. Rudi Schönfeld, 'Gesamteinschätzung des vorliegenden Manuskriptes "Kurs Ganymed"', [12 November 1961], BArch, DR-1/3360.
35. Rudi Schönfeld, 12 November 1961, 'Einzelbemerkungen zu dem Manuskript nach den jeweiligen Seiten', BArch, DR-1/3360.
36. Oberstudienrat Hans-Joachim Laabs, 'Ganymed auf falschem Kurs: Bemerkungen zur utopischen Literatur in der DDR', *Neues Deutschland,* 9 March 1963.
37. Ruth Krenn, 'Stellungnahme', 13 March 1963, BArch, DR-1/3360.
38. Gert Prokop, *Wer stiehlt schon Unterschenkel?* (Berlin: Neues Berlin, 1977), p. 207.

39. Steinmüller and Steinmüller, *Vorgriff,* p. 168.

40. *Berichte aus der Parallelwelt: Die Geschichte des Science Fiction-Fandoms in der DDR,* ed. by Wolfgang Both and others (Passau: EDFC, 1998), pp. 39–55.

41. Ekkehard Redlin, 'Verlagsgutachten', 10 January 1985, BArch, DR-1/3633a.

42. Udo Birkenholz, 'Lektorat: Titel: Der Irrtum des großen Zauberers', 5 December 1971, BArch, DR-1/3545.

43. Fritzsche, *Science Fiction,* pp. 126–28.

44. Adolf Sckerl, 'Zu dem Manuskript', 30 November 1972, BArch, DR-1/3630.

45. Adolf Sckerl, 'Zu dem Manuskript "Conviva Ludibundus"', 23 October 1977, BArch, DR-1/5431.

46. Ekkehard Redlin, 'Gutachten' on *Die Geburt des Pantamannes* (1988), 3 December 1986, BArch, DR-1/3635.

47. Helmut Fickelscherer, 'Verlagsgutachten', 24 July 1981, BArch, DR-1/3557a.

48. Angela and Karlheinz Steinmüller, '"Dieser Satz hat das Buch gerettet": Der lange Weg zu Andymon', in Angela and Karlheinz Steinmüller, *Andymon: Eine Weltraum-Utopie* (Berlin: Shayol, 2004), pp. 291–302.

49. Angela and Karlheinz Steinmüller, *Andymon: Eine Weltraum-Utopie* (Berlin: Neues Leben, 1982), p. 276.

50. Annette Breitenfeld, *Die Begegnung mit außerirdischen Lebensformen: Untersuchungen zur Science-Fiction-Literatur der DDR* (Wetzlar: Förderkreis Phantastik, 1994), pp. 157-58.

51. Hartung, *Science Fiction,* pp. 78–79.

52. Fritzsche, *Science Fiction,* pp. 166–68 and 191.

53. Heinz Entner, 'Gutachten', n.d., BArch, DR-1/2157.

54. Steinmüller and Steinmüller, *Vorgriff,* p. 35.

# 15

# Funerals in Berlin
## The Geopolitical and Cultural Spaces of the Cold War
### *James Chapman*

> James Bond had always found Berlin a glum, inimical city varnished on the Western side with a brittle veneer of gimcrack polish, rather like the chromium 'trim' on American motor cars. He walked to the Kurfürstendamm, sat in the Café Marquardt, drank an espresso and moodily watched the obedient queues of pedestrians waiting for the 'Go' sign on the traffic lights while the shiny stream of cars went through their dangerous quadrille at the busy intersection. It was cold outside and the sharp wind from the Russian steppes whipped at the girls' skirts and at the waterproofs of the impatient hurrying men each with the inevitable briefcase tucked under his arm.
>
> —'The Living Daylights' (1962)

There are two dominant images of Berlin in Anglo-American popular culture.[1] One is the Berlin of the Weimar years: the hedonistic, libidinous nightlife capital of Europe imagined in films such as Josef von Sternberg's *Der blaue Engel* (*The Blue Angel*, 1930) and evoked in Christopher Isherwood's semi-autobiographical novel *Goodbye to Berlin* (1939), which in turn provided the source for the films *I Am a Camera* (Henry Cornelius, 1955) and *Cabaret* (Bob Fosse, 1972). This is a Berlin of vice and promiscuity, a society caught between the economic problems that beset Germany in the aftermath of the First World War and the rise of National Socialism. The other is the divided city of the Cold War: the bleak, austere urban landscape described in spy stories by authors like Ian Fleming, Len Deighton and John le Carré, which received its definitive representation in the novel (1963) and film *The Spy Who Came in from the Cold* (Martin Ritt, 1965). This is a Berlin of political intrigue and moral duplicity, a world of treachery and paranoia, a city on the front line of the Cold War that has become a battleground for competing ideologies, a place of existential anxieties and despair.

A prominent trend in the recent historiography of the Cold War has focused on what is sometimes termed 'the battle for hearts and minds'. The Cold War was not won or lost on the battlefield but was contested in diplomatic and cultural arenas. Historians have only recently begun to acknowledge the role of political and cultural propaganda during the Cold War.[2] Propaganda did not win the Cold War, but it did play an important role in mobilizing public opinion and, in the West, in discrediting communism in the eyes of publics at home and abroad. The role of propaganda (or public diplomacy, as it has come to be known in current US discourse) was particularly significant when tensions were at their height in the two decades following 1945. This was the period when the Cold War threatened to erupt into a 'hot war' over flashpoints such as the Berlin blockade of 1948–49 and the Cuban Missile Crisis of 1962. State agencies were proactive in commissioning film and popular fiction that could be employed for ideological ends: the US Central Intelligence Agency, for example, covertly financed an animated film version of George Orwell's anti-Stalinist novel *Animal Farm* (John Halas and Joy Batchelor, 1954).[3] As in the Second World War, however, cultural providers were also happy to turn their hands to Cold War propaganda without official encouragement. This is particularly evident in the ideological and cultural politics of spy fiction in literature and film during the 1950s and 1960s.

Cold War themes characterize a range of genres from science fiction – exemplified by Hollywood invasion narratives of the 1950s such as *War of the Worlds* (Byron Haskin, 1953) and *Invasion of the Body Snatchers* (Don Siegel, 1955) – to the Biblical epic, where they were overlaid onto the contest between religious freedom and oppression in *The Robe* (Henry Koster, 1953) and *The Ten Commandments* (Cecil B. DeMille, 1956). However, the archetypal Cold War genre was the spy thriller, its very subject matter – espionage, intrigue, international politics – ideally suited to dramatizing the conflict. Geopolitics are at the heart of the spy genre. As Michael Denning observes in *Cover Stories,* his cultural history of the British literary spy thriller:

> Since the turn of the [twentieth] century, spy thrillers have been 'cover stories' for our culture, collective fantasies in the imagination of the English-speaking world, paralleling reality, expressing what they wish to conceal, and telling the 'History of Contemporary Society'. Thrillers use cover stories about assumed identities and double agents, and take their plots from cover stories of the daily news; and their tales of spies, moles and the secret service

have become a cover story, translating the political and cultural transformations of the twentieth century into the intrigues of a shadow world of secret agents.[4]

The spy thriller, of course, predates the Cold War – the genre emerged in the late Victorian and Edwardian periods in the work of authors such as William Le Queux, E. Phillips Oppenheim and Erskine Childers. But it underwent its most overtly propagandistic phase during the 1950s and 1960s, when it became the perfect vehicle for dramatizing the ideological and cultural contests of the Cold War.

The Cold War was significant in other ways for the development of the spy thriller. In general the genre has divided into two lineages. Denning posits a difference between, on the one hand, 'magical thrillers where there is a clear contest between good and evil with a virtuous hero defeating an alien and evil villain' and, on the other, 'existential thrillers which play on a dialectic of good and evil overdetermined by moral dilemmas, by moves from innocence to experience, and by identity crises, the discovery in the double agent that the self may be evil'.[5] This difference may also be described as that between the 'sensational' and the 'realist' spy thriller. The 'magical' or 'sensational' spy thriller emphasizes action and adventure via narratives of rapid movement and pursuit, and is posited on a relatively straightforward Manichean universe of 'good' and 'evil'. It is exemplified by the novels, and films based on them, of John Buchan and 'Sapper' (pen name of H.C. McNeile) – and, preeminently, by the James Bond adventures of Ian Fleming. Non-British examples include the novels of Robert Ludlum and Tom Clancy. The 'existential' or 'realist' thriller, by contrast, is characterized by greater psychological realism and uses the motif of spying to explore ethical and moral questions. It inhabits the seedier side of the secret world of espionage and is notable for its sense of ambiguity. It is exemplified by the works of W. Somerset Maugham, Graham Greene, John le Carré and Len Deighton. The characteristic protagonist of Cold War fiction is the professional spy, a figure crossing both the sensational and realist lineages who is exemplified by such diverse archetypes as Fleming's high-living Bond (who first appeared in *Casino Royale* in 1953), William Haggard's levelheaded Charles Russell (1958), le Carré's anonymous George Smiley (1961), Deighton's nameless anti-hero (1962), christened Harry Palmer in the films, and Adam Hall's hard man Quiller (1965).

Cold War spy fiction was typically posited on a set of ideological oppositions that map onto the geopolitical landscape of a divided Europe. The same basic structures underpin both the sensational and realistic tendencies. Umberto Eco has argued that the Bond novels are structured around an overlapping set of structural oppositions between characters (Bond/villain) and ideologies (free world/Soviet Union).[6] Bond was conceived as a cold warrior: all but one of the novels written during the 1950s were set against a Cold War background in which the villain was employed directly or indirectly by the Soviet organ of vengeance SMERSH (a contraction of *'Smiert Spionam'* – 'Death to Spies' – which had been a wartime counter-espionage agency responsible for tracking down and killing traitors and deserters). While, following the relatively realistic *Casino Royale,* the plots of the Bond books became increasingly far-fetched, including attempts to destroy London with a nuclear rocket (*Moonraker,* 1955) and to 'topple' US missile tests by radio-beam from a base in the Caribbean (*Dr No,* 1958), they all remained rooted in Cold War geopolitics until *Thunderball* (1961), which introduced a new adversary for Bond in the form of the international criminal syndicate SPECTRE (the Special Executive for Counter-Intelligence, Terrorism, Revenge and Extortion).

Sensational and melodramatic devices are entirely absent from the novels of John le Carré, yet the secret world his recurring protagonist, George Smiley, inhabits is the same as Bond's. Smiley, too, is engaged in combating the Soviet bloc, masterminding schemes to penetrate East German intelligence (*The Spy Who Came in from the Cold*) and to trick enemy spymaster 'Karla' into defecting to the West (*Smiley's People,* 1979). Despite their downbeat tone, these plots assert British mastery of the secret war as surely as Fleming's self-consciously mythical *From Russia, with Love* (1957). Le Carré's narratives are structured along lines similar to Fleming's in their representation of opposing ideologies (Englishness/communism), but there is more of a grey area in between that allows for greater psychological complexity and moral ambiguity. In *Tinker, Tailor, Soldier, Spy* (1974) the traitor Bill Haydon (inspired by Kim Philby) is motivated not by affection for communism but by his dislike of America. Both Fleming and le Carré had first-hand knowledge of the world they described: Fleming had been assistant to the Director of Naval Intelligence during the Second World War, while le Carré is the pseudonym of David Cornwell, a former MI5 British intelligence officer.

A further characteristic of Cold War British spy fiction is the extent to which the secret war between East and West is mapped onto a history of Anglo-German enmity. In *The Spy Who Came in from the Cold,* for example, the East German intelligence service, rather than the Soviet Union, is the target of a British conspiracy. And in *Moonraker* the villain, Drax, turns out to be a fanatical ex-Nazi with a pathological hatred of the British whose conspiracy to destroy their capital is backed by the Soviets. To an extent this reflects the fact that German villains had figured prominently in British spy fiction since before the First World War. The displacement of Cold War narratives onto Anglo-German relations also serves an ideological purpose in so far as it suggests that Britain is engaged in a continuous struggle against the same enemy.

This ideological context helps to explain the prominence of Berlin as a site of Cold War *Realpolitik* in the spy thriller. Berlin was on the front line of the conflict, both geographically and figuratively, ever since the division of the city into zones of occupation as agreed at the Yalta Conference of February 1945. Thereafter Berlin became the focal point of tensions in the deteriorating relationship between East and West. The Soviet blockade in 1948–49 cemented the division of Berlin – and effectively of the whole of Germany – into two administrative and political units. Between the end of the blockade in 1949 and the building of the Berlin Wall in August 1961 there was relatively free traffic between the sectors. The Berlin Wall became a physical symbol of the 'Iron Curtain' across Europe described some fifteen years earlier by Winston Churchill in his famous speech at Fulton, Missouri (5 March 1946). The motif of the border crossing, through a military checkpoint or across the Wall itself, became a recurring device of spy fiction during these years. It represented, from a Western perspective, escape from the oppression of the East to the freedom of the West. From a German perspective, furthermore, it represented the possibility of mobility across an artificial border that divided one nation into two.

Berlin prior to the building of the Wall had been the location for many minor US spy films, including *Berlin Express* (Jacques Tourneur, 1948) and *Night People* (Nunnally Johnson, 1954), and one major British film: Carol Reed's *The Man Between* (1953). *The Man Between* was a follow-up to Reed's classic *The Third Man* (1949), scripted by Graham Greene, and like the earlier film it was produced for London Films by Alexander Korda. The Hungarian émigré Korda had been involved in British wartime propaganda activities, producing and directing films such as *The Lion Has Wings* (1939) and *Lady Hamilton* (1941), an association that continued in the postwar period when he produced *State Secret* (Sidney Gilliat, 1950), a thriller set in the fictitious East European state of 'Vosnia' and the first British film to dramatize life behind the Iron Curtain. Korda was involved in Cold War propaganda: in 1953 he acted as a front for donations to the magazine *Encounter* from the Information Research Department of the Foreign Office, the British government's covert anti-communist propaganda agency.[7] There is reason to believe that *The Man Between* may have been officially sanctioned, since much of it was shot on location in West Berlin (as *The Third Man* had been in Vienna), which required cooperation from various authorities. Reed was denied permission to film in East Berlin, however, and so re-created it in areas like the Moritzplatz that were close to the Soviet sector.

Tony Shaw describes *The Man Between* as 'the most graphic cinematic dramatization of Berlin's schizophrenic personality during the whole of the Cold War'.[8] The film has too often been seen as an inferior imitation of *The Third Man*. While it lacks the atmospheric expressionist cinematography of Robert Krasker and the scripting hand of Graham Greene, it is notable for its realistic locations and tensely plotted narrative. James Mason starred as Ivo Kern, a black marketeer (shades of Orson Welles' Harry Lime in *The Third Man*) who is paid by the East German authorities to track down fugitives in the West. Kern blackmails his ex-wife Bettina (Hildegard Knef), now married to a British army doctor, to lure her friend Kastner (Ernst Schroeder) into the Eastern zone. Kastner is wanted by the authorities for spiriting refugees out of East Berlin. When the English visitor Susanne Mallison (Claire Bloom) is mistaken for Bettina and kidnapped by the East German police, Kern's conscience is pricked. He rescues Susanne and Kastner, who escape back to the West through the Brandenburg Gate, though Kern is shot just short of the frontier.

*The Man Between* prompted mixed reviews and was only a modest success at the box office. Reed later acknowledged that it 'wasn't a particularly good story ... It didn't come out quite right because we were forced back from Berlin before the location work was finished and we had to match a lot in the studio.'[9] Its release in September 1953 was topical, coming as it did soon after the popular uprising in the GDR in June that year. Ideologically *The Man Between* endorses an official view of Eastern-bloc oppression with its anonymous trench-coated secret police and ubiquitous posters of Lenin and Stalin. However, later filmic treatments of Cold War Berlin would be characterized by a greater sense of moral ambiguity that suggests some distancing from official discourses of the Cold War.

It is no coincidence that the building of the Berlin Wall in 1961 was followed by what Denning calls the 'golden age of the spy novel', marked by the publication of Len Deighton's *The Ipcress File* in 1962 and John le Carré's *The Spy Who Came in from the Cold* in 1963.[10] These two books represented a significant ideological shift in the genre: they were by authors who had come of age after the Second World War and were interested in examining changes in British society and the decline of British power following the Suez Crisis (1956) and the retreat from empire. However, one of the first spy stories to respond to the situation in Berlin following the building of the Wall came from the older school of thriller fiction. Fleming's 'The Living Daylights' (originally published in the inaugural *Sunday Times* magazine in February 1962) is something of an aberration in the Bond sequence. The Bond novels in the wake of *Thunderball* in 1961 belong firmly to the 'magical' lineage of the spy thriller with their implausible plots and megalomaniac villains. 'The Living Daylights', however, marked a return to 'the treacherous life of moral meditation and psychological anger' that had characterized the first novel, *Casino Royale,* but was absent from later stories.[11]

Bond is sent to Berlin to cover the escape of a British agent fleeing with Soviet atomic secrets. The agent has travelled to East Berlin and plans to cross the Wall at a given time on one of three successive evenings. The KGB (Soviet intelligence agency), however, have learned of his plan and have sent their top marksman, codenamed 'Trigger', to stop him. Bond's job is to kill Trigger first. For two nights Bond surveys the 'killing ground' between East and West, and takes a fancy to a young blonde cellist playing in an orchestra that practises in a building on the Soviet-controlled side. On the third evening the agent makes a dash for it and Bond locates Trigger, who turns out to be the blonde girl. At the last moment Bond alters his aim to wound rather than kill her. Reprimanded for disobeying his orders to shoot to kill, Bond rationalizes his decision: 'That girl won't do any more sniping. Probably lost her left hand. Certainly broke her nerve for that kind of thing. Scared the living daylights out of her.'[12] 'The Living Daylights' was located in a specific time and place – 1961 on the Zimmerstraße – and its narrative of the crossing from East to West provided a template for the spy fictions of the 1960s.

In the mid 1960s, however, a cluster of films appeared that did much to establish the popular image of Berlin during the Cold War: *The Spy Who Came in from the Cold* (1965), *Funeral in Berlin* (Guy Hamilton, 1966) and *The Quiller Memorandum* (Michael Anderson, 1966). *The Spy Who Came in from the Cold* is the best of these and stands as the definitive Cold War spy thriller. It was directed by American Martin Ritt, a former teacher from the Actors Studio in New York who had been blacklisted in the 1950s. The screenplay by Paul Dehn and Guy Trosper stuck closely to the novel, which, with its terse and economical style, reads not unlike a film treatment. Some critics felt the film was too close to the novel: one American reviewer found it a 'complexly plotted, curiously dull film, puzzling where it should be interesting, boring where it should be exciting'.[13] But a more typical response came from British critic Penelope Huston, who saw it as a realistic alternative to the narrative extravagance and visual excess of the Bond films: 'Part of the success of John le Carré's novel was surely the matter of its timing: cold, anti-romantic disenchantment, dry biscuits and railway coffee, as a necessary antidote to the euphoric champagne of 007.'[14]

*The Spy Who Came in from the Cold* exemplifies the existential trend within the spy thriller. Its core theme is the ethics of the Cold War. Leamas (Richard Burton) is an embittered, alcoholic agent on one last mission before he is brought 'in from the cold'. He is sent to East Germany, posing as a defector to discredit intelligence chief Mundt (Peter Van Eyck). At a show trial, where Mundt acts as prosecutor and Leamas is defended by the kindly Fiedler (Oskar Werner), Leamas is exposed when his girlfriend Nan (Claire Bloom), a member of the Communist Party, appears as a witness and is tricked into revealing that Leamas' defection was fake. This discredits Leamas and Fiedler too. Leamas realizes that he has been an actor in 'the lousy end to a lousy, filthy operation to save Mundt's skin'. Mundt, it transpires, is a British mole inside the East German security services, and the aim has been to discredit Fiedler, who was becoming suspicious of Mundt. To this extent the mission is successful: Fiedler is arrested, only to be shot by his own side. Leamas and Nan are released and brought to Berlin, where Mundt has arranged for them to cross the Wall. Nan is shot dead – Mundt fears that she might reveal the truth once back in the West – whereupon Leamas climbs back down to the Eastern side and is also shot.

*The Spy Who Came in from the Cold* is an unremittingly pessimistic film. It presents the Cold War as a morally equivocal business in which each side is as duplicitous as the other. Leamas is set up by his own side; the gullible Nan is duped into a charade that gets her killed; the agent whom the whole point is to protect is a thoroughly unpleasant character (Mundt is a bully and an anti-Semite) while the sympathetic Fiedler (a Jew) is set up to die. As Leamas' superior (Cyril Cusack) tells him: 'You can't be less wicked than your enemy simply because your government's policies are benevolent, can you?' Leamas characterizes the members of his profession as 'seedy, squalid bastards like me – little men, drunkards, queers, hen-pecked husbands, civil servants playing cowboys and Indians to brighten their rotten little lives'. This gloominess is also expressed in the film's visual style. Its low-key black-and-white cinematography (by Oswald Morris) creates a feeling of austerity: scenes are set at night or during overcast days, and the action takes place in either bleak exteriors or shadowy rooms. Appropriately, the film begins and ends in Berlin, represented as a grim landscape of barriers and barbed wire. In the opening sequence an agent is shot attempting to cross at Checkpoint Charlie (a studio set – the film was made at Shepperton Studios near London and Ardmore Studios in Ireland). It ends with a double death on the Berlin Wall as Nan and Leamas are killed, their deaths in long shot suggesting their smallness in the wider geopolitical context.

*The Spy Who Came in from the Cold* was preceded in cinemas by *The Ipcress File* (Sidney J. Furie, 1965), adapted from the novel by Len Deighton and introducing Michael Caine as the insubordinate working-class spy Harry Palmer, whose investigation of a 'brain drain' among British scientists leads him to uncover internal treachery within the British security services. It was produced by Harry Saltzman, venturing outside the partnership with Albert R. Broccoli that had produced the series of Bond films. *Funeral in Berlin* in 1966, the first sequel to *The Ipcress File*, sent Palmer to Berlin to arrange the defection of KGB intelligence chief Colonel Stok (Oscar Homolka). The films are very different stylistically – Guy Hamilton's direction of *Funeral in Berlin* seems anodyne compared with Sidney J. Furie's self-conscious camera placements in *Ipcress* – though both have a strong sense of place. Unlike *The Spy Who Came in from the Cold, Funeral in Berlin* used real locations and colour. Hamilton and cinematographer Otto Heller contrast the shining modern tower blocks of West Berlin with the graffiti-strewn ugliness of the Wall, which again provides the backdrop for the climax.

*Funeral in Berlin* interweaves two narratives. Palmer realizes that Colonel Stok's defection is fake when the coffin carried across the border turns out not to be Stok alive but a dead criminal called Kreutzman. Kreutzman was a leading escape expert, and Stok has used British Intelligence to find his escape route and dispose of him. In the second parallel narrative Palmer becomes involved with an Israeli agent (Eva Renzi) who is tracking down Nazi war criminals. That the film attempted to do something different with the genre is evident in its inversion of the usual escape narrative – it ends with the Nazi villain trying to enter East Berlin to escape Israeli vengeance – and in its characterization of KGB chief Stok as a warm, likeable character. In this respect *Funeral in Berlin* might be seen as an early example of the détente narratives that featured in later Bond movies such as *The Spy Who Loved Me* (Lewis Gilbert, 1977). Indeed, the third Harry Palmer film, *Billion Dollar Brain* (1967), extravagantly directed by Ken Russell, took this theme even further by having Palmer and Stok join forces to foil a megalomaniac American anti-communist's attempt to invade the Soviet Union and trigger a third world war.

The legacy of the Nazi past also informs *The Quiller Memorandum*. This was adapted by playwright Harold Pinter, a frequent collaborator of Joseph Losey, from the novel *The Berlin Memorandum* by Adam Hall (pen name of Elleston Trevor), and directed by Michael Anderson. Its protagonist Quiller (George Segal) is an American spy sent to Berlin to investigate the murder of two British agents. His brash professionalism is contrasted with the eccentricities of his British handlers. Pinter's screenplay strips away the melodramatic elements of the novel to focus on the motif of the agent as a man in the middle caught between two blocs, exemplified in a scene where his handler Pol (Alec Guinness) explains the Cold War using two ashtrays and a peanut. (This theme also featured in *The Ipcress File*, where Palmer is threatened both by enemy heavies and by the CIA because he has accidentally killed one of their men.) The *Monthly Film Bulletin* disliked what it called Pinter's 'eliptical dialogue' and the 'funereal pace' of the film, in which 'every shot is held a fraction too long'.[15] Yet this might be seen as a deliberate stylistic choice by Anderson and his cinematographer Erwin Hillier. The most striking feature of *The Quiller Memorandum* is its eerie atmosphere of deserted streets and anonymous high-rise hotels. It eschews the obvious landmarks, including the Wall, but uses the Olympic Stadium to good effect. The setting of the 'Nazi Olympics' of 1936 – sounds of cheering crowds are heard on the soundtrack as Quiller and Pol meet in the empty stadium – once again suggests that the Cold War is the continuation of a longer historical process.

The significance of these films was that they packaged the German experience of the Cold War for wider consumption. They helped to shape the image of Germany as being on the front line of the Cold War – with Berlin as its no-man's-land – in Western popular culture beyond the borders of the Federal Republic itself. They represented Berlin in terms of what, to cite Thomas Elsaesser, we might call 'Germany's historical imaginary'.[16] Through them Berlin became a cultural and geopolitical 'space' as well as a real place. This idea was perhaps best demonstrated in the most unlikely of films: *Casino Royale* (1967), which bore no relation to the Bond series produced by Broccoli and Saltzman for United Artists. Producer Charles K. Feldman had acquired the screen rights to Fleming's first novel and, unable to come to terms with Broccoli and Saltzman or to hire the services of Sean Connery, decided to make *Casino Royale* the spy spoof to end all spy spoofs. The result was uneven, its episodic narrative featuring the input of five directors (John Huston, Ken Hughes, Robert Parrish, Val Guest, Joseph McGrath), three credited writers (Wolf Mankowitz, John Law, Michael Sayers) and numerous uncredited writers (including Billy Wilder, Ben Hecht and Joseph Heller). The finished film has been described as 'a self-indulgent mess – an inferior Monty Python sketch stretched way beyond its limits'.[17]

Yet *Casino Royale* contains one sequence very relevant to this discussion. Mata Bond (Joanna Pettet), the daughter of James Bond and Mata Hari, is sent to Berlin by British Intelligence to infiltrate a SMERSH school for spies. She arrives (in a black London taxi) on a studio set divided by a wall. One side is replete with neon lights, clubs with names like

'Der Sexy Blaue Engel' and 'Die Striptease Raserei', the streets packed with US servicemen and miniskirt-clad prostitutes. The other side is painted entirely red. Mata gains entry to the school – all tilted angles and sloping walls in a spoof of the visual style of German Expressionist cinema – and succeeds in stealing a set of compromising photographs that are being auctioned to the highest bidder before making her escape. The auctioneer (Vladek Sheybal, a sinister-faced Polish character actor who found frequent employment in spy films) is killed in an exploding telephone booth that blows a hole in the Wall. Immediately hordes of East Berliners flock through the hole with suitcases and prams. The sight of East Berliners literally falling over themselves to flee 'the red side' fits perfectly with Western images of the GDR as a society yearning for the consumerist delights of the West. That it might also reflect a communist view of the FRG as a decadent society overrun with Americans and vice is one of the many contradictions of this film.

It was in the mid 1960s, then, that the enduring filmic image of Cold War Berlin was established. Later representations have adhered to the visual conventions established in films such as *The Spy Who Came in from the Cold*. Berlin continued to be a popular location for the spy genre. The authentic James Bond got to Berlin in *Octopussy* (John Glen, 1983), a film that maps tensions arising from a revival of the nuclear arms race in the early 1980s onto a jewel-smuggling narrative.[18] It includes a brief location sequence as 'M' drops Bond off near Checkpoint Charlie. *Octopussy* was one of several latter-day Bond movies that featured a conspiracy hatched between a renegade Soviet general and a capitalist partner in the West; others are *The Living Daylights* (John Glen, 1987) and *GoldenEye* (Martin Campbell, 1995). *The Living Daylights* employs the Fleming short story as a starting point, though the location is switched to Bratislava (shot in Vienna) and the girl Bond shoots is not a professional assassin. *Game, Set, Match* (Ken Grieve and Patrick Lau, 1988) was a costly thirteen-part television miniseries based on Len Deighton's first Bernard Sampson trilogy, *Berlin Game, Mexico Set, London Match*, that again featured much location shooting. It was produced for the PBS network in the US and failed to make much of an impact on viewers.

Rather more successful were two serial adaptations of John le Carré – *Tinker, Tailor, Soldier, Spy* (John Irvin, 1979) and *Smiley's People* (Simon Langton, 1982) – by the British Broadcasting Corporation. In the novels le Carré promoted the character of spymaster George Smiley, who appeared as a supporting character in his earlier books, to centre stage. Alec Guinness played Smiley in both serials, and his chameleon-like ability to inhabit a role is perfectly suited to the part of the modest, anonymous grand old man of British Intelligence. *Tinker, Tailor, Soldier,*

*Spy* follows Smiley's hunt to find a mole in the 'Circus', which is loosely based on the unmasking of Kim Philby as a KGB agent. In *Smiley's People* he investigates the murder of a defector and in the process learns that his opposite number in Moscow Centre, Karla, has a secret daughter in a Swiss sanatorium – knowledge he uses to blackmail Karla into defecting. The conclusion of *Smiley's People* recalls the opening of *The Spy Who Came in from the Cold* as the British spymaster waits in a hut near the border while Karla crosses a bridge to the West. It is a victory for British Intelligence ('You won, George'), though there is no triumphalism: Smiley knows he has won only by acting as ruthlessly as his enemy ('Be like Karla'). It is entirely fitting that a snowy Berlin should be the location for this Cold War endgame.

The end of the Cold War, following the fall of the Berlin Wall in 1989 and the collapse of the Soviet Union in 1991, inevitably impacted upon the spy film. The main trends in the genre in recent years have been the emergence of terrorism as the principal geopolitical threat to the West and the rise of the techno-thriller in films like *The Net* (Irwin Winkler, 1995) or the television series *The Last Enemy* (Iain B. MacDonald, 2008). The front lines of geopolitical and ideological conflict within the genre have shifted to the Middle East and the Internet. Berlin continues to feature as a location in spy thrillers such as *The Bourne Supremacy* (Paul Greengrass, 2004) and *Mission: Impossible 3* (J.J. Abrams, 2006), though it tends to be employed for its photogenic opportunities rather than as a space where geopolitics and culture meet. In *The Bourne Supremacy,* the second of (to date) three films based loosely on the Jason Bourne novels of Robert Ludlum, starring Matt Damon as an amnesiac ex-CIA assassin, the Berlin locations such as Alexanderplatz function not for any specific narrative purpose but rather as part of an extended travelogue that includes India and Moscow. Just as Berlin has reinvented itself following the Cold War, so too has the spy thriller. And the old, divided Berlin of *The Spy Who Came in from the Cold* and other films now belongs to Germany's historical imaginary rather than to its modern and unified present.

## Notes

1. I am indebted to Krista Cowman for the essay's subtitle, coined in March 2004 when we took time off from the European Social Sciences and History Conference at the Humboldt University to trace the path of the Berlin Wall in the company of urban historian Bob Morris. The discovery that large parts of the old West Berlin were in fact further east than the westernmost parts of East Berlin prompted us – after

a couple of happy-hour cocktails in a neighbourhood café – to discuss whether this made Berlin a 'conceptual rather than a geographical space'.

2. The literature is now extensive, but see in particular: David Caute, *The Dancer Defects: The Struggle for Cultural Supremacy during the Cold War* (Oxford: Oxford University Press, 2003); *Across the Blocs*, ed. by Mitter and Major; Tony Shaw, *British Cinema and the Cold War: The State, Propaganda and Consensus* (London: I.B. Tauris, 2001); and Tony Shaw, *Hollywood's Cold War* (Edinburgh: Edinburgh University Press, 2007).

3. See Daniel J. Leab, *Orwell Subverted: The CIA and the Filming of* Animal Farm (University Park: Pennsylvania State University Press, 2007).

4. Michael Denning, *Cover Stories: Narrative and Ideology in the British Spy Thriller* (London: Routledge & Kegan Paul, 1987), pp. 1–2.

5. Ibid., p. 34.

6. Umberto Eco, 'The Narrative Structure in Fleming', in *The Bond Affair*, ed. by Oreste Del Buono and Umberto Eco, trans. by R.A. Downie (London: Macdonald, 1966), pp. 35–75.

7. Saunders, *Who Paid the Piper?*, pp. 175–77.

8. Shaw, *British Cinema and the Cold War*, p. 70.

9. Quoted in Nicholas Wapshott, *The Man Between: A Biography of Carol Reed* (London: Chatto & Windus, 1990), p. 268. For an analysis of the film see Peter William Evans, *Carol Reed* (Manchester: Manchester University Press, 2005), pp. 127–30.

10. Denning, *Cover Stories*, p. 117.

11. Eco, 'The Narrative Structure in Fleming', p. 37.

12. Fleming, *Octopussy and the Living Daylights* (London: Cape,1966), p. 95.

13. Elinor Halprin, review of *The Ipcress File* and *The Spy Who Came in from the Cold, Film Quarterly* 19.4 (1966), 60–64 (p. 64).

14. *Monthly Film Bulletin* 33.385 (1966), 20.

15. *Monthly Film Bulletin* 34.396 (1967), 6.

16. Thomas Elsaesser, *Weimar Cinema and After: Germany's Historical Imaginary* (London: Routledge, 2000), pp. 4–5. Elsaesser uses the term 'historical imaginary' as an alternative to 'national identity' in discussing how German films of the Weimar period helped to create a sense of community based on shared media images, memory and invented traditions. It seems to me that spy films do something similar for Cold War Berlin.

17. Clive Hirschhorn, *The Columbia Story* (London: Pyramid, 1989), p. 266.

18. See James Chapman, *Licence to Thrill: A Cultural History of the James Bond Films,* 2nd edn (London: I.B. Tauris, 2007), pp. 179–84.

# Select Bibliography

Abendroth, Wolfgang, *Aufstieg und Krise der deutschen Sozialdemokratie* (Frankfurt/Main: Stimme, 1964)
Achten, Udo, *Zum Lichte empor* (Bonn: J.H.W. Dietz Nachf., 1980)
Ahonen, Pertti, *After the Expulsion: West Germany and Eastern Europe 1945–1990* (Oxford: Oxford University Press, 2003)
Angster, Julia, *Konsenskapitalismus und Sozialdemokratie: Die Westernisierung von SPD und DGB* (Munich: Oldenbourg, 2003)
Appadurai, Arjun, *Modernity at Large: Cultural Dimensions of Globalization* (Minneapolis: University of Minnesota Press, 1996)
Badstübner, Ralf, 'Die sowjetische Deutschlandpolitik im Lichte neuer Quellen', in *Die Deutschland Frage in der Nachkriegszeit,* ed. by Wilfried Loth (Berlin: Akademie, 1994), pp. 114–23
Balbier, Uta Andrea, '"Die Grenzlosigkeit menschlicher Leistungsfähigkeit" – Planungsgläubigkeit, Konkurrenz und Leistungssportförderung in der Bundesrepublik und der DDR in den 1960er Jahren', *Historical Social Research,* 32 (2007), 137–53
———, *Kalter Krieg auf der Aschenbahn. Der deutsch-deutsche Sport 1950–1972: Eine politische Geschichte* (Paderborn: Schöning, 2007)
Bald, Detlef, *Die Bundeswehr: Eine kritische Geschichte 1955–2005* (Munich: Beck, 2005)
Barck, Simone, Martina Langermann and Siegfried Lokatis, *'Jedes Buch ein Abenteuer': Zensur-System und literarische Öffentlichkeiten in der DDR bis Ende der sechziger Jahre* (Berlin: Akademie, 2002)
Bartel, Walter, *Die Linken in der deutschen Sozialdemokratie im Kampf gegen Militarismus und Krieg* (East Berlin: Dietz, 1958)
Behn, Manfred, and Hans-Michael Bock, *Film und Gesellschaft in der DDR,* 2 vols (Hamburg: Cinegraph, 1989)
Behrends, Jan C., and Patrice Poutrus, 'Xenophobia in the Former GDR: Explorations and Explanation from a Historical Perspective', in *Nationalisms Across the Globe: An Overview of Nationalisms in State-Endowed and Stateless Nations,* ed. by Wojciech Burszta and Tomasz Kamusella (Poznan: Wysza Szkola Nauk Hymanistycznych I Dziennikarstwa, 2005), pp. 155–70
Bell, Daniel, *The Coming of Post-Industrial Society: A Venture in Social Forecasting* (New York: Basic Books, 1973)
Bennewitz, Inge, and Rainer Potratz, *Zwangsaussiedlungen an der innerdeutschen Grenze: Analysen und Dokumente* (Berlin: Links, 1994)

Berg, Leo van den, Jan van der Borg and Jan van der Meer, *Urban Tourism: Performance and Strategies in Eight European Cities* (Aldershot: Ashgate, 1995)

Berger, Stefan, 'National Paradigm and Legitimacy: Uses of Academic History Writing in the 1960s', in *The Workers' and Peasants' State: Communism and Society in East Germany under Ulbricht, 1945-71,* ed. by Patrick Major and John Osmond (Manchester: Manchester University Press, 2002), pp. 244-61

——, *The Search for Normality: National Identity and Historical Consciousness in Germany since 1800* (Oxford: Berg, 1997)

Berghahn, Daniela, *Hollywood behind the Wall* (Manchester: Manchester University Press, 2005)

Bertram, Mathias, *Enzyklopädie der DDR: Personen, Institutionen und Strukturen in Politik, Wirtschaft, Justiz, Wissenschaft und Kultur,* Digitale Bibliothek, 32 (Berlin: Directmedia, 2000)

Bezner, Lili Corbus, *Photography and Politics in America: From the New Deal into the Cold War* (Baltimore: John Hopkins University Press, 1999)

Biess, Frank, 'Survivors of Totalitarianism: Returning POWs and the Reconstruction of Masculine Citizenship in West Germany, 1945-1955', in *The Miracle Years: A Cultural History of West Germany, 1949-1968,* ed. by Hanna Schissler (Princeton: Princeton University Press, 2001), pp. 57-82

Blasius, Tobias, *Olympische Bewegung, Kalter Krieg und Deutschlandpolitik 1949-1972* (Frankfurt/Main: Lang 2001)

Both, Wolfgang, and others, eds, *Berichte aus der Parallelwelt: Die Geschichte des Science Fiction-Fandoms in der DDR* (Passau: EDFC, 1998)

Bradley, Laura, 'A Different Political Forum: East German Theatre and the Construction of the Berlin Wall', *Journal of European Studies,* 36 (2006), 139-56

Breitenfeld, Annette, *Die Begegnung mit außerirdischen Lebensformen: Untersuchungen zur Science-Fiction-Literatur der DDR* (Wetzlar: Förderkreis Phantastik, 1994)

Brinks, Jan Herman, *Paradigms of Political Change: Luther, Frederick II, and Bismarck* (Milwaukee: Marquette University Press, 2001)

Brochhagen, Ulrich, *Nach Nürnberg: Vergangenheitsbewältigung und Westintegration in der Ära Adenauer* (Hamburg: Junius, 1994)

Büch, Martin-Peter, 'Elite Sport', in *Sport and Physical Education in Germany,* ed. by Roland Naul and Ken Hardman (London: Routledge, 2002), pp. 132-52

Buffet, Cyril, *Mourir pour Berlin: La France et l'Allemande 1945-1949* (Paris: Armand Colin, 1991)

Byg, Barton, 'DEFA and the Traditions of International Cinema', in *DEFA: East German Cinema, 1946-1992,* ed. by Seán Allan and John Sandford (Oxford: Berghahn, 1999), pp. 22-42

Carew, Anthony, 'Towards a Free Trade Union Centre: The International Confederation of Free Trade Unions (1949-1972)', in *The International Confederation of Free Trade Unions,* ed. by Anthony Carew and others (New York: Lang, 2000), pp. 187-339

Caute, David, *The Dancer Defects: The Struggle for Cultural Supremacy during the Cold War* (Oxford: Oxford University Press, 2003)

Chandler, Andrea, *Institutions of Isolation: Border Controls in the Soviet Union and its Successor States 1917-1993* (Montreal: McGill-Queens Press, 1998)

Chapman, James, *Licence to Thrill: A Cultural History of the James Bond Films,* 2nd edn (London: I.B. Tauris, 2007)

Ciesla, Burghard, Michael Lemke and Thomas Lindenberger, *Sterben für Berlin?: Berliner Krisen 1948-1958* (Berlin: Metropol, 1999)
Classen, Christoph, 'Fremdheit gegenüber der eigenen Geschichte: Zum öffentlichen Umgang mit dem Nationalsozialismus in beiden deutschen Staaten', in *Fremde und Fremd-Sein in der DDR: Zu historischen Ursachen der Fremdenfeindlichkeit in Deutschland*, ed. by Jan C. Behrends, Thomas Lindenberger and Patrice Poutrus (Berlin: Metropol, 2003), pp. 101-26
Clemens, Walter C., *Baltic Independence and the Russian Empire* (London: Macmillan, 1990)
Coeuré, Sophie, and Sabine Dullin, eds, *Frontières du communisme: Mythologies et réalités de la division de l'Europe de la revolution d'Octobre au mur de Berlin* (Paris: La Découverte, 2007)
Cooke, Paul, '*Dresden* (2006), TeamWorx and *Titanic* (1997): German Wartime Suffering as Hollywood Disaster Movie', *German Life and Letters*, 61.2 (2008), 279-94
——, *Representing East Germany since Unification: From Colonization to Nostalgia* (Oxford: Berg, 2005)
Cooke, Paul, and Christopher Young, 'Selling Sex or Dealing with History? German Football in Literature and Film and the Quest to Normalize the Nation', in *German Football: History, Culture, Society*, ed. by Alan Tomlinson and Christopher Young (London: Routledge, 2006), pp. 181-203
Crew, David, ed., *Consuming Germany in the Cold War* (Oxford: Berg, 2003)
Darnton, Robert, *Berlin Journal, 1989-90* (New York: Norton, 1991)
Decker, Bernard H., *Gewalt und Zärtichkeit: Einführung in die Militärbelletristik der DDR* (New York: Lang, 1989)
Denning, Michael, *Cover Stories: Narrative and Ideology in the British Spy Thriller* (London: Routledge & Kegan Paul, 1987)
Diedrich, Torsten, Hans Ehlert and Rüdiger Wenzke, eds, *Im Dienste der Partei: Handbuch der bewaffneten Organe der DDR* (Berlin: Links, 2004)
Dorpalen, Andreas, *German History in Marxist Perspective: The East German Approach* (Detroit: Wayne University Press, 1985; London: I.B. Tauris, 1986)
Doßmann, Axel, *Begrenzte Mobilität: Eine Kulturgeschichte der Autobahnen in der DDR* (Essen: Klartext, 2003)
Dülffer, Jost, 'Cold War History in Germany', *Cold War History*, 8.2 (2008), 135-56
Eco, Umberto, 'The Narrative Structure in Fleming', in *The Bond Affair*, ed. by Oreste Del Buono and Umberto Eco, trans. by R.A. Downie (London: Macdonald, 1966), pp. 35-75
Eley, Geoff, 'The SPD in War and Revolution, 1914-1919', in *Bernstein to Brandt: A Short History of German Social Democracy*, ed. by Roger Fletcher (London: Arnold, 1987), pp. 65-74
Elsaesser, Thomas, *Weimar Cinema and After: Germany's Historical Imaginary* (London: Routledge, 2000)
Endy, Christopher, *Cold War Holidays: American Tourism in France* (Chapel Hill: University of North Carolina Press, 2004)
Erickson, Kenneth Paul, and Patrick V. Peppe, 'Dependent Capitalist Development, U.S. Foreign Policy, and Repression of the Working Class in Chile and Brazil', *Latin American Perspectives*, 3.1 (1976), 19-44
Evans, Peter William, *Carol Reed* (Manchester: Manchester University Press, 2005)

Evans, Richard J., 'Introduction', in *Society and Politics in Wilhelmine Germany*, ed. by Richard J. Evans (London: Croom Helm, 1978), pp. 11–39

Feinstein, Joshua, *The Triumph of the Ordinary: Depictions of Daily Life in the East German Cinema, 1949–1989* (Chapel Hill: University of North Carolina Press, 2002)

Feldner, Heiko, 'History in the Academy: Objectivity and Partisanship in the Marxist Historiography of the German Democratic Republic', in *The Workers' and Peasants' State* (see Berger, 'National Paradigm and Legitimacy', above), pp. 262–77

Fetzer, Thomas, 'Die gesellschaftliche Akzeptanz des Leistungssportsytems', in *Sport in der DDR: Eigensinn, Konflikte, Trends,* ed. by Hans Joachim Teichler (Cologne: Sport und Buch Strauß, 2003), pp. 273–357

Fischer, William Baldwin, *The Empire Strikes Out: Kurd Lasswitz, Hans Dominik and the Development of German Science Fiction* (Bowling Green: Bowling Green State University Popular Press, 1984)

Fisher, Peter S., *Fantasy and Politics: Visions of the Future in the Weimar Republic* (Madison: University of Wisconsin Press, 1991)

Fletcher, M.D., *Contemporary Political Satire: Narrative Strategies in the Post-Modern Context* (Lanham, MD: University Press of America, 1987)

Fox, Thomas, *Stated Memory: East Germany and the Holocaust* (Rochester, NY: Camden House, 1999)

Frank, Mario, *Walter Ulbricht: Eine deutsche Biographie* (Berlin: Seidler, 2001)

Frei, Norbert, *Adenauer's Germany and the Nazi Past: The Politics of Amnesty and Integration,* trans. by Joel Golb (New York: Columbia University Press, 2002)

Frevert, Ute, *A Nation in Barracks: Modern Germany, Military Conscription and Civil Society* (Oxford: Berg, 2001)

Fricke, Dieter, 'Friedrich Stampfer und der "demokratische Sozialismus"', *ZfG*, 6.4 (1958), 749–74

Fritzsche, Sonja, *Science Fiction Literature in East Germany* (Bern: Lang, 2006)

Fülberth, Georg, and Jürgen Harrer, *Die deutsche Sozialdemokratie, 1890–1933* (Darmstadt: Luchterhand, 1974)

Fulda, Daniel, and Martin Andree, 'Anticommunism and (West) German Identity: An Analysis of Metaphors and Concepts of History in the F.A.Z., 1949–1952', *Yearbook of European Studies,* 13 (1999), 94–129

Furet, François, *The Passing of an Illusion: The Idea of Communism in the Twentieth Century* (Chicago: University of Chicago Press, 1999)

Gaddis, John Lewis, *We Know Now: Rethinking Cold War History* (Oxford: Oxford University Press, 1997)

Gemünden, Gerd, 'Between Karl May and Karl Marx: The DEFA Indianerfilme (1965–1983)', *Film History,* 10 (1998), 399–407

Goeckel, Robert F., 'The Luther Anniversary in East Germany', *World Politics,* 37.1 (1984), 118–20

Granville, Johanna, 'Ulbricht in October 1956: Survival of the *Spitzbart* during Destalinization', *Journal of Contemporary History,* 41.3 (2006), 477–502

Gray, William Glenn, *Germany's Cold War: The Global Campaign to Isolate East Germany, 1949–1969* (Chapel Hill: University of North Carolina Press, 2003)

Grazia, Victoria de, 'Mass Culture and Sovereignty: The American Challenge to European Cinemas, 1920–1960', *Journal of Modern History,* 61.1 (1989), 53–87

Grebing, Helga, *Geschichte der deutschen Arbeiterbewegung* (Munich: Nymphenburger, 1966)

———, 'Gewerkschaften: Bewegung oder Dienstleistungsorganisation – 1955 bis 1965', in *Geschichte der Gewerkschaften in der Bundesrepublik Deutschland: Von den Anfängen bis heute,* ed. by Hans-Otto Hemmer and Kurt Thomas Schmitz (Cologne: Bund, 1990), pp. 149–82

Grieder, Peter, *The East German Leadership, 1946–73: Conflict and Crisis* (Manchester: Manchester University Press, 1999)

Gries, Rainer, 'Zur Ästhetik und Architektur von Propagemen: Überlegungen zu einer Propagandageschichte als Kulturgeschichte', in *Kultur der Propaganda: Überlegungen zu einer Propagandageschichte als Kulturgeschichte,* ed. by Rainer Gries and Wolfgang Schmale (Bochum: Winkler, 2005), pp. 9–35

Groh, Dieter, *Negative Integration und revolutionärer Attentismus: Die deutsche Sozialdemokratie am Vorabend des Ersten Weltkrieges* (Frankfurt/Main: Propyläen, 1973)

Grunert, Horst, *Für Honecker auf glattem Parkett: Erinnerungen eines DDR-Diplomaten* (Berlin: Edition Ost, 1995)

Habermas, Jürgen, *Autonomy & Solidarity: Interviews with Jürgen Habermas,* ed. by Peters Dews, rev. edn (London: Verso, 1992)

Hall, B. Welling, 'The Church and the Independent Peace Movement in Eastern Europe', *Journal of Peace Research,* 23.2 (1986), 193–208

Han, Un-Suk, ed., *Geschichte der Teilung. Wie ist sie zu betrachten?: Vergleich der Nordkorea- und DDR-Forschung* (Seoul: Sangji University, 2004)

Hardman, Ken, and Roland Naul, 'Sport and Physical Education in the Two Germanies, 1945–90', in *Sport and Physical Education in Germany* (see Büch, above), pp. 29–76

Harford, James, *Korolev: How One Man Masterminded the Soviet Drive to Beat America to the Moon* (New York: Wiley, 1997)

Hartley, John, *Communication, Cultural and Media Studies: The Key Concepts* (London: Routledge, 2005)

Hartung, Thomas, *Die Science Fiction der DDR von 1980–1990: Eine unterhaltungsliterarische Bestandsaufnahme unter thematischem und wirkungsspezifischem Aspekt* (Magdeburg: Block, 1992)

Haun, Horst, *Kommunist und 'Revisionist': Die SED-Kampagne gegen Jürgen Kuczynski (1956–1959)* (Dresden: Sächsisches Druck- und Verlagshaus, 1999)

Häussermann, Hartmut, and Claire Columb, 'The New Berlin: Marketing the City of Dreams', in *Cities and Visitors: Regulating People, Markets, and City Space,* ed. by Lily M. Hoffman, Susan S. Fainstein and Dennis R. Judd (Malden, MA: Blackwell, 2003), pp. 200–218

Haydock, Michael D., *City under Siege: The Berlin Blockade and Airlift, 1948–1949* (Washington, DC: Brassey's, 1999)

Heidegger, Hermann, *Die deutsche Sozialdemokratie und der nationale Staat, 1870–1920* (Göttingen: Musterschmidt, 1956)

Heimann, Thomas, *Bilder von Buchenwald: die Visualisierung des Antifaschismus der DDR (1945–1990)* (Cologne: Böhlau, 2005)

Herf, Jeffrey, *Divided Memory: The Nazi Past in the Two Germanys* (Cambridge, MA: Harvard University Press, 1997)

Hertle, Hans-Hermann, 'Volksaufstand und Herbstrevolution: Die Rolle der West-Medien 1953 und 1989 im Vergleich', in *Aufstände im Ostblock,* ed. by Henrik Bispinck and others (Berlin: Links, 2004), pp. 163–92

Hindenburg, Hannfried von, *Demonstrating Reconciliation: State and Society in West German Foreign Policy toward Israel, 1952–1965* (Oxford: Berghahn, 2007)

Hirschhorn, Clive, *The Columbia Story* (London: Pyramid, 1989)

Hochscherf, Tobias, and Christoph Laucht, '"Every Nation Needs a Legend": The *Miracle of Bern* and the Formation of a Postwar Foundational Myth', in *All-Stars and Movie Stars: Sports in Film & History,* ed. by Ron Briley, Michael K. Schoenecke and Deborah A. Carmichael (Lexington: University Press of Kentucky, 2008), pp. 279–302

Hodenberg, Christina von, *Wo 1968 liegt: Reform und Revolte in der Geschichte der Bundesrepublik* (Göttingen: Vandenhoeck & Ruprecht, 2006)

Howell, Yvonne, *Apocalyptic Realism: The Science Fiction of Arkady and Boris Strugatsky* (New York: Lang, 1994)

Internationaler Bund Freier Gewerkschaften, *Zwanzig Jahre IBFG* (Brussels: Internationaler Bund Freier Gewerkschaften, 1969)

Jäger, Jens, *Photographie: Bilder der Neuzeit. Einführung in die Historische Bildforschung* (Tübingen: Edition Diskord, 2000)

Jarausch, Konrad H., *After Hitler: Recivilizing Germans, 1945–1995* (Oxford: Oxford University Press, 2006)

Jarausch, Konrad H., Hinrich C. Seeba and David P. Conradt, 'The Presence of the Past: Culture, Opinion and Identity in Germany', in *After Unity: Reconfiguring German Identities,* ed. by Konrad H. Jarausch (Oxford: Berghahn, 1997), pp. 25–60

Kaiser, Alexandra, 'Performing the New German Past: The *Volkstrauertag* and 27th January as Commemoration Days in United Germany', in *The Dynamics of Memory in Contemporary Germany,* ed. by Eric Langenbacher, Bill Niven and Ruth Wittlinger, forthcoming special edition of *German Politics and Society*

Kansteiner, Wulf, *In Pursuit of German Memory: History, Television, and Politics after Auschwitz* (Athens: Ohio University Press, 2006)

Keßler, Mario, *Exilerfahrung in Wissenschaft und Politik: Remigrierte Historiker in der frühen DDR* (Cologne: Böhlau, 2001)

Killian, Werner, *Die Hallstein-Doktrin: der diplomatische Krieg zwischen der BRD und der DDR 1955–1973* (Berlin: Duncker and Humblot, 2001)

Kleßmann, Christoph, 'Introduction', in *The Divided Past: Rewriting Post-War German History,* ed. by Christoph Kleßmann (Oxford: Berg, 2001), pp. 1–9

———, *Zwei Staaten, eine Nation: Deutsche Geschichte 1955–1970,* 2nd rev. edn (Bonn: Bundeszentrale für politische Bildung, 1997)

Klotz, Katharina, 'Foto – Montage – Plakat: Zur politischen Ikonographie der "sozialistischen Sichtagitation" in der frühen DDR', in *Die DDR im Bild: Zum Gebrauch der Fotografie im anderen deutschen Staat,* ed. by Karin Hartewig and Alf Lüdtke (Göttingen: Wallstein, 2004), pp. 29–50

Kluge, Volker, *Olympische Sommerspiele. Die Chronik III: Mexico-Stadt 1968 – Los Angeles 1984* (Berlin: Sportverlag Berlin, 2000)

Knight, Charles, *The Literature of Satire* (Cambridge: Cambridge University Press, 2004)

Knoch, Habbo, *Die Tat als Bild: Fotografien des Holocaust in der deutschen Erinnerungskultur* (Hamburg: Hamburger Edition, 2001)

Koller, Christian, 'Der "Eiserne Vorhang": Zur Genese einer politischen Zentralmetapher in der Epoche des Kalten Krieges', *ZfG,* 54.4 (2006), 366–84

Koshar, Rudy, *German Travel Cultures* (Oxford: Berg, 2000)

Kott, Sandrine, 'Der Beitrag der französischen Sozialwissenschaften zur Erforschung der ostdeutschen Gesellschaft', in *Die ostdeutsche Gesellschaft: eine transnationale Perspektive,* ed. by Sandrine Kott and Emmanuel Droit (Berlin: Links, 2006), pp. 13–23

Kowalczuk, Ilko-Sascha, *Legitimation eines neuen Staates: Parteiarbeiter an der historischen Front. Geschichtswissenschaft in der SBZ/DDR, 1945–1961* (Berlin: Links, 1997)

Krasmann, Susanne, 'Gouvernementalität: Zur Kontinuität der Foucaultschen Analytik der Oberfläche', in *Geschichte schreiben mit Foucault,* ed. by Jürgen Martschukat (Frankfurt/Main: Campus, 2002), pp. 79–98

Krebs, Hans-Dieter, 'Die "doppelten Deutschen" (1965 bis 1988)', in *Deutschland in der Olympischen Bewegung: Eine Zwischenbilanz,* ed. by Manfred Lämmer (Frankfurt/Main: Nationales Olympisches Komitee für Deutschland, 1999), pp. 267–99

Kruschel, Karsten, *Spielwelten zwischen Wunschbild und Warnbild: Eutopisches und Dystopisches in der SF-Literatur der DDR in den achtziger Jahren* (Passau: EDFC, 1995)

Kruse, Wolfgang, *Krieg und nationale Integration: Eine Neuinterpretation des sozialdemokratischen Burgfriedensschlusses 1914/15* (Essen: Klartext, 1993)

Kuczynski, Jürgen, *Der Ausbruch des ersten Weltkrieges und die deutsche Sozialdemokratie: Chronik und Analyse* (East Berlin: Akademie, 1957)

——, 'Parteilichkeit und Objektivität in Geschichte und Geschichtsschreibung', *ZfG,* 4.5 (1956), 873–88

Kuznick, Peter J., and James Gilbert, *Rethinking Cold War Culture* (Washington, DC: Smithsonian, 2001)

Ladd, Brian, *The Ghosts of Berlin: Confronting the German Past in the Urban Landscape* (Chicago: University of Chicago Press, 1997)

Landsberg, Alison, *Prosthetic Memory: The Transformation of American Remembrance in the Age of Mass Culture* (New York: Columbia University Press, 2004)

Langer, Josef, ed., *Euroregions: The Alps-Adriatic Context* (Frankfurt/Main: Lang, 2007)

Large, David Clay, *Germans to the Front: West German Rearmament in the Adenauer Era* (Chapel Hill: University of North Carolina Press, 1996)

Larkey, Edward, *Rotes Rockradio: Populare Musik und die Kommerzialisierung des DDR-Rundfunks* (Münster: LIT, 2007)

Lazar, Marc, *Maisons Rouges: les partis communistes français et italiens de la Libération à nos jours* (Paris: Aubier, 1992)

Leab, Daniel J., *Orwell Subverted: The CIA and the Filming of* Animal Farm (University Park: Pennsylvania State University Press, 2007)

Leide, Henry, *NS-Verbrecher und Staatssicherheit: Die Geheime Vergangenheitspolitik der DDR* (Göttingen: Vandenhoeck & Ruprecht, 2005)

Lemberg, Hans, and K. Erik Franzen, *Die Vertriebenen: Hitlers letzte Opfer* (Munich: Propyläen, 2001)

Lindau, Rudolf, 'Arbeiterklasse und SPD-Führung beim Ausbruch des Ersten Weltkrieges: Kritik einer unmarxistischen Darstellung in einem Buch von Jürgen Kuczynski', *Einheit,* 13.3 (1958), 381–95

Lindenberger, Thomas, '"Asoziale Lebensweise": Herrschaftslegitimation, Sozialdisziplinierung und die Konstruktion eines "negatives Milieus" in der SED-Diktatur', *Geschichte und Gesellschaft,* 32 (2005), 227–54

———, '"Asociality" and Modernity: The GDR as a Welfare Dictatorship', in *Socialist Modern: East German Everyday Culture and Politics,* ed. by Katherine Pence and Paul Betts (Ann Arbor: University of Michigan Press, 2008), pp. 211–33

———, 'Geteilte Welt, geteilter Himmel? Der Kalte Krieg und die Massenmedien in gesellschaftsgeschichtlicher Perspektive', in *Zwischen Pop und Propaganda: Radio in der DDR,* ed. by Klaus Arnold and Christoph Classen (Berlin: Links, 2004), pp. 27–44

Link, Werner, *Deutsche und amerikanische Gewerkschaften und Geschäftsleute 1945–1975* (Düsseldorf: Droste, 1978)

Lokatis, Siegfried, *Der rote Faden: Kommunistische Parteigeschichte und Zensur unter Walter Ulbricht* (Cologne: Böhlau, 2003)

Lyotard, François, *The Postmodern Condition* (Manchester: Manchester University Press, 1984)

Major, Patrick, *Behind the Berlin Wall: East Germany and the Frontiers of Power* (Oxford: Oxford University Press, 2010)

———, 'Communist Science Fiction in the Cold War', in *Across the Blocs: Cold War Cultural and Social History,* ed. by Rana Mitter and Patrick Major (London: Cass, 2004), pp. 71–96

———, 'Going West: The Open Border and the Problem of Republikflucht', in *The Workers' and Peasants' State* (see Berger, 'National Paradigm and Legitimacy', above), pp. 190–208

———, '"Trash and Smut": Germany's Culture Wars against Pulp Fiction', in *Mass Media, Culture and Society in Twentieth-Century Germany,* ed. by Karl-Christian Fuehrer and Corey Ross (London: Palgrave, 2006), pp. 234–50

———, 'Vor und nach dem 13. August 1961: Reaktionen der DDR-Bevölkerung auf den Bau der Berliner Mauer', *Archiv für Sozialgeschichte* 39 (1999), 325–54

Marcuse, Harold, *Legacies of Dachau: The Uses and Abuses of a Concentration Camp, 1933–2001* (Cambridge: Cambridge University Press, 2001)

Marszolek, Inge, ed., *100 Jahre Zukunft: Zur Geschichte des 1. Mai* (Frankfurt/Main: Büchergilde Gutenberg, 1990)

May, Lary, 'Inventing Cold War America: Global Hollywood and the Politics of Memory', in *European Cold War Cultures: Perspectives on Societies in the East and the West,* ed. by Thomas Lindenberger and others (New York: Berghahn), publication forthcoming.

Meier, Helmut, and Walter Schmidt, eds, *Erbe und Tradition in der DDR: Die Diskussion der Historiker* (Cologne: Pahl-Rugenstein, 1989)

Meinecke, Friedrich, *The German Catastrophe: Reflections and Recollections,* trans. by Sidney B. Fray (Wiesbaden: Brockhaus Verlag, 1946; Cambridge, MA: Harvard University Press, 1950)

Mergel, Thomas, 'Europe as Leisure Time Communication: Tourism and Transnational Interaction since 1945', in *Conflicted Memories: Europeanizing Contemporary Histories,* ed. by Konrad H. Jarausch and Thomas Lindenberger (New York: Berghahn, 2007), pp. 133–53

Merker, Paul, *Sozialdemokratie und Gewerkschaften, 1890–1920* (East Berlin: Dietz, 1949)

Merkl, Peter H., *German Foreign Policies, West and East: On the Threshold of a New European Era* (Santa Barbara: ABC-Clio Press, 1974)
Merta, Klaus-Peter, 'Uniformierung als Mittel der Politik', in *Parteiauftrag: Ein Neues Deutschland: Bilder, Rituale und Symbole der frühen DDR,* ed. by Dieter Vorsteher (Berlin: Koehler & Amelang, 1996), pp. 175–86
Meuschel, Sigrid, *Legitimation und Parteiherrschaft* (Frankfurt/Main: Suhrkamp, 1992)
Meusel, Alfred, 'Der Ausbruch des Ersten Weltkriegs und die deutsche Sozialdemokratie: Kritische Betrachtungen zu dem Buch von Jürgen Kuczynski', *ZfG,* 6.5 (1958), 1049–68
——, *Thomas Müntzer und seine Zeit* (Berlin: Aufbau, 1952)
Meyen, Michael, *Denver Clan und Neues Deutschland: Mediennutzung in der DDR* (Berlin: Links, 2003)
Meyen, Michael, and Ute Nawratil, 'The Viewers: television and everyday life in East Germany', *Historical Journal of Film, Radio and Television,* 24.3, (2004), 355–64
Mietkowska-Kaiser, Ines, 'Zur brüderlichen Zusammenarbeit zwischen polnischen und deutschen Kommunisten und Antifaschisten nach dem Sieg über den deutschen Faschismus (1945–1949)', *Jahrbuch für Geschichte der sozialistischen Länder Europas,* 23. 1 (1979), 49–67
Mihelj, Sabina, 'Drawing the East-West Border: Narratives of Modernity and Identity in the Julian Region, 1947–1954', in *European Cold War Cultures: Perspectives on Societies in the East and the West,* ed. by Thomas Lindenberger and others (New York: Berghahn), publication forthcoming
Miller, Roger G., *To Save a City: The Berlin Airlift 1948–1949* (Washington, DC: GPO, 1998)
Miller, Susanne, *Burgfrieden und Klassenkampf: Die deutsche Sozialdemokratie im Ersten Weltkrieg* (Düsseldorf: Droste, 1974)
Mitschein, Thomas, *Die Dritte Welt als Gegenstand gewerkschaftlicher Theorie und Praxis* (Frankfurt/Main: Campus, 1981)
Mitter, Rana, and Patrick Major, eds, *Across the Blocs: Cold War Cultural and Social History* (London: Cass, 2004)
——, 'East is East and West? Towards a Comparative Socio-Cultural History of the Cold War', in *Across the Blocs: Cold War Cultural and Social History* (see Mitter and Major above), pp. 1–20
Mujal-Leon, Eusebio, 'The West German Social Democratic Party and the Politics of Internationalism in Central America', *Journal of Inter-American Studies and World Affairs,* 29.4 (1987–88), 89–123
Münkler, Herfried, 'Das kollektive Gedächtnis der DDR', in *Parteiauftrag* (see Merta, above), pp. 458–68
Naimark, Norman, *The Russians in Germany: A History of the Soviet Zone of Occupation, 1945–1949* (Cambridge, MA: Harvard University Press, 1995)
Nehring, Holger, 'The British and West German Protests against Nuclear Weapons and the Cultures of the Cold War, 1957–64', *Contemporary British History,* 19.2 (2005), 223–41
——, 'National Internationalists: British and West German Protests against Nuclear Weapons, the Politics of Transnational Communications and the Social History of the Cold War, 1957–1964', *Contemporary European History,* 14.4 (2005), 559–82

Neuhäußer-Wespy, Ulrich, *Die SED und die Historie: Die Etablierung der marxistisch-leninistischen Geschichtswissenschaft der DDR in den fünfziger und sechziger Jahren* (Bonn: Bouvier, 1996)

Niethammer, Lutz, 'Privat-Wirtschaft: Erinnerungsfragmente einer anderen Umerziehung', in *Lebensgeschichte und Sozialkultur im Ruhrgebiet 1930–1960*, ed. by Lutz Niethammer, 3 vols (Bonn: J.H.W. Dietz Nachf., 1983–85), II (1983), 17–105

Niethammer, Lutz, Alexander von Plato and Dorothee Wierling, *Die Volkseigene Erfahrung: Eine Archäologie des Lebens in der Industrieprovinz der DDR* (Berlin: Rowohlt, 1991)

Niven, Bill, *Facing the Nazi Past: United Germany and the Legacy of the Third Reich* (London: Routledge, 2001)

———, 'The GDR and Memory of the Bombing of Dresden', in *Germans as Victims: Remembering the Past in Contemporary Germany*, ed. by Bill Niven (Basingstoke: Palgrave Macmillan, 2006), pp. 109–29

Noelle, Elisabeth, and Erich Peter Neumann, eds, *Allensbacher Jahrbuch der öffentlichen Meinung 1958–1964* (Allensbach: Verlag für Demoskopie, 1965)

Pagenstecher, Cord, *Der bundesdeutsche Tourismus. Ansätze zu einer Visual History: Urlaubsprospekte, Reiseführer, Fotoalben, 1950–1990* (Hamburg: Dr. Kovac, 2003)

Paul, Gerhard, 'Von der historischen Bildkunde zur Visual History: Eine Einführung', in *Visual History: Ein Studienbuch*, ed. by Gerhard Paul (Göttingen: Vandenhoeck & Ruprecht, 2006), pp. 7–36

Pinto-Duschinsky, Michael, 'Foreign Political Aid: The West German Political Foundations and their U.S. Counterparts', *International Affairs*, 67.1 (1991), 33–63

Plowman, Andrew, '*Staatsbürger in Uniform*? Looking back at the Bundeswehr in Jochen Missfeldt *Gespiegelter Himmel* (2001) and Sven Regener *Neue Vahr Süd* (2004)', *Seminar*, 43.2 (2007), 163–75

Poiger, Uta, *Jazz, Rock and Rebels: Cold War Politics and American Culture in a Divided Germany* (Berkeley: University of California Press, 2000)

Poock-Feller, Ulrike, and Andrea Krausch, '"Berlin lebt – Berlin ruft!" Die Fremdenverkehrswerbung Ost- und West-Berlins in der Nachkriegszeit', in *Goldstrand und Teutonengrill: Kultur- und Sozialgeschichte des Tourismus in Deutschland 1945–1989*, ed. by Hasso Spode (Berlin: Moser, 1996), pp. 105–16

Poutrus, Patrice, 'Die DDR, ein anderer deutscher Weg? Zum Umgang mit Ausländern im SED-Staat', in *Zuwanderungsland Deutschland: Migrationen 1500–2005*, ed. by Rosmarie Beier-de Haan (Wolfratshausen: Minerva, 2005), pp. 118–31

Raich, Silvia, *Grenzüberschreitende und interregionale Zusammenarbeit in einem "Europa der Regionen": Dargestellt anhand der Fallbeispiele Grossregion Saar-Lor-Lux, EUREGIO und "Vier Motoren für Europa": Ein Beitrag zum europäischen Integrationsprozess* (Baden-Baden: Nomos, 1995)

Rakowski, Mieczyslaw, *The Foreign Policy of the Polish People's Republic* (Warsaw: Interpress, 1975)

Raundalen, Jon, 'A Communist Takeover in the Dream Factory: Appropriation of Popular Genres by the East German Film Industry', *I: Slavonica*, 11.1 (2004), 69–86

Reich, Ines, and Kurt Finker, 'Reaktionäre oder Patrioten? Zur Historiographie und Widerstandsforschung in der DDR bis 1990', in *Der 20. Juli: Das andere Deutschland in der Vergangenheitspolitik nach 1934*, ed. by Gerd R. Ueberschär (Berlin: Elefanten Press, 1998), pp. 158–78

Reichel, Peter, *Vergangenheitsbewältigung in Deutschland: Die Auseinandersetzung mit der NS-Diktatur von 1945 bis heute* (Munich: Beck, 2001)
Reinisch, Jessica, '"Zurück zu unserem Virchow!": Medizinische Karrieren, Nationalhelden und Geschichtsschreibung in Deutschland nach 1945', in *Gesundheit und Staat: Studien zur Geschichte der Gesundheitsämter in Deutschland, 1870–1950*, ed. by Axel C. Hüntelmann, Johannes Vossen and Herwig Czech (Husum: Matthiesen, 2007), pp. 255–74
Rentschler, Eric, 'From New German Cinema to the Post-Wall Cinema of Consensus", in *Cinema and Nation*, ed. by Mette Hjort and Scott MacKenzie (London: Routledge, 2000), pp. 260–77
Richards, Yvette, 'African and African-American Labor Leaders in the Struggle over International Affiliation', *International Journal of African Historical Studies*, 31.2 (1998), 301–34
Richie, Alexandra, *Faust's Metropolis: A History of Berlin* (New York: Carroll & Graf, 1998)
Ritter, Andreas, *Wandlungen in der Steuerung des DDR-Hochleistungssports in den 1960er und 1970er Jahren* (Potsdam: Universitätsverlag Potsdam, 2003)
Ritter, Gerhard, *Carl Goerdeler und die deutsche Widerstandsbewegung* (Stuttgart: Deutsche Verlags-Anstalt, 1955)
——, *Die Dämonie der Macht: Betrachtungen über Geschichte und Wesen des Machtproblems im politischen Denken der Neuzeit*, 6th edn (Munich: Leibniz, 1948)
——, *Staatskunst und Kriegshandwerk: Das Problem des Militarismus in Deutschland*, 4 vols (Munich: Oldenbourg, 1954–68)
Rudolph, Rolf, 'Die nationale Verantwortung der Historiker in der DDR', *ZfG*, 10.2 (1962), 253–85
Sabrow, Martin, 'Confrontation and Co-operation: Relations between the Two German Historiographies', in *The Divided Past* (see Kleßmann, 'Introduction', above), pp. 127–47
——, *Das Diktat des Konsenses: Geschichtswissenschaft in der DDR, 1949–1969* (Munich: Oldenbourg, 2001)
Sahlins, Peter, *Boundaries: The Making of France and Spain in the Pyrenees* (Berkeley: University of California Press, 1989)
Sälter, Gerhard, 'Rituelle Inszenierung staatlicher Anerkennung: Konferenzen der freiwilligen Grenzhelfer (1956–1989)', *Horch und Guck*, 56.4 (2006), 15–16
——, 'Loyalität und Denunziation in der ländlichen Gesellschaft der DDR: Die Freiwilligen Helfer der Grenzpolizei im Jahr 1952', in *Der willkommene Verrat: Beiträge zur Denunziationsforschung*, ed. by Michael Schröter (Weilerswist: Velbrück, 2007), pp. 159–84
Saunders, Frances Stonor, *Who Paid the Piper? The CIA and the Cultural Cold War* (London: Granta, 1999)
Schenk, Ralf, 'Mitten im Kalten Krieg', in *Das zweite Leben der Filmstadt Babelsberg: DEFA Filmspiele 1946–1992*, ed. by Ralf Schenk (Berlin: Henschel, 1994), pp. 50–157
Schildt, Axel, *Zwischen Abendland und Amerika: Studien zur Erfolgsgeschichte der Bundesrepublik* (Munich: Oldenbourg, 1999)
Schmelz, Andrea, *Migration und Politik im geteilten Deutschland während des Kalten Krieges: die West-Ost-Migration in die DDR in den 1950er und 1960er Jahren* (Opladen: Leske + Budrich, 2002)

Schmundt-Thomas, Georg, 'Hollywood's Romance of Foreign Policy: American G.I.s and the Conquest of the German Fräulein', *Journal of Popular Film and Television*, 19.4 (1992), 187–97

Schönhoven, Klaus, *Die deutschen Gewerkschaften* (Frankfurt/Main: Suhrkamp, 1987)

Schroeder, Wolfgang, *Gewerkschaftspolitik zwischen DGB, Katholizismus und CDU 1945 bis 1960* (Cologne: Bund, 1990)

Schulz, Brigitte, *Development Policy in the Cold War Era: The Two Germanies and Sub-Saharan Africa, 1960–1985* (Münster: Lit, 1995)

Schütz, Erhard, Klaus Siebenhaar and Cornelia Kunkat, eds, *Berlin wirbt! Metropolenwerbung zwischen Verkehrsreklame und Stadtmarketing, 1920–1995* (Berlin: FAB, 1995)

Scott-Smith, Giles, and Hans Krabbendam, *The Cultural Cold War in Western Europe, 1945 – 1960* (London: Cass, 2003)

Selvage, Douglas, 'Introduction to Khrushchev's November 1958 Berlin Ultimatum: New Evidence from the Polish Archives', *Bulletin: Cold War International History Project,* 10 (1998), 200–203

Shaw, Tony, *British Cinema and the Cold War: The State, Propaganda and Consensus* (London: I.B. Tauris, 2001)

——, *Hollywood's Cold War* (Edinburgh: Edinburgh University Press, 2007)

——, 'The Politics of Cold War Culture', *Journal of Cold War Studies*, 3.3 (2001), 59–76

Shearer, David, 'Elements Near and Alien: Passportization, Policing, and Identity in the Stalinist State, 1931–1952', *The Journal of Modern History*, 76 (2004), 835–81

Sikora, Franz, *Sozialistische Solidarität und nationale Interessen* (Cologne: Verlag für Wissenschaft und Politik, 1977)

Silberman, Marc, 'Post-Wall Documentaries: New Images from a New Germany?', *Cinema Journal*, 33 (1994), 22–41

Simon, Erik, and Olaf R. Spittel, *Die Science-Fiction der DDR: Autoren und Werke: Ein Lexikon* (East Berlin: Das Neue Berlin, 1988)

Spalding, Hobart A., *Organized Labor in Latin America* (New York: Harper & Row, 1977)

Spitzer, Giselher, 'Anfang und Ende der Lex Ewald 1955–1989', in *Goldkinder: Die DDR im Spiegel ihres Spitzensports,* ed. by Grit Hartmann (Leipzig: Forum, 1998), pp. 260–81

——, 'Der innerste Zirkel: Von der Leistungssportkommission des Deutschen Turn- und Sportbundes zur LSK der DDR', *Sportwissenschaft,* 25.4 (1995), 360–75

Spode, Hasso, and Matthias Gutbier, 'Berlin-Reise als Berlin-Geschichte', in *Die Reise nach Berlin,* ed. by Berliner Festspiele GmbH (Berlin: Siedler, 1987), pp. 25–41

Stahl, Heiner, *Jugendhörfunk im kalten Ätherkrieg: Jugendstudio DT 64, s-f-beat und RIAS-Treffpunkt und die Herausbildung einer Klanglandschaft des Pop in Berlin (1962–1973),* (unpublished doctoral dissertation, University of Potsdam, 2007).

Staritz, Dietrich, *Geschichte der DDR, 1949–1985* (Frankfurt/Main: Suhrkamp, 1985)

Steinbach, Peter, 'Widerstand im Dritten Reich – die Keimzelle der Nachkriegsdemokratie?', in *Der 20. Juli* (see Reich, above), pp. 98–124

Steiner, André, ed., *Überholen ohne einzuholen: die DDR-Wirtschaft als Fußnote der deutschen Geschichte* (Berlin: Links 2006)

Steinmüller, Angela, and Karlheinz Steinmüller, *Vorgriff auf das Lichte Morgen: Studien zur DDR-Science Fiction* (Passau: EDFC, 1995)
Stern, Leo, *Martin Luther and Philipp Melanchthon* (East Berlin, Rütten & Loening, 1953)
Stibbe, Matthew, 'The Fischer Controversy over German War Aims in the First World War and its Reception by East German Historians, 1961-1989', *The Historical Journal*, 46.3 (2003), 649-68
Stivers, William, 'The Incomplete Blockade: Soviet Zone Supply of West Berlin, 1948-49', *Diplomatic History*, 21.4 (1997), 569-602
Stokłosa, Katarzyna, 'Two Sides of the Border and One Regional Identity: The Identity Problem in the German-Polish and Ukrainian-Slovak Border Regions', in *Crossing the Border: Boundary Relations in a Changing Europe*, ed. by Thomas Lundén (Gdansk: Förlags ab Gondolin, 2006), pp. 117-33.
Stott, Rosemary, 'Entertained by the Class Enemy: Cinema Programming Policy in the German Democratic Republic', in *100 Years of European Cinema: Entertainment or Ideology?*, ed. by Diana Holmes and Alison Smith (Manchester: Manchester University Press, 2000), pp. 27-39
——, 'Zwischen Sozialkritik und Blockbuster: Hollywood-Filme in den Kinos der DDR zwischen 1970 und 1989', in *Umworbener Klassenfeind: Das Verhältnis der DDR zu den USA*, ed. by Uta A. Balbier and Christiane Rösch (Berlin: Links, 2006), pp. 144-60
Stöver, Bernd, *Der Kalte Krieg 1947-1991: Geschichte eines radikalen Zeitalters* (Munich: Beck, 2007)
——, 'Radio mit kalkuliertem Risiko: RIAS als amerikanischer Sender für die DDR', in *Zwischen Pop und Propaganda* (see Lindenberger, 'Geteilte Welt, geteilter Himmel', above), pp. 209-28
Streim, Alfred, 'Vorwort', in Christa Hoffmann, *Stunden Null? Vergangenheitsbewältigung in Deutschland 1945 und 1989*, Extremismus & Demokratie, 2 (Bonn: Bouvier, 1992), pp. 7-24
Strom, Elizabeth A., *Building the New Berlin: The Politics of Urban Development in Germany's Capital City* (Lanham, MD: Lexington, 2001)
Süssmuth, Hans, 'Luther 1983 in beiden deutschen Staaten: Kritische Rezeption oder ideologische Vereinnahmung?', in *Das Luther – Erbe in Deutschland: Vermittlung zwischen Wissenschaft und Öffentlichkeit*, ed. by Hans Süssmuth (Düsseldorf: Droste, 1985), pp. 16-40
Teichler, Hans Joachim, 'Sport in der DDR.: Systemmerkmale, Folgen und offene Forschungsfragen', *Deutschland Archiv: Zeitschrift für das vereinigte Deutschland*, 37.3 (2004), 414-21
——, *Die Sportbeschlüsse des Politbüros: Eine Studie zum Verhältnis von SED und Sport mit einem Gesamtverzeichnis und einer Dokumentation ausgewählter Beschlüsse* (Cologne: Sport und Buch Strauß, 2002)
Timm, Angelika, 'Juden in der DDR und der Staat Israel', in *Zwischen Politik und Kultur: Juden in der DDR*, ed. by Moshe Zuckermann (Göttingen: Wallstein, 2002), pp. 17-33
Toplin, Robert Brent, *History by Hollywood: The Use and Abuse of the American Past* (Urbana and Chicago: University of Illinois Press, 1996)
Torner, Evan, 'To the End of a Universe: The (Brief) History of the DEFA Science Fiction Film', in *From Weimar to Christiania: German and Scandinavian Studies*

*in Context*, ed. by Florence Feiereisen and Kyle Frackman (Newcastle upon Tyne: Cambridge Scholars Publishing, 2007), pp. 89–106

Trachtenberg, Marc, *A Constructed Peace: The Making of the European Settlement 1945–1963* (Princeton: Princeton University Press, 1999)

Uecker, Matthias, 'Fractured Families – United Countries? Family, Nostalgia and Nation-building in *Das Wunder von Bern* and *Goodbye Lenin!*', *New Cinemas: Journal of Contemporary Film*, 5.3 (2007), 189–200

Ullrich, Maren, *Geteilte Ansichten: Erinnerungslandschaft deutsch-deutsche Grenze* (Berlin: Aufbau, 2006)

Wagner, Christoph, 'Die offiziöse Außen- und Entwicklungspolitik der deutschen politischen Stiftungen in Lateinamerika', in *Deutschland – Lateinamerika: Geschichte, Gegenwart und Perspektiven*, ed. by Manfred Mols and Christoph Wagner (Frankfurt/Main: Vervuert, 1994), pp. 167–228

Wandel, Paul, *Der deutsche Imperialismus und seine Kriege – das nationale Unglück Deutschlands* (East Berlin: Dietz, 1955)

Wapshott, Nicholas, *The Man Between: A Biography of Carol Reed* (London: Chatto & Windus, 1990)

Weiler, Peter, *Ernest Bevin* (Manchester: Manchester University Press, 1993)

Weinke, Annette, *Die Verfolgung von NS-Tätern: Vergangenheitsbewältigungen 1949–1969, oder, eine deutsch-deutsche Beziehungsgeschichte im Kalten Krieg* (Paderborn: Schöningh, 2002)

Weinstein, Raymond M., 'Occupation G.I. Blues: Post-war Germany During and After Elvis Presley's Tour', *Journal of Popular Culture*, 39.1 (2006), 126–49

Wendauer, Friedemann, and Alan Morris, 'The Politics of Laughter: Problems of Humor and Satire in the FRG Today', in *Laughter Unlimited: Essays on Humor, Satire and the Comic*, ed. by Reinhold Grimm (Madison: University of Wisconsin Press, 1991), pp. 56–78

Wiesener, Albrecht, 'Halle an der Saale – Chemiemetropole oder "Diva in Grau": Zur bildlichen Repräsentation einer Stadt im Sozialismus', in *Die DDR im Bild* (see Klotz, above), pp. 51–68

Wilke, Jürgen, 'Radio im Geheimauftrag: Der Freiheitssender 904 und der Deutsche Soldatensender 935 als Instrumente des Kalten Krieges', in *Zwischen Pop und Propaganda: Radio in der DDR* (see Lindenberger, 'Geteilte Welt, geteilter Himmel', above), pp. 249–66

Wirsching, Andreas, *Abschied vom Provisorium: Die Geschichte der Bundesrepublik Deutschland 1982–1990* (Munich: Deutsche-Verlagsanstalt, 2006)

Wolf, Werner, *Untersuchungen über Schulen und Unterrichtsmittel in Ghana* (Berlin: Verein zur Förderung der Bildungshilfe in Entwicklungsländern e.V., 1966)

Wolffsohn, Michael, *Die Deutschland Akte: Tatsachen und Legenden* (Munich: Edition Ferenczy bei Bruckmann, 1995)

Wolle, Stefan, 'Die Welt der verlorenen Bilder: Die DDR im visuellen Gedächtnis', in *Visual History* (see Paul, above), pp. 333–52

Zec, Peter, *Mythos aus der Flasche: Coca-Cola Culture im 20. Jahrhundert* (Essen: Design Zentrum NRW, 1994)

Ziegler, Melanie M., *U.S.-Cuban Cooperation Past, Present, and Future* (Florida: Florida University Press, 2007)

# Notes on Contributors

**Seán Allan** is Reader in German Studies at the University of Warwick. He is co-editor (with John Sandford) of *DEFA: East German Cinema, 1946–1992* (Oxford: Berghahn, 1999) and has written a wide range of articles on representations of East Germany and post-unification German identity in contemporary German cinema. He has also written extensively on eighteenth- and nineteenth-century drama, including *The Plays of Heinrich von Kleist: Ideals and Illusions* (Cambridge: CUP, 1996) and *The Stories of Heinrich von Kleist: Fictions of Security* (Rochester, NY: Camden House, 2001).

**Sheldon Anderson** is Professor of History at Miami University, Ohio. He has authored three books, including *Condemned to Repeat It: "Lessons of History" and the Making of U.S. Cold War Containment Policy* (Lanham, MD: Rowman & Littlefield, 2008). He is currently writing a history of sport in international affairs.

**James Chapman** is Professor of Film Studies at the University of Leicester. He has wide-ranging research interests in British cinema, television and popular culture. His books include *Past and Present: National Identity and the British Historical Film* (London: I.B. Tauris, 2005), *Licence To Thrill: A Cultural History of the James Bond Films* (London: I.B. Tauris, 2nd edn 2007), *War and Film* (London: Reaktion, 2008) and, co-authored with Nicholas J. Cull, *Projecting Empire: Imperialism and Popular Cinema* (London: I.B. Tauris, 2009).

**Tobias Hochscherf** is Professor of Audio-Visual Media at the University of Applied Sciences at Kiel, Germany. His research interests focus on European film and television cultures. He is particularly interested in film practices across borders, émigrés and British cinema, and representations of the Cold War in film and television. His research has been published widely in academic journals and edited collections.

**Christoph Laucht** is Lecturer in History at the University of Liverpool. His research interests include the cultural history of the nuclear age, the transnational history of the Cold War and film and history. He is currently completing a book on the impact of German émigré scientists on British nuclear culture.

**Thomas Lindenberger** is Director of the Ludwig Boltzmann Institute for European History and Public Spheres in Vienna and Associate Professor at the University of Potsdam. He has been published widely in German and international journals and anthologies. His books include *Volkspolizei: Herrschaftspraxis und öffentliche Ordnung im SED-Staat, 1952–1968* (Cologne: Böhlau, 2003) and *Straßenpolitik: Zur Sozialgeschichte der öffentlichen Ordnung in Berlin, 1900–1914* (Bonn: J.H.W. Dietz Nachf., 1995). His latest co-edited book (with Muriel Blaive and Christian Gerbel) is *Clashes in European Memories. The Case of Communist Repression and the Holocaust* (Innsbruck: Studienverlag, 2010).

**Patrick Major** is Professor at the University of Reading. His research interests are primarily the political, social and cultural history of divided Germany in the Cold War. He has written *The Death of the KPD: Communism and Anti-Communism in West Germany, 1945–1956* (Oxford: OUP, 1998) and *The Rise and Fall of the Berlin Wall: A Concrete History* (Oxford: OUP, 2009).

**Inge Marszolek** is Professor in the Department of Cultural Studies at Bremen University. She is the author of various studies on twentieth-century history, mainly in Germany. Her research focuses on media history, power and society in the National Socialist and postwar eras and on images (mainly photography) in the Cold War.

**Bill Niven** is Professor of Contemporary German History at Nottingham Trent University. His books include *The Buchenwald Child: Truth, Fiction and Propaganda* (Woodbridge: Boydell & Brewer, 2007) and *Facing the Nazi Past: United Germany and the Legacy of the Third Reich* (London: Routledge, 2002). He has, among others, edited the anthology *Germans as Victims: Remembering the Past in Contemporary Germany* (London: Palgrave Macmillan, 2006).

**Jon Berndt Olsen** is Assistant Professor in the Department of History at the University of Massachusetts at Amherst, where he teaches courses on German History, Public History and New Media. His research specialization is in the area of memory cultures and historical consciousness in modern Germany, especially in the former GDR.

**Andrew Plowman** is Senior Lecturer in German at the University of Liverpool. He is the author of a study on German autobiography and of numerous articles on contemporary German literature. His current research focuses on the cultural representation of the Bundeswehr.

**Quinn Slobodian** is Assistant Professor of History at Wellesley College in Massachusetts. He is currently completing a manuscript on Third World politics and the New Left in 1960s West Germany.

**Michelle A. Standley** is completing a doctoral dissertation in Modern European History at New York University. Her thesis examines the relationship between the Cold War and mass tourism in East and West Berlin from 1945–1979.

**Matthew Stibbe** is Professor of Modern European History at Sheffield Hallam University. He has written several books and articles on Germany's role in the First World War, and has co-edited (with Kevin McDermott) two volumes of essays on the post-1945 era – *Revolution and Resistance in Eastern Europe: Challenges to Communist Rule* (Oxford: Berg, 2006); and *Stalinist Terror in Eastern Europe: Elite Purges and Mass Repression* (Manchester: Manchester University Press, 2010).

**Rosemary Stott** is Principal Lecturer in Film Studies at London Metropolitan University. She has published widely in the field of film policy in the GDR, in particular the exhibition and reception of Western films there.

**Christopher Young** is Reader in Modern and Medieval German Studies, and Head of the Department of German and Dutch at the University of Cambridge. He has authored and co-edited over a dozen volumes on German culture and modern European sport. His *The 1972 Munich Olympics and the Making of Modern Germany* (with Kay Schiller) appeared with the University of California Press in 2010.

# Index

Abendroth, Wolfgang, 37, 46n16
Abteilung Sport beim ZK der SED, 153
Academy of Sciences (GDR), 42, 67
Actors Studio (New York), 226
Adams, R.A., 81
Adenauer, Konrad, 34, 36, 50–60, 78
    Konrad Adenauer Foundation
    (Konrad-Adenauer-Stiftung),
    82
Africa, 38, 78–86, 110
Ahonen, Pertti, 52
Airlift Memorial, 109. *See also* Berlin
    Airlift
Akademie Verlag (GDR), 42–43
*Aktion Ungeziefer* (operation vermin),
    15
Aldiss, Brian, 215
Alexanderplatz (Berlin), 231
Algeria, 82
All-African Trade Union Federation,
    82
Allianz Film Company, 167, 172
Allies, 178, 180
    and division of Germany, 1, 4, 15,
        17, 52, 58, 77, 97, 113, 123, 188,
        190, 195–96
American Farm Security
    Administration, 177
American Federation of Labor and
    Congress of Industrial Organizations
    (AFL-CIO), 84
American Institute for Free Labor
    Development (AIFLD), 84
Americanization, 7, 178, 183–88,
    194–96, 200
Andernach, 185–86

Anderson, Michael, 226, 228–29
*Andymon: Eine Weltraum-Utopie*
    (*Andymon: A Space Utopia*, 1982),
    214–15
Anglican faith, 71
*Animal Farm* (1954), 221
Anti-Americanism, 200, 207, 212, 223
Anti-communism, 58, 60, 78–79, 86,
    195. *See also* Bolsheviks
*Antifaschistischer Schutzwall, see* Wall
anti-fascism, 20–21, 37–38, 51, 173,
    179, 182–88, 206
    anti-fascist film, 120, 166–73
    anti-fascist resistance, 49, 168,
        178
Anti-GDR rhetoric, 55
Anti-German sentiment, 108
anti-Slavism, 20. *See also* Bolsheviks
anti-Semitism, 53–54, 58, 227
anti-socialism, 20
Antonio, Eberhardt del', 208, 210
Apartheid, 81
Arbeitsgruppe Sport (GDR), 153
*Armee auf der Erbse, Die* (*The Army on
    the Pea*), 135, 141–45
Art-house films, 169
*Arzt von Stalingrad, Der* (*The Doctor of
    Stalingrad*, 1958), 184
Asia, 26, 78–86, 107
Astronaut, 210–11
Aufbau publishing house (GDR), 39
*Aufrecht Gehen, Rudi Dutschke, Spuren*
    (*Standing Tall, Rudi Dutschke,
    Traces*, 1988), 173
*Auf Wiedersehen Kinder* (*Au revoir les
    enfants*, 1987/1989), 167

Index ■ 251

*Augenzeuge, Der* (GDR newsreel), 180
Auschwitz concentration camp, 56–57
    trials in Frankfurt, 56
Austria, 91, 100, 167, 207
Axen, Hermann, 53, 101

Bach, Johann Sebastian, 64, 172
Baden-Württemberg, 18
Balhaus, Carl, 121
Ballard, J.G., 208, 215
Baltic (region), 26
Baltic (sea), 209
Baptist faith, 71
Bärmeier, Erich, 137
Batchelor, Joy, 221
Baum, Bruno, 95
BBC (British Broadcasting Corporation), 230
Becker, Wolfgang, 197, 209
Behrens, Fritz, 43
Bartel, Horst, 67
*Beil von Wandsbek, Das* (*The Axe of Wandsbek*, 1952), 122
Belgium, 18
Bergen-Belsen concentration camp, 55
Berger, Stefan, 39, 44
Bergman, Ingmar, 167, 169
Bergman, Ingrid, 197
Berlin
    and Berlin Airlift, 2, 7, 8, 178, 183, 190–203. *See also* Airlift Memorial *and* Soviet Blockade of Berlin (1948–49)
    Berlin Wall, *see* Wall
    as a divided city, 2, 6, 15, 16, 25, 30n6, 34, 44, 113, 119–133, 183, 195, 224. *See also* Wall
    East Berlin, 39, 66, 70, 72, 90, 90–102, 108–110, 119–33, 165, 171–72, 180–81, 209, 225–26, 228, 230
    as former German capital, 34, 183, 220
    as image in Anglo-American popular culture, 220–32, 8
    Olympics (1936), 153
    750th anniversary of, 64
    and Soviet Blockade of (1948–49), 17, 25, 123, 180, 191, 193, 196–97, 221
    West Berlin, 4, 6, 16–17, 55, 66, 105–116, 119–132, 170–73, 178, 190, 193–200, 206, 220–32, 228
*Berlin – Ecke Schönhauser* (*Berlin – Schönhauser Corner*, 1957), 119, 126
*Berlin Express* (1948), 224
*Berlin Game*, 230
*Berlin Memorandum, The*, 228
Berlin Republic, 191, 196–97, 200, 231. *See also* Foundation myth
Bertelsmann/RTL Group, 192
Bethmann Hollweg, Theobald von, 36
Beyer, Frank, 120–21
Bible, 67, 71
Biess, Frank, 184
*Big Lift, The* (1950), 196, 198
*Bild Zeitung*, 149–50
*Bild des Soldaten, Das* (*The Image of the Soldier*), 141
*Billion Dollar Brain* (1967), 228
*Bitterfisch* (*Bitter Fish*, 1974), 214
*blaue Engel, Der* (1930), 168, 220
*Blechtrommel, Die* (*The Tin Drum*, 1979), 166
Bloch, Ernst, 43, 205
Bloom, Claire, 225, 227
Bogart, Humphrey, 197
Bohm, Hark, 172
Bohn, Thomas, 144
Böll, Heinrich, 52, 135, 184
Bolsheviks, 178, 184. *See also* anti-communism and anti-Slavism
Bolz, Lothar, 93, 98
Bond, James, 109, 220, 222–223, 226, 228–30
Böttcher, Jürgen, 124, 129–31
Bonn (as capital of the FRG), 54, 20, 61n19, 90, 93, 98–102, 106, 113, 135, 178
Border cinemas, 156
Borderlines, 14
*Bourne Supremacy, The* (2004), 231
Bräutigam, Otto, 52
Bradbury, Ray, 207, 215
Bramarbas, Miles, 134, 141–45

## 252 ■ Index

*Brand, der* (*The Fire*), 198
Brandenburg Gate, 123, 130–31, 209, 225
Brandt, Willy, 3, 49, 55, 59, 63, 66, 73, 85, 113, 165. *See also Ostpolitik*
Branstner, Gerhard, 213
Braun, Johanna and Günter, 213–14
Brazil, 73
Bremerhaven, 183
British Broadcasting Corporation, *see* BBC
Broccoli, Albert R., 228–29
Buchan, John, 222
Buchenwald Concentration Camp, 178
  Memorial at, 51, 59, 178
Bundesausschuß Leistungssport (Federal Committee for Competitive Sport, FRG), 150
Bundesgrenzschutz (FRG), 185
Bundesinstitut für Sportwissenschaft (Federal Insititute for Sports Science, FRG), 151
Bundeswehr, 6, 134–47 182, 185. *See also* Rearmament
Burma, 79
Burton, Richard, 227

*Cabaret* (1972), 174n7, 220
Caine, Michael, 228
Capitalism, 81, 99, 110, 125, 135, 178, 206–9
Carow, Heiner, 120, 163,
Carpentier, Karlheinz, 128
Carré, John le, 8, 220–30
Carstens, Karl, 66, 72
*Casablanca* (1942), 197
*Casino Royale* (novel 1954, film 1967), 222–23, 226, 229
Catholic faith, 66, 71, 94, 96
Censorship, 43, 71, 205–7, 215–6
Central Film Authority (GDR), 166, 170–1
Central Intelligence Agency (USA), *see* CIA
Central Institute of History (GDR), 67
Checkpoint Charlie, 109, 116, 124, 227, 230
Childers, Erskine, 222
Chile, 84
China, 26, 38
Christian Democratic Party (CDU), 52, 82
Churchill, Winston, 91, 224,
CIA, 221, 229, 231
Cinema, *see* Film
Clancy, Tom, 222
Clausewitz, Carl von, 64–65
Clay, Lucius D., 194, 200,
Coca-Cola, 109, 183
Coal, 81, 191
Cold War
  battle of legitimacy, 44, 49–62
  ethics of, 227
  as experience, 1–21, 28–9
  mediascape of, 22–28
  as predicament, 11–21
  and reductionism, 13
  as system, 11
  tourism, *see* Tourism
Cold Warriors, 86
Comedy Film, 128, 165, 170, 199
Communism, 21, 27, 49, 55–60, 74, 78, 83–6, 90, 110, 148, 187, 200, 208, 211, 221, 223
Communist Party of the Soviet Union (CPSU), 35
  Twentieth Party Congress of (1956), 42
Concentration camp, 34, 53, 55, 99, 108, 127. *See also* Auschwitz, Bergen-Belsen, Buchenwald and Dachau, 56
Connery, Sean, 229
Conrad, Bernt, 51
Consensual capitalism, 78
Consumption, 17, 23, 93, 111, 115–6, 119, 130, 176, 183, 229
Consumerism, 168, 183, 187, 212, 230
*Conviva Ludibundus* (1978), 214
Cooperative societies, 81
Cornelius, Henry, 220
Cornwell, David, 223
'Cor Serpentis' (1959), 211
Cosmonaut, 209–10
Costa Rica, 84
*Cover Stories*, 221

Crime film, 169, 172
Cuba, 26, 126, 171, 221
Cuban Missile Crisis, 221
Cultural legacy, 65
Cultural memory, 5, 7–8
Cultural policy, 6, 129
Currency, 68, 178, 199, 207
Curtiz, Michael, 197
Cusack, Cyril, 227
Czechoslovakia, 18–19, 92, 97–98, 100–101

Dachau concentration camp, 56
*Daily Mirror,* 183
Damon, Matt, 231
Daume, Willi, 149,153, 159
David, Vaclav, 100
Dean, James, 187
Decolonization, 28, 79,
Defection, 227–8
Dehn, Paul, 226
Deighton, Len, 220, 222, 225, 228, 230
Denning, Michael, 221-2, 225
Denazification (FRG), 182
   See also reeducation
De-Stalinization, 39, 94, 96, 211
Détente, 24–25, 73, 78, 85, 91, 100, 142, 171, 228
Deutsche Film Aktiengesellschaft (DEFA), 23, 69, 120, 122-3, 127–31, 132n13, 163–75, 205
Deutsche Hochschule für Körperkultur (DHfK, German University of Physical Culture, GDR), 153, 158
Deutsche Olympische Gesellschaft (DOG, German Olympic Society, FRG), 150, 152
Deutsche Sportkonferenz (The German Sports Conference, FRG), 150
Deutsche Turn- und Sportbund der DDR (DTSB, German Gymnastics and Sports Federation, GDR), 153, 155, 162n52
   Leistungskomission des DTSB (Performance Commission of the DTSB), 155

Deutscher Gewerkschaftsbund (DGB, the Confederation of German Trade Unions), 78–86
Deutscher Sportbund (DSB, German Sports Association, FRG), 150, 152
DeMille, Cecile B., 221
de Roche, Alex, 172
Development aid, 2, 88n33
Dick, Philip K, 208, 213, 215
dictatorship, 15–20, 25, 50, 55, 57, 177–8, 212
Dietrich, Marlene, 168
diplomacy, 3, 18, 26, 53–4, 80, 84–85, 92–97, 100–101, 149, 152, 163, 166, 207, 221
documentary film, 6, 123–5, 129–31, 173, 185, 199, 202n12
Dörrie, Doris, 170
Dominik, Hans, 206
Dominican Republic, 84
Domröse, Angelica, 127
Dorst, Christiane, 172
DreamWorks, 192
*Drehort Berlin* (*Location Berlin,* 1987), 173
*Dresden* (TV film, 2006), 190
Dresden (city of) 166, 172, 208
   bombing of, 57
   Technical University of, 213
*Dritte, Der* (*The Third,* 1972), 165
*Dr No* (novel 1958), 223
Drugs, performance enhancing in sport, 157–8
Dudow, Slatan, 121
Dürrfeld, Walter, 57
*Dutschke* (2009), 192

East Berlin, *see Berlin*
East German parliament, 72, 97
East Germany, *see* GDR
Eastern bloc, 18, 27–28, 59, 150–51, 205, 211, 215, 225
Friedrich Ebert Foundation (Friedrich-Ebert-Stiftung), 78, 82–86
Eco, Umberto, 222
Economic Miracle, *see Wirtschaftswunder*
Efremov, Ivan, 211

*Ehe der Maria Braun, Die* (*The Marriage of Maria Braun*, 1978), 166–8
*Ehe im Schatten* (*Marriage in the Shadow*, 1947), 122
1848 revolution, 38, 178
Eighth Plenum, 95
*Einheit* (journal), 42
*Ein Kessel Buntes* (*The Variety Show*), 171
Eisenach (city of), 68, 70–71
Eisenhower, Dwight D., 99, 136, 192, 200
Eisleben (city of) 68, 70–72
Elbe (river of) 93
Elsaesser, Thomas, 229, 232n16
Emergency Decrees of 1972 (FRG), 59
Emilia Romana, 27
*Encounter* (journal) 224
*Ende einer Dienstfahrt* (*End of a Mission*), 135
Engels, Friedrich, 37, 40, 44, 181, 205
Entertainment film, 23–24, 164, 169
environmental pollution, 212, 216
Esche, Eberhard, 129
Estonia, 26
Ethnicity, 29
*Eulenspiegel*, 135, 159
Europe, 1, 13–15, 18–20, 22, 26–29, 31n14, 38, 49, 64, 69, 73, 77, 82, 86, 91–92, 94, 97–102, 105–9, 115, 119, 148, 160, 178, 188, 220, 222, 224
European Common Market, *see* European economic integration
European economic integration, 25, 82, 101
European integration, 18
European Economic Community, 18
Ewald, Manfred, 155–6, 159
Evangelical Church, 66, 68, 70–4
Eyck, Peter Van, 227

Fahlberg, H.L., 208
*Fahrenheit 451*, 207
*Fall Gleiwitz, Der* (*The Gleiwitz Affair*, 1961), 120
Fassbinder, Rainer Werner, 167–8, 172
Febrista Party, 85
Feldman, Charles K., 229

Ferch, Heino, 190, 192–3
Film, 6, 23, 109, 191–2, 195, 197–9, 224–5, 227–9, 230
  import of, 163–75
  programming of, 173
  and representations of the wall, 119–33
Finland, 26
First World War, 5, 13, 34–48, 91, 171, 220, 224
Fischer, Fritz, 35–6, 45n5
Fischer, Joachim, 134, 139, 141
Fleming, Ian, 8, 220, 222–3, 225, 229, 230
*Foreign Affair, A* (1948), 196
Foreign aid, 77
Fosse, Bob, 220
Foucault, Michel, 176–7
  *Gouvernementalité*, 177
Foundation Myth, 191, 194, 197
Four Allies' Conference, 180
*456 und der Rest von heute* (*456 and the Rest of Today*), 144
France, 18, 26–28, 77, 100, 160, 164–5, 183, 194
*Frau vom Checkpoint Charlie, die* (*The Woman from Checkpoint Charlie*, 2007), 201
*Fräulein* (1958), 196
Frederick the Great, 64
Free Democratic Party (FDP), 83
Freedom, 19, 66, 105–18, 134, 137, 139, 178, 221, 224
Freedom Bell, 107, 109
Freie Deutsche Jugend (FDJ, Free German Youth, GDR), 179, 210
'Freiheitssender 904' (liberty station 904, GDR), 22
FRG
  western integration of, 1–2, 4, 15, 18–19, 25, 36, 82, 182, 187, 199
  West German economic model, 113, 150
  West German Foreign Ministry (Auswärtiges Amt, AA), 79, 84–85
  West German standard of living, 23, 127

Friedrich, Jörg, 198
Fritzsche, Sonja, 205, 208
Frölich, Paul, 42
*From Russia, with Love* (novel 1957), 223
*Frühlingssinfonie* (*Spring Symphony*, 1983), 172
Fühmann, Franz, 216
*Funeral in Berlin* (film 1966), 226, 228
Funke, Christoph, 126, 128
Furie Sidney J., 228

Gaddis, John Lewis, 3
Gagarin, Juri Alexejewitsch, 204, 211
*Game, Set, Match* (1988), 230
Gass, Karl, 6, 119, 123–4, 131
Gdansk (Danzig), 91
GDR
    as dictatorship, 15–17, 19, 50, 55, 57, 177–8
    economy, 63, 95–97, 166–7, 206–7, 212–3, 215
    Ministry of the Interior, 211
    1974 constitution, 3
    as people's republic, 27, 98
    policy of demarcation from the FRG, 3
    and *Republikflucht* (flight from the Republic), 15
    as Workers' and Peasants' State, 177
*Gefangene des ewigen Kreises* (*Prisoners of the Eternal Circle,* 1956), 210
*Geheimnis des Transpluto, Das* (*The Secret of Transpluto,* 1962), 211
George, Götz, 120
German Academy of Sciences (GDR), 42
Deutsche Zentrale für Fremdenverkehr (German Agency for Tourism), 108
German Expressionist cinema, 225, 230
German language, 67
German question (Deutschlandfrage), 1, 2, 80, 85, 90, 100–101
German unification, 3, 9, 25–26, 29, 49, 59, 92, 131, 182, 191, 196–7

German victimhood, 57–8, 184, 198
Germany
    as border region of the Cold War, 4, 8, 11–33
    as border zone of the Cold War, 14, 17
    division of, 13, 19, 25, 29, 34, 73, 106, 113, 191, 224. *See also* Potsdam Conference
    Federal Republic of, *see* FRG
    German Democratic Republic of, *see* GDR
    inner-German border, 1, 5–6, 8, 24, 97, 119. *See also* Wall
    Nazi Germany, 14, 19–21, 27, 43, 49–62, 99, 130, 166–8, 177–8, 180–7, 196, 198, 223, 228–9. *See also* Third Reich
    occupation zones, 13, 15, 28, 123, 134, 179, 182, 193–4, 197, 199, 224
    post-Wall Germany, 191, 197–8, 200. *See also* Berlin Republic
    unification of, *see* German unification
*Geschichten jener Nacht* (*Stories from that Night,* 1967)
    *Der große und kleine Willi* (*Big Billy and Little Billy*)
    *Phönix* (*Phoenix*)
    *Die Prüfung* (*The Test*)
    *Materna* (Materna)
Geschonneck, Erwin, 121, 128–9
Ghana, 82–83
*GI Blues* (1960), 196
*Gigantum* (1957), 208, 210
Gilliat, Sidney, 224
Glid, Nandor, 56
Globke, Hans, 52
*Glocke von Friedland, Die* (*The Bell of Friedland,* 1957), 185
*Glos Ludu* (*Voice of the People*), 91
Glück, Wolfgang, 167
Görlitz agreement, 92–93
Goethe, Johann Wolfgang von, 64–65
*Die goldene Kugel* (*The Golden Sphere,* 1949), 207
*GoldenEye* (1995), 230

Gomulka, Wladyslaw, 39, 44, 90–91, 94–96, 99–101
*Good Bye, Lenin!* (2002), 197, 209
*Goodbye to Berlin* (1939), 220
Gorbachev, Mikhail, 171
Graf, Dominik, 119, 131
Grass, Günter, 34, 198
Great Britain, 38, 43, 52, 77, 100, 224
    and Berlin airlift, 194
Grebing, Helga, 36
Greene, Graham, 222, 224–5
Gremm, Wolfgang, 167
*Grenzgänger* (border crossers), 14–17, 124–5
*Grenzgebiet* (border zone), 15
*Grenztruppen* (specialist military border guards, GDR), 16
Grönemeyer, Herbert, 172
Groh, Dieter, 36
*Große Flucht, Die* (*The Great Flight*, 2002), 199
*Die große Grenze* (*The Great Frontier*, 1960), 210
Grotewohl, Otto, 51, 99–100, 181
*Grünstein-Variante, Die* (*The Grünstein Variant*, 1984), 167, 172
Guatemala, 85
Günther, Egon, 123, 165
Guest, Val, 229
Guinness, Alec, 229–30

Händel, Georg Friedrich, 64
Hager, Kurt, 64–65
Haggard, William, 222
Halas, John, 221
Hall, Adam (Elleston Trevor), 222, 228
Halle, city of, 70
Hallstein Doctrine, 53, 152
Halvorsen, Gail S., 195–6
Hamilton, Guy, 226, 228
*Hammett* (1982), 172
*Handbuch der Inneren Führung* (*Handbook of Inner Leadership*, FRG), 141–2
Harich, Wolfgang, 39, 43
Harmon, Robert, 192
Haskin, Byron, 221
Hasler, Joachim, 121

*Hauch von Truppe, Ein* (*A Whiff of Troops*), 135, 141–3
Hauff, Reinhard, 169
*Hauptmann von Köpenick, Der* (*The Captain of Köpenick*), 144
'Hauptstädtisches Journal' ('Bonn Diary'), 135
Haydon, Bill, 223
Heartfield, John, 179
Hecht, Ben, 229
Hegen, Josef, 100
Heidegger, Hermann, 41
Heinemann, Gustav (FRG President), 178
Heintje (Hendrik Nikolaas Theodoor Simons), 164
*Heißes Metall* (*Hot Metal*, 1952), 208
Heller, Otto, 228
Heller, Joseph, 229
Helsinki Agreement, 163
Heritage, 64
Herzog, Erich, 84
*Hexer, Der*, 169
Heymann, Stefan, 98
Hillier, Erwin, 229
*Himmel über Berlin, Der* (*Wings of Desire*, 1987), 173
Hindenburg, Paul von, 36
*Hiroshima mon Amour* (1959), 125
Hirschmeier, Alfred, 172
Historical event film, 197
Historical materialism, 204
*Historische Zeitschrift*, 41
Histotainment, *see* Historical event film
Hitler, Adolf, 36, 38, 49, 56–58, 93, 99, 108, 139, 179, 181
    assessination attempt of (20 July 1944), 57–58
Hofmann, Nico, 191, 193. *See also* TeamWorx
Holocaust, 21, 54, 58, 198
Hollywood, 23, 169–70, 196–8, 221
Homolka, Oscar, 228
Honecker, Erich, 17, 67, 72, 102, 153, 155–6, 165, 212–3
Hoppe, Rolf, 172
Howley, Frank, 195
Hoyerswerda (city of), 213

Hungary, 18, 39, 95, 149
Hungarian Revolution (1956), 94, 96
Hughes, Ken, 229
Hürrig, Hans-Jürgen, 193
Huston, John, 229
Huston, Penelope, 226

*I Am a Camera* (1955), 220
IG-Farben, 56–57
IG Metall, 85
*Ike: Countdown to D-Day* (2004), 192
*Im Krebsgang*, 198
*Im Tornister: Ein Marschallstab (Destined to Become a Field Marshall)*, 135
Imperialism, 16, 24, 37, 38, 40, 42, 44, 51, 53–55, 57, 59, 135, 154, 156, 205–8, 212
India, 79–80, 83, 231
*Indianerfilme* (Native Indian films), 23, 169
Industrial relations, 79
*Innere Führung* (inner leadership), concept of (Bundeswehr), 137, 139, 140–2
Intelligence service, 84, 208, 221, 223, 226–31
International Congress of Free Trade Unions (ICFTU), 79
International Olympic Committee (IOC), 148, 153
*Invasion of the Body Snatchers* (1955), 221
*Ipcress File, The* (novel 1962, film 1965), 225, 228–9
Iraq War, 200
Iron Curtain, 5, 13, 24, 41, 44, 97, 107, 109–10, 160, 206, 224. *See also* Wall
*Irrtum des großen Zauberers, Der (The Grand Sorcerer's Mistake,* 1972), 213
Isherwood, Christopher, 220
Israel, 54, 228
Italy, 26–27, 164, 194
Izydorczyk, Jan, 99

Jähn, Sigmund, 209
*Jahr der ruhigen Sonne, Das (Year of the Quiet Sun,* 1984), 167

Janka, Walter, 39
Jews, 43, 50, 53–58, 167, 178, 227, 230
*Johann Sebastian Bachs vergebliche Reise in den Ruhm (Johann Sebastian Bach's Futile Journey into Fame,* 1980), 172
Johnson, Nunnally, 224
Journalists, *see* Press
Jugendgesetz, (Youth Law, GDR), 152

Kailembo, A. M., 81
*Kaiserreich*, 35, 204
*Kampfmai* (Fighting May Day), 180
Karst, Heinz, 141
Kasernierte Volkspolizei (KVP, People's Barracked Police, GDR), 98
Kaul, Friedrich Karl, 56
Kautsky, Karl, 40, 42
Kennedy, John F., 112, 123, 136
Kenneth Kaunda Foundation, 83
Kenya, 81–82, 156
Kellermann, Bernhard, 204
KGB, 226, 228, 231
Khrushchev, Nikita, 35, 41, 44, 94, 112, 123
*Kinnhaken, Der (The Punch to the Jaw,* 1962), 124–5
Kinski, Natassja, 172
Kirst, Hans Hellmuth, 186
Klagemann, Eugen, 122
Klaußner, Burghart, 200
*Kleid, Das (The Robe,* 1961), 123
Klein, Gerhard, 119–21, 127–9
Klemperer, Victor, 43
Kleßmann, Christoph, 4
and asymmetrical entanglement, 3, 24
Klippel, Christian, 144
Klüh, Gerhard, 185
Knef, Hildegard, 225
Knietzsch, Horst, 164
Knoch, Habbo, 186
Knopp, Guido, 199, 222n12
Kohl, Helmut, 66
Kohlhaase, Wolfgang, 127–8, 172
Kopa, Stanislaw, 92
Korda, Alexander, 224
Korea, 25–26

Korean War (1950–1953), 34, 36
Koster, Henry, 196, 221
Kommunistische Partei Deutschlands (KPD, German Communist Party), 35, 37–38, 42, 91–92, 179
Krämer-Badoni, Rudolf, 184
Kranz, Erhard, 170
Krasker, Robert, 225
Krebs, Mario, 172
Kreis- und Jugend-Sportschulen (KJS, children's and youth sports schools, GDR), 154–55, 158
Kremlin, 94, 101, 195
*Kristall* (journal), 186
Krohn, Rolf, 213
Krupkat, Günther, 208–9, 215
Krug, Manfred, 124, 132n18
Kruse, Wolfgang, 37
Kuczynski, Jürgen, 35, 39–44, 48n56
*kugeltranszendentale Vorhaben, Das* (*The Spherical Transcendental Project*, 1980), 214
Kulturbund (GDR), 212
Kultusministerkonferenz (the collective body of Education and Culture Ministers in the federal states, FRG), 151–2
Kunkel, Klaus, 208
Kurfürstendamm, 107, 109–10, 114, 120
*Kurs Ganymed* (*Vector Ganymede*, 1962), 211-2

Labour internationalism, 77–89
Labour unions, 77–89
*Lady Hamilton* (1941), 224
Landsberg, Alison, 191
'Landser', figure of, 186
Larkey, Edward, 23
Lassalle, Ferdinand, 179
*Last Enemy, The* (2008), 231
Laternser, Hans, 56
Latin America, 83–86, 88–89
Law, John, 229
*Legende von Paul und Paula, Die* (*The Legend of Paul and Paula*, 1973), 163, 165
Legitimacy, 63
LeGuin, Ursula, 215

Leistungssportkommission (Commission for Competitive Sport, GDR), 155
Lem, Stanislaw, 205
Lenin, Vladimir Ilyich, 36–37, 40–41, 44, 95, 181, 183, 204–205, 225
  *See also Good Bye, Lenin!*
  *See also* Marxism-Leninism
Leninism, *see* Lenin, Vladimir Ilyich
Le Queux, William, 222
*Lichtjahr* (*Light Year*), 213
Liebknecht, Karl, 37, 41–42
Lilienthal, Peter, 166
Lindau, Rudolf, 42
Lindenberger, Thomas, 1, 4, 5, 34, 119, 179
*Lion Has Wings, The* (1939), 224
*Living Daylights, The* (story 1962), 220, 225–26
  (film 1987), 230
*London Match*, 230
Lorenz, Peter, 212
Loriot (Vicco von Bülow), 170
Losey, Joseph, 228
Lübeck, 185
Ludendorff, Erich, 36
Ludlum, Robert, 231
Lübke, Heinrich, 53, 55
*Luftbrücke, Die* (*The Airlift*, 2005), 190–203
  production context of, 191–93
  and new German national identity, 196–200
  and view of Communism, 195
  and West German and American views of the Berlin Airlift, 193–96
Luther, Martin, 6, 63–76
Luxemburg, Rosa, 37

Mach, Josef, 169
*Männer* (*Men*, 1985), 170
Maetzig, Kurt, 120–22, 164
Magdeburg, 93
Major, Patrick, 2, 3, 7
Male body, 177–89
  visualization of in Soviet-occupied zone (GDR), 179–82

visualization of in Western
  occupation zones (FRG), 182–87
Male hero, 177–89
  visualization of, 177–89
Malle, Louis, 167
*Malou* (1980), 167
Malthusianism, 210
*Man Between, The* (1953), 224–25
Mankowitz, Wolf, 229
*Mann aus der Pfalz, Der* (*The Man from Palatinate*, 2009), 192
Margarete, Queen of Denmark, 72
Markowitsch, Erich, 56
Marx, Karl, 37, 40, 44, 67, 174, 183
  Karl Marx University, 103
  *See also* Marxism-Leninism
Marxism, 39–40, 42–43, 47, 64, 94, 99, 205, 212
Marxism-Leninism, 5, 7, 39–40, 42–44, 46, 48, 65, 67, 69, 94, 96–97, 205
Mason, James, 225
Mass media, *see* media
*Mauer, Die* (*The Wall*, 1990), 124, 129, 131
*Mauer – Berlin '61, Die* (*The Wall – Berlin '61*, 2006), 119, 192
Maugham, W. Somerset, 222
May, Karl, 23, 170
May Day, 180. *See also* Kampfmai (Fighting May Day)
McGrath, Joseph, 229
McNeile, H.C., *see* 'Sapper'
Meerapfel, Jeanine, 167
*Meine Dienstzeit in der Bundeswehr* (*My Service in the Bundeswehr*), 134, 139–40, 142, 144–45
Meinecke, Friedrich, 35–36
Melanchthon, Philipp, 68
Melzer, Andrea, 215
*Mephisto* (1981), 167
Merker, Paul, 53
*Messer im Kopf* (*Knife in the Head*, 1978), 169
Meusel, Alfred, 44
*Mexico Set*, 230
Meyer, Horst, 151
Meyer, Julius, 53
Michel, Jannis, 193

MI5 (Military Intelligence, Section 5, UK), 223
Militarism, 51
  American, 207
  German, 36, 98, 123, 135
  Prussian, 38
Military Reform, 7, 135–36, 138, 143, 144–45
  *See also* Bundeswehr
Miller, Susanne, 36
Ministry of Economic Cooperation and Development (BMZ, Das Bundesministerium für wirtschaftliche Zusammenarbeit und Entwicklung, FRG), 84
Ministry of State Security (Ministerium für Staatssicherheit, GDR), *see* Stasi
'miracle years', *see Wirtschaftswunder* (Economic Miracle)
*Mission: Impossible 3* (2006), 231
Mitter, Rana, 3
Moewig publishing house, *see* Perry Rhodan
*Mogadischu* (2008), 192
*Monthly Film Bulletin*, 228
Monty Python, 229
*Moonraker* (novel 1955), 223
Morris, Oswald, 227
*Mosaik* comics, 210
Müller, Hans, 120
Müller, Horst, 211
Müller-Stahl, Armin, 125
Müntzer, Thomas, 67
Münckler, Herfried, 178
*Munich* (2005), 192
Museum for German History (Berlin), 72
Mussolini, Benito, 36

*Nach Mitternacht* (*After Midnight*, 1981), 167
*nackte Mann auf dem Sportplatz, Der* (*The Naked Man on the Sports Field*, 1974), 165
Nagold, 136–40
Nagy, Imre, 95
Natalis, Leo, 193

National identity, 7, 44, 45n. 7, 124, 196, 232n. 16
National Revolutionary Movement Party (El Salvador), 86
National Socialism, 5, 7, 49–62, 107, 141, 178–79, 181, 183–84, 187–88, 198, 206, 220
    crimes of, 52, 188. *See also* Holocaust
    memory of, 7, 49–62
Nationale Volksarmee (NVA, National People's Army, GDR), 17, 135, 137, 141–42, 145, 182. *See also* Rearmament
Nationalism, 57, 99
Native American Films, *see Indianerfilme*
Naumann, Friedrich, 82–83
    Friedrich Naumann Foundation (Friedrich-Naumann-Stiftung), 82–83
Nazis, *see* National Socialism
Nazi-Soviet Pact (also known as Molotov–Ribbentrop Pact and Hitler-Stalin Pact), 92, 93
Neckermann, Josef, 150–52, 159
Neo-fascism, 213
*Net, The* (1995), 231
New Economic System (GDR), 213
Neue Berlin, Das, 206
*Neue Vahr Süd*, 145, 147
*Neues Deutschland*, 41, 95, 100–101, 164, 211
Neues Leben, 210, 214
New Deal, 177
New German Cinema, 165, 169, 172
New Urban Traveller, concept of, 114–16
Neyer, Harry, 140
*Nick's Film-Lightning Over Water* (*Lightning Over Water*, 1980), 172
*Night People* (1954), 224
Nikel, Hans A., 137
Nkrumah, Kwame, 82
Nörvenich, 185
Noethen, Ulrich, 192–93
Norden, Albert, 50, 53
Normandy, Allied invasion of, 192

North Atlantic Treaty Organization (NATO), 18, 34, 51, 56, 78, 81–82, 91, 97–99, 101, 134–37, 141–42
North Rhine-Westphalia, state of (FRG), 66
Norway, 72
Nuclear arms, 9, 44, 78, 87, 97, 99–100, 113, 136, 138, 193, 205, 207
    Nuclear arms race, 44, 230
    Protest against, 78, 113
Nuclear weapons, *see* nuclear arms
*08/15* (film series), 186
Nuremberg, 66
    Nuremberg trial, 184
Nyasaland, 80

Oberländer, Theodor, 50
Obote, Milton, 83
    Milton Obote Foundation, 83
*Octopussy* (film 1983), 230
Oder-Neiße border, 6, 14, 55, 91–94, 96–98, 100
*Ödipussi* (*Oedipussy*, 1988), 170
*Offensive im Eimer, Die* (*The Offensive down the Pan*), 135, 141–43, 146
Oil crisis (1973), 190
Olympic Games / Olympics, 7, 105, 148–62, 229
    in Munich 1972, 7, 148–62
Olympic Stadium (Berlin), 229
Oppenheim, E. Phillips, 222
Opitz, Karlludwig, 135
Orwell, George, 212
Ost, Günter, 125
*Ostpolitik*, 3, 21, 49, 59, 63, 73, 82, 86, 113, 156
*Otto – Der Film* (*Otto – the Film*, 1985), 170–71

Pakistan, 85, 89
Palmer, Harry, 222
Pankow, 20
Paraguay, 85, 89
*Pardon*, 134–35, 137–40, 144–46
Paris, 105, 208
    *banlieues*, 27
    Peace Conference, 91
    Treaty, 98

Paris, Helga, 177
Parrish, Robert, 229
Pastewka, Bastian, 190
  *Pastewka* (television series), 190
Paul, Gerhard, 176
PBS, 230
Peasants' War, 67, 178
Pehnert, Horst, 170–71
People's Day of Mourning, The (GDR), 58
People's Police (GDR), *see* Volkspolizei
*Peppermint Frieden* (*Peppermint Peace*, 1983), 167
Perrey, Siegfried, 149–50
Pershing II missiles, 63
Pettet, Joanna, 229
Petzold, Konrad, 123
Pfemfert, Franz, 42
Philby, Kim, 223, 231
Pieck, Wilhelm, 92, 181
Pierzchala, Jan, 95
Pinter, Harold, 228
Piotrowski, Roman, 93
Ploog, Arno, 134, 139, 141
Pohl, Arthur, 120
Poland, 6, 18–19, 28, 34, 39, 44, 59, 90–104, 120, 167, 205, 213
  Polish October (1956), 90, 95–96
  Polish Workers' Party (Polska Zjednoczona Partia Robotnicza, PZPR), 96
    Central Committee of, 96
  and relations with GDR, 90–104.
  *See also* Oder-Neiße border
Politburo (SED), 42, 64, 95–96, 154–55, 161
Political Academy Eichholz (Politische Akademie Eichholz, FRG), 82
*Polityka,* 100
Popular culture, 2, 5, 109, 173, 178, 183–84, 229. *See also* Americanization
Popular memory, 191
Porten, Henny, 120
Portugal, 81–82
Potsdam, 1, 91, 95, 172
  Potsdam Conference, 1, 91

Potsdam Treaty (also known as Potsdam Agreement), 54, 93
Poznan, 95
*Prager Botschaft* (*Prague Embassy,* 2001), 82
Prague, 97
Presley, Elvis, 183, 187–88, 196
Press, 8, 80, 95, 144, 186, 216
Prisoners, 51, 56, 184, 198, 210
  of Nazi regime, 51, 56
  of War (POW), 58, 184, 198
Pröttel, Dr. Dieter, 170
Prokop, Gert, 212
Propaganda, 24, 50–51, 55–56, 59, 69, 92–93, 95, 97, 106–108, 112, 126, 164, 177, 179–181, 185, 188, 209, 221, 224
Protestantism, 66, 71, 73
Pro7/Sat1 Group, 192
Prosthetic memory, *see* Landsberg, Alison
Prussia, 36, 38, 64, 91, 182, 186

*Queerschläger, Der* (*Ricochet*), 144
Quiller, 222
*Quiller Memorandum, The* (film 1966), 226, 228–29

Radio, 22–23, 26, 98, 121, 126, 172
Radványi, Géza von, 184
Ragwitz, Ursula, 64
Rakowski, Mieczyslaw, 100
Ranke, Leopold von, 35
Rapacki, Adam, 93, 100
Rapacki Plan, 100
Rapallo Treaty, 92–93
Rau, Johannes, 66
Rauhaus, Martin, 193
*Realpolitik,* Cold War as, 224
Rearmament, 6, 34, 36–37, 82, 91, 97–98, 134–35, 145, 182, 186. *See also* Bundeswehr. *See also* Nationale Volksarmee
Red Army, 57, 178–81
Redlin, Ekkehard, 213
Reed, Carol, 224
Reeducation, 182. *See also* denazification

Reformation, 67–68, 72
Regener, Sven, 145, 147
Rehahn, Rosemarie, 125, 168
Reichswehr, 134, 136
Reidemeister, Helga , 173
Reisch, Günter, 120–21
Remilitarization, 97, 182. *See also* Rearmament
Rentschler, Eric, 198
Renzi, Eva, 228
*Republikflucht* (flight from the Republic), *see* GDR
Resnais, Alain, 125
Restitution payments, 54
*Rettet die Bundeswehr* (*Save the Bundeswehr*), 142
Reusse, Peter, 129
Reuter, Ernst, 194, 200
*Revue*, 186
Rhodan, Perry, 206
Ries, Henry, 196
Ritt, Martin, 220
Ritter, Gerhard, 36, 41
*Robe, The* (1953), 221
Robespierre, Maximilien, 36
Rodenberg, Hans, 122, 127
Roman Catholic, *see* Catholic
Roosevelt, Franklin Delano, 177
 and New Deal, 177
Rosenbaum, Marianne S. W., 167
Rosenberg, Ludwig, 78
*rote Kakadu, Der* (*The Red Cockatoo*, 2006), 119, 131
Rundfunk im Amerikanischen Sektor (RIAS, Radio in the American Sector), 22, 193
Runze, Ottokar, 167
Rupkalwis, Jörg, 177
Rusk, Dean (U.S. Secretary of State), 84, 86
Russel, Charles, 222
Russell, Ken, 228
Russia, 32, 58, 71, 91, 178, 181–82, 184, 186–87, 194–95, 220, 223. *See also* Soviet Union
Russian Orthodox Church, 71
Russian Realism, 181

Saale (river), 212
Saarland, state of (FRG), 18
Saban, Haim, 192
*Saiäns-Fiktschen* (1981), 216
Sabrow, Martin, 43–44
Saltzman, Harry, 228
Sandinista Party, 86
'Sapper' (H.C. McNeile), 222
Satire, 6, 134–47
*Saving Private Ryan* (1998), 193
Sayers, Michael, 229
Schamoni, Peter, 172
*Schaut auf diese Stadt* (*Look at this City*, 1962), 6, 119, 123–24, 131
Schön, Hartmut, 119, 131
Schiller, Friedrich, 64
Schirdewan, Karl, 96
*Schlangenei, Das* (*The Serpent's Egg*, 1977), 167
Schlöndorff, Volker, 166, 169
Schmöing, Richard, 94
Schnez, Albert, 137
*Schokoladenflieger* (chocolate flier), 195–96. *See also* Halvorsen, Gail S.
Schöbel, Heinz, 155
Schreiner, Albert, 41
Schröder, Gerhard, 200
Schüle, Erwin, 52
Schütz, Heinrich, 64
Schütz, Klaus, 56
Schumacher, Kurt, 39
Schumann, Robert, 172
Schwarzenberger, Xaver, 170
*schweigende Stern, Der* (*The Silent Star*, 1960), 121
Schweiger, Til, 190
*Schwestern oder die Balance des Glücks* (*Sisters or the Balance of Luck*, 1979), 169
Science fiction, 2, 7, 204–19
Sckerl, Adolf, 214
Seaton, George, 196
Second World War, 7, 11, 13, 14, 19, 21, 22, 27–28, 49–50, 57, 90–91, 107, 120, 167, 179, 186–87, 194, 198, 221, 223, 225

SED (Sozialistische Einheitspartei
    Deutschlands, German Socialist
    Unity Party, GDR), 15–17, 19, 21,
    23, 37–39, 40–43, 50, 53–59, 63–65,
    67–68, 70, 72, 92–99, 121, 124, 127,
    129, 153, 155, 161, 179–81, 188,
    209, 212
  Central Committee (ZK,
      Zentralkommittee) of, 41–43,
      47, 53, 95, 129, 153, 155–56
  Fifth Party Congress, 181
  Politburo of, 42, 64, 95–96, 154
Seebohm, Hans-Christoph, 52
Seeckt, Hans von, 93
Segal, George, 228
Seghers, Anna, 216
*Seitenstechen* (*In Stitches,* 1985), 170
*Septemberliebe* (*September Romance,*
    1961), 121
17 June 1953, uprising of, 56, 95
Shaw, Tony, 225
Sheybal, Vladek, 230
Siegel, Don, 221
Siemens, 206
Simon, Harald, 85
*singende, klingende Bäumchen, Das*
    (*The Singing, Ringing Tree,* 1957),
    122
Slevogt, Max, 180
Smiley, George, 222
*Smiley's People* (novel 1979, film 1982),
    223, 230
Social Democratic Party, *see* SPD
Socialist International, 85
Socialist states, 69, 156, 158. *See also*
    Eastern bloc
Sociodemographic segregation, 27
*Söhne der Großen Bärin, Die* (*The Sons
    of Big Bear,* 1966), 169
Solidarnoćś, 19
Sonderausschuß für Sport und
    Olympische Spiele (Parliamentary
    Special Committee for Sport and the
    Olympic Games, FRG), 150
*Sonntagsfahrer* (*Sunday Drivers,* 1963),
    127–28
South Africa, 81–82, 110

Soviet Union, 15, 18, 26, 35, 39,
    42–43, 90, 92–93, 96–101, 106, 108,
    138, 149–150, 156, 163, 178–81,
    183, 187, 195, 205, 223, 228, 231
Sozialdemokratische Partei
    Deutschlands, *see* SPD
*Spätheimkehrer. See also* Prisoners of
    War (POW), 184, 198
SPD (Sozialdemokratische Partei
    Deutschlands), 5, 35–37, 39–42, 44,
    52, 56, 78, 82, 84, 91–92, 137, 179
  Bad Godesberg programme of
      (1959), 36
Spielberg, Steven, 192
*Spiegel, Der,* 52, 86, 136–37, 139,
    183–85, 188
  *Spiegel* affair, 136–37, 188
*Spy Who Came in from the Cold* (novel
    1963; film 1965), 220, 223, 225,
    227–28, 230–31
Spree, 209
Sputnik, 209
SS (Schutzstaffel), 56
Staatliches Komitee für Körperkultur
    (SKKS), 153, 155
Staatsbürger in Uniform (citizen in
    uniform), concept of (FRG), 135, 147
Staatsoper (Berlin), 72
Staatssekretäriat für Körperkultur und
    Sport (StKS), 153
Stahl, Heiner, 23
Stalin, Joseph, 35, 41, 91–92, 94, 96,
    99, 101, 178–86, 193, 195, 208, 211,
    221, 225. *See also* Nazi-Soviet Pact.
    *See also* Soviet Union
Stalingrad, Battle of, 139, 184
Stalinism, 31, 40, 48n. 56, 53, 94, 96,
    180, 182, 184, 208
  and de-Stalinization, 39, 211, 221
Stampfer, Friedrich, 36, 39
*Stand der Dinge, Der* (*The State of
    Things,* 1982), 172
Stanislaw-Lem-Klub, 213
Starfighter crisis (Bundeswehr), 136,
    138–39
Starnberg, Josef von, 168, 220
Stasi, 17, 51, 59, 155, 212

*State Secret* (1950), 224
Steinmüller, Angela and Karlheinz, 207
*Stern, Der,* 185–86
*Stern ohne Himmel,* 167, 174n. 9
Stiftung Deutsche Sporthilfe (Foundation for German Sports Aid, FRG), 150–51, 159–60
Stöver, Bernd, 11
Stolze, Lena, 172
Strauß, Franz Josef, 51
Stroessner, Alfredo, 85
Struggle against Atomic Death (Kampf dem Atomtod, FRG), 78
Students, 213
Student protests, 56
Studnitz, Hans Georg, 142, 144
Strugatsky brothers (Arkady Natanovich and Boris Natanovich), 205
*Sturmflut, Die* (*The Flood,* 2006), 190
*Suchkind 312* (*Foundling 312,* 2007), 201
Sweden, 72, 100
Switzerland, 207
Sybel, Heinrich von, 35
Szabó, István, 167

Tacke, Bernhard, 78
Tanganyika, 81
Tanzania, 73
*Tanzmusik* (dance music), 23
*Taschenbuch für Wehrpflichtige* (*Handbook for Conscripts*), 141
Taurog, Norman, 196
Television, 190–203
*Ten Commandments, The* (1956), 221
Territorial disintegration, 23
Thälmann, Ernst, 51
Teheran Conference (1943), 91
Thein, Ulrich, 128
Thiel, Heinz, 121, 124
*Third Man, The* (1949), 225
Third Reich, 61, 166, 182, 186. See also Hitler, Adolf and National Socialism.
Third World, 77–89
*38 – Heim ins Reich* (*Back Home to the Fatherland,* 1988), 167
*Thunderball* (novel 1961), 223

*Tinker, Tailor, Soldier, Spy* (novel 1974, film 1979), 223, 230
Tito-Stalin split, 101
Titov, Gherman Stepanovich, 211
Tobis Film, 171
Torner, Evan, 205
*toten Augen von London, Die* (*The Dead Eyes of London,* 1961), 169
Touré, Sekou, 171
Tourism, 105–18
Tourneur, Jacques, 224
Trainingszentren (TZ, Training Centres, GDR), 154–55, 158
Transnationalism, 206
Travel, 6, 17–19, 26, 86, 105–118, 122, 204, 214–15, 226
    Restriction of by GDR, 17–19
Travel Bureau Berlin, 105–108, 111–112, 114–16
Treptow Park, memorial in, 180
Trier Historians' Congress (1958), 41
Trimborn, Gerd, 136, 140
Trosper, Guy, 226
Trotta, Margarethe von, 169, 172
Truman, Harry S., 193
    and Truman administration, 193
Tukur, Ulrich, 192, 194
*Tunnel, Der* (*The Tunnel*) (novel 1913), 204
*Tunnel, Der* (film 2006), 190
Tunner, William H., 194
Turek, Ludwig, 207
Tuscany, 27

Uganda, 83
Ulbricht, Walter, 17, 34, 38–39, 42, 50, 92–96, 99, 101, 123, 127, 153, 156, 159, 179, 181, 212–13
*Ultrasymet bleibt geheim* (*Ultrasymet Stays Secret, 1955*), 208
*Und deine Liebe auch* (*And Your Love Too,* 1962), 124–27, 131
*Unheimliche Erscheinungsformen auf Omega XI* (*Uncanny Creatures on Omega XI,* 1974), 214
Union Marocaine du Travail (Moroccan Labour Union, UMT), 80
United Artists, 229

United States, 22, 77, 84, 106, 108, 136, 140, 151, 164, 195, 200, 203
  United States Air Force (USAF), 193–94, 196
  United States military, 140
    inconography of, 182–87, 196–200
Universum Film Aktiengesellschaft (UFA), 165, 191
United Nations (UN), 100, 200
*Unsichtbaren, Die* (*The Invisible Ones*, 1958), 209
Unter den Linden, 109, 209
Upper Volta, 82
USPD (Unabhängige Sozialdemokratische Partei Deutschlands, Independent Social Democratic Party), 37
USSR, *see* Soviet Union
Utopia-Klub, 213

VEB Domowina, 212
*Vergangenheitsbewältigung* ('coming to terms with the past'), 21
*Vergangenheitspolitik* ('politics of the past'), 50
Verhoeven, Michael, 167–68, 172
*verlorene Ehre der Katharina Blum, Die* (*The Lost Honour of Katharina Blum*, 1975), 169
Verner, Waldemar, 98
Vicas, Victor, 172
Vieweg, Heinz, 208
Virchow, Rudolf, 38
Vogel, Frank, 124–25, 127–29, 131, 133
Vohrer, Alfred, 169
Volkspolizei (People's Police; GDR), 98, 182
*Von einem der auszog und das Fürchten lernte* (*Of One Who Left Home and Learnt to Fear*), 144, 147
'Vorstoß nach Andromeda' ('Advance to Andromeda'), 215

Waalkes, Otto, 167, 170–71
Wall, the (*Die Mauer*), 1–6, 8–9n. 11, 15–17, 22, 25, 30n9, 55, 57, 108–13, 116–17, 119–20, 122–33, 165, 206, 224–31
  representations of, 119–33, 224–31
  as symbol of German division, 1–6, 8–9, 15–17, 22–23, 25, 55, 224
  as tourist attraction, 105–18
  *See also Mauer, Die*
  *See also Mauer – Berlin '61, Die*
Waller, Angelika, 129
Wallraff, Günter, 144–45
War of Liberation, 178
*War of the Worlds* (1953), 221
Warner Brothers, 193
Warsaw, 90–91, 94, 96, 97–98, 100–101. *See also* Poland
Warsaw Pact, 6, 35, 88–104
Wartburg Castle (Eisenach), 68
Wehrmacht, 58, 98–99, 134, 137–38, 141–44, 184–86, 196
Weimar Germany, *see* Weimar Republic
Weimar Republic, 7, 49, 92, 107–108, 114, 134, 136, 165, 180, 182, 205
Weise, Lothar, 210–1
*weiße Rose, Die* (*The White Rose*, 1982), 167, 172
Welfare state, 81
Welles, Orson, 225
*Welt, Die*, 51
Wenders, Wim, 172–73
Werner, Oskar, 227
West Berlin, *see* Berlin
Western (film genre), 165, 169–70. *See also* anti-western
Western liberalism, 49
West Germany, *see* FRG
Whitehall, 194–95
Wicki, Bernhard, 167, 172–73
*Wie stehst Du zur Bundeswehr* (*Where Do You stand on the Bundeswehr*), 140–41
Wieck, Clara, 172
Wieke, Johannes, 129
Wilder, Billy, 196, 229
Wilhelmshaven, 185
Wilkening, Alfred, 122

*Winnetou*, 23
Winzer, Otto, 101
*Wirtschaftswunder* (Economic Miracle), 113, 168, 178, 187, 199
Wischnewski, Klaus, 121
Wittenburg, 70
*Wochenpost*, 125, 168
Wolf, Christa, 216
Wolff, Ilse, 106, 111
Wolf, Konrad, 165, 173
Working class, 36, 39–40, 64, 69, 88
Works councils, 81
World Cup
   (1954) West German victory in, 152, 196
   (2006) Germany as host of, 206
World Federation of Free Trade Unions (WFTU), 79, 82
World Games of Youth and Students in Berlin and Moscow, 181
Worms, 66
Wortmann, Sönke, 197
*Wunder von Berlin, Das* (*The Miracle of Berlin*, 2008), 192

*Wunder von Bern, Das* (*The Miracle of Bern*, 2003), 197, 199

Yalta Conference, 224
'Year Zero', 108
Yugoslavia, 97

Zahavi, Dror, 7, 190
Zambia, 83
Zander, Erich, 122
Zanussi, Krzystof, 167
*Zeitschrift für Geschichtswissenschaft (ZfG)*, 41
Zgorzelec, 93
Ziergiebel, Herbert, 213
Ziller, Gerhart, 42
Zimmermann, Bettina, 192–93
Zionism, 53
*Zonenrandgebiet* (zonal border area), 25
*Zonengrenze* (zonal border), 15
Zuckmayer, Carl, 144
*zweite Sonne, Die* (*The Second Sun*, 1958), 208

www.ingramcontent.com/pod-product-compliance
Lightning Source LLC
Chambersburg PA
CBHW072148100526
44589CB00015B/2134